Preparing for Disunion

ALSO BY ALLEN H. MESCH

*Teacher of Civil War Generals:
Major General Charles Ferguson Smith,
Soldier and West Point Commandant* (McFarland, 2015)

Preparing for Disunion

*West Point Commandants
and the Training
of Civil War Leaders*

ALLEN H. MESCH

McFarland & Company, Inc., Publishers
Jefferson, North Carolina

Special thanks go to Sharlyn K. Mesch, who drove while I
edited and checked drafts while I checked calculations.

LIBRARY OF CONGRESS CATALOGUING-IN-PUBLICATION DATA

Names: Mesch, Allen H., author.
Title: Preparing for Disunion : West Point Commandants
and the Training of Civil War Leaders / Allen H. Mesch.
Description: Jefferson, North Carolina : McFarland & Company, Inc.,
Publishers, 2019. | Includes bibliographical references and index.
Identifiers: LCCN 2018048521 | ISBN 9781476674254 (softcover :
acid free paper) ∞
Subjects: LCSH: United States Military Academy—Biography. |
United States. Army—Officers—Biography. | Military education—
United States—History—19th century. | Military education—
United States—Biography. | United States—History—Civil War,
1861–1865.
Classification: LCC U410.M1 A37 2019 | DDC 355.0092/273—dc23
LC record available at https://lccn.loc.gov/2018048521

BRITISH LIBRARY CATALOGUING DATA ARE AVAILABLE

ISBN (print) 978-1-4766-7425-4
ISBN (ebook) 978-1-4766-3365-7

© 2019 Allen H. Mesch. All rights reserved

*No part of this book may be reproduced or transmitted in any form
or by any means, electronic or mechanical, including photocopying
or recording, or by any information storage and retrieval system,
without permission in writing from the publisher.*

Front cover images *left to right* William J. Worth,
Ethan Allen Hitchcock, Charles Ferguson Smith, William J. Hardee,
Henry B. Clitz, John F. Reynolds; West Point, from above
Washington Valley, looking down the river, painted by Geo. Cooke,
engraved by W.J. Bennett (all images Library of Congress)

Printed in the United States of America

*McFarland & Company, Inc., Publishers
Box 611, Jefferson, North Carolina 28640
www.mcfarlandpub.com*

To the instructors at the United States Military Academy at West Point, New York. Although this work focuses on the Commandant of Cadets at West Point, it also honors the faculty at the other service academies and at Reserve Officer Training Corps programs at colleges and universities throughout the United States. Thank you for preparing the military commanders who defend our country.

And to the memory of
Helen I. (Grenell) Williams
June 20, 1918–September 15, 2017

Table of Contents

Preface	1
The United States Military Academy	5
Military Training	13
The Department of Tactics	23
West Point in the Civil War	37
Commandant of Cadets	46
George W. Gardiner	54
John Bliss	58
John R. Bell	62
William J. Worth	65
Ethan A. Hitchcock	71
John Fowle	79
Charles F. Smith	84
John A. Thomas	93
Bradford R. Alden	98
Robert S. Garnett	106
William H. T. Walker	111
William J. Hardee	117
John F. Reynolds	124
Christopher C. Augur	129
Kenner Garrard	133
Henry B. Clitz	138
The Commandant's Role in Preparing Civil War Generals	143

Appendices:
   Major Campaigns and Strategic Battles
      of the Civil War   165
   U.S. Military Academy Graduating Classes   169
   Notable West Point Graduates Who Served
      in the Civil War   217
   Highest Rank Prior to the Civil War   251

Notes   255

Bibliography   271

Index   277

Preface

History records the successes of military commanders but ignores the teachers who gave them the knowledge and character necessary to achieve these honors. Colonel Charles W. Larned focused on these issues in his address "The Genius of West Point," presented at the June 12, 1902, graduation exercises. Colonel Larned described war as "a science whose details must be mastered in advance."[1] Before an officer leads soldiers to engage the enemy, he must be properly trained in the principals of military science and command. Larned portrayed the Military Academy as "a machine in which a heterogeneous mass of raw material is transformed in the short space of four years into a finished product, molded, tested, and stamped with the sterling mark which has come to be recognized the world over."[2]

> This brand of the Military Academy stands primarily for character. It does not mean that the individual is a finished expert in mathematics or engineering, or even in the science of war. It does not mean that he is a perfect automaton in military drill, a superior marksman, a rough rider, or a

Military Academy West Point, New York, as viewed from above Washington Valley (Library of Congress).

skilled artillerist. It means that, having had a sound, exacting grounding in all these things and in many more covering the whole field of usefulness of a soldier, he has had also the inestimable seasoning of his moral fiber which results from four years' immersion in an atmosphere of hard work; unsparing criticism; strict personal accountability for every act, large or small; simplicity of life; an exalted ideal of integrity, of duty, of truth telling; a tradition of a century of honor upheld by hundreds of names borne on the pages of his country's story.[3]

The colonel's remarks remind us that West Point training provides the graduate officer with a foundation on which to continue his education and he is not a polished commander skilled in all aspects of warfare. Larned spoke about three constituent principals: morale, mental discipline, and the military university. The colonel reduced the morale principal to making "a soldier who shall be an honorable, courageous, self-reliant, clear-thinking man, having a broad grasp of all the essentials of his profession." Molding character at West Point consists of four traits: honor, courage, subordination, and hard work. Regarding honor, the colonel said, "The views of rectitude and personal accountability, which have grown into the marrow of the institution, which are fostered by its authorities and have become its sacred code of honor, have a formative power impossible to be understood other than by experience." Courage is divided into physical courage, the ability to be physically brave, and moral courage, the ability to stand and face the enemy. West Point demands both traits. Subordination guides "the entire existence of the Cadet" and he is "surrounded by a hierarchy of graded responsibility and obligation." The last point is hard work. The cadet faces the "unending, uncompromising exactions of duty from reveille to taps." The requirements for graduation can only be achieved through persistent and consistent hard work. These principles of character are instilled in the cadet during his time at the Academy and impart the character necessary to command men in battle.[4]

West Point is fundamentally unique among military schools. West Point stands for "something" more than European military schools. This "something" was well done, abundantly proved, and acclaimed in its achievements over the nineteenth century. The "something" has three essential principles: (1) Morale—The molding of character by a thorough, consistent, and continued discipline; (2) Mental Discipline—A thorough general training of the rational faculties; and (3) The Military University—A general and comprehensive instruction of officers of all arms of the service in the elements of every military branch.[5]

The West Point system is built on these core values:

> The purpose of West Point is to make a soldier who shall be an honorable, courageous, self-reliant, clear-thinking man, having a broad grasp of all the essentials of his profession.

Character building (morale) is composed of honor (integrity and accountability), courage (physically and morally brave), subordination (obeying orders), and hard work (exact performance of every military and academic requirement).

Mental discipline is achieving the Academy's standard in everything with no deficiencies. Therefore, the academic course is based upon three fundamentals: (1) Every man in every subject; (2) Every man proficient in everything; and (3) Every man every day. In other words, every cadet must take the whole course and there are no optional or exceptional studies. Every cadet must complete the standard in everything and deficiency in one subject is deficiency in the course. Each cadet must be prepared to recite every day on all the subjects he is now studying.[6]

As to the role of the military university, Larned pronounced, "the quality of mind and character with which the Military Academy has equipped its graduates in the past has made of them a grade of officers of general intelligence and resourcefulness superior to that of any other similar body of officers in the world."[7]

> Four years of constant drill, practical instruction in military operations, and respectful submission to the will of his superiors makes him a soldier in the true meaning of the word. He may or may not have the talents of a great general, but he has at least the instincts of a soldier and a knowledge of the duties and technical requirements of his profession. He has, above all, an understanding of the term duty, which makes it the motive power of his professional life and simplifies for him all complex questions of practical ethics. The motto of his alma mater is the philosophy of his life. To do his duty, keep bright his honor, and serve faithfully his country is the hereditary ideal of every son of West Point.[8]

On June 11, 1902, General Horace Porter presented the orator of the day address in the Centennial Exercise. He directed his closing remarks to "the Corps of Cadets, the departure of whose graduating class marks the close of the first century of the Academy's life." General Porter reminded the Corps of their roots and potential. "The boy is father to the man. The present is the mold in which the future is cast. The dominant characteristics of the cadet are seen in the future general."[9] Porter admonished the graduates that the Academy taught them "how to command" and, more importantly, "how to obey":

General Horace Porter (Library of Congress).

> Not the least valuable part of your education is your service in the cadet ranks, performing the duties of a private soldier. That alone can acquaint you with the feelings and the capabilities of the soldiers you will command. It teaches you just how long a man can carry a musket[10] in one position without overfatigue [sic], just how hard it is to keep awake on sentry duty after an exhausting day's march. You will never forget this part of your training.[11]

Porter's comments emphasize that before a cadet can become a great officer, he must be a great soldier.

This book is about the West Point commandants of cadets who prepared the young cadets for the most challenging conflict of the Military Academy's first century—the American Civil War.

The United States Military Academy

Antebellum Colleges

The typical antebellum college believed its mission to be the general education of "gentlemen." This "general education" consisted of extensive lessons in Greek and Latin, some mathematics, literature, natural science, and a capstone course in ethics or moral philosophy. Except for law and medicine, the colleges rejected utilitarian or practical courses. In contrast, the military academy offered a functional education designed to produce professional soldiers, or more accurately, engineers capable of functioning as soldiers. Although the Academy emphasized scholarly, general education aspects over military topics, the West Point curriculum was basically practical and not classical.[1]

While the academic emphasis was different, students at antebellum colleges and the military academy had to obey an exacting list of regulations. These rules were essen-

Battalion on review, 1890 (Library of Congress).

tially the same ones enacted when the schools tightened discipline early in the nineteenth century. While the regulations were the same, the enforcement was very different. In the antebellum colleges, the faculty had generally "lost the will to enforce these rules." Prohibitions against shouting, loud-talking, and boisterous noise in the entries or rooms of the college were not effective or not enforced in practice. The rules against visiting taverns and restaurants in town were not enforced because of impact on the students' social lives. In the 1850s, absences from recitations were recorded and entered onto student report cards. The faculty made routine visits to student living quarters to report on those absent during study hours. Although the colleges had the authority to punish violations, they were reluctant to reprimand the offenders. However, the threat of penalties hung over the students and set ambiguous boundaries to student behavior.[2] The military academy had similar rules, but the staff enforced them rigorously with demerits, extra duty, and discharge.

Military Academy Philosophy

The military classes at the Academy had two basic goals: (1) to teach the fundamentals and (2) to build the foundation for future study, competence, and knowledge. Although introduced to military strategy and the art of war, there was never any attempt to instruct cadets on adapting past strategies in future battles with unknown adversaries, new technologies, and unfamiliar terrains.

West Point cadets marching to dinner, 1889 (Library of Congress).

Curriculum

Although West Point was primarily an engineering and military school, the superintendents introduced classical topics to enrich and broaden the cadets.

> Military instruction deserves to be an assured feature of education in this country. Its influence in developing mind and body, in teaching method and precision, self-control and obedience, discipline and manliness are incalculable; and the blending of classical with military education is also pregnant with happy results.[3]

The 1825 West Point curriculum included, in order of importance, mathematics, natural philosophy, mechanics, astronomy, engineering, chemistry, French, tactics, principles of artillery,[4] mineralogy, ethics, and history. Some attempt was made to change the school to be like higher education in civilian institutions, but the object of West Point was to prepare graduates for life in the military not in the civilian world.[5]

Curriculum at the U.S. Military Academy[6]

Class Year	1833	1840	1850	1860
Fifth Year				Mathematics English Studies and Literature Tactics of Artillery and Infantry Use of Small Arms
Fourth Class[7] (First Year)	Mathematics French	Mathematics French	Mathematics French English Studies	Mathematics French English Studies and Literature Tactics of Artillery and Infantry Ethics
	Military Drill	Military Drill	Military Drill	Military Drill
Third Class (Second Year)	Mathematics French Drawing	Mathematics French Drawing	Mathematics French Drawing	French Drawing Natural and Experimental Philosophy Tactics of Artillery, Cavalry, and Infantry
	Ethics Military Drill	Ethics Military Drill	Military Drill	Military Drill
Second Class (Third Year)	Natural and Experimental Philosophy Chemistry Drawing Infantry and Artillery Tactics[8]	Natural and Experimental Philosophy Chemistry Drawing Infantry and Artillery Tactics	Natural and Experimental Philosophy Chemistry Drawing Infantry and Artillery Tactics and	Ethics Chemistry Drawing Tactics of Infantry and Artillery and

Class Year	1833	1840	1850	1860
			Equitation	Equitation, Strategy, Out Post Duty, and Military Organization and Administration
First Class (Fourth Year)	Military Drill	Military Drill	Military Drill	Military Drill
	Military and Civil Engineering and Science of War	Military and Civil Engineering and Science of War	Military and Civil Engineering and Science of War	Military Engineering and Science of War
	Ethics	Ethics	Ethics	
	Infantry and Artillery Tactics	Infantry and Artillery Tactics	Infantry Tactics	Tactics of Artillery, Cavalry and Infantry and Equitation
		Equitation, Infantry and Artillery	Artillery and Cavalry	
	Chemistry	Mineralogy and Geology	Mineralogy and Geology	Mineralogy and Geology
				Law and Literature
			Practical Military Engineering	Practical Military Engineering
				Ordnance[9] and Gunnery[10]
	Military Drill	Military Drill	Military Drill	Military Drill

Technical subjects dominated the instructional time. In 1833, 71 percent of total classroom hours were devoted to mathematical, scientific, and engineering topics. The remaining time was distributed among French, drawing of the human figure, moral and political science, rhetoric, and tactics. In calculating the cadet rankings, 55 percent of the grade depended on performance in engineering, mathematics, and scientific classes. Only 14 percent of the score was from tactics.[11]

Other Military Schools

Although the U.S. Military Academy supplied most of the Civil War generals, other colleges also trained graduates who became generals. Southern military schools contributed twenty-three officers who became general officers.

Virginia Military Institute

- James Robert Jones, Class of 1841, Brigadier General, Confederate
- Reuben Lindsay Walter, Class of 1845, Brigadier General, Confederate
- Ralph Edward Colston, Class of 1846, Brigadier General, Confederate
- Gabriel Colvin Wharton, Class of 1847, Brigadier General, Confederate
- William Mahone, Class of 1847, Major General, Confederate
- Robert Emmett Rhodes, Class of 1848, Brigadier General, Confederate

- William H.F. Payne, Class of 1849, Brigadier General, Confederate
- Samuel Garland, Jr., Class of 1849, Brigadier General, Confederate
- William Richard Terry, Class of 1850, Brigadier General, Confederate
- William Y.C. Humes, Class of 1851, Brigadier General, Confederate
- Alfred Jefferson Vaughan, Jr., Class of 1851, Brigadier General, Confederate
- James Henry Lane, Class of 1854, Brigadier General, Confederate
- John McCausland, Class of 1857, Brigadier General, Confederate
- James Barbour Terrill, Class of 1858, Brigadier General, Confederate
- Birkett Davenport Fry, Attended, 1845, Brigadier General, Confederate
- James Edwin Slaughter, Attended 1845, 1846, Brigadier General, Confederate
- James Alexander Walker, Dismissed on Charges, Brigadier General, Confederate[12]

South Carolina Military Academy (The Citadel)

- Johnson Hagood, Class of 1847, Brigadier General, Confederate
- Ellison Capers, Class of 1857, Brigadier General, Confederate
- Evander McIvor Law, Class of 1856, Brigadier General, Confederate
- Micah Jenkins, Class of 1854, Brigadier General, Confederate[13]

Georgia Military Institute

- Pierce M.B. Young, Class Unknown, Brigadier/Major General, Confederate[14]

Kentucky Military Institute

- Robert Frederick Hoke, Class of 1854, Major General, Confederate[15]
- Stephen Gano Burbridge, Class Unknown, Major General, Union[16]

Nashville Military Institute

- Thomas Benton Smith, Class Unknown, Brigadier General, Confederate[17]

Western Military Institute

- George Washington Gordon, Class of 1859, Brigadier General, Confederate[18]

In the north, Norwich University was another source of Civil War officers.

- Horatio Seymour, Class of 1828, Brigadier General, Union[19]
- Robert H. Milroy, Class of 1843, Major General, Union[20]
- Thomas E.G. Ransom, Class of 1851- brevet Major General, Union[21]
- George C. Strong, Class of 1850, Major General, Union[22]
- Edmund Rice, Medal of Honor, Class of 1858 (Awarded degree in 1874), Brigadier General, Union[23]

Jacksonian Democracy

The expansion of the right to vote to include all white men was an important movement from 1800 to 1830. States started removing voting restrictions, and, by the mid–1820s, only Rhode Island, Virginia, and North Carolina limited voting to white men who owned property. From 1824 to 1830, the American political landscape changed, and the Whigs and newly formed Democratic Party became the cornerstones of the Second Party System.²⁴

The 1828 election of Andrew Jackson began a period of greater democracy for the common man.

> The Democrats represented a wide range of views but shared a fundamental commitment to the Jeffersonian concept of an agrarian society. They viewed a central government as the enemy of individual liberty and they believed that government intervention in the economy benefited special-interest groups and created corporate monopolies that favored the rich. They sought to restore the independence of the individual—the artisan and the ordinary farmer—by ending federal support of banks and corporations and restricting the use of paper currency.²⁵

The Jacksonians wanted to abolish the existing socio-economic system, which granted special benefits to the few and replace it with one in which political freedom led to social and economic opportunity. This philosophy quickly targeted American colleges.

Andrew Jackson (Library of Congress).

Antebellum Colleges Under Fire

Attacks on antebellum colleges focused on their exclusive characteristics. After Jackson's election, antebellum colleges became targets of Jacksonian Democracy's "war on privilege" and "artificial or accidental advantage."²⁶ In the 1830s, the public was very hostile toward colleges. The dissatisfaction with colleges was wide spread and the schools had to defend themselves from these attitudes. This resentment resulted in declining enrollments.²⁷ Democrats led the assault on higher education because it was restrictive—open to some but not all. They believed the "rich and well-born" were receiving significant educational benefits. Davey Crockett complained in a speech before Congress: "This college system went into practice to draw a line of demarcation between the two classes of society—it separated the children of the rich from the children of the poor."²⁸

American colleges and their graduates were isolated from the "mainstream" of American social and cultural development. College graduates accounted for no more than one percent of the male workforce before the Civil War. Most college graduates had careers in the clergy, education, government, medicine, and the law.²⁹ The small and limited number of graduates also supported the public's negative view of higher education. The high failure rates at public universities and the Military Academy enhanced the exclusiveness of the institutions.

Attacks on the Military Academy

The U.S. Military Academy was an easy target for the Jacksonians because it was totally dependent on federal funds. Since its founding in 1802, the public and their elected officials had criticized the Academy and its graduates. These attacks focused on funding, exclusivity, states' rights, and free education.

Many of these complaints led to motions in Congress to change or abolish the Academy. Representative Newton Cannon of Tennessee called for a committee in 1820 to "inquire into the expediency of abolishing the military academy at West Point."[30] In 1821, the House Committee on Military Affairs was asked to investigate reducing the number of cadets at West Point "educated at public expense" to a level needed by the Army.[31]

President Jackson's attacks led to Superintendent Sylvanus Thayer's[32] resignation on January 19, 1833. However, the assaults continued even after Thayer left West Point on July 1, 1833.[33] In 1834, Kentucky representative Albert G. Hawes asked for a committee to examine "whether it would not comport with the public interests to abolish said institution [*West Point*]."[34] The Tennessee legislature in 1833 and the Ohio legislature in 1834 voted to abolish the military academy.[35] In 1843, the governor of Maine sent a resolution from the state legislature to Congress calling for the abolition of the Military Academy.[36] In the House of Representatives, George O. Rathbun from New York State announced he was willing to abolish West Point to obtain funds to build forts in the West.[37] Representative John P. Hale from New Hampshire issued a resolution in 1844 declaring the National Military Academy at West Point ought to be abolished, instructing the Military Committee to report a bill for this purpose, and applying the money now appropriated to its support, for the diffusion of military science among the States and territories.[38]

The actions to abolish the Academy came from the Jacksonian's desire to limit the powers of the federal government. President Jackson said he would guard against "all encroachments upon the legitimate sphere of State sovereignty." President Jackson believed, "Thayer's engineering school" was wrong in its focus and dangerous in its encouragement of an elite group of officers. An 1836 letter to the *Army and Navy Chronicle* noted "the contempt in which the military service is held by Congress."[39]

The public criticized the Academy for creating an aristocracy of "haughty" and "insolent" officers.

WEST-POINT MILITARY

This institution is growing unpopular in many parts of the country, and we do not think it improbable, that it will be finally abolished.—

This school been well conducted, there is no institution in the country that has sent out riper [readier] or more accomplished scholars; but we do think that it is calculated [to] foster a spirit that had better not exist in a government such as ours.

The feelings of him who is educated and bred a soldier, are very different from those obtained in civil life. He feels he is better than his fellows and that he was born to command.—

It is true, that in this kind of schools the cadet is taught the virtue of obedience, but he knows that such obedience is due only to superiors, but he comes into the world, with a warrant to command those over whom he is placed, and he is apt to fancy that those whom he commands are as good as the mass of the community. He has high notions of the dignity of his profession, and in consequence of it, assumes haughty, and if be a weak man, often an insolent deportment towards those with whom he associates; and few, except the sons the rich and influential are able to obtain admission: besides the existence of such an institution shuts up the avenues of promotion, in the army, to all such as not its graduates. It may be urged in its favor, that it is a strong arm of defense, by reason of its furnishing the army with intelligent and scientific men. This. argument has some weight; but the advantage that is gained by the science of the cadets, is more than lost by the discouragement that others receive from the preference given to such as have been educated in this institution. The requisites of a great commander are not acquired by study or training for these are in vain. The history of the great military men confirms this view of the case; many of them having risen from the ranks to supreme command. It has often happened, that in the midst of great national danger, some master-spirit has risen from obscurity to wield the truncheon of command with an energy and success that would have been vainly sought for in the schools of military science.

We do the not condemn science, but we think that the preference given to those who have been educated at West Point, is calculated to damp its pursuit in those who have not had the disposition or means to pursue it within its walls, and that adding this to the aristocratic features of the institution, it would be well to abolish it or place it under new regulations.[40]

On November 26, 1833, the Tennessee Legislature passed resolutions in favor of abolishing the Academy with the argument that "a few young men, sons of distinguished and wealthy families, through the intervention of members of Congress, are educated at this institution at the expense of the great body of the American people, which entitle them to privileges, and elevate them above their fellow-citizens, who have not been so fortunate as to be educated under the patronage of this aristocratical institution."[41]

Jacksonians believed the cadets were taking advantage of the free education. After graduation, the cadets became snobbish officers in a "caste-ridden army" or resigned their commission to "cash in on the mathematical and engineering knowledge" provided by the government.[42]

Horace Greeley, editor of the *New York Tribune* said, "The atmosphere, the fume of the bivouac, not an academy education, is what produces military genius."[43] Politicians and the public idealized the citizen-soldier and "natural talents of the common man provided all the means necessary for military success, and had a long-standing antipathy toward standing armies."[44]

A cadet responded to a newspaper's criticism.

All I want of those Editors who say that "the lily-fingered cadets lounge on their velvet lawns, attend their brilliant balls & take pay for it," is that they may go through but one plebe encampment.[45]

Military Training

The Department of Tactics trained the cadets in the duties of the soldiers and how to maneuver on the battlefield. The Department of Engineering and the Science of War taught practical military engineering. The responsibilities of the Department of Engineering were taken over by the Department of Practical Military Engineering in 1842. The Department of Artillery presented practical artillery instruction. The Department of Ordnance and Gunnery taught the science of gunnery and ordnance. The Department of Tactics is discussed in the next chapter, and descriptions of the other departments are presented below.

Department of Engineering

Instruction in military engineering began when Congress established Military Academy. Congress formally created the Department of Engineering on April 29, 1812.

Fortifications at Centreville, Virginia (Library of Congress).

The department emphasized the elements of fortification. Until 1818, instruction in military engineering was done with lectures illustrated by a small model of the front of a fortification and by field exercises in practical engineering. The only textbook was a translation from the French of a fifty-page pamphlet.

In 1818, the department began using a translation of the textbook *A Treatise on the Science of War and Fortification* written by Colonel de Vernon, professor of fortification in the Polytechnic School in France. Vernon's two-volume book presented the science of war in general, field fortifications, permanent fortifications, and a summary of the principles and maxims of grand tactics and operations. This book was used until Professor Dennis. H. Mahan introduced his textbooks.

Professor Mahan was appointed head of the Engineering Department on January 1, 1832. Initially, he used his notes and lectures from his studies of European military schools. Mahan began teaching his course on Military and Civil Engineering and the Science of War in 1833. His textbooks first appeared in 1841. Mahan prepared a book on field fortifications and seven lithographs.[1] In 1848, the department introduced Mahan's *Advanced Guard and Outposts* followed by Moseley's *Mechanics of Engineering* in 1858.

Pontoon bridge (Library of Congress).

Professor Mahan's course on civil and military engineering was taught in two parts: civil engineering in the first term and military engineering and the art and science of war in the second term. Military engineering covered fixed and field fortifications. The art of war included discussions on: Army organization and discipline, tactics, minor tactics in relation to logistics, grand tactics, minor operations, logistics, and strategy.

The department staff included one professor, head of the department; three instructors, one of which was appointed as assistant professor; and one draftsman, employed by the department.[2]

Department of Practical Military Engineering

From the establishment of the Military Academy until around 1842, the Department of Engineering and the Science of War taught practical military engineering, under the title of "actual (or practical) operations on the ground." In August 1842, the Army assigned Captain Alex J. Swift, Corps of Engineers, as instructor in practical military engineering.[3]

The Department of Practical Military Engineering existed from 1844 until the Civil War, when it was "probably merged in a greater or less degree" into the Department of Engineering and the Science of War. The first detailed outline of the course appeared in the Academic Regulations of 1853. The Academy expanded the program in 1857, and cadets in the First Class had instruction in practical military engineering until after the Civil War. In 1863, the Army sent signal officer Captain S.T. Cushing to West Point to introduce "instruction in military signaling and telegraphy as a part of the regular course of instruction for Cadets." Captain Cushing was on duty at West Point from July 24, 1863, to January 24, 1864, but the Army did not assign him to a specific duty. The Academy added instruction in military signaling and telegraphy to the course in practical military engineering in October 1867.[4]

Engineer Company A, which the Army formed for service in the war with Mexico, returned to West Point on June 22, 1848. The company helped instruct the cadets until January 18, 1861, when the Army transferred the unit to Washington, D.C. The company returned on September 30, 1861, and stayed for a month before it joined the Army of the Potomac. During the absence of this company, a small detachment of engineers stayed at West Point until September 10, 1863. The Army kept a small group of engineers in the Department of Practical Military Engineering until Company A returned in 1865.[5]

During the first two years of the Civil War, between October 30, 1861, and September 10, 1863, the Academy combined the Department of Practical Military Engineering with the Department of Civil and Military Engineering.[6]

Instructors in the Department of Practical Military Engineering[7]

Instructor	Rank and Department	Assigned	Relieved
Alex. J. Swift[8]	Captain Corps of Engineers	August 1842	September 12, 1846
Fred. A. Smith	Captain Corps of Engineers	September 12, 1846	March 25, 1848

Instructor	Rank and Department	Assigned	Relieved
George W. Cullum	Captain Corps of Engineers	March 25, 1848	May 19, 1851
Alex. H. Bowman	Captain Corps of Engineers	May 19, 1851	June 1, 1852
George W. Cullum	Captain Corps of Engineers	June 1, 1852	January 1, 1855
John G. Barnard[9]	Captain Corps of Engineers	March 2, 1855	September 8, 1856
Andrew J. Donelson	First Lieutenant Corps of Engineers	September 9, 1856	October 15, 1858
James C. Duane	First Lieutenant Corps of Engineers	October 16, 1858 September 30, 1861	January 18, 1861 October 30, 1861
Miles D. McAlester	Captain Corps of Engineers	September 10, 1863	June 22, 1864
William P. Craighill	Captain Corps of Engineers	June 22, 1864	August 31, 1864
George H. Mendell	Captain Corps of Engineers	September 21, 1864	July 3, 1865
Henry M. Robert	Captain Corps of Engineers	August 31, 1865	August 31, 1867

Signal Corps and tower (Library of Congress).

Department of Artillery

From 1812 to 1817, General George Cullum reported instruction in artillery tactics was limited by the "few pieces of ordnance for drill or target practice." There was very little theoretical instruction in ordnance in the early days of the department. Initially, the Department of Tactics taught the artillery course. At this time, there was very little scientific knowledge on artillery and ordnance. The instruction focused on practical applications learned in drills with little attention to the principles. This emphasis changed as artillerists learned more about the underlying theory. By 1839, understanding of the technology had increased to the extent that the course included lessons on the theory of artillery, the determination of initial velocity,[10] proof of gunpowder,[11,12] rifling,[13] and causes of deviation in firing.[14,15] Most of lessons were practical and taught by the Department of Tactics instead of the Department of Ordnance. The Department of Artillery began in 1817 and presented practical instruction. General Cullum said, "The first principles of artillery were taught with the drill of field pieces, target practice, and a little laboratory duty. The artillery was not studied in detail. The department only taught definitions from Scheele's *Artillery*,[16] practical pyrotechny,[17] and preparation of fixed ammunition, and practiced the use of field pieces and mortars[18] during drills and target practice."[19]

The first instructor was Second Lieutenant George W. Gardiner of the Corps of Artillery. His assignment was from September 15, 1817, to February 1, 1820. Gardiner also served as commandant of cadets from September 15, 1817, to April 2, 1818.

In January 1820, the Academic Board formed a committee to revise the course of

Union Field Artillery Unit in position (Library of Congress).

studies and classification rules. The committee outlined a course in artillery and military science consisting of "the knowledge and use of the various kinds of ordnance and military projectiles,[20] principles of gunnery, experiments on the strength of powder, and calculation of the initial velocity of balls."[21]

The 1821 Academic Regulations stipulated, "There shall be detailed a captain or field officer and attached to the Academy as instructor of tactics; and the captain or commandant of artillery to be stationed at West Point shall perform the duty of instructor of artillery."[22] The regulations of 1839 and 1853 authorized "a captain or lieutenant may be detailed as instructor of artillery."[23]

Between 1820 and 1826, the Academy transferred "scientific instruction" to the Department of Engineering. On June 26, 1826, the Academic Board returned scientific instruction to the Department of Artillery. In 1839–1840, the chief engineer ordered the preparation of a new program of studies. The revised artillery course included the following subjects:

Pyrotechny—This class presented theoretical and practical lessons. The course included "making of slow match,[24] quick match,[25] portfires,[26] priming tubes,[27] cannon cartridges, musket, rifle,[28] and pistol cartridges,[29] canister shot,[30] grape shot, strap shot, leaden balls, fuses,[31] rock fire, light balls, fireballs,[32] incendiary balls, the mousse, sulphur [*sic*] matches,[33] thundering barrels,[34] carcasses,[35] and signal rockets; to the loading of bombs, howitzers,[36] and grenades,[37] and putting up ammunition for transportation. The manner of making petards,[38] powder sacks, smoke balls,[39] suffocating balls,[40] alarm signals, Congreve rockets,[41] and parachute rockets[42] was studied but not applied to practice."[43]

Artillery Tactics—This subject presented the organization of a field battery[44] and duties of the company of artillerists needed to service the guns. The cadets had theoretical instruction and practical exercise in the School of the Gunner, School of the Piece, and School of the Battery. Cadets studied the evolutions of the batteries,[45] but did not practice the evolutions in the field.

Passing cartridge (Library of Congress).

Gunnery—In this class, cadets studied the theory of gunnery and applied the lessons during practice with guns, howitzers, and mortars.

Manufacture of Gunpowder, Percussion Powder, Cannon,[46] and Projectiles—Topics in this subject area included preparation of gunpowder materials; manufacture and inspection of gunpowder; proof of gunpowder; proof of gunpowder by the mortar *eprouvette*,[47] spring (traction) *éprouvette*,[48] ballistic pendulum, cannon pendulum,[49] and rotary machine[50]; storage and preservation of gunpowder; restoration of damaged gunpowder; inflammation and properties of gunpowder; description of the principals of the different fulminating powders; manufacture of percussion caps[51] and wafers; preparation of metals used in the fabrication of arms[52]; manufacture of cannon of cast iron, wrought iron, and bronze; inspection and proof of iron guns, howitzers, and mortars; inspection and proof of guns, howitzers, and mortars of bronze; preservation of cannon; and manufacture, inspection, and proof of shot and shell.[53,54]

General Subject of Artillery—This part of the course described the different types of guns, howitzers, and mortars; the various kinds of hollow projectiles[55] and of the manner of filling and preserving them; the nomenclature and forms of gun carriages, caissons,[56] etc., with an explanation of their forms; propositions with respect to strength and ease of draft. The lessons included the manner of spiking and unspiking[57] cannon; manner of repairing and destroying the material of artillery; theory of firing; manner of determining initial velocities; effects of recoil[58]; aiming of guns, howitzers, mortars, and stone mortars[59]; firing of grapeshot,[60] Congreve rockets, and grenades; throwing of hand grenades; different modes of firing; manner of firing by night; causes of deviation in firing; effect of rifling in correcting the inaccuracy of small arms; effects produced by balls, howitzers, bombs, grapeshot, etc.; composition of siege trains; construction of siege batteries; manner of battering in breach[61] and counter battering; and construction of coast batteries[62] and defense of coasts.[63]

The textbooks used included Jacques P. Thiroux's *Instruction théorique et pratique d'artillerie à l'usage des élèves de l'École militaire de Saint-Cyr* and a *System of Exercise and Instruction of Field Artillery*, prepared by a board of officers at Washington in 1826. The instructors taught the remaining parts of the course from notes prepared and lithographed at the Military Academy.

The Academy made the following changes to the course in 1853.

Artillery instruction included nomenclature and description of the different kinds and parts of artillery (gun carriages, caissons, and other artillery carriages) of artillerists' implements, and military projectiles; exercise of the fieldpiece and of mortars, howitzers, siege, garrison,[64] and seacoast guns; maneuvers of a field battery of artillery; mechanical maneuvers.

The lessons in gunnery presented the theory of gunnery and target practice with the gun, howitzer, and mortar.

Training in pyrotechny dealt with preparing musket, rifle, pistol, cannon, and howitzer cartridges; making strap, grape, and canister shot, priming tubes, fuses, slow and quick match, portfire, rockets, carcasses, fireballs, light balls, and incendiary composition; loading shells, shrapnel[65] shot, and grenades; casting musket balls; putting up stores for transportation; loading caissons; and the manner of proving powder.

The 1853 Regulations ordered artillery tactics "be taught according to the most approved system." The "best qualified" cadets served as commissioned and noncommissioned officers and helped the instructor during drill. The instructor selected "passages from the best works in the different subjects of the course" for study and recitation.

The gunnery lessons included practical instruction with various exercises. In the laboratory, the cadets learned gunnery duties and, through practice, achieved "facility and correctness" in performing them.[66]

The Department of Artillery continued until 1857 under the following instructors:

Instructors in the Department of Artillery[67]

Name	Rank and Department	Assigned	Relieved
George W. Gardiner	Second Lieutenant Corps of Artillery	September 17, 1817	February 1, 1820
Fabius Whiting	Captain Corps of Artillery	August 15, 1820,	August 7, 1821
Z.J.D. Kinsley	Second Lieutenant Third Artillery	December 18, 1823	December 1, 1835
Robert Anderson	First Lieutenant Third Artillery	December 1, 1835	November 6, 1837
Minor Knowlton	First Lieutenant First Artillery	November 9, 1837	July 1, 1844
E.D. Keyes	Captain Third Artillery	July 25, 1844	December 24, 1848
William H. Shover	Captain and Brevet[68] Major Third Artillery	December 24, 1848	September 7, 1850
George H. Thomas	First Lieutenant and Brevet Major Third Artillery	April 2, 1851	May 1, 1854
Fitz John Porter	First Lieutenant and Brevet Major Fourth Artillery	May 1, 1854	September 11, 1855
Henry F. Clarke	First Lieutenant and Brevet Captain Second Artillery	September 11, 1855	August 6, 1856

Department of Ordnance and Gunnery

In December 1856, the Academic Board organized the Department of Ordnance and Gunnery. The Board resolution said, "the portion of the present course of artillery which comprises the science of gunnery, and what is known in our service as ordnance, be disconnected from that which relates to tactics merely, and be made the subject of a separate department, and that the additional time necessary for the development and improvement of this department be taken from that now given to practical engineering...." On December 9, 1856, the Board completed the course schedule. "Ordnance and gunnery [*would be held*] from 11 a.m. to 1 p.m. from October 1 to [*the*] end of the first week in March, alternating every other week day with cavalry tactics during October and two weeks in November, and with riding during the rest of the term."[69]

The Academic Regulations specified the appointment of an instructor of ordnance and gunnery and assigned Captain James G. Benton, Ordnance Department, as the first instructor.[70]

Mortar and artillery at Broadway Landing, Appomattox River, Virginia (Library of Congress).

Instructors in the Department of Ordnance and Gunnery

Name	Rank and Department	Assigned	Relieved
James G. Benton	Captain Ordnance Department	February 27, 1857	April 26, 1861
Stephen V. Benet	First Lieutenant Ordnance Department	April 26, 1861	February 1, 1864
Thomas J. Treadwell	Captain Ordnance Department	February 1, 1864	September 13, 1864
George T. Balch	Captain Ordnance Department	September 22, 1864	July 12, 1865

The 1857 course in ordnance and the science of gunnery presented nomenclature and descriptions of the different kinds and parts of artillery (gun carriages, caissons, and other artillery carriages), of artillerists' implements, and military projectiles.[71] The program covered the theory of gunnery, pyrotechny, and the ordnance and the science of gunnery.

Heinrich Otto Sheele's *Treatise on Artillery* was the first textbook used in the artillery course. In 1841, the Academy added Robert Anderson's *United States Artillery Tactics*; Edward van Schoonhoven Kinsley's *Pyrotechny*; Jacques P. Thiroux's *Instruction Theorique et pratique d'artillerie*; and Miner Knowlton's *Notes on Gunpowder, Percussion Powder, Cannon, and Projectiles*. The books used in 1850 included *Tactics for Garrison, Siege, and Field Artillery*; Kinsley's *Pyrotechny*; Thiroux's *Instruction theorique et pratique d'artillerie*; Knowlton's *Notes on Gunpowder, Cannon, and Projectiles*; and Alfred Mordecai's *Experiments on Gunpowder, by means of the Gun and Ballastic* [sic] *Pendulum*.

In 1859, the textbooks in ordnance and gunnery were Thiroux's *Instruction theorique et pratique d'artillerie*; Ordnance Manual; Mordecai's *Experiments on Gunpowder*; Notes on Fabrication of Cannon and Projectiles. In 1863 and 1864, the Academy added James G. Benton's *Course of Ordnance and Gunnery*.[72]

A major change in the program occurred in 1857 when the Academy divided the course into two parts. The Department of Tactics taught the practical lessons and a separate course explained the theoretical principles of ordnance.[73]

The first instructor of ordnance and gunnery, Colonel J.G. Benton, organized the Ordnance Department and wrote the basic textbook, *Ordnance and Gunnery.* Colonel Alfred Mordecai published a series of pamphlets to update chapters in Benton's book.[74]

Like other courses at the Academy, the object of the ordnance and gunnery program was to teach general principles and their application. This provided the graduating officers with the practical knowledge of the weapons he employed in performing his duties. The course presented a broad foundation on which to learn more about the subject.[75]

The Department of Tactics

Tactics, Strategy and the Art of War

Tactics and strategy are two components of how countries conduct wars. Although often confused or treated as synonymous military terms, tactics and strategy are distinct planning levels in military science.[1] Strategy and tactics are part of a hierarchical relation where government policy defines a grand *strategy* that leads to *strategy* that produces *operations* to achieve this strategy and finally the *tactics* employed to win individual battles.[2]

Strategy

Strategy is the highest level of *military* planning. Strategy employs all a nation's military capabilities through high level and long-term planning, development, and procurement of materials[3] to guarantee a desired outcome.

The father of Western modern strategic studies, Carl von Clausewitz,[4] defined military strategy as "the employment of battles to gain the end of war." B.H. Liddell Hart's[5] definition put less emphasis on battles and described strategy as "the art of distributing and applying military means to fulfill the ends of policy." Both men believed political aims were superior or more important than military goals.

Strategy defines and drives the operations to implement the strategy and achieve the strategic goals. Operational planning creates campaigns and missions and defines the goals to be met in these operations. These operations may result in battles to defeat enemy forces, capture property, demolish military supplies, and destroy supporting logistical and economic systems. Even if confrontations are not part of the operational plan, enemy forces may launch counter measures such as building defensive works to block the army's advancement, destroying the line of supply, and/or launching strikes against other targets to force units to withdraw and diminish the effectiveness of the campaign.

The Art of War

According to Antoine Henri baron de Jomini,[6] the art of war consists of six distinct parts: (1) Statesmanship in its relation to war; (2) Strategy, or the art of properly directing masses upon the theater of war, either for defense or for invasion; (3) Grand Tactics; (4) Logistics, or the art of moving armies; (5) Engineering, or the attack and defense of fortifications; and (6) Minor Tactics.[7]

Tactics

Tactics is the lowest level of military planning. Tactics defines the actions opposing commanders use on the battlefield. These actions are intended to achieve a battlefield victory often by attacking the enemy where he is weakest. These vulnerable points are on the sides and rear of the opposing forces. In these assaults, the army must be capable of rapid movement and effective fire power. Therefore, tactics governs how battles are fought during operations (campaigns). Tactics focuses on the means which infantry, artillery, and cavalry are employed and directed against an enemy.[8]

The United States Department of Defense Dictionary of Military Terms defines tactics as "the level of war at which battles and engagements are planned and executed to accomplish military objectives assigned to tactical units or task forces. Activities at this level focus on the ordered arrangement and maneuver of combat elements in relation to each other and to the enemy to achieve combat objectives."[9]

Tactical decisions are those made to achieve the greatest immediate value; strategic decisions are those made to achieve the greatest overall value, irrespective of the immediate results of a tactical decision.[10]

Tactics are the actions of individual soldiers and groups of soldiers. This is the level where combat and fighting takes place. The contest is a personal struggle where men meet, fight, and live or die.

Jomini divides tactics into minor tactics and grand tactics. Grand tactics is the art of placing troops on the battlefield according to the nature of the ground, bringing them into action, and the art of fighting upon the ground, in distinction to planning upon a map.[11] Minor tactics consists of the manual of arms and movement of troops in companies, battalions, and regiments. Simply put, minor tactics includes the actions of soldiers and movement of soldiers on the battlefield, while grand tactics deals with where these troops should be placed and how they should perform during a battle.

It is extremely important to understand the difference between strategy and tactics and their place in the hierarchy of warfare in evaluating the intent and effectiveness of military education at the United States Military Academy. The West Point curriculum focused on minor and grand tactics with little time spent on military strategy. The Academy's goal was to prepare officers who led and took part in the fighting and not those who designed the overall battle and stayed behind the front line with their staff to monitor the actions. Bluntly said, soldiers and junior officers were meant to fight and die, and generals were expected to plan and report.

Criticism of Tactical Training

> "Mankind is divided into two classes, those who go ahead and do something and those who sit back and criticize them for not doing it better."—General Horace Porter[12]

Since its founding in 1802, the military training conducted at the Academy has been criticized by politicians, the public, and alumni. These complaints focused on the utility of military training, lack of military experience in the peacetime army, relevance of tactical training, curriculum, and defection of West Point graduates to the Confederacy. These criticisms were in addition to those already made on the U.S. Military Academy by Jacksonians. Cadets disparaged tactical instruction. In 1832, Jacob W. Baily said, "Artillery and Infantry Tactics are disgusting. I would as soon commit to memory a table of logarithms as some of the lessons in these studies."[13]

Are Generals Made or Born?

One of the core questions concerning military training is whether the Academy prepares the cadets to be general officers in the Army.

> Graduation at West Point does not make one a good general. A man must have natural aptitude or adaptability, or he will not succeed. Graduation at West Point equips a young man and enables him to apply to advantage whatever talents he possesses, but without aptitude it will never make him a safe general.—William C. Oates[14]

Can the Academy educate cadets to become generals? Some believed "a man can no more be made a first-class general than a first-class painter, or a great poet, by professors and text-books; he must be born with the genius of war in his breast."[15]

> The best material for commanders in this civil strife may have never seen West Point. There is something in the remark that a good general is "born to command." We have experienced that some of our best-educated officers have no faculty to govern, control, and direct an army in offensive warfare.—Gideon Welles, Diary, 1:85[16]

Perhaps the public's expectations were too high. Was it reasonable for the typical Academy graduate to have all the knowledge and skills to lead an army?

> It was assumed that West Point officers knew the whole art of war and were ready-made generals. A few—but not too many—of those officers read military books.—Ben Butler, *Butler's Book*, 863.[17]

Graduates complained the training focused on the soldier and not the officer.

> For nearly all, it was the education of the soldier in the ranks and not the officer—Jacob Cox, *Military Reminiscences*, vol. I, p. 178.[18]

Some critics complained about the lack of stimulation provided in the peacetime military.

> Take a boy sixteen from his mother's apron strings, shut him up under constant surveillance for four years at West Point, send him out to a two-company post upon the frontier where he does little but play seven-up[19] and drink whiskey at the sutler's,[20] and by the time he is forty-five years old he will furnish the most complete illustration of suppressed mental development of which human nature is capable, and many such specimens were made generals on both sides when the war began.[21]

Citizen-soldier brevet Major General Alvin Voris thought little of the professional-trained officer who lacked real-world experience.

I grant there is an advantage in favor of the man who has made the art of war his study, but that is only the advantage of theory. And where that theory has never had any better opportunity to develop into practical knowledge than the lazy limited routine offered by the little standing army of this Republic, I must say that advantage is not very great over a thorough, intelligent, practical business man.[22]

Relevance of Tactical Training

Tactical training was also chastised for not keeping up with changing technology. "To the small extent that West Point taught them to wage on a large scale at all, it was as Napoleon had waged it. But when the war came, those tactics and strategies had either gone out of date or required drastic amendment in the face of more powerful weaponry and the peculiar requirements of the geography and the times."[23]

Outsiders said West Point was "more concerned with social status and outward appearances than with hard objective realities." They concluded the Academy's emphasis on "rote-learning and style" did not prepare graduates with the ability to adapt to "the rapidly changing military universe." If the lessons the Academy taught were those of past wars, then West Point officers might be expected to commit "anachronistic" errors on Civil War battlefields. Many officers were "completely divorced from tactical reality" and functioned under "some remote theoretical system." Respected Civil War historian Grady McWhiney stated, "Losses were so staggering because officers on both sides fought by the books, and the books were wrong."[24] Compounding this reliance on the past, the generals and government were accused of being "strangely stupid" and "slow to learn."[25]

The tactical manuals received much of the blame for the quality of military training. The textbooks were criticized because they were obsolete, unrealistic, or too complex. The manuals were based on Napoleonic armies and had not been greatly altered until General William Hardee's revisions in 1855. They were unrealistic because they did not consider actual combat conditions. "It is only in pictures and civilian novels that brigades and regiments charge at the double with even front over any distance above sixty or eighty yards." The manuals were criticized as being too complex and should be "significantly reduced and simplified."

The manuals were also disparaged because they did not instruct officers on how to win battles. The instruction in tactics and practice preached by the commandants of cadets provided Civil War officers with the ability "to change the front to face an attack or to retreat to avoid fighting in one direction when the foe attacked in another."[26]

In 1840, the *Citizen Soldier* accused the Academy of being "monopolizing, aristocratic, unconstitutional, and worse than useless."[27]

Curriculum

The United States Military Academy was built as an engineering college and not as a military school. West Point graduates "might not have been particularly well versed in the art of commanding infantry or cavalry in battle," but they had a "solid grounding in mathematics and military engineering."[28] The focus on engineering led to constructing defensive works to guard the coasts.

An important factor was that the Military Academy was under the jurisdiction of the Corps of Engineers and its Chief of Engineers, Joseph Totten.[29] Brigadier General Totten served as Chief Engineer from 1838 until 1864.[30] His influence is shown in the West Point curriculum and its superintendents and commandants of cadets. From 1817 until 1864, every superintendent graduated as a member of the Corps of Engineers and served as a military engineer.[31]

The Army rewarded the highest-ranking graduates with commissions in the Corps of Engineers. The poorest performing cadets were assigned to infantry regiments. The Army was controlled by military engineers and there was a bias toward them. Naturally, this created conflicts among the various branches.

The Academy's technical orientation was challenged by critics who wanted a broader, classical curriculum. As early as 1819, Inspector General John E. Wool recommended more attention to history, geography, and languages, especially in the training of infantry officers. In his opinion, the great victories of history "were not achieved by the 'rule and compass' or the 'measurement of angles.' They were the product of enlarged minds, highly cultivated and improved by a constant survey of human events." Criticism of this kind continued through the antebellum period and in the 1850s led to a brief experiment with a five-year course of instruction, which allowed greater emphasis on liberal arts and military topics.[32]

Civil War Defections and Battle Failures

The resignation of West Point graduates in 1861 to join the Confederacy launched a new attack on the Academy. Secretary of War Simon Cameron[33] blamed the Academy for the defection. He asked, "whether its promoting cause may not be traced to a radical defect in the system of education itself." Cameron referred to a report of the Board of Visitors which found problems with the disciplinary system. The Board said the system ignores differences between "acts wrong in themselves" and "acts wrong because permitted by special regulations." The report showed there was no distinction in punishment for "either class of offenses." Cameron argued this causes confusion in the minds of cadets. Cameron said the disaffection, or the "extraordinary treachery" displayed, might be traced to a "radical defect in the system of education at the Academy."[34]

In 1862, Ohio Congressman John Hutchens presented a proposal in the House of Representatives "to inquire into the propriety of dispensing with the military academy at West Point, and aiding the endowment of military academies under the control of the several States." The motion was rejected, by a vote of 79 to 48.[35] Henry Barnard, editor of the *American Journal of Education*, noted of West Point, "It was not to be expected that schools of refined, scientific art should be found by small colonies in the wilderness of a new world. When even their clergymen must resort to Europe for education, and their lawyers for license, it was in vain to expect their soldiers to be accomplished engineers."[36]

Early Tactical Training

Cadets received practical instruction in tactics from the founding of the Military Academy in 1802. However, it took an act of Congress on June 12, 1858, to officially recognize the department and authorize the commanding officer of the corps or battalion of cadets as commandant of cadets and instructor of artillery, cavalry, and infantry tactics. Over time, the department changed in response to requirements at the Academy.[37]

Instruction

From 1802 to 1812, the academic term time began in April and ended in November. The cadets were absent the rest of the year. After 1805, the study hours were from 8 a.m. to 1 p.m., 2 to 4 p.m., and in the evening. Drills and practical exercises took place from 4 p.m. to sunset and occasionally before breakfast.[38]

Generally, the number of tactical instructors ranged from one to four. The infantry tactical instruction included manual exercises with the musket. The tactical instructors trained the cadets on the School of the Company.[39] The cadets also practiced with field pieces and mortars, which included "a little target practice."[40] The cavalry assistant

West Point Cadets before Civil War (Library of Congress).

taught cavalry tactics, equitation,[41] and outpost duty.[42] The senior infantry assistant taught infantry tactics, strategy, grand tactics, and logistics. The senior artillery assistant taught artillery tactics and army organization and administration.[43]

The first Academic Regulations were very brief and "adapted to the small requirements of the institution." After eight years of experience with the first regulations, the Military Academy approved an "extended code'" on April 30, 1810. These early rules became the basis "upon which the school rests." The regulations defined fifteen to twenty years as the age of entrance; made cadets serve in the United States military for four years unless discharged; abolished furloughs except during vacations or under peculiar circumstances; prescribed the same uniform for all cadets of the different arms of the service; and defined rules for interior police and discipline. Before these regulations, the Academy admitted cadets without mental or physical examinations. Some of the cadets, who enrolled between 1802 and 1810, had a good preliminary education before coming to West Point. A few of the candidates were college graduates, one had been an officer in the British army, and another had practiced law in the supreme court of New York. Generally, they had "more knowledge and maturity of mind than those of the present day." They were of all ages from twelve to thirty-four years, and one or two men were married with several children.[44]

Cadets shared quarters with Regular Army soldiers, stationed at West Point, in the old "Long Barracks" of the Revolution (near the site of the Thayer Hotel). Classes were held in a two-story wooden building, which served both as an academy and post headquarters.

Discipline was irregularly enforced during the early years of the Academy. When Superintendent Colonel Jonathan Williams was at West Point (1801–1803 and 1805–1812), he personally enforced discipline. However, when Williams was absent, "great irregularities took place from want of proper control on the part of the commanding officer" and because the instructors were "all civilians and foreigners."[45]

Evolution of Tactical Instruction

Between its founding in 1802 and the Civil War, military instruction evolved with changing technology and military responsibilities.

- 1802—Thomas Jefferson signed the bill creating the United States Military Academy. The Academy formally opened on July 4. Joseph Gardner Swift and Simon Magruder Levy became the first graduates after only seven months attendance.[46]
- 1803—Three cadets graduated after stays at the Academy ranging from ten to thirteen months.[47]
- 1808—Future Superintendent Sylvanus Thayer graduated after an eleventh-month stay.[48]
- April 29, 1812—Congress authorized appointing 250 cadets and the necessary academic staff. However, at the end of September 1812, only one officer and one new cadet were at the Academy.[49]

1812—The Army named Colonel Joseph G. Swift[50] superintendent.[51]

1812–1814—The war of 1812 diverted potential cadets and trained officers from the classroom to the battlefield.

April 15, 1813—The Academy resumed operations with less than a dozen Cadets.

1814—The Academy appointed a civilian to manage the cadet commons. The required cadet uniform consisted of blue coat and pantaloons, round hat with black silk cockade and gilt eagle, a black hat, and Jefferson shoes. The coat was single-breasted, with one row of bullet buttons and a standing collar. Cadets used the same muskets as those used by soldiers, but the Academy allowed small boys to use a lighter model. The Academy expected each cadet to wear a sword, but few owned the weapon.

May 1814—The Academy appointed Pierre Thomas as the first sword master. Sword exercises were restricted to specially selected cadets. During the summer of 1814, the cadets made an excursion to Governors Island, New York Harbor.[52]

1815—Alden Partridge was named superintendent.[53]

Summer 1816—Cadets made a three-day excursion to New York.

July 2, 1816—The regulations for military instruction prescribed infantry and artillery tactics, practical gunnery, camp duties, and broad and small sword exercises.

September 4, 1816—The Academy adopted a new uniform for cadets.

1812–1817—During this period, the staff "practically ignored" the course of instruction outlined in the Regulations. However, the acting superintendent taught infantry and artillery drills. The small number of cadets and the few pieces of ordnance for drill and target practice limited the exercises.

1814–1817—Prior to 1818, the Academy did not have an officer who was specially designated as instructor of tactics. From 1814 to 1817, the acting superintendent was commander, professor, and chaplain.

July 28, 1817—The Army named brevet Major Sylvanus Thayer superintendent. The tactics department officially began when Thayer assumed command. He organized the cadets into a battalion of two companies. Members from the Corps of Cadets served as junior officers in the battalion.

September 15, 1817—Thayer appointed an Army officer to command the battalion, instruct the cadets in infantry tactics, enforce "soldierly discipline," and administer the interior police. The Army temporarily assigned Second Lieutenant G.W. Gardiner, of the Corps of Artillery, to command the battalion, instruct the cadets in infantry tactics, enforce discipline, and supervise the interior police.[54]

1818—The Military Academy assigned the commanding officer of the Battalion of Cadets as the inspector of the cadet commons. He was named permanent president of the board to audit the accounts of the cadets' mess and the board of inspectors of supplies.[55]

April 2, 1818—The Army appointed Captain John Bliss, of the Sixth Infantry, as commanding officer of the battalion of cadets and instructor of infantry tactics.

November 22, 1818—Cadets mutinied over discipline.[56]

1820—The Academy assigned two junior officers as assistant instructors of infantry tactics.

1821—The Regulations of 1821 provided that a captain or field officer be designated as instructor of infantry tactics.[57]

July 20, 1821—The corps of cadets under the command of commandant of cadets, Major William J. Worth, marched to Boston during the summer and spent two weeks encamped on Boston Common. The cadets visited former President John Adams on August 14.[58]

1821—The Academy introduced the study of infantry tactics as a formal course. Cadet recitations on tactics took place between 2 and 4 p.m. The cadets used the "infantry rules and regulations for the infantry branch of service" as the textbook.[59]

1825—The Regulations of 1825 specified the instruction in the system of U.S. Army infantry tactics. The curriculum included the School of the Soldier, School of the Company, School of the Battalion, and the evolutions of the line,[60] and the exercises and maneuvers of light infantry and riflemen. The training also included the duties in camp, garrison, and as guards and police for privates, noncommissioned officers, and officers.[61] The regulations also specified formation of a cadet battalion of four companies and designated the instructor of infantry tactics and commanding officer of the battalion of cadets as "Commandant of Cadets." The regulations mentioned the "officer in charge" and defined his duties. The commandant also served as the permanent president of the board to audit the accounts of the cadets' mess and board of inspectors of supplies.[62] The Military Academy divided the corps of cadets "into as many squads as there are tables in the mess hall." "They also stipulated that when the signal for breakfast, dinner, and supper sounded, these squads assembled under the direction of the first or second carver,[63] and marched to the mess hall as directed by the superintendent of the mess hall."[64]

July 4, 1825—Colonel Thayer saw the drunken behavior of cadets and forbid alcohol.[65]

December 26, 1826—Cadets engaged in the "Egg-Nog [sic] Riot." Cadets chased officers at sword point, threw missiles through windows, and destroyed stairs and railings. Several cadets were court-martialed.[66]

1827—The Academy increased the number of assistant instructors of infantry tactics to three.[67]

1829—The regulations specified that explanations for offenses had to be presented in writing. The rule changed in 1857 and the Academy ordered explanations be given verbally. If the explanation was unsatisfactory to the commandant, he could ask for a written clarification. Initially, the format used to present the account began by first declaring the "offense" and then giving the "excuse." Later the Academy changed the form to first saying the "delinquency" which was followed by the "explanation." Subsequently, the terms were altered to first the "report" which was followed by the "explanation."

1837—The Academy appointed an instructor of cavalry tactics.

1838—The Army increased the term of service of cadets to eight years, "unless sooner discharged."[68]

1839—The Academy Regulations prescribed that during the encampment the First Class cadets should study the evolutions of the line in the system of infantry tactics prescribed for the Army. Cadets had to recite and explain the evolutions to the instructor. In addition, the cadets had to study and recite on selected portions of the General Regulations of the Army. This training continued until the summer of 1862.

1839—The Army sent a sergeant and five dragoons to West Point from Carlisle Barracks, Pennsylvania to help present riding instruction and exercises for cadets. The Quartermaster's Department supplied twelve horses. The Army discharged the sergeant from the service and appointed him as civilian riding master. The Academy bought horses and harness for the light battery. Before 1839, cadets had to haul the pieces and carriages around using a rope harness.

1840—The Army said the commander of the Corps of Cadets should be either the instructor of infantry tactics, cavalry and artillery, or practical military engineering.

1842—The Academy Regulations authorized an officer as instructor of artillery and cavalry tactics.

1849—The Academy appointed the instructor of cavalry as instructor in riding. The Academy dropped the position of riding master in 1852.

1852—The Academy increased the number of assistant instructors of infantry tactics to four.[69]

1857—The Regulations specified that at the hour appointed for breakfast, dinner, and supper, a senior cadet officer would form the companies and march them to the mess hall.

June 12, 1858—Congress recognized the title of "Commandant of Cadets," and ordered that, "The Commandant of Cadets shall have the local rank and the pay and allowances of a lieutenant-colonel of engineers, and besides his other duties shall be charged with the duties of instructor in the tactics of the three arms of the service."[70]

February 28, 1858—From February 28, 1858, until April 24, 1861, the Academy added instruction in small arms and military gymnastics[71] to the curriculum. They placed a commissioned officer, not attached to the tactical department, in charge of the program. After 1861, this instruction returned to the commandant of cadets with a civilian as sword master, but without gymnastics.[72]

September 12, 1859—When the Academy increased training from four to five years; the Secretary of War transferred the study of strategy, grand tactics, outpost duty, army organization and administration, equitation and veterinary science to the Second Class in the Department of Tactics. The secretary also requested the commandant of cadets to prepare a program for instruction. Because the tactical department did not have the required number of assistant tactical instructors, the commandant recommended keeping the subjects of strategy, grand tactics, and outpost duty in the Department of Engineering and taught to First Class cadets. The Army approved these changes on October 20, 1859. These subjects, together with infantry and cavalry tactics, were taught in the First Class course through the June 1860 examinations. From January 1860 to May 1861, the Department of Tactics taught these subjects in the Second Class.[73]

April 1861—After Confederate forces captured Fort Sumter, many cadets from the South left the Military Academy and obtained commissions in the Confederate States Army.[74]

May 1861—When the Academy returned to a four-year program in 1861, strategy, grand tactics, and outpost duty returned to the Department of Engineering and were taught to the First Class. The Academy stopped teaching organization, administration, and veterinary science, but the remaining subjects continued to be presented in the Second Class course.[75]

Tactics in the Classroom

The Academy taught drill regulations in varying levels from its founding. However, the Department of Tactics officially began on September 15, 1817, when the Academy organized the cadets into a battalion and Lieutenant G.W. Gardiner was temporarily detailed to command the battalion. The position of commandant of cadets was not "officially" defined until the regulations of 1825. The department was not formally recognized until July 12, 1858.[76]

The Regulations of 1821 provided that a captain or field officer should be assigned as instructor of infantry tactics. These regulations authorized the Department of Tactics to give instruction in "the system of infantry tactics established for the Army of the United States." This system included instruction in the School of the Soldier, School of the Company, and School of the Battalion. The lessons also involved the evolutions of the line, the exercises and maneuvers of light infantry and riflemen, and the duties in camp and garrison of privates, noncommissioned officers, and officers, including guard and police responsibilities.[77]

There were two assistant instructors of infantry tactics from 1820 to 1827, three assistants from 1827 to 1852, and four assistants after 1852. The 1840 regulations provided that the commander of the Corps of Cadets should be either the instructor of infantry tactics, instructor of cavalry and artillery, or instructor of practical military engineering. In 1842, the regulations authorized an officer as instructor of artillery and cavalry tactics. The 1849 regulations named the instructor of cavalry as instructor in riding. The Military Academy ended the riding master position in 1852.[78]

Before the start of the Civil War, cadets used the following textbooks: Carl von Decker's *Tactics of Three Arms*; *Tactics for Garrison, Siege, and Field Artillery*; William Youatt's *The Horse*; Dennis H. Mahan's *Treatise on Advanced Guards and Outposts*; Antoine-Henri Jomini's *The Art of War*; Thomas Thackeray's *Army Organization and Administration*, and the United States Army Regulations.[79]

Hardee's *Rifle and Light Infantry Tactics*

The formulation of standardized tactics was as important as it was mundane. The nineteenth-century tactical manual served as the indispensable grammar of battle field maneuver. There is nothing "natural" about lining up in long lines with one's fellows and tramping around a battlefield shooting at the other groups of soldiers doing the same; furthermore, the inherent tendency toward chaos in war requires a special degree of regimentation. A manual could be better, or it could be worse; a general might choose the right evolution at the appropriate time, or he might not; but without some system of standardized tactics, an army was only a disorganized body of individuals with weapons, incapable of the intense trials of strength in battle that nation-state wars demanded. Furthermore, a common manual would greatly facilitate the training of citizen-soldier volunteers by the Regular Army in wartime.[80]

The commandants used several textbooks to teach tactics. However, the principle source of drill field training were manuals written by Winfield Scott and William Hardee to explain the fundamentals of managing groups of soldiers. General Hardee's manual illustrates the range in topics covered in tactical instruction.

Secretary of War Jefferson Davis transmitted the president's approval of William Hardee's *Rifle and Light Infantry Tactics* on March 29, 1855. The U.S. Army and state militias adopted the manual for instructing troops "acting as light infantry or riflemen." The lessons presented in Hardee's manual illustrate the scope of tactical education provided by the commandants.

Volume I presents the "Schools of the Soldier and Company" and "Instruction for Skirmishers." The First Article describes the "formation of a regiment in order of battle, or in line." The lessons on regiments show the Academy designed the instruction to prepare officers who might become colonels. With the small size of the army before the Civil War, this instruction would train officers for the largest command they were likely to lead. Most of the instruction dealt with the "posts" of officers, regimental staff, musicians, and color guard.

The Second Article explains "Instruction of the Battalion"[81]

RIFLE

AND

LIGHT INFANTRY TACTICS:

FOR

THE EXERCISE AND MANŒUVRES

OF

TROOPS WHEN ACTING AS LIGHT INFANTRY OR RIFLEMEN.

PREPARED UNDER THE DIRECTION OF THE WAR DEPARTMENT,

BY

BREVET LIEUT.-COL. W. J. HARDEE,
U. S. ARMY.

VOL. II.
SCHOOL OF THE BATTALION.

PHILADELPHIA:
LIPPINCOTT, GRAMBO & CO.
1855.

The title page of Hardee's *Rifle and Light Infantry Tactics* (Philadelphia: Lippincott, Grambo & Co., 1855).

Drilling troops near Washington, D.C. (Library of Congress).

and assigns the responsibility for instruction to various officers. The article defines the chain of command used for training soldiers, non-commissioned officers, and officers. This part of the manual emphasizes the importance of proper training. The manual states, "The instruction of officers can be perfected only by joining theory to practice."

The Third Article describes the basic military training, which encompasses the "School of the Soldier." This school presented (1) lessons for recruits "without arms"; (2) the "manual of arms"[82] and loading and firing muskets and rifles; and (3) principles of alignment, marching by the front, different marching steps, marching by the flank, principles of wheeling, changing direction, and "long marches in double quick time and the run." This part of the training guide explained the "manual of arms" and the "load in nine times," which are step-by-step instructions for loading a muzzle musket or rifle. Then, the manual describes the procedure to aim and fire the weapon. Training is also included on fixing bayonets and preparing to charge with bayonets. This part of the textbook has descriptions for direct, oblique, file, and rank firing. It also has directions for firing from kneeling and prone positions. The section explains the procedures for "marching to the front, right or left oblique, front in double quick time, face about, backwards, flank, file left or right, and flank in double quick time" and "wheeling from a halt, wheeling in marching, and wheeling in double quick time."[83]

This section of Hardee's manual presents the "School of the Company," which describes the various movements and firing operations used in platoon and company size[84] units. The guide presents directions for the deployment, movement, and firing of skirmishers.

The tactics textbook has a "Manual of the Sword or Sabre, for Officers" with the procedure to salute and present a color salute. Another section explains how to relieve sentinels. This article lists twenty-five general calls and twenty-three calls for skirmishers for the chief bugler and drum major to play, with the music for each of the calls.[85]

Volume II focuses on the "School of the Battalion." Hardee explained, "This school has for its object the instruction of battalions singly, and thus to prepare them for manoeuvers [sic] in line." He divided the "School of the Battalion" into five parts: (1) opening and closing ranks and executing different fires; (2) different modes of passing from the order in battle to the order in column; (3) marching in column and the other associated movements; (4) the different modes of passing from the order in column to the order in battle; and

Private Louis H. Benz, chief bugler, West Point Military Academy (Library of Congress).

(5) marching in line of battle, in advance, and in retreat, passing of defiles[86] in retreat, marching by the flank,[87] forming by file into line of battle, changing the front; doubling the column on the center, dispositions against cavalry, rallying, and maneuvering by the rear rank.[88]

Hardee's manual does not explain how to use this training to *attack* and *defeat* an enemy in the field. Figuratively speaking, it explains how to hold the saw and cut a board but not how to build a table or a house. Of course, one cannot construct a table or house without the basic knowledge of how to hold the saw and cut a board. Cadets practiced these fundamental skills until they understood how to apply them and how to instruct subordinates in their use.

West Point in the Civil War

Before the beginning of the Civil War, West Point cadets came from all over the country. Naturally, the cadets presented the attitudes and values of their homes. They adhered to the political doctrines, traditions, and prejudices of their native state. Emotions ran high and fierce at the Academy. Even in the North, opposing political opinions divided the region. The Corps of Cadets reflected the nation's political disharmony.

West Point Officers in the Civil War

State and family loyalties divided the West Point alumni. One hundred and sixty-two Academy graduates from the South (twenty percent of the Southern graduates from West Point) "withstood the terrible strain of kin and birth and stood by the flag." This statistic contrasts with fifty percent of the Confederate officers who came from civilian careers in the South and "flocked en masse to their native states."[1]

When the war ended in April 1865, West Point–trained officers commanded the Union and Confederate armies. Academy graduates led nearly all the corps, most of the divisions, most of the staffs of organization, supply, and science of both forces; and many of the brigades. West Point graduates commanded forces in every important battle of the war on one or both sides and usually both. Only five of the sixty engagements on the following list of very important battles and campaigns were not commanded on both sides by West Point graduates. Of the five exceptions, a West Point officer commanded the army on one side and was victorious in four of the battles.

Officers Serving in the Civil War[2]

Category	Number
Number of graduates who became general officers in the Regular and Volunteer armies of the United States	294
Total number of general officers of each grade in the Regular and Volunteer armies of the United States who were graduates of the Military Academy:	
Generals	3
Lieutenant Generals	1
Major Generals	85
Brigadier Generals	205
Total	294

Category	Number
Number of graduates who served as general officers in the U.S. Army:	
Commanded separate armies	24
Commanded army corps	46
Commanded divisions	88
Commanded brigades	105
Number of graduates who served as general officers in the Confederate Army	
Generals	8
Lieutenant Generals	15
Major Generals	40
Brigadier Generals	88
Total	151
Number of graduates who became general officers in foreign armies	3
Grand total of general officers in both armies who were graduates of the United States Military Academy	448[3]

The following West Point graduates became high-ranking officers in the Confederate Army.[4]

Generals	*Lieutenant Generals*
Beauregard, P.G.T.	Anderson, Richard H.
Hood, John B.	Buckner, Simon B.
Lee, Robert E.	Early, Jubal A.
Bragg, Braxton	Ewell, Richard S.
Johnston, Albert S.	Hardee, William J.
Cooper, Samuel	Hill, Daniel H.
Smith, Edmund K.	Hill, A.P.
Johnston, Joseph E.	Holmes, Theophilus H.
	Jackson, Thomas J.
	Lee, Stephen D.
	Longstreet, James
	Pemberton, John C.
	Polk, Leonidas
	Stewart, Alexander P.
	Wheeler, Joseph

The following West Point graduates became high-ranking officers in the Union Army.[5]

Lee and his generals, chromolithograph by W.B. Matthews (Library of Congress).

Generals
Grant, Ulysses S.
Sheridan, Philip H.
Sherman, William T.

Lieutenant Generals
Schofield, John M.

Major Generals (U.S. Army)
McClellan, George B.
Meade, George G.

Major Generals (U.S. Volunteers)
Augur, Christopher C.
Buell, Don Carlos
Buford, John
Burnside, Ambrose E.
Canby, Edward R.S.
Casey, Silas
Couch, Darius N.
Crook, George
Curtis, Samuel R.
Dana, Napoleon J.T.
Doubleday, Abner
Foster, John G.
Franklin, William B.
French, William H.
Gibbon, John
Parke, John G.
Peck, John J.
Pleasonton, Alfred
Pope, John
Porter, Fitz-John

Major Generals
Gillmore, Quincy A.
Granger, Gordon
Griffin, Charles
Halleck, Henry W.
Hamilton, Charles S.
Hancock, Winfield S.
Hartsuff, George L.
Hazen, William B.
Heintzelman, Samuel P.
Hitchcock, Ethan A.
Hooker, Joseph
Howard, Oliver O.
Humphreys, Andrew A.
Hunter, David
Keyes, Erasmus D.
Mansfield, Joseph K.F.
Mansfield, Joseph K.F.
McCook, Alexander McD.
McDowell, Irvin
McPherson, James B.
Merritt, Wesley
Mitchel, Ormsby Mc-Knight
Newton, John
Ord, Edward O.C.
Smith, Charles F.
Smith, William F.
Stanley, David S.
Steele, Frederick
Stevens, Isaac I.
Stoneman, George v
Strong, George C. v
Sykes, George v

Grant and his generals on horseback, chromolithograph by E. Boell (Library of Congress).

Major Generals (U.S. Volunteers)
Reno, Jesse L.
Reynolds, John F.
Reynolds, Joseph J.
Richardson, Israel B.
Rosecrans, William S.
Ruger, Thomas H.
Sedgwick, John
Slocum, Henry W.
Smith, Andrew J.

Major Generals
Thomas, George H. v
Warren, Gouverneur K. v
Weitzel, Godfrey v
Whipple, Amiel V. v
Wood, Thomas J. v
Wright, Horatio G. v

Important Battles of the Civil War, with the Names of Commanders and the Forces Engaged on Both Sides[6]

Battle	Date	Union Commander	Union Force	Confederate Commander	Confederate Force
1861					
Bull Run	July 2, 1861	I. McDowell*	28,452	J. E. Johnston* P.T. Beauregard*	32,232
Wilson Creek	August 10, 1861	N. Lyon*	5,400	Ben. McCulloch	6,000
1862					
Fort Donelson	February 12–16, 1862	U.S. Grant*	27,000	John B. Floyd	21,000
Pea Ridge	March 7, 1862	S.R. Curtis*	11,250	Earl van Dorn*	14,000
Shiloh	April 6–7, 1862	U.S. Grant*	62,682	A.S. Johnston* P.T. Beauregard*	40,335
Williamsburg	May 4–5, 1862	G. McClellan*	40,768	J.E. Johnston*	31,823
Fair Oaks	May 31–June 1, 1862	G. McClellan*	41,797	J.E. Johnston*	41,816
Mechanicsville	June 26, 1862	G. McClellan*	15,631	R.E. Lee*	16,356
Gaines' Mill	June 27, 1862	G. McClellan*	34,214	R.E. Lee*	57,018
Peach Orchard, Malvern Hill	June 29–July 1, 1862	G. McClellan*	83,345	R.E. Lee*	86,748

Fort Sumter before the bombardment (Library of Congress).

Battle	Date	Union Commander	Union Force	Confederate Commander	Confederate Force
Seven Days' Battles	June 25–July 1, 1862	G. McClellan*	91,169	R.E. Lee*	16,868
Cedar Mountain	August 9, 1862	J. Pope*	8,030	R.J. Jackson*	48,527
Manassas and Chantilly	August 27–September 2, 1862	J. Pope*	7,569	R.E. Lee*	48,527
South Mountain	September 14, 1862	G. McClellan*	28,480	R.E. Lee*	18,714
Antietam	September 16–17, 1862	G. McClellan*	75,316	R.E. Lee*	51,844
Corinth	October 3–4, 1862	W. Rosecrans*	21,147	Earl Von Dorn*	22,000
Perryville	October 8, 1862	D.C. Buell*	36,940	B. Bragg*	16,000
Fredericksburg	December 13, 1862	A.E. Burnside*	100,007	R.E. Lee*	72,497
Chickasaw Bayou	December 27–29, 1862	W.T. Sherman*	30,720	J.C. Pemberton*	13,792
Stone River	December 31, 1862	W. Rosecrans*	41,400	B. Bragg*	34,732
1863					
Chancellorsville	May 1–4, 1863	J. Hooker*	97,382	R.E. Lee*	57,352
Champion Hill	May 6, 1863	U.S. Grant*	29,373	J.C. Pemberton*	20,000
Vicksburg	May 22, 1863	U.S. Grant*	45,556	J.C. Pemberton*	22,301
Port Hudson	May 27, 1863	N. Banks	13,000	F. Gardner*	4,192
Port Hudson	June 14, 1863	N. Banks	6,000	F. Gardner*	3,487
Gettysburg	July 1–3, 1863	G.G. Meade*	83,289	R.E. Lee*	75,054
Fort Wagner	July 18, 1863	Q.A. Gillmore*	5,264	P.T. Beauregard*	1,785
Chickamauga	September 19–20, 1863	W. Rosecrans*	58,222	B. Bragg*	66,326
Chattanooga	November 23–25, 1863	U.S. Grant*	56,359	B. Bragg*	46,165
Mine Run	November 27–December 1, 1863	G.G. Meade*	69,643	R.E. Lee*	44,426
1864					
Wilderness and Spotsylvania	May 5–2, 1864	U.S. Grant*	88,892	R.E. Lee*	61,025
Wilderness	May 5–7, 1864	U.S. Grant*	101,895	R.E. Lee*	61,025
Spotsylvania	May 10, 1864	U.S. Grant*	37,822	R.E. Lee*	52,000
Spotsylvania	May 12, 1864	U.S. Grant*	65,785	R.E. Lee*	52,000
Drewry's Bluff	May 12–16, 1864	B.F. Butler	15,800	P.T. Beauregard*	18,025
Atlanta Campaign	May 1864	W.T. Sherman*	110,123	J.E. Johnston*	66,089
Cold Harbor	June 1–3, 1864	U.S. Grant*	107,907	R.E. Lee*	59,000–62,000
The Mine	July 30, 1864	U.S. Grant*	20,708	R.E. Lee*	11,466
Deep Bottom	August 14–19, 1864	U.S. Grant*	27,974	R.E. Lee*	20,008
Weldon Railroad	August 18–21, 1864	U.S. Grant*	20,289	R.E. Lee*	14,787
Kennesaw Mountain	June 2, 1864	W.T. Sherman*	16,225	J.E. Johnston*	17,733
Tupelo	July 13–15, 1864	A.J. Smith*	14,000	S.D. Lee*	6,600
Peach Tree Creek	July 20, 1864	W.T. Sherman*	20,139	J.B. Hood*	18,832
Atlanta	July 22, 1864	W.T. Sherman*	30,477	J.B. Hood*	36,934
Atlanta	July 28, 1864	W.T. Sherman*	13,226	J.B. Hood*	18,450
Jonesboro	August 31, 1864	W.T. Sherman*	14,170	J.B. Hood*	23,811
Jonesboro	September 1, 1864	W.T. Sherman*	20,460	J.B. Hood*	12,661

Battle	Date	Union Commander	Union Force	Confederate Commander	Confederate Force
Winchester	September 19, 1864	P. Sheridan*	37,711	J.A. Early*	17,103
Chaffin's Farm	September 29–30, 1864	U.S. Grant*	19,639	R.E. Lee*	10,836
Cedar Creek	October 19, 1864	P. Sheridan*	30,829	J.A. Early*	18,410
Boydton Plank Road	October 27–28, 1864	U.S. Grant*	42,823	R.E. Lee*	20,234
Franklin	November 30, 1864	J.M. Schofied*	27,939	J.B. Hood*	26,897
Nashville	December 15–16	G.H. Thomas*	49,773	J.B. Hood*	23,207
1865					
Fort Fisher	January 15, 1865	A. Terry*	9,632	W.C. Whiting*	7,800
Hatchers Run	February 5–7, 1865	U.S. Grant*	34,517	R.E. Lee*	13,835
Bentonville	March 19, 1865	W.T. Sherman*	16,127	J.E. Johnston*	16,895
Appomattox Campaign	March 29–April 5, 1865	U.S. Grant*	114,826	R.E. Lee*	49,496
Dinwiddie	March 29–31, 1865	U.S. Grant*	45,247	R.E. Lee*	20,030
Petersburg	April 2, 1865	U.S. Grant*	63,299	R.E. Lee*	9,652

*United States Military Academy graduates

Comparison of Northern and Southern Officers

During the Civil War, the South supposedly benefited from a "generally superior level of military leadership." Some believe cadets from the South dominated the antebellum Military Academy. There was a difference between the academic performance of cadets from the North and the South. This disparity might have given the Confederacy an advantage during the early stages of the Civil War. Northern students tended to perform better at the technically oriented Military Academy. Consequently, after graduation they were assigned to the more prestigious engineering and artillery units. Those Southern graduates whose academic performance placed them in the lower half of the class obtained less prized assignments in the cavalry, dragoons, mounted rifles, and infantry. This gave an initial advantage for the Confederacy, because the Southern graduates gained valuable experience leading infantry and the Civil War was an "infantryman's war."[7]

The evidence from the classes between 1818 and 1860 supports this proposition. Of the 373 West Point graduates who became Civil War generals,[8] fifty-five percent graduated in the top half of their classes. This shows academic performance was an indicator of wartime advancement. Sixty-one percent of future Union generals in the Civil War ranked in the top half of their graduating classes. This compares with fifty-one percent of Confederate generals who were in the top half of their classes. An examination of the top and bottom graduates shows eighty-six percent of the cadets who were first in their class obtained commissions in the Corps of Engineers. In contrast, eighty-one percent of the cadets who were the class goats (last in their class) received commissions in the U.S. Infantry. Of the cadets at the top of the class, fourteen (33 percent) became generals compared to only five (12 percent) at the bottom.

The status of the West Point-trained military officer was a source of friction on both sides throughout the war. The Union and the Confederacy benefited greatly from the professional knowledge and expertise of the West Pointers. However, neither the Northern or Southern society completely appreciated or understood the specialized skills and standards the professionals considered essential for conducting a "modern" war. In the North, suspicion of professional officers increased when many Southern officers joined the Confederate army. In the South, President Jefferson Davis displayed a "clear preference" for West Pointers. The contempt for politicians and civilians shown by professional officers added to their arrogant reputation. The officers expressed their disrespect in a "haughty cliquishness," contempt for volunteer troops, and unnecessarily harsh enforcement of military discipline.

Perhaps the most glaring problem was the inability of West Point officers to adjust and adapt to the innovations in military technology, which revolutionized warfare. From both a tactical and strategic perspective, they did not understand the impact of rifled muskets. The longer ranges and widespread use of rifled guns significantly improved firepower and gave an "overwhelming advantage to forces operating on the tactical defensive" and "rendered traditional assault tactics obsolete." The unanticipated increase in the use of field fortifications also favored defensive tactics.[9]

Three factors influenced Civil War operational and strategic planning: earlier training, the nature of the terrain, and the weapons used. The lessons learned at the Military Academy gave fundamental training in tactics (minor tactics) and operational planning (grand tactics). Some officers did not understand the West Points classes were the first steps in learning about the art of war. They stayed stuck in time, tied to Napoleonic principles and Professor Dennis Mahan's concepts. They implemented textbook teachings without considering the impact of terrain or technical innovations. Those who learned from each battle succeeded while those who held fast to antiquated thinking continued to fail.[10]

Civil War Generalship

Historians have often criticized the Military Academy for the deficiency of time devoted to military strategy. Dennis Hart Mahan taught the session on grand military strategy or the "art of war." Professor Mahan only allocated a small amount of time to the study of the great historical campaigns. In fact, his contributions to military strategy were more from his writing than his classroom instruction. W.J. Wood, in *Civil War Generalship*, attributed the lack of emphasis on strategy to three reasons. First, only a small part of the West Point curriculum was devoted to the art of war. Second, the curriculum focused on military engineering. Third, "the faculty at West Point did not have as its principle goal ... the production of future generals, but it had its hands full simply trying to turn out second lieutenants qualified to fill vacancies in the branches of the army."[11]

This last point is worth emphasizing especially when considering the limited opportunities for advancement in the peacetime military. The goal of preparing graduates for their first assignment in "the real world" is not unique to military education. Colleges and universities offer the fundamentals necessary to begin a career; they do not train students to perform the tasks of heads of businesses, governments, religious organizations, or academic institutions. Their graduates are equipped with a basic "tool box" of knowledge to which they can add new "tools" (skills and expertise). How well they add new skills and apply the skills in their "tool box" will determine how far they advance in their field of study.

However, there are unique educational aspects, which separates the military graduate from other baccalaureate graduates. West Point emphasized competition among the cadets. This contest went beyond classroom grades and extended to personal responsibility and leadership. Every day, cadets "fought" each other for honors. This competitive spirit helped prepare them for the limited opportunities in the peacetime army. The Military Academy, unlike non-military colleges and universities, instilled personal discipline in their students to control their emotions and think logically. The Academy stressed both giving and obeying orders.

Most of the West Point officers did not have the opportunity or inclination to study the art of war. Some remembered Mahan's comments on "the use of judgement" or Jomini's warning against "slavish obedience to abstract rules."[12]

The estimates of the number of Civil War generals range from 952 to 1,008. The number of Union generals range from 554 to 583 and Confederate generals from 398 to 425.[13] West Point trained officers accounted for 58 percent of Union and 42 percent of Confederate commanders. Thirty percent of West Point trained Union generals were major generals or above and 42 percent of Confederate generals were major generals or above.

During the Civil War, Southern generals performed better than their Union counterparts. Truman Seymour suggested that, "The South owes whatever of successful resistance it has made to her proper employment of her military education, and the North has failed in using its overpowering strength to insure quick success, because of its entire inappreciation [sic] of its military duties and its abusive or willful perversion of its military skill. The best possible vindication of the Military Academy is to be found in the history of the Confederacy."[14]

Civil War Service of Commandants

Not only did the commandants of cadets prepare the officers who served in the Civil War, they also held senior positions in the Union and Confederate Armies.

Name	Term as Commandant	Civil War Service
George W. Gardiner	September 15, 1817, to April 2, 1818	Killed on December 28, 1835, in Dade's Massacre
John Bliss	April 2, 1818, to January 11, 1819	Resigned on September 6, 1837
John R. Bell	February 8, 1819, to March 17, 1820	Died on April 11, 1825
William J. Worth	March 17, 1820, to December 2, 1828	Died on May 7, 1849
Ethan A. Hitchcock	March 13, 1829, to June 24, 1833	Union, Major General
John Fowle	July 10, 1833, to March 31, 1838	Killed on April 25, 1838, in boiler explosion on steamer *Moselle*
Charles F. Smith	April 1, 1838, to September 1, 1842	Union, Major General
J. Addison Thomas	September 1, 1842 to December 14, 1845	Died on March 26, 1858

Name	Term as Commandant	Civil War Service
Bradford R. Alden	December 14, 1845, to November 1, 1852	Resigned on September 29, 1853
Robert S. Garnett	November 1, 1852, to July 31, 1854	Confederate, Brigadier General
William H.T. Walker	July 31, 1854, to May 27, 1856	Confederate, Major General
William J. Hardee	July 22, 1856, to September 8, 1860	Confederate, Lieutenant General
John F. Reynolds	September 8, 1860, to June 25, 1861	Union, Major General
Christopher C. Augur	August 26, 1861, to December 5, 1861	Union, Major General
Kenner Garrard	December 5, 1861, to September 25, 1862	Union, Brigadier General
Henry B. Clitz	October 23, 1862, to July 4, 1864	Union, Colonel

Six former commandants fought for the Union and three fought for the South. Of the nine officers who served as commandants from 1817 to 1864, six served in the Union Army: three were major generals, one a brigadier, and another a colonel. Three commandants fought for the Confederacy: one lieutenant general, one a major general, and the other a brigadier general. Future Confederate officers were commandants for 92 months while their Union counterparts served for 146 months. Charles F. Smith held the post longest (52 months) followed by Ethan A. Hitchcock (51 months) and William J. Hardee (49 months).

Commandant of Cadets

In the decades before the Civil War, the commandant of cadets at the United States Military Academy was a highly desired position. Only the most accomplished Army officers received this respected assignment. Many in the Army considered the commandant to be the most important person on the Military Academy faculty because he directed the military program and administered discipline. The commandant had three distinct but overlapping responsibilities. First, he oversaw military training as Commander of the Corps of Cadets and Instructor of Infantry Tactics. Second, he enforced military regulations on cadets, faculty, Regular Army soldiers, and civilians. Third, he served as a communication link between the cadets and the Superintendent by presenting their grievances and reporting their infractions.

In addition to these tasks, the Commandant served as an unofficial role model for the cadets on how to conduct themselves as officers and gentlemen. As a former commandant explained: "It is thus by constantly and unceasingly, patiently and earnestly placing before the Cadet his obligations to duty, and impressing upon him the qualities of mind and character that constitute the high-minded, truthful, and conscientious officer, that the commandant of cadets … fulfills the most important part of his many responsible duties."[1] More than any other individual, he exercised an "important influence on the military character and opinions of the junior officers of the Army."[2]

Tactical Training

The Commander of the Corps of Cadets directed drill and military exercises for the four-company battalion at the Military Academy. The battalion provided the cadets with practical experience in military training and tactics as soldiers and officers and offered leadership opportunities for deserving cadets.[3] The superintendent and commandant selected the corps officers based on their military bearing and qualifications. They picked the adjutant, quartermaster, four company captains, and twelve lieutenants from the First Class; the sergeants from the Second Class; and the corporals from the Third Class. With the small garrisons at most army posts, the battalion presented the only opportunity for the future officers to study and practice "large unit" tactics. With an enrollment of around 250 cadets, the future officers gained experience directing company and battalion units. The system also created a competitive environment which prepared the prospective officers for the limited positions in the peacetime army.[4] Cadets had no experience in directing 1,000-man regiments. In addition, as cadet officers they were used to dealing with disciplined young men. Following graduation, the officers would be leading with an entirely different type of soldier—the enlisted man.

In his role as Instructor of Tactics, the commandant taught the First Class course on Army Infantry Tactics. Tactics and military Engineering and Science of War were the capstone modules in a cadet's military education, which began with the first roll call. The commandant presented lessons on minor tactics and managed the practice of these principles.[5] Professor Mahan presided over the class on grand tactics and the art of war. The cadets applied the commandant's lessons "on the drill field, in the barracks, and in summer encampments."[6] The tactics instructor and his assistants (TACs) used General Winfield Scott's three-volume textbook *Rules and Regulations for the Exercise and Maneuvers of the United States Infantry*.[7]

Infantry instruction began with the school of the soldier and progressed through the School of the Company and Battalion to "evolutions of the line." During the four-year program, cadets were drilled 204 times in artillery, 268 in equitation, and 540 in infantry.[8]

In terms of military proceedings, the commandant was "God" and the manuals of Army and Academy Regulations were his "Bibles." The commandant showed the depth and breadth of his knowledge of rules and conventions through his battalion orders. He quoted the pertinent sections from the handbooks to show there was a guideline for every aspect of military life and to encourage his young charges to commit these rules to memory.[9]

While the commandant was omnipresent at the Academy, his personal domain was the West Point parade ground. Drill was particularly important to the commandants because it was a reflection on their stewardship of the military program. The commandants were proud of the corps' reputation as a marching unit, and the cadets spent many hours each day working to maintain this proficiency. The commandant usually

Encampment at West Point, by John R. Smith, 1820 (Library of Congress).

Battalion passing in review (Library of Congress).

introduced a new system during the academic year. He made the cadets work long and hard to learn and master the new procedure, so he could demonstrate their skills to the superintendent and the Board of Visitors[10] during the annual review.[11]

Directing the annual summer encampment was an important part of the commandant's duties. The instructors and student officers used the camp to teach the cadets as much as possible about practical soldiering and to indoctrinate the plebes[12] into military life. The encampment focused on the fundamentals: the manual of arms, marching in various formations, and maneuvering on the field.[13]

Discipline

Superintendent Sylvanus Thayer developed the West Point disciplinary system. He considered "the maintenance of Discipline as a first principle in Military Economy." Thayer believed "the observance of its rules is at least as essential to the prosperity of the Military Academy as to the wellbeing of the Army." Therefore, Thayer said the Academy must instill the "habits of obedience" in the candidates for the Army before the officers enter upon the "Theater of Military Life."[14]

The commandant of cadets was responsible for maintaining obedience, discipline, and self-control. Under the Thayer system, the commandant "would watch over and inflict the punishments for all minor delinquencies."[15] The commandant applied lessons he learned as a cadet, educator, staff officer, and field commander to administer military law and order. Henry Coppee wrote of Commandant Charles F. Smith, "We all feared him, but thoroughly respected him, and we believed no commandant ever accomplished as much for the discipline of the corps as he did."[16] Commandant William J. Hardee's cadets praised him for his "unbending discipline."[17]

To instill the importance of discipline, the final ranking for cadets included a conduct grade, which included the total number of demerits. Additionally, the weight of the conduct grades increased as cadets advanced into the next class. The offenses counted more by adding one sixth of the cadet's total to the number of demerits for his second year, one third for his third, and one half for his fourth.[18] If a cadet received more than 200 demerits in a year or 100 demerits in a semester, the Academy considered him to be "deficient in conduct" and recommended his expulsion.[19]

Officers issued demerits for various offensives, which regulated every aspect of their behavior. The fledgling officers earned demerits for tardiness or absence at roll calls for meals, chapel, drill, and inspections; for dirty quarters or equipment; for visiting after taps; for disturbances during study hours; for unshaven faces and uncut hair; for smoking; for improper behavior toward cadet officers and Academy officers; and for altercations or fights.[20] Thayer devised the concept of additional tours, which were "walked" during a cadet's free time, and could reduce a cadet's number of demerits. Punishments for more serious violations included extra tours of duty, confinement to quarters, imprisonment, and dismissal. The Academy held courts-martial for cadets guilty of disobeying orders, disrespecting officers, and violating the code of honor.[21]

One of the undesirable side effects of the "minutely regulated" cadet life was it did little to "develop maturity or judgement." In many cases, cadets did not develop self-discipline at West Point.[22]

Communication Link

The commandant served as an unofficial link between the Corps of Cadets and the superintendent. Most of the communications were complaints about the food in the cadet mess.[23] The commandant also acted as a conduit for suggestions and ideas from the cadets. Casual conversations might lead to new or revised policies and added amusements. Commandant William J. Hardee substituted two five-week vacations in place of the one ten-week furlough. Commandants also instituted cadet balls three nights a week during the summer encampment. In this role, the commandant might also serve as adviser, mentor, or counselor and take the place of fathers, uncles, teachers, or clergymen.

Role Model

The commandant of cadets was also a role model. The cadets studied how he gave orders, talked, and walked. Cadets saw in the commandant the *beau ideal* of the perfect soldier. The commandant's bearing and knowledge of Army Regulations became a goal cadets could aspire to but probably not obtain. The descriptions from former students gives a glimpse into this role.

- Major Worth is "by far the most captivating man."—Ethan Allen Hitchcock[24]
- "Genl Worth is my earliest admiration as a military man & has always shown the kindest disposition for me."—Joseph Johnston[25]
- "In fact I regarded General Scott and Captain C.F. Smith, the Commandant of

Cadets, as the two men most to be envied in the nation. I retained a high regard for both up to the day of their death."—Ulysses S. Grant[26]

- "Hardee was the best commandant the Corps of Cadets ever had.... Whatever control I have of myself I attribute to the relentless teaching of that unbending student."—unknown student[27]

Professor Peter Michie described the characteristics of the ideal commandant:

His example should be that of the ideal soldier, officer, and gentleman. He should cultivate soldierly honor among the cadets until it attains vigorous growth. He should rebuke with severity the first tendency to prevarication or dishonesty in word or act. With a system of divided responsibility, which ultimately rests on one or two comrades, he should control all by strict and increasing exactions. To make his government successful he should be endowed with the highest soldierly qualities in personal bearing at drill, and even in every act while subject to vision of his corps.[28]

Other Duties

The commandants served on military boards to revise current lessons and develop new ones. They might compose books on military subjects, translate French and German books into texts for the Army and cadets, and/or conduct scientific or philosophical studies.

The commandant of cadets oversaw the department aided by from two to four assistants. The cavalry assistant taught cavalry tactics, equitation, and outpost duty. The senior infantry assistant taught infantry tactics, strategy, grand tactics, and logistics. The senior artillery assistant taught artillery tactics and army organization and administration.[29]

Initially, the department taught infantry tactics, interior police and discipline, and supervised the cadet commons. The department's functions remained unchanged until the law of 1858, which made the commandant of cadets instructor of tactics for the three arms of the service (infantry, artillery, and cavalry). The course load for the next two years increased when the Academy transferred the subjects taught by the Department of Engineering to this department. The commandant of cadets supervised the civilian sword master who gave instruction in the saber and broadsword. From February 28, 1858, until April 24, 1861, the Department of Engineering offered instruction in small arms and military gymnastics by a commissioned officer not attached to the tactical department. After 1861, this instruction was returned to the commandant of cadets with a civilian as sword master, but gymnastics instruction was dropped.[30]

Battlefield Applications of Tactical Lessons

Perhaps the best description of the role of tactics instruction appeared in the departmental overview prepared for the Academy's centennial celebration:

The present course designs to give to the Cadet the elements of a military education, as comprehended in the drill regulations of the three arms of the Service and in the other manuals and lectures referred to in the theoretical course; and in the practical work to impress upon him a thorough knowledge and appreciation of discipline and of military police, both in barracks and in camp; to educate him in the important qualities of attention to detail and of promptness in all his work; to give him the physical training necessary for the work and hardships he may be called upon to endure; and in conjunction with the other departments, to instill into his mind during his four years at the Academy a proper spirit of subordination and obedience to authority and to develop his confidence and capacity for command.[31]

The description does not mention how to attack an enemy, win a battle, or formulate and execute campaign strategy. The exclusions are deliberate. The emphasis is on mastering the *military basics* in the three schools, recognizing the importance of *discipline*, paying attention to *detail*, completing work *promptly*, preparing *physically* for the work and hardships, understanding the *command structure*, *obeying orders*, developing *confidence*, and demonstrating the *capacity to command*.

During the four years of instruction, each cadet had the opportunity to exercise command in all the grades of noncommissioned and commissioned officers including captain of a company. The progressive method assigned cadet supervision and command in any drill or exercise as he became proficient in it. For example, the Third Class provided the drillmasters for the Fourth Class cadets in the School of the Soldier. Cadet officers from the First Class supervised the Third Class drillmasters. The First Class officers received their instructions from a commissioned officer in charge of the drill. This process offered the cadet the combination of practice of command and the exercise of authority in drills in which he was proficient and further instruction and practice in drills not yet mastered.[32]

Superintendents from 1817 to 1864

The commandants served under the superintendent of military academy. They implemented the superintendent's academic philosophy and disciplinary methods. The most influential superintendents were Sylvanus Thayer, Richard Delafield, and Harry Brewerton. Thayer served as superintendent for sixteen years, Delafield held this post for terms amounting to 11½ years, and Brewerton served as superintendent for seven years. These three officers oversaw the Academy 72 percent of the time between 1817 and 1864.

Superintendent U.S. Military Academy[33]

Name	Rank and Department	Term
Sylvanus Thayer	Captain, Corps Engineers Brevet Major, U.S. Army	July 28, 1817–July 1,1833
Rene E. DeRussy	Major, Corps of Engineers	July 1, 1833–September 1, 1838
Richard Delafield	Major, Corps of Engineers	September 1, 1838–August 15, 1845
Henry Brewerton	Captain, Corps of Engineers	Aug. 15, 1845–September 1, 1852
Robert E. Lee	Captain, Corps of Engineers Brevet Colonel, U.S. Army	September 1, 1852–March 31, 1855
John G. Barnard	Captain, Corps of Engineers Brevet Major, U.S. Army	March 31, 1855–September 8, 1856
Richard Delafield	Major, Corps of Engineers	September 8, 1856–March 1, 1861,
Alexander H. Bowman	Major, Corps of Engineers	March 1, 1861–July 8, 1864

Commandants from 1817 to 1864

The following officers served as commandants from 1817 to 1864. The officer's tenure varied from three months to eight-years-eight months. The time in this position affected the impact each commandant had on the program. Men who served less than a year (Gardiner, Bliss, Bell, Reynolds, Augur, and Garrard) trained fewer future generals and were less influential than those whose terms were more than four years (Worth, Alden, Hitchcock, Fowle, Hardee, and Smith).

Commandants of Cadets[34]

Name	Rank and Department	Time
George W. Gardiner	Second Lieutenant, Corps of Artillery	September 15, 1817, to April 2, 1818
John Bliss	Captain, Sixth Infantry	April 2, 1818, to January 11, 1819
John R. Bell	Captain, Light Artillery	February 8, 1819, to March 17, 1820
William J. Worth	Captain, Second Infantry Brevet Major	March 17, 1820, to December 2, 1828
Ethan A. Hitchcock	Captain, First Infantry	March 13, 1829, to June 24, 1833
John Fowle	Major, Third Infantry	July 10, 1833, to March 31, 1838
Charles F. Smith	First Lieutenant, Second Artillery	April 1, 1838, to September 1, 1842
J. Addison Thomas	First Lieutenant, Third Artillery	September 1, 1842, to December 14, 1845
Bradford R. Alden	Captain, Fourth Infantry	December 14, 1845, to November 1, 1852
Robert S. Garnett	Captain, Seventh Infantry Brevet Major, U.S. Army	November 1, 1852, to July 31, 1854
William H.T. Walker	Captain, Sixth Infantry Brevet Lieutenant Colonel, U.S. Army	July 31, 1854, to May 27, 1856
William J. Hardee	Major, Second Cavalry Brevet Lieutenant Colonel	July 22, 1856, to September 8, 1860
John F. Reynolds	Captain, Third Artillery Brevet Major	September 8, 1860, to June 25, 1861
Christopher C. Augur	Major, Thirteenth Infantry	August 26, 1861, to December 5, 1861
Kenner Garrard	Captain, Fifth Cavalry	December 5, 1861, to September 25, 1862
Henry B. Clitz	Major, Twelfth Infantry	October 23, 1862, to July 4, 1864

Format and Criteria

The following chapters profile the life and achievements of the commandants of cadets. The descriptions follow the order of subjects below:

- Name—Name and Cullum Number
- Service at the Academy—Period the individual served as commandant and in other positions at the Academy
- Superintendent—Name of the Military Academy superintendent(s) who directed the Academy during the commandant's term
- Significant Contributions—How the commandant improved the position, enhanced the Department of Tactics, and/or the Military Academy. This

topic also includes events during the commandant's term and the opinions of cadets and others about commandant
- Notable Cadets—Individual West Point graduating classes are assigned to commandants using the following criteria. The commandant presented the capstone course on Infantry Tactics to the graduating class or the commandant led the Corps of Cadets and directed drill for the graduating class during their Fourth, Third, and Second classes or First, Second, and Third classes. The notable members of each class were selected based on their contributions or rank as general officers. Promotions awarded as part of the March 13, 1865, announcements were not used in the selection process. In other words, a Union colonel who was promoted to a brigadier general on March 13, 1865, would not be considered a general officer. The author included men who contributed as government officials, commanders of supporting units, and military instructors. The officers' contributions were limited to his achievements in the American Civil War. The list of students is based on the names in volumes I and II of the Cullum *Biographical Register of the Officers and Graduates of the U.S. Military Academy at West Point, NY* and Ezra Warner's *Generals in Gray*.[35]
- Promotions—Ranks held by the commandant in military service
- Assignments—Posts, missions, campaigns, and battles where the commandant served
- Biographical Sketch—A brief biographical sketch based on information from the George Cullum *Biographical Register of the Officers and Graduates of the U.S. Military Academy at West Point, NY*, Ezra Warner *Generals in Gray*, Bruce S. Allardice *More Generals in Gray*, Joe A. Mobley *Confederate Generals of North Carolina*, Gerard A. Patterson *Rebels from West Point*, and James S. Robbins *Last in Their Class*.

> The Cullum number is a reference and identification number assigned to each graduate of the United States Military Academy. The system was developed by Brevet Major General George W. Cullum, USMA Class of 1833. In 1850, Cullum started preparing assigning Cullum numbers in class order to create a register with biographies of every graduate.

George W. Gardiner
(September 15, 1817–April 2, 1818)
Cullum Number: 91

Service at the Academy

George W. Gardiner was at the Academy from 1816 to 1820. He was Adjutant from October 12, 1816, to September 15, 1817. After Major Sylvanus Thayer became superintendent, he promoted Gardiner to commandant of cadets and instructor of infantry tactics. Gardiner held this position from September 15, 1817, to April 2, 1818. He also served as Instructor of Artillery from September 15, 1817, to February 1, 1820.

Superintendent

Brevet Brigadier General Sylvanus Thayer was the superintendent of the U.S. Military Academy from July 28, 1817, to July 1, 1833. After he became superintendent, he began organizing the Academy and dismissing cadets who did not meet his standards. He formed the cadets into a battalion of two companies under an Army officer designated the "Commandant of Cadets." The commandant handled tactical instruction and soldierly discipline. Thayer instituted many changes in the academic program including: ranking cadets, dividing classes into small sections, requiring weekly cadet progress reports, adding more thorough recitations, improving the curriculum, adding new departments, organizing a "proper" Academic Board, introducing the check-book system to control cadet expenditures, instituting a rigorous program of cadet discipline, and establishing the summer encampment of cadets. He enlarged the library, added new buildings, and assembled a skilled faculty. Historians regard Thayer as the "Father of the Military Academy." He resigned on July 1, 1833, following several years of conflict with President Andrew Jackson.[1]

Significant Contributions

Lieutenant Gardiner has the distinction of being the first officer assigned to the duties, which became those of the commandant of cadets. Major Thayer asked Gar-

Dade Monument at West Point (Library of Congress).

diner to command the cadet battalion, instruct cadets in infantry tactics, enforce "soldierly discipline," and administer the interior police. Gardiner helped transform Superintendent Thayer's ideas into duties that became the foundation of the commandant of cadets and instructor of tactics. During Gardiner's term, the Military Academy appointed the commanding officer of the Battalion of Cadets as the inspector of the cadet commons. The commandant was also designated as the permanent president of the boards that audited the accounts of the cadets' mess and oversaw inspectors of supplies.

Notable Cadets

Please see "Notable West Graduates Who Served in the Civil War" for more information.

- Class of 1818 (23 Graduates)
  - Richard Delafield (1), Union, Brigadier General
  - Harvey Brown (6), Union, Brigadier General
  - Hartman Bache (19), Union, Colonel, Bureau of Topographical Engineers
- Class of 1819 (29 graduates)
  - Daniel Tyler (14), Union, Brigadier General

Promotions

- Third Lieutenant, First Artillery, March 11, 1814
- Second Lieutenant, First Artillery, May 1, 1814

- First Lieutenant, Corps of Artillery, April 20, 1818
- First Lieutenant, Second Artillery, June 1, 1821
- Brevet Captain, April 20, 1828, for faithful service ten years in one grade
- Captain, Second Artillery, November 3, 1832

Assignments

- Cadet at the Military Academy, September 2, 1812, to March 11, 1814
- Served in the War of 1812–1815 with Great Britain
- Transferred to Corps of Artillery, May 12, 1814
- In the garrisons at Fort Columbus, New York, 1814–1815, and Portsmouth, New Hampshire, 1815–1816
- At the Military Academy, 1816–1820
    - Adjutant, October 12, 1816, to September 15, 1817, and February 10, 1819, to March 9, 1820
    - Commandant of Cadets and Instructor of Infantry Tactics, September 15, 1817, to February 1, 1820
    - Instructor of Artillery, September 15, 1817, to April 2, 1818
- In the garrison at New York harbor, 1820
- On commissary duty, 1820–1821
- In the garrisons at Fort Mifflin, Pennsylvania, 1821–1824; Fort Delaware, Delaware, 1824–1827; and Augusta Arsenal, Georgia, 1827–1830
- In operations in the Cherokee Nation, 1830–1831
- In the garrisons at Fort Marion, Florida, 1831–1832, and Augusta Arsenal, Georgia, 1832–1833
- In operations in the Cherokee Nation, 1833
- In the garrisons at Fort Mitchell, Alabama, 1833–1834; Fort Jackson, Louisiana, 1834; Covington, Louisiana, 1834; Fort Jackson, Louisiana, 1834–1835; and Fort Pickens, Florida, 1835
- In the Florida War, 1835, where the Seminole Indians killed "the whole command, save three, fell without an attempt to retreat" at Dade's Massacre, Florida, December 28, 1835.[2]

Biographical Sketch

George Gardiner entered the U.S. Military Academy on September 2, 1812, and graduated on March 11, 1814. The Army promoted him to third lieutenant in the First Artillery Regiment. The War of 1812 was being fought between Great Britain and the United States during his attendance at West Point. After graduation, the Army sent him to Fort Columbus, New York. On May 1, 1814, he received a promotion to second lieutenant in the First Artillery Regiment. Several days later, on May 14, he transferred to the Corps of Artillery. After a year at Fort Columbus, Gardiner went Portsmouth, New Hampshire where he stayed until his transfer on October 12, 1816, to serve as adjutant at the U.S. Military Academy. He was adjutant until September 15, 1817, when he was appointed to the post of commandant of cadets and instructor of infantry tactics. While at West Point, the Army promoted him to first lieutenant in the Corps of Artillery on April 20, 1818. He served as both instructor of infantry tactics and instructor of artillery from September 15, 1817, until April 2, 1818. He continued to serve as instructor of artillery from April 2, 1818, until February 1, 1820.

The Army assigned Gardiner to garrison duty at several different posts. He was on commissary duty from 1820 to 1821 at Fort Columbus, New York. He was reassigned to the Second Artillery Regiment on June 1, 1821, as part of the Army reorganization. He served in the garrisons at Fort Mifflin, Pennsylvania (1821–1824); Fort Delaware, Delaware (1824–1827); and Augusta Arsenal, Georgia (1827–1830). He received a brevet promotion to captain for faithful service, ten years in one grade. Captain Gardiner served in the Cherokee Nation (1830–1831) and in the garrison at Fort Marion, Florida (1831–1832). He was promoted to captain in the Second Artillery on November 3, 1832. He returned to the Augusta Arsenal (1832–1833). He served in the Cherokee Nation (1833) before being sent to the garrisons at Fort Mitchell, Alabama (1833–1834); Fort Jackson, Louisiana (1834); Covington, Louisiana (1834); Fort Jackson, Louisiana (1834–1835); and Fort Pickens, Florida (1835). He fought in the Florida War in 1835 and was killed on December 28, 1835, in "Dade's desperate Battle with the Seminole Indians, where 'the whole command, save three, fell without an attempt to retreat.'"[3]

John Bliss
(April 2, 1818–January 11, 1819)
Cullum Number: 24

Service at the Academy

John Bliss was commandant of cadets and instructor of infantry tactics from April 2, 1818, to January 11, 1819.

Superintendent

Bliss reported to Sylvanus Thayer who was superintendent of the Military Academy from July 28, 1817, to July 1, 1833.

Significant Contributions

Captain Bliss' term at the Academy began on April 2, 1818. On April 20, 1818, Superintendent Thayer wrote to General Joseph Swift with the news the Academy had received twelve thousand copies of an essay on the science of war. One copy was to be given to each cadet when they graduated.[1]

On November 22, 1818, the Corps of Cadets decided to complain about the brutality by the commandant of cadets, Captain John Bliss. Bliss dragged cadets out of formations, pushed them off railings, and threw stones at them. Bliss' treatment was approved under former superintendents, Alden Partridge and Joseph Swift. The Corps elected a committee of five members to ask Superintendent Thayer to correct the situation. These five cadets were leaders, had no dispute with the commandant, and had exemplary records. They gathered evidence and presented a petition to Major Thayer.

The cadets were surprised by the outcome of their request to the superintendent. The military establishment responded aggressively. The cadets were arrested, exiled, and excluded from their studies. A court of inquiry and a court-martial tried the cadets. Although the five were expelled from the Academy, their actions brought about changes in the treatment of cadets.[2]

Notable Cadets

See "Notable West Point Graduates Who Served in the Civil War" in the Appendices for more information.

- Class of 1818 (23 Graduates)
  - Richard Delafield (1), Union, Brigadier General
  - Harvey Brown (6), Union, Brigadier General
  - Hartman Bache (19), Union, Colonel, Bureau of Topographical Engineers
- Class of 1819 (29 graduates)
  - Daniel Tyler (14), Union, Brigadier General
- Class of 1820 (30 Graduates)
  - Andrew J. Donelson (2), Diplomat, Publisher, *chargé d'affaires*[3] to Texas
  - John H. Winder (11), Confederate, Brigadier General
  - George D. Ramsay (26), Union, Brigadier General
  - William W. Morris (30), Union, Brigadier General

John Bliss (Find a Grave).

Promotions

- First Lieutenant Eleventh Infantry, March 12, 1812
- Captain Eleventh Infantry, May 13, 1813
- Brevet Major, May 13, 1823, for faithful service, ten years in one grade
- Major, First Infantry Regiment, July 15, 1831
- Lieutenant Colonel, Sixth Infantry, October 30, 1836

Assignments

- Served in the War of 1812–1815 with Great Britain
- While on the Northern frontier, he was wounded in the Battle of Niagara, July 25, 1814
- Transferred to Sixth Infantry, May 17, 1815
- In command of company at Plattsburg, New York, 1815–1818
- In the garrisons at Rouse's Point, New York, 1818, and Plattsburg, New York, 1818
- At the Military Academy, as commandant of cadets and instructor of infantry tactics, April 2, 1818, to January 11, 1819

- On frontier duty at Bellefontaine, Missouri, 1819; on the Missouri River, 1819–1820; and at Council Bluffs, Iowa, 1820–1821
- Transferred to Fifth Infantry, 1821
- On leave of absence, 1821–1822
- Transferred to Third Infantry, 1822
- On frontier duty at Fort Howard, Wisconsin, 1822–1825
- On recruiting service, 1825–1826
- On frontier duty at Fort Winnebago, Wisconsin, 1826
- In the garrison at Jefferson Barracks, Missouri, 1826–1827, and at Fort Leavenworth, Kansas, 1827–1829
- On leave of absence, 1829–1830
- On frontier duty at Des Moines, Iowa, 1830
- In the garrison at Fort Armstrong, Illinois, 1830–1832
- In the Black Hawk War, in command of a regiment in the Battle of the Bad Axe, August 2, 1832
- On leave of absence, 1832–1833
- On frontier duty at Fort Snelling, Minnesota, 1833–1836
- In the garrison at Newport Barracks, Kentucky, 1836–1837
- Resigned, September 6, 1837[4]

Biographical Sketch

John Bliss was born on September 2, 1785, in Lebanon, New Hampshire. He graduated twenty-fourth in the class of 1811 from the U.S. Military Academy. On March 12, 1812, the Army appointed him a first lieutenant in the Eleventh Infantry Regiment. He served on the northern frontier in the War of 1812–1815 with Great Britain. Bliss received a promotion to captain in the Eleventh Infantry on May 13, 1813. Captain Bliss fought in the Battle of Niagara (July 25, 1814) where he was wounded. The Army transferred him to the Sixth Infantry on May 17, 1815, and placed him in command of a company at Plattsburg, New York (1815–1818). He was in the garrisons at Rouse's Point, New York and Plattsburg, New York during 1818.

Captain Bliss returned to the Military Academy as commandant of cadets and instructor of infantry tactics. He held in this position from April 2, 1818, to January 11, 1819. On November 22, 1818, the Corps of Cadets elected a five-man committee to complain about Commandant Bliss' cruel and harsh treatment. Captain John Bliss dragged cadets out of formations, pushed them off railings, swore at them, and threw stones at them. The cadets presented a petition to Major Thayer. The five cadets were expelled from the Academy, but their protest changed the treatment of cadets.[5]

Bliss served on frontier duty at Bellefontaine, Missouri (1819); on the Missouri River (1819–1820); and at Council Bluffs, Iowa (1820–1821). He transferred to the Fifth Infantry in 1821. Bliss went on a leave of absence from 1821–1822. Bliss transferred to the Third Infantry in 1822. Captain Bliss returned to frontier duty at Fort Howard, Wisconsin in 1822. The Army awarded him with a brevet promotion to major on May 13, 1823, for faithful service, ten years in one grade. After leaving Fort Howard, he served in recruiting service (1825–1826). Bliss returned to frontier duty with assignments at Fort Winnebago, Wisconsin (1826); Jefferson Barracks, Missouri (1826–1827); and at Fort Leavenworth, Kansas, (1827–1829). He had a leave of absence from 1829 to 1830. Major Bliss was on frontier duty at Des Moines, Iowa (1830) and Armstrong, Illinois (1830–1832). He received a promotion to major in the First Infantry on July 15, 1831. Major Bliss commanded a regiment at the Battle of the Bad Axe on August 2, 1832, during the Black Hawk War. He was on a leave of absence (1832–1833). Bliss was on garrison duty at Fort Snelling, Minnesota (1833–1836) and Newport Barracks, Kentucky (1836–1837). The Army promoted him to lieutenant colonel in the Sixth Infantry on October 30, 1836. Colonel Bliss resigned on September 6, 1837.[6]

John R. Bell
(February 8, 1819–March 17, 1820)
Cullum Number: 76

Service at the Academy

John R. Bell was commandant of cadets and instructor of infantry tactics from February 8, 1819, to March 17, 1820.

Superintendent

Brevet Brigadier General Sylvanus Thayer was the superintendent of the Military Academy from July 28, 1817, to July 1, 1833.

Significant Contributions

Bell's greatest contribution to the Academy was changing discipline from his predecessor John Bliss. John H.B. Latrobe, from the class of 1822, described Commandant Bell as "a tall, handsome and soldierly-looking man, who was with us for little more than a year, and who, without abating the rigor of the discipline, showed how it could be maintained consistently with a proper regard for the feelings of those under him."[1]

Captain Bell received additional help when the Academy assigned two junior officers as assistant instructors of infantry tactics in 1820.[2]

Notable Cadets

See "Notable West Point Graduates Who Served in the Civil War" in the Appendices for more information.

- Class of 1819 (29 graduates)
  - Daniel Tyler (14), Union, Brigadier General

Fort Moultrie, South Carolina (Library of Congress).

- Class of 1820 (30 Graduates)
  - Andrew J. Donelson (2), Diplomat, Publisher, *chargé d'affaires* to Texas
  - John H. Winder (11), Confederate, Brigadier General
  - George D. Ramsay (26), Union, Brigadier General
  - William W. Morris (30), Union, Brigadier General
- Class of 1821 (24 Graduates)
  - Charles Dimmock (5), Confederate, Brigadier General

Promotions

- Second Lieutenant, Light Artillery, January 3, 1812
- First Lieutenant, Light Artillery, August 24, 1812
- Major, Staff, Assistant Inspector-General, July 29, 1813
- Captain, Light Artillery, October 10, 1814
- Colonel, Staff, Inspector-General, October 28, 1814
- Captain, Fourth Artillery, in reorganization of Army, June 1, 1821
- Brevet Major, for faithful service, ten years in one grade, October 10, 1824

Assignments

- Cadet at the Military Academy, June 15, 1808, to Jan. 3, 1812
- In the War of 1812–1815 with Great Britain
  - Engaged in the Campaign of 1812
  - On the Niagara Frontier, in 1813
  - On the St. Lawrence River, taking part in the capture of Fort George, British Canada, May 27, 1813
  - With General Izard's division, 1814

- In the garrison at Castine, Maine, 1815–1816, and Boston Harbor, Massachusetts, 1816–1818
- Superintendent of the Recruiting Service, 1818
- In the garrison at Boston Harbor, Massachusetts, 1818–1819
- At the Military Academy, as commandant of cadets and instructor of infantry tactics, February 8, 1819, to March 17, 1820
- On special duty in Missouri, 1820–1821
- In East Florida in command of U.S. troops at St. Augustine, 1821
- Acting governor of West Florida, July 11, 1821, to August 20, 1821
- In the garrison at Savannah Harbor, Georgia, 1822–1824, and Fort Moultrie, South Carolina, 1824
- Died, April 11, 1825[3]

Biographical Sketch

John R. Bell was an Army officer who served as provisional secretary and interim governor of East Florida between July and August 1821.

Bell was a cadet at the Military Academy from June 15, 1808, to January 3, 1812. He graduated fifth in his class, and the Army promoted him to second lieutenant in the Light Artillery. Lieutenant Bell fought in the War of 1812–1815. He received a promotion to first lieutenant in the Light Artillery. Bell fought in the 1812 campaign on the Niagara Frontier. In 1813, he helped capture Fort George on the St. Lawrence River. The Army promoted him to major on July 29, 1813, and assigned him to staff duties as inspector general. He served in General Izard's division in 1814. Bell received a promotion to captain in the Light Artillery on October 10, 1814, and the Army increased his rank to colonel and inspector general on October 28, 1814. He was in the garrison at Castine, Maine from 1815 to 1816, and at Boston Harbor, Massachusetts from 1816 to 1818. He was superintendent of the Recruiting Service in 1818 and in the garrison at Boston Harbor from 1818 to 1819. Bell returned to the Military Academy on February 8, 1819, as commandant of cadets and instructor of infantry tactics. He held this post until March 17, 1820. Bell was on special duty in Missouri (1820–1821).

In 1821, the Army sent Bell to East Florida in command of U.S. troops at St. Augustine. Bell became a temporary agent to the Seminoles. In early 1822, he estimated there were 22,000 Native Americans and 5,000 slaves in Florida. He reckoned two-thirds of them were refugees from the Creek War. In his opinion, they had no valid claim to Florida. Bell wrote to Secretary of War John C. Calhoun reporting he had gone to government warehouses to collect provisions to help move the Seminoles. On July 11, 1821, the government appointed Bell as acting governor of West Florida. He held this office until August 20, 1821.

The Army promoted him to captain in the Fourth Artillery on June 1, 1821. He was in the garrisons at Savannah Harbor, Georgia (1822–1824) and Fort Moultrie, South Carolina in 1824. On October 10, 1824, the Army promoted Bell to brevet major for faithful service, ten years in one grade. Major Bell died on April 11, 1825.[4]

William J. Worth
(March 17, 1820–December 2, 1828)
Cullum Number: None

Service at the Academy

William J. Worth was commandant of cadets and instructor of infantry tactics from March 17, 1820, to December 2, 1828.

Superintendent

Colonel Sylvanus Thayer was the superintendent of the Military Academy from July 28, 1817, to July 1, 1833.

Significant Contributions

> The military commandant of cadets at the time of my visit was Major, afterwards General Worth, whose military bearing in the presence of troops filled the very ideal of a gallant soldier in the field. To young and impulsive natures designed for the military profession, Major Worth was by far the most captivating man, while graver men could see in Major Thayer deeper and more valuable qualities which made him an object of enthusiastic admiration.—Ethan Allen Hitchcock[1]

Commandant William Worth presided over the Corps of Cadets and taught tactics from March 17, 1820, to December 2, 1828. In 1821, the Academy introduced the study of infantry tactics as a formal course and the regulations ordered that "a captain or field officer would be appointed as instructor of infantry tactics." In July 1821, Major Worth marched the Corps of Cadets to Boston and spent two weeks encamped on Boston Common. This inaugural march was the first of many to introduce the Military Academy to the public and gain citizen support. The Army Regulations of 1825 refined and defined instruction in infantry tactics. The curriculum included the School of the Soldier, School of the Company, School of the Battalion, evolutions of the line, and the exercises and maneuvers of light infantry and riflemen. The training also included the duties in camp, garrison, and as guards and police for privates, noncommissioned officers, and officers. The 1825 Regulations authorized a cadet battalion of four companies, and officially appointed the instructor of infantry tactics and commanding officer of the battalion of cadets as "Commandant of Cadets." In 1827, the Academy increased the number of assistant instructors of infantry tactics to three. During Worth's term as commandant, the Army formalized the position's role and provided structure to the instruction in infantry tactics. In this time of refinement and clarification, Worth gave the stability necessary to implement the changes. His long tenure as commandant allowed him to add his personal touches to the position and provide a pattern on which future commandants could model their behavior.[2]

William J. Worth (Library of Congress).

Worth had a large measure of knowledge and experience, and was full of martial spirit and generosity, which, with his handsome person and gallant bearing, made him a model for these young soldiers. He always treated [Joseph] Johnston with marked consideration.[3]

The cadets showed their esteem for Major Worth on December 10, 1828. The cadets requested permission to present a sword to Commandant Worth. Unfortunately, the president of the United States and secretary of war refused the cadet's appeal.[4]

Notable Cadets

See "Notable West Point Graduates Who Served in the Civil War" in the Appendices for more information.

- Class of 1820 (30 Graduates)
    - Andrew J. Donelson (2), Diplomat, Publisher, *chargé d'affaires* to Texas
    - John H. Winder (11), Confederate, Brigadier General
    - George D. Ramsay (26), Union, Brigadier General
    - William W. Morris (30), Union, Brigadier General
- Class of 1821 (24 Graduates)
    - Charles Dimmock (5), Confederate, Brigadier General
- Class of 1822 (40 Graduates)
    - Joseph K.F. Mansfield (2), Union, Major General
    - Walter Gwyn (8), Confederate, Major General
    - Isaac R. Trimble (17), Confederate, Major General
    - George Wright (24), Union, Brevet Brigadier General
    - David Hunter (25), Union, Major General

- George A. McCall (26), Union, Brigadier General
- John J. Abercrombie (37), Union, Brigadier General
- Class of 1823 (35 Graduates)
  - George S. Greene (2), Union, Brigadier General
  - Alfred Beckley (9), Confederate, Brigadier General
  - Lorenzo Thomas (17), Union, Brigadier General
- Class of 1824 (31 Graduates)
  - Dennis H. Mahan (1), Union, Second Lieutenant, U.S. Military Academy, Professor of Engineering
  - Robert P. Parrott (3), Union, U.S. Military Academy, Rifled Ordnance
- Class of 1825 (37 Graduates)
  - Alexander D. Bache (1), Union, Second Lieutenant, Assistant Professor of Engineering, U.S. Military Academy
  - Daniel S. Donelson (5), Confederate, Major General
  - Benjamin Huger (8), Confederate, Major General
  - Robert Anderson (15), Union, Brevet Major General
  - Charles F. Smith (19), Union, Major General
  - William R. Montgomery (28), Union, Brigadier General
- Class of 1826 (41 Graduates)
  - Albert S. Johnston (8), Confederate, General
  - Samuel P. Heintzelman (17), Union, Major General
  - Augustus J. Pleasonton (20), Union, Brigadier General
  - John B. Grayson (22), Confederate, Brigadier General
  - Amos Eaton (36), Union, Brigadier General
  - Silas Casey (39), Union, Major General
- Class of 1827 (38 Graduates)
  - Napoleon H. Buford (6), Union, Brigadier General
  - Leonidas Polk (8), Confederate, Lieutenant General
  - Gabriel J. Rains (13), Confederate, Brigadier General
  - Philip St. George Cooke (23), Union, Brigadier General
- Class of 1828 (33 Graduates)
  - Albert E. Church (1), Union, First Lieutenant, Professor of Mathematics, U.S. Military Academy
  - Hugh Mercer (3), Confederate, Brigadier General
  - Jefferson Davis (23), Confederate, President of the Confederate States of America
  - Thomas F. Drayton (28), Confederate, Brigadier General
- Class of 1829 (46 Graduates)
  - Robert E. Lee (2), Confederate, General
  - James Barnes (5), Union, Brigadier General
  - Cathanarinus P. Buckingham (6), Union, Brigadier General
  - Joseph E. Johnston (13), Confederate, General
  - O. McKnight Mitchell (15), Union, Major General
  - William Hoffman (18), Union, Brevet Brigadier General
  - Thomas A. Davies (25), Union, Brigadier General

- Albert G. Blanchard (26), Confederate, Brigadier General
- Benjamin W. Brice (40), Union, Brevet Brigadier General
- Theodolphilus H. Holmes (44), Confederate, Lieutenant General

Promotions

- First Lieutenant, Twenty-Third Infantry, March 19, 1813
- Brevet Captain, for gallant and distinguished conduct in the Battle of Chippewa, July 5, 1814
- Brevet Major, for gallantry and good conduct in the Battle of Niagara, July 25, 1814
- Captain, Twenty-Third Infantry, August 19, 1814
- Major, Ordnance Corps, May 30, 1832
- Colonel, Eighth Infantry, July 7, 1838
- Brevet Brigadier General, U.S. Army, for gallantry and highly distinguished service as commander of the forces in the War against the Florida Indians, March 1, 1842
- Brevet Major General, U.S. Army, for gallant and meritorious conduct in the several conflicts at Monterey, Mexico, September 23, 1846

Assignments

- In the War of 1812–1815 with Great Britain
  - *Aide-de-Camp*[5] to Major General Lewis, 1813
  - *Aide-de-Camp* to Brigadier General Scott, 1814
  - Fought in the campaign on the Northern frontier and was severely wounded in the Battle of Niagara, July 25, 1814
- Transferred to First Artillery during reorganization of Army, May 17, 1821
- In the garrisons at Sackett's Harbor, New York, 1815–1817; Greenbush, New York, 1817–1819; Plattsburg, New York, 1819; and Sackett's Harbor, New York, 1819–1820
- Superintendent of Recruiting Service, 1820
- At the Military Academy, as commandant of cadets and instructor of infantry tactics, March 17, 1820–December 2, 1828
- In the garrison at Fort Monroe, Virginia, 1829
- Member of the Board of Visitors to the Military Academy, 1829
- On leave of absence, 1829
- In the garrison at Fort Monroe, Virginia, 1829–1832
- In command of Fort Monroe Arsenal, Virginia, 1832; Frankfort Arsenal, Pennsylvania, 1832–1835; and Watervliet Arsenal, New York 1835–1838
- Served during Canada Border Disturbances, 1838–1839
- In command of Eighth Infantry, July 1838–October 1838, and Northern Department, October 1838–December 1839
- In the Florida War against the Seminole Indians, 1840–1842

- In command of the District of Tampa, January 1841–May 1841, and the Army in Florida, May 1841–August 1842
- Engaged in the attack on Halleck Tustenuggee's Band at Pilaklikaha, April 19, 1842
- In command of the Department of Florida, 1842–1846
- In command of brigade, 1846–1847
- In the War with Mexico[6]
  - In command of a division, 1847–1848
  - Battle of Monterey, September 21–23, 1846
  - Siege of Vera Cruz, March 9–29, 1847
  - Battle of Cerro Gordo, April 17–18, 1847
  - Capture of San Antonio, August 20, 1847
  - Battle of Churubusco, August 20, 1847
  - Battle of Molino del Rey, September 8, 1847
  - Battle of Chapultepec, September 13, 1847
  - Assault and Capture of the City of Mexico, September 13–14, 1847
- In command of the Department of Texas and New Mexico, November 7, 1848–May 7, 1849
- Died on May 7, 1849, at San Antonio, Texas at the age of 55[7]

Biographical Sketch

William Jenkins Worth (March 1, 1794–May 7, 1849) was an U.S. Army officer in the War of 1812, Mexican-American War, and Second Seminole War.

Worth was born in 1794 in Hudson, New York, to Thomas Worth and Abigail Jenkins. Although both of his parents were Quakers, he rejected the pacifism of their faith. He received common schooling as a child. He moved to Albany and was working as a merchant when the War of 1812 began.

The Army commissioned Worth as a first lieutenant in March 1813. He served as an aide to Brigadier General Winfield Scott during the war and became good friends with him. He named his son Winfield Scott Worth. Worth distinguished himself at the battles of Chippewa and Lundy's Lane during the Niagara campaign. He was seriously wounded in the thigh by grapeshot in the Battle of Lundy's Lane. He recovered after a year, but his wound left him with a limp. The Army awarded him a promotion to brevet major. As a brevet major, Worth spoke his famous words that are now inscribed in West Point's "Bugle Notes," a book of knowledge all cadets must learn by heart:

> But an officer on duty knows no one—to be partial is to dishonor both himself and the object of his ill-advised favor. What will be thought of him who exacts of his friends that which disgraces him? Look at him who winks at and overlooks offences in one, which he causes to be punished in another, and contrast him with the inflexible soldier who does his duty faithfully, notwithstanding it occasionally wars with his private feelings. The conduct of one will be venerated and emulated, the other detested as a satire upon soldiership and honor.

After the War of 1812, he served as commandant of cadets at the U.S. Military Academy. The Army promoted him to colonel in 1838 and placed him in command of the newly created Eighth Infantry Regiment.

Using his own tactics, he successfully directed military operations in the Second Seminole War in Florida and received a brevet promotion to brigadier general in 1842. Eventually, he convinced Secretary of War John C. Spencer[8] to allow the remaining Indians in the territory to agree to confine themselves to the region south of Peace Creek and officially end the war.

When the Mexican-American War began, Worth was serving under Zachary Taylor in Texas. Worth negotiated the surrender of Matamoros, Mexico. He commanded the Second Regular Division of the Army of Occupation at the Battle of Monterrey. In 1847, the Army transferred Worth to Winfield Scott's army and placed him in command of the First Division. During the landings at Veracruz, he jumped from his boat into shoulder deep water and waded ashore to become the first American to make an amphibious landing.

He took part in the siege of Veracruz and commanded the First Division in the battles of Cerro Gordo, Contreras, and Churubusco as Scott's Army of Invasion crossed Mexico to Mexico City. During the advance on the Mexican capital, Scott ordered Worth to seize the enemy works at Molino del Rey. Worth and Scott's friendship ended when Scott refused to allow Worth to change the attack. The battle resulted in severe casualties for the First Division. Worth later changed his son's name from Winfield Scott to William. After the disaster at Molino del Rey, Worth led his division against the San Cosme Gate at Mexico City. When U.S. forces entered Mexico City, Worth climbed to the roof of the National Palace and took down the Mexican flag. A U.S. Marine raised the Stars and Stripes as celebrated in the first line of the Marine Corps Hymn.

The congress awarded Worth with a sword of honor for his service at the Battle of Chapultepec. In 1847, the New York Society of the Cincinnati admitted Worth as an honorary member.

In 1848, a group of Cuban Freemasons known as the Havana Club, composed of sugar plantation owners and aristocrats, approached Worth to help overthrow the Spanish colonial government in Cuba. The Havana Club sent college professor Ambrosio José Gonzales to ask Worth to lead an invasion of Cuba. Knowing Worth was also a Freemason, Gonzales greeted the war hero with the Masonic secret handshake, and later offered him three million dollars to lead an invasion force of five thousand American veterans of the Mexican-American War against the Spanish in Cuba. Worth accepted the offer, but before the plot could be put into effect, the War Department transferred him to Texas.

He was in command of the Department of Texas when he died of cholera in 1849 in San Antonio. His remains were reinterred in a fifty-one-foot granite monument on Worth Square on a traffic island between Fifth Avenue and Broadway at 25th Street in New York City's borough of Manhattan.[9]

Ethan A. Hitchcock
(March 13, 1829–June 24, 1833)
Cullum Number: 177

Service at the Academy

Ethan Allen Hitchcock returned to West Point on February 1, 1824. For the next three years (February 1, 1824, to April 20, 1827), he was an assistant instructor of tactics. He was assigned to recruiting duties from 1827 to 1829. Hitchcock returned to the Academy as commandant of cadets and instructor of infantry tactics from March 13, 1829, to June 24, 1833.

Ethan Allen Hitchcock (Library of Congress).

Superintendent

Sylvanus Thayer was the superintendent of the Military Academy from July 28, 1817, to July 1, 1833.

Significant Contributions

Like many of his successors, Hitchcock had no combat experience when he assumed command of the Corps of Cadets. He was on garrison duty at Mobile, Alabama (1817–1818), New Orleans, Louisiana (1818–1819), the Bay of St. Missouri (1821–1822), and Baton Rouge, Louisiana (1822–1823). He served three stints on recruiting service in 1819, 1823–1824, and 1827–1829. Hitchcock returned to the Military Academy on February 1, 1824, and he was an assistant instructor of tactics until April

20, 1827. He brought firsthand experience as a junior garrison officer. He spent his time preparing the monthly reports and dealing with the volumes of paperwork associated with running a military post. His recruiting duties brought him in contact with the caliber of men who joined the Regular Army. He divided his time between drilling the enlisted men and filling out paperwork. His prior experience allowed him to prepare his cadets for the soldiers they would command and the boring tasks they would perform.

Notable Cadets

See "Notable West Point Graduates Who Served in the Civil War" in the Appendices for more information.

- Class of 1829 (46 Graduates)
    - Robert E. Lee (2), Confederate, General
    - James Barnes (5), Union, Brigadier General
    - Cathanarinus P. Buckingham (6), Union, Brigadier General
    - Joseph E. Johnston (13), Confederate, General
    - O. McKnight Mitchell (15), Union, Major General
    - William Hoffman (18), Union, Brevet Brigadier General
    - Thomas A. Davies (25), Union, Brigadier General
    - Albert G. Blanchard (26), Confederate, Brigadier General
    - Benjamin W. Brice (40), Union, Brevet Brigadier General
    - Theodolphilus H. Holmes (44), Confederate, Lieutenant General
- Class of 1830 (42 Graduates)
    - William N. Pendleton (5), Confederate, Brigadier General
    - John B. Magruder (15), Confederate, Major General
    - Albert Taylor Bledsoe (16), Confederate, Colonel, Assistant Secretary of War
    - Meriwether L. Clark (23), Confederate, Brigadier General
    - Robert C. Buchanan (31), Union, Brevet Brigadier General
- Class of 1831 (33 Graduates)
    - Jacob Ammen (12), Union, Brigadier General
    - Andrew A. Humphreys (13), Union, Major General
    - William H. Emory (14), Union, Brevet Major General
    - Thomas J. McKean (19), Union, Brigadier General
    - Lucius B. Northrop (22), Confederate, Brigadier General
    - Horatio P. van Cleve (24), Union, Brigadier General
    - Samuel R. Curtis (27), Union, Major General
- Class of 1832 (45 Graduates)
    - Philip St. George Cocke (6), Confederate, Brigadier General
    - Erasmus D. Keyes (10), Union, Major General
    - George B. Crittenden (26), Confederate, Major General
    - Randolph B. Marcy (29), Union, Brigadier General
    - Richard C. Gatlin (35), Confederate, Brigadier General
    - Humphrey Marshall (42), Confederate, Brigadier General

- Class of 1833 (43 Graduates)
  - John G. Barnard (2), Union, Brevet Major General
  - George W. Cullum (3), Union, Brigadier General
  - Rufus King (4), Union, Brigadier General
  - Francis Smith (5), Confederate, Colonel
  - Edmund Schriver (17), Union, Brevet Brigadier General
  - Alexander E. Shiras (20), Union, Brevet Brigadier General
  - Benjamin Alvord (22), Union, Brigadier General
  - Henry W. Wessells (29), Union, Brigadier General
  - Abraham C. Myers (32), Confederate, Colonel, Quartermaster General
  - Daniel Ruggles (34), Confederate, Brigadier General
  - Benjamin Du Bose (39), Confederate, Brigadier General
- Class of 1834 (36 Graduates)
  - Thomas A. Morris (4), Union, Brigadier General
  - Robert T.P. Allen (5), Confederate, Colonel
  - Gabriel R. Paul (18), Union, Brigadier General
  - Goode Bryan (25), Confederate, Brigadier General
  - William Scott Ketchum (32), Union, Brigadier General

Promotions

- Third Lieutenant, Corps of Artillery, July 17, 1817
- Second Lieutenant, Eighth Infantry, February 13, 1818
- First Lieutenant, Eighth Infantry, October 31, 1818
- First Lieutenant, First Infantry, in reorganization of the Army, June 1, 1821
- Captain, First Infantry, December 31, 1824
- Major, Eighth Infantry, July 7, 1838
- Lieutenant Colonel, Third Infantry, January 31, 1842
- Brevet Colonel, for gallant and meritorious conduct in the Battles of Contreras and Churubusco, Mexico, August 20, 1847
- Brevet Brigadier General, for gallant and meritorious conduct in the Battle of Molino del Rey, Mexico, September 8, 1847
- Colonel, Second Infantry, April 15, 1851
- Resigned, October 18, 1855
- Major General, U.S. Volunteers, February 10, 1862

Assignments

- Cadet of the Military Academy, October 11, 1814–July 17, 1817
- In the garrisons at Mobile, Alabama, 1817–1818, and New Orleans, Louisiana, 1818–1819
- Adjutant, Eighth Infantry, June 1, 1819–June 1, 1821
- On recruiting service, 1819

- In garrisons at the Bay of St. Louis, Missouri, 1821–1822, and Baton Rouge, Louisiana, 1822–1823
- On recruiting service, 1823–1824
- At the Military Academy, as assistant instructor of infantry tactics, February 1, 1824–April 20, 1827
- On recruiting service, 1827–1829
- At the Military Academy, as commandant of cadets and instructor of infantry tactics, March 13, 1829–June 24, 1833
- On frontier duty at Fort Crawford, Wisconsin, 1834–1835
- Served in a campaign in the Florida War against the Seminole Indians, 1836
- Fought in the skirmishes at Camp Izard on February 27–29, 1846, and March 5, 1836
- Acting Inspector General of the Western Department, February 10–July 5, 1836
- On recruiting service, 1836–1837
- Acted as disbursing Indian Agent, March 2, 1837–December 31, 1839
- On Northern Frontier, at Madison Barracks, New York during Canada Border disturbances, 1840
- In the garrison at Jefferson Barracks, Missouri, 1840
- In the Florida War, 1840
- On special duty in the War Department, September 29, 1841–August 29, 1842
- In the garrison at Fort Stansbury, Florida, 1842
- In command of the Western District of Florida, from which he removed Pascofa's band of hostile Indians, 1842–1843
- In the garrison at Fort Stansbury, Florida, 1843, and Jefferson Barracks, Missouri, 1843–1844
- On frontier duty at Fort Jesup (Camp Wilkins), Louisiana, 1844–1845
- In the Military Occupation of Texas, 1845–1846
- On sick leave of absence, 1846–1847
- In the War with Mexico, 1847–1848
  - Siege of Vera Cruz, March 9–29, 1847
  - Battle of Cerro Gordo, April 17–18, 1847
  - Battle of Churubusco, August 20, 1847
  - Battle of Molino del Rey, September 8, 1847
  - Storming of Chapultepec, September 13, 1847
  - Assault and Capture of the City of Mexico, September 13–14, 1847
  - Acting Inspector General of the Army commanded by Major General Scott, 1847–1848
- In mustering out Mexican War volunteers at Independence, Missouri, 1848
- On sick leave of absence, 1849–1850
- On detached service at Washington, D.C., 1850–1851
- In command of the Pacific Division, July 9, 1851–May 21, 1854
- In the garrison at Carlisle Barracks, Pennsylvania, 1854–1855

- Served during the Rebellion of the Seceding States, 1862–1866
  - On Special Duty, under the direction of the Secretary of War, at Washington, D.C., March 17, 1862–October 1, 1867
  - Commissioner for the Exchange of Prisoners of War, November 15, 1862–October 1, 1867[1]

Biographical Sketch

Major General Ethan Allen Hitchcock was born on May 18, 1798, at Vergennes, Vermont and died on August 5, 1870, at Sparta, Georgia at the age of seventy-two. His remains were re-interred on December 14, 1871, at West Point, New York. His father was Samuel Hitchcock, a U.S. Circuit Judge during the Washington Administration, and his mother was a daughter of the famous Revolutionary War General Ethan Allen. General Hitchcock inherited the name, general appearance, and many marked characteristics from the old hero of Ticonderoga and Crown Point.

At sixteen, Hitchcock became a cadet at the Military Academy on October 11, 1814. He graduated seventeenth in his class on July 17, 1817. The Army promoted him to third lieutenant in the Corps of Artillery. Lieutenant Hitchcock believed advancement in the infantry was faster than in other branches, and he applied and obtained a transfer to the Eighth Infantry Regiment on February 13, 1818. He entered the regiment as a second lieutenant and was promoted to first lieutenant on October 31, 1818. Hitchcock served in the regiment at Mobile and New Orleans until June 1, 1819. He was the regimental adjutant until the Army reorganization on June 1, 1821. The Army transferred him to the First Infantry where he received a promotion to captain on December 31, 1824.

Captain Hitchcock returned to West Point in 1824 as an assistant instructor of infantry tactics from 1824 to 1827. From 1827 to 1829, he was assigned recruiting and garrison duty. On March 13, 1829, he became commandant of cadets at the Military Academy. At the Academy, his "soldierly qualities and marked intelligence" became noticeable. The Army relieved him from this responsible position on June 24, 1833. Hitchcock was assigned to Fort Crawford, Wisconsin and served on frontier duty until the outbreak of the Florida War. He volunteered for assignment in the Florida War and served as acting inspector general during "Gaines' Campaign of 1836" against the Seminole Indians. The conflict ended after a few skirmishes at Camp Izard, near the site of "Dade's Massacre." This campaign was another blunder in the Florida War and finally reached a court of inquiry. Hitchcock testified, the "continuance of the war was in no small degree due to the want of concert; between the rival generals, Scott and Gaines." His testimony might have caused General Scott's unfriendliness toward him.

In 1833 and 1837, Hitchcock declined the American Colonization Society's appointment as Governor of Liberia.

From Florida, Hitchcock went with General Gaines to the Western Department where Hitchcock served as acting inspector general from February 10 to July 5, 1836. The Army transferred Hitchcock to recruiting service in 1836–1837. He performed "invaluable" services as disbursing agent to the Indians of the Northwest Territory from

March 2, 1837, to December 31, 1839. This assignment was "marked by the inflexible justice and unflinching firmness characteristic of the performance of all his public duties." Hitchcock strictly adhered to his instructions and determinedly fulfilled his responsibilities as agent. His efforts on behalf of the Indians saved a large part of their annuities. Prior to Hitchcock's presence, the Indians had naively assigned their annuities to men whose intent was to deceive and swindle them. While protecting the weak by "this firm, honest, and humane course," he made enemies of these swindlers, who became influential men in the Northwest Territory. However, Hitchcock was satisfied that Secretary of War Joel Roberts Poinsett[2] approved his actions. Poinsett complimented Hitchcock's efforts and appointed him major in the newly created Eighth Infantry Regiment on July 8, 1838. He held this position until December 31, 1839.

For the next two years, he was assigned to garrison duty. On September 29, 1841, Secretary of War John Bell[3] assigned Hitchcock to direct the Indian Bureau in Washington, D.C. He directed the bureau for about a year and exposed frauds and discharged unworthy agents, despite the efforts of men who fought these changes.

After he left Washington, he joined his regiment in Florida. In 1842–1843, his command removed Pascofa's band of hostile Indians. On January 31, 1842, the Army promoted him to lieutenant colonel of the Third Infantry Regiment. The regiment was assigned to operations on the Western frontier from 1843 to 1845. He assumed command of the Third Regiment and returned to Florida. Colonel Hitchcock turned the Third into a "crack" infantry regiment in drill, discipline, and in high mental culture. In April 1843, the regiment was transferred to Jefferson Barracks where Hitchcock introduced evolutions of the lines. He increased the interest in military exercises and duties and encouraged a "spirit of generous rivalry" between the Third and Fourth Infantries. Under Hitchcock's guidance, the barracks became a school for officers to apply their higher duties and instilled pride in being in the military profession.

In 1844, the Army sent Hitchcock's regiment to Fort Jesup on the Louisiana frontier in anticipation of the annexation of Texas. After Texas joined the United States in 1845, the Third Regiment became part of General Zachry Taylor's Army of Occupation at Corpus Christi, Texas. While in Texas awaiting developments with Mexico, Hitchcock wrote his paper on "Brevet and Staff Rank and Command." This analysis was signed by many officers and sent as a petition to Congress. Hitchcock's regiment advanced to the Rio Grande River. However, Hitchcock's health failed, and he was granted a sick leave of absence.

After his health improved, Hitchcock returned to the Rio Grande in January 1847 and assumed command of his regiment. The Third joined General Winfield Scott's new army at Brazos Santiago, Texas. Scott prepared his Army of Invasion for a campaign to capture Mexico City. The plan was to land at Vera Cruz, Mexico, seize the city, and march west to attack the Mexican capital.

The feud between Scott and Hitchcock grew from Hitchcock's actions as major of the Eighth Infantry under Colonel Worth and his involvement the "Buell Court Martial."[4] Hitchcock protested General Scott's right to retry Don Carlos Buell. Scott and Hitchcock resolved their differences and aligned "against the common enemy." Scott offered Hitchcock the important appointment as inspector general. Scott believed, "he [Hitchcock] could be of greater service to the Army and his country [as inspector general] than in any other position." Hitchcock ably performed his civilian and military duties, and Scott rewarded the inspector general's efforts with brevet promotions to colonel and brigadier general.

After the Mexican War, Hitchcock traveled in Europe and the East to recover his health. General Hitchcock returned home in 1850 with "bright memories of scenic and artistic beauty" and "much intellectual wealth." The Army assigned General Hitchcock to detached service at Washington and promoted him to colonel of the Second Infantry on April 15, 1851. He was sent to San Francisco, California in command of the Military Division of the Pacific. He managed this department from July 9, 1851, to May 21, 1854. Hitchcock protected the many Indian tribes from "plundering politicians and reckless adventurers." He broke up William Walker's plans to send men and arms to Guaymas, Mexico to incite the inhabitants of Sonora in Northern Mexico to declare their independence and set up a new government. The plotters intended to seize Sonora, attack Mexico, and establish a Southern slavery republic. Hitchcock's seizure of the brig *Arrow*, which planned to ship men and supplies for the revolution, effectively ended Walker's adventure. The conspirators obtained a measure of revenge when the Secretary of War Jefferson Davis transferred Hitchcock from his high command to a nominal one at Carlisle Barracks, Pennsylvania.

Previously, Hitchcock tried to improve his health and reduce the threat of paralysis at clinics in Wiesbaden, Germany and the Arkansas Hot Springs. In July 1855, he asked and obtained a four-month leave from General Scott to continue to improve his heath. Secretary of War Davis asked Scott why he granted this "indulgence." Davis retracted Scott's permission and ordered Hitchcock to Fort Pierre, South Dakota. In response, Hitchcock asked for an extension of his leave of absence. Hitchcock offered his resignation if Davis refused to grant the extension. However, if his services were considered "indispensable," he would go to Fort Pierre at all hazards, "as nothing would be further from his purpose than to jeopardize a reputation which had continued unblemished during a period of nearly forty years in the Army." Davis refused Hitchcock's request and accepted his resignation on October 18, 1855. General Scott said, "A most meritorious officer [*was*] forced out of service by the Secretary's oppressive orders in denying a simple indulgence at a time when there was no urgent reason for his presence at a remote post."

After resigning, Hitchcock lived in St. Louis where he read extensively and conducted philosophical investigations. He was a life-long student and never had enough books in his library. He examined the great works of philosophy and theology. He published the *Problem of Life* in eight volumes.

Hitchcock was in St. Louis when the Civil War began. Missouri was a slave state, and many of her prominent citizens advocated secession. In this turbulent environment, Hitchcock stayed loyal to the United States and preservation of the Union. Despite his poor health, he travelled to Washington and offered his services to the government. General Scott urged the authorities to grant Hitchcock a high commission, but the Secretary of War refused the request. Hitchcock returned to St. Louis and became an adviser to General William S. Harney,[5] who commanded the Military Department of the Missouri. Hitchcock wrote Harney's proclamation denouncing the legislature's "Military Bill" as "an indirect secession ordnance."

When General Henry W. Halleck assumed command of the Department of Missouri on November 15, 1861, he renewed the request for Hitchcock to receive a high commission. General Scott enthusiastically supported this application. Halleck and Scott's efforts resulted in Hitchcock's appointment and confirmation as major general of U.S. Volunteers on February 10, 1862. Hitchcock appreciated the compliment, but he declined the commission because he believed his poor health would not allow him to perform the duties of a major general. Subsequently, Halleck and Scott convinced him to keep his commission and serve in the War Department in Washington. On November 15, 1862, he was appointed Commissioner for the Exchange of Prisoners of War. The authorities assigned him to the added position of Commissary-General of Prisoners on November 3, 1865. He continued with these responsibilities until October 1, 1867, when he was mustered out of service.

Hitchcock and his wife moved to Georgia to improve his health. He died on August 5, 1870, at Sparta, Georgia at 72 years old.[6]

John Fowle
(July 10, 1833–March 31, 1838)
Cullum Number: None

Service at the Academy

John Fowle was commandant of cadets and instructor of infantry tactics from July 10, 1833, to March 31, 1838.

Superintendent

Major Rene E. DeRussy was superintendent from July 1, 1833, to September 1, 1838. DeRussy served as an engineering officer in the War of 1812–1815. He supervised fortifications at East Coast and Gulf Coast harbors.[1]

Significant Contributions

Two former cadets taught by Fowle received the Thanks of Congress: Major General George G. Meade (Class of 1835) and Major General Joseph Hooker (Class of 1837).[2] On May 10, 1838, cadets who were appointed non-commissioned officers in the Corps of Cadets resigned their positions. The Secretary of War ordered the cadets to return to their "appointed assignments."[3]

Notable Cadets

See "Notable West Point Graduates Who Served in the Civil War" in the Appendices for more information.

- Class of 1834 (36 Graduates)
  - Thomas A. Morris (4), Union, Brigadier General
  - Robert T.P. Allen (5), Confederate, Colonel
  - Gabriel R. Paul (18), Union, Brigadier General
  - Goode Bryan (25), Confederate, Brigadier General
  - William Scott Ketchum (32), Union, Brigadier General

- Class of 1835 (56 Graduates)
  - George W. Morrell (1), Union, Brigadier General
  - John H. Martindale (3), Union, Brigadier General
  - Montgomery Blair (18), Union, U.S. Postmaster General
  - George G. Meade (19), Union, Major General
  - Henry M. Naglee (23), Union, Brigadier General
  - Henry Prince (30), Union, Brigadier General
  - Herman Haupt (31), Union, Colonel, Chief of Construction and Transportation of U.S. Military Railroads
  - John M. Withers (44), Confederate, Major General
  - Larkin Smith (47), Confederate, Brigadier General
  - Marsena R. Patrick (48), Union, Brigadier General
  - Benjamin S. Roberts (53), Union, Brigadier General
- Class of 1836 (49 Graduates)
  - Danville Leadbetter (3), Confederate, Brigadier General
  - Joseph R. Anderson (4), Confederate, Brigadier General
  - Montgomery C. Meigs (5), Union, Brevet Major General
  - Daniel P. Woodbury (6), Union, Brevet Major General
  - James Lowry Donaldson (15), Union, Brevet Brigadier General
  - Thomas W. Sherman (18), Union, Brigadier General
  - Henry H. Lockwood (22), Union, Brigadier General
  - John W. Phelps (24), Union, Brigadier General
  - Robert Allen (33), Union, Brigadier General
  - George C. Thomas (35), Union, Major General
  - Richard G. Stockton (44), Union, Brigadier General
  - Lloyd Tilghman (46), Confederate, Brigadier General
- Class of 1837 (50 Graduates)
  - Henry W. Benham (1), Union, Brigadier General
  - Braxton Bragg (5), Confederate, General
  - Alexander B. Dyer (6), Union, Brigadier General, U.S. Ordnance Bureau
  - William W. Mackall (8), Confederate, Brigadier General
  - E. Parker Scammon (9), Union, Brigadier General
  - Lewis G. Arnold (10), Union, Brigadier General
  - Israel Vogdes (11), Union, Brigadier General
  - Thomas Williams (12), Union, Brigadier General
  - Edward D. Townsend (16), Union, Brigadier General
  - Jubal Early (18), Confederate, Lieutenant General
  - Bennett H. Hill (21), Brevet Brigadier General
  - William H. French (22), Union, Major General
  - John Sedgwick (24), Union, Major General
  - Joshua H. Bates (25), Union, Brigadier General
  - John C. Pemberton (27), Confederate, Lieutenant General
  - Joseph Hooker (29), Union, Major General
  - Arnold Elzey (Jones) (33), Confederate, Major General
  - John B.S. Todd (39), Union, Brigadier General

- William H.T. Walker (46), Confederate, Major General
  - Robert H. Chilton (48), Confederate, Brigadier General
- Class of 1838 (45 Graduates)
  - P.G.T. Beauregard (2), Confederate, General
  - James H. Trapier (3), Confederate, Brigadier General
  - Henry C. Wayne (14), Confederate, Brigadier General
  - William F. Barry (17), Union, Brevet Brigadier General
  - Milton A. Haynes (18), Confederate, Lieutenant Colonel
  - Langdon C. Easton (22), Union, Brevet Brigadier General
  - Irvin McDowell (23), Union, Major General
  - William J. Hardee (26), Confederate, Lieutenant General
  - Robert S. Granger (28), Union, Brigadier General
  - Henry S. Sibley (31), Confederate, Major General
  - Edward Johnson (32), Confederate, Major General
  - Alexander W. Reynolds (35), Confederate, Brigadier General
  - Andrew J. Smith (36), Union, Major General
  - Justus McKinstry (40), Union, Brigadier General
  - Carter L. Stevenson (42), Confederate, Major General
- Class of 1839 (31 Graduates)
  - Isaac I. Stevens (1), Union, Major General
  - Henry W. Halleck (3), Union, Major General
  - Jeremy F. Gilmer (4), Confederate, Major General, Chief Engineer
  - Joseph A. Haskin (10), Union, Brigadier General
  - Alexander R. Lawton (13), Confederate, Brigadier General
  - James B. Ricketts (16), Union, Major General
  - Edward O.C. Ord (17), Union, Major General
  - Henry J. Hunt (19), Union, Brevet Major General
  - Eleazer A. Paine (24), Union, Brigadier General
  - Edward R.S. Canby (30), Union, Major General

Promotions

- Second Lieutenant, Ninth Infantry, April 9, 1812
- First Lieutenant, Ninth Infantry, April 16, 1813
- Captain, Ninth Infantry, June 10, 1814
- Captain, Fifth Infantry, May 17, 1815
- Brevet Major, for faithful service, ten years in one grade, June 10, 1824
- Major, Third Infantry, March 4, 1833
- Lieutenant Colonel, Sixth Infantry, December 25, 1837

Assignments

- Regimental Paymaster in the Ninth Infantry, July 3, 1812
- In the War of 1812–15 with Great Britain, in the campaigns on the Northern frontier, being wounded in the Battle of Niagara, July 25, 1814

- On frontier duty at Detroit, Michigan, 1815–1818; Fort Gratiot, Michigan, 1818–1819; Green Bay, Wisconsin, 1819; and Fort Crawford, Wisconsin, 1819–1822
- On recruiting duty, 1822–1823
- On frontier duty at Council Bluffs, Iowa, 1823–1824, and Fort Edwards, Illinois, 1824
- On leave of absence, 1824–1825
- On recruiting duty, 1825
- On frontier duty at Fort Snelling, Minnesota, 1825–1826
- On recruiting duty, 1826
- On frontier duty at Fort Snelling, Minnesota, 1826
- On leave of absence, 1826–1827
- On frontier duty at Fort Crawford, Wisconsin, 1827–1828; Jefferson Barracks, Missouri, 1828; and Fort Dearborn, Michigan, 1828
- On leave of absence, 1830–1832
- On frontier duty at Fort Brady, Michigan, 1832–1833
- Commandant of cadets and instructor of infantry tactics at the U.S. Military Academy, July 10, 1833–March 31, 1838
- Killed enroute to his new post when the boiler burst on the steamer *Moselle* on the Ohio River near Cincinnati, April 25, 1838

Biographical Sketch

John Fowle joined the U.S. Army on April 9, 1812, as second lieutenant in the Ninth Infantry Regiment. He served as the regimental paymaster from July 3, 1812, until May 17, 1815. He fought in campaigns on the Northern frontier in the War of 1812. The Army promoted him to first lieutenant in the Ninth Infantry on April 16, 1813. Lieutenant Fowle was wounded at the Battle of Niagara on July 25, 1814. The Army promoted him to captain in the Ninth on June 10, 1814. Captain Fowle served on the frontier at Detroit, Michigan (1815–1818); Fort Gratiot, Michigan (1818–1819); Green Bay, Wisconsin (1819), and Fort Crawford, Wisconsin (1819–1822). He was on recruiting duty (1822–1823) and returned to frontier duty at Council Bluffs, Iowa (1823–1824) and Fort Edwards, Illinois (1824). The Army promoted him to brevet major on June 10, 1824, for ten years of faithful service in one grade. Fowle had a leave of absence (1824–1825) and worked in recruiting operations (1825).

He was on frontier duty at Fort Snelling, Minnesota (1825–1826) and spent part of 1826 on recruiting service. Fowle was back on frontier duty at Fort Snelling, in 1826 before going on a leave of absence from 1826 to 1827. The Army assigned Major Fowle to frontier duty at Fort Crawford, Wisconsin (1827–1828); Jefferson Barracks, Missouri (1828); and Fort Dearborn, Illinois (1828). He was on a leave of absence from 1830 to 1832 before returning to frontier duty at Fort Brady, Michigan (1832–1833).

On March 4, 1833, Fowle received a promotion to major in the Third Infantry. The Army assigned him to the Military Academy as commandant of cadets and instructor of infantry tactics from July 10, 1833, to March 31, 1838. Fowle was promoted to lieutenant colonel in the Sixth Infantry on December 25, 1837.

Colonel Fowle was killed enroute to his new post when the boiler burst on the steamer *Moselle* on the Ohio River near Cincinnati on April 25, 1838.[4]

Charles F. Smith
(April 1, 1838–September 1, 1842)
Cullum Number: 410

Service at the Academy

Charles F. Smith held several posts at the Military Academy from 1829 to 1842. He was assistant instructor of infantry tactics (June 25, 1829, to September 1, 1831); adjutant to Superintendent Thayer (September 1, 1831, to April 1, 1838); and commandant of cadets and instructor of infantry tactics (April 1, 1838, to September 1, 1842).

Superintendent

Rene E. DeRussy was superintendent from July 1, 1833, to September 1, 1838. DeRussy was succeeded by Captain Richard Delafield who held the post from September 1, 1838, to August 15, 1845. Delafield supervised construction of harbor defenses on the East and Gulf Coasts and improvements to rivers and roads.[1]

Significant Contributions

During his thirteen years at the U.S. Military Academy, he "won the golden opinions of all over and under him."[2]

General Grant considered "General Scott and Captain C.F. Smith, the Commander of Cadets, as the two men most to be envied in the nation."[3]

Five former cadets taught by Smith received the Thanks of Congress: Major General W.T. Sherman (Class of 1840), Major General George H. Thomas (Class of 1840), Brigadier General Nathaniel Lyon (Class of 1841), Major General William S. Rosecrans (Class of 1842), and Major General Ulysses S. Grant (Class of 1843).[4]

In two-thirds of the "Important Battles of the Civil War," one or both commanders were Smith's students.

Several changes occurred at the Academy in 1839 while Smith was commandant. The Army sent a sergeant and five dragoons to West Point to help with riding instruction, and appointed a riding master in September. The commandant drilled the cadets in infantry and artillery tactics. However, "unfavorable circumstances" caused the cadets to be "less skilled" in artillery. The cadet examinations were regarded as "thorough and impartial." Mathematics was considered as "the basis on which a military education must rest." All cadets were treated equally, and discipline was imposed uniformly on all students. The only distinctions between cadets were the grades of merit, which were open to all cadets and only awarded when deserved.[5]

Charles Ferguson Smith (Library of Congress).

Notable Cadets

See "Notable West Point Graduates Who Served in the Civil War" in the Appendices for more information.

- Class of 1838 (45 Graduates)
    - P.G.T. Beauregard (2), Confederate, General
    - James H. Trapier (3), Confederate, Brigadier General
    - Henry C. Wayne (14), Confederate, Brigadier General
    - William F. Barry (17), Union, Brevet Major General
    - Milton A. Haynes (18), Confederate, Lieutenant Colonel
    - Langdon C. Easton (22), Union, Brevet Brigadier General
    - Irvin McDowell (23), Union, Major General
    - William J. Hardee (26), Confederate, Lieutenant General
    - Robert S. Granger (28), Union, Brigadier General
    - Henry S. Sibley (31), Confederate, Major General
    - Edward Johnson (32), Confederate, Major General
    - Alexander W. Reynolds (35), Confederate, Brigadier General
    - Andrew J. Smith (36), Union, Major General
    - Justus McKinstry (40), Union, Brigadier General
    - Carter L. Stevenson (42), Confederate, Major General
- Class of 1839 (31 Graduates)
    - Isaac I. Stevens (1), Union, Major General
    - Henry W. Halleck (3), Union, Major General
    - Jeremy F. Gilmer (4), Confederate, Major General
    - Joseph A. Haskin (10), Union, Brigadier General

- Alexander R. Lawton (13), Confederate, Brigadier General
- James B. Ricketts (16), Union, Major General
- Edward O.C. Ord (17), Union, Major General
- Henry J. Hunt (19), Union, Brevet Major General
- Eleazer A. Paine (24), Union, Brigadier General
- Edward R.S. Canby (30), Union, Major General

- Class of 1840 (42 Graduates)
  - Paul O. Hebert (1), Confederate, Brigadier General
  - William T. Sherman (6), Union, Major General
  - Stewart van Vliet (9), Union, Brigadier General
  - John P. McCown (10), Confederate, Major General
  - George H. Thomas (12), Union, Major General
  - Richard S. Ewell (13), Confederate, Lieutenant General
  - James G. Martin (14), Confederate, Brigadier General
  - George W. Getty (15), Union, Brevet Major General
  - William Hays (18), Union, Brigadier General
  - Bushrod R. Johnson (23), Confederate, Major General
  - William Steele (31), Confederate, Brigadier General
  - Robert Plunket Maclay (32), Confederate, Brigadier General
  - James Green Martin (39), Confederate, Brigadier General
  - Thomas Jordan (41), Confederate, Brigadier General

- Class of 1841 (52 Graduates)
  - Zealous B. Tower (1), Union, Brigadier General
  - Horatio G. Wright (2), Union, Major General
  - Amiel W. Whipple (5), Union, Brevet Major General
  - Josiah Gorgas (6), Confederate, Brigadier General
  - Albion Powell (8), Union, Brigadier General
  - Nathaniel Lyon (11), Union, Brigadier General
  - Samuel Jones (19), Confederate, Major General
  - Joseph B. Plummer (22), Union, Brigadier General
  - John M. Brannan (23), Union, Brevet Major General
  - Schuyler Hamilton (24), Union, Major General
  - James Totten (26), Union, Brigadier General
  - John F. Reynolds (26), Union, Major General
  - Robert S. Garnett (27), Confederate, Brigadier General
  - Richard B. Garnett (29), Confederate, Brigadier General
  - Claudius W. Sears (31), Confederate, Brigadier General
  - Don Carlos Buell (32), Union, Major General
  - Alfred Sully (34), Union, Brevet Brigadier General
  - Israel B. Richardson (38), Union, Major General
  - John M. Jones (39), Confederate, Brigadier General
  - William T.H. Brooks (46), Union, Brigadier General
  - Abraham Buford (51), Confederate, Brigadier General

- Class of 1842 (56 Graduates)
  - Henry Eustis (1), Union, Brigadier General

- John Newton (2), Union, Brigadier General
- William S. Rosecrans (5), Union, Major General
- Gustavus W. Smith (8), Confederate, Major General
- Mansfield Lovell (9), Confederate, Major General
- Alexander P. Stewart (12), Confederate, Lieutenant General
- Martin L. Smith, Confederate, Major General
- John Pope (17), Union, Major General
- Seth Williams (23), Union, Brevet Brigadier General
- Abner Doubleday (24), Union, Major General
- Daniel H. Hill (28), Confederate, Lieutenant General
- Napoleon J.T. Dana (29), Union, Major General
- George Sykes (39), Union, Major General
- Richard H. Anderson (40), Confederate, Lieutenant General
- George W. Lay (41), Confederate, Colonel, Chief of Bureau of Conscription
- Lafayette McLaws (48), Confederate, Major General
- Earl van Dorn (52), Confederate, Major General
- James Longstreet (54), Confederate, Lieutenant General
- Class of 1843 (39 Graduates)
  - William B. Franklin (1), Union, Major General
  - Isaac F. Quinby (6), Union, Brigadier General
  - Roswell S. Ripley (7), Confederate, Brigadier General
  - John J. Peck (8), Union, Major General
  - Joseph J. Reynolds (10), Union, Major General
  - Samuel Gibbs French (14), Confederate, Major General
  - Christopher C. Augur (16), Union, Major General
  - Franklin K. Gardner (17), Confederate, Major General
  - Ulysses S. Grant (21), Union, Lieutenant General
  - Charles S. Hamilton (26), Union, Major General
  - Frederick Steele (30), Union, Major General
  - Rufus Ingalls (32), Union, Brevet Brigadier General
  - Henry M. Judah (35), Union, Brigadier General

Promotions

- Brevet Second Lieutenant, Second Artillery, July 1, 1825
- Second Lieutenant, Second Artillery, July 1, 1825
- First Lieutenant, Second Artillery, May 30, 1832
- Captain, Second Artillery, July 7, 1838
- Brevet Major, for gallant and distinguished conduct in the Battles of Palo Alto and Resaca-de-la-Palma, Texas, May 9, 1846
- Brevet Lieutenant Colonel, for gallant conduct in the several conflicts at Monterey, Mexico, September 23, 1846
- Brevet Colonel, for gallant and meritorious conduct in the Battles of Contreras and Churubusco, Mexico, August 20, 1847
- Major, First Artillery, November 25, 1854

- Lieutenant Colonel, Tenth Infantry Regiment, March 3, 1855
- Brigadier General, U.S. Volunteers, August 31, 1861
- Colonel, Third Infantry, September 9, 1861
- Major General, U.S. Volunteers, March 21, 1862

Assignments

- Cadet at the Military Academy, July 1, 1820, to July 1825
- In garrison at Fort Delaware, Delaware, 1825–1827, and Augusta Arsenal, Georgia, 1827–1829
- At the U.S. Military Academy, 1829–1842
  - Assistant Instructor of Infantry Tactics, June 25, 1829, to September 1, 1831
  - Adjutant to Superintendent Sylvanus Thayer, September 1, 1831, to April 1, 1838
  - Commandant of cadets and instructor of infantry tactics, April 1, 1838, to September 1, 1842
- In garrison at Fort Columbus, New York, 1843–1844, and Frankford Arsenal, Pennsylvania, 1844–1845
- In Military Occupation of Texas, 1845–1846
- In the War with Mexico, 1846–1848
  - Battle of Palo Alto, May 8, 1846
  - Battle of Resaca-de-la-Palma, May 9, 1846
  - Battle of Monterey, in command of the storming' party which carried Federation Hill, September 21–23, 1846
  - Siege of Vera Cruz, March 9–29, 1847
  - Battle of Cerro Gordo, April 17–18, 1847
  - Skirmish of Amazoque, May 14, 1847
  - Capture of San Antonio, August 20, 1847
  - Battle of Churubusco, August 20, 1847
  - Storming of Chapultepec, September 13, 1847
  - Assault and capture of the City of Mexico, September 13–14, 1847
  - In command of Light Infantry Battalion, May 1 to November 3, 1847
  - In command of the Police Guard of the City of Mexico, September 1847 to June 4, 1848
- In garrison at Fort Marion, Florida, 1849
- Member of a Board of Officers, 1849–51, to devise "A Complete System of Instruction for Siege, Garrison, Seacoast, and Mountain Artillery," which was adopted on May 10, 1851, for the service of the United States
- President of Board of Claims for supplies, etc., furnished by Colonel John C. Frémont, in 1846, to California Volunteers, September 7, 1852, to April 3, 1855
- In garrison at Carlisle Barracks, Pennsylvania, 1855
- On frontier duty at Fort Snelling, Minnesota, 1855; Fort Crawford, Wisconsin, 1855–1856: and Fort Snelling, Minnesota, 1856

- In command of the Expedition to the Red River of the North, 1856
- On frontier duty at Fort Snelling, Minnesota, 1856–1857
- Utah Expedition, 1857–1861
- In command of the Department of Utah, February 29, 1860, to February 28, 1861
- Served during the Rebellion of the Seceding States, 1861–1862
  - In command of the Department of Washington, April 10–28, 1861
  - Superintendent of General Recruiting Service at Fort Columbus, New York, April 28 to August 19, 1861
  - In command of District of Western Kentucky, with headquarters at Paducah, Kentucky, September 8, 1861, to January 31, 1862
  - In the Federal Penetration up the Cumberland and Tennessee Rivers, 1862
  - Engaged in the operations about Fort Henry, February 4–6, 1862
  - Assault and Capture of Fort Donelson, February 13–16, 1862
  - In command of the advance upon Shiloh, March 1862
  - Received a severe injury before the Battle of Shiloh and died from infection at Savannah, Tennessee, April 25, 1862[6]

Biographical Sketch

Major General Charles F. Smith was born on April 24, 1807, in Philadelphia, Pennsylvania. He was a grandson of a colonel of the Continental Army and son of Assistant Surgeon Samuel B. Smith of the U.S. Army. He graduated nineteenth in the class of 1825 from the United States Military Academy, and the Army commissioned him as a second lieutenant in the Second U.S. Artillery Regiment. He attended artillery schools at Fort Delaware, Delaware (1825–1827) and Augusta Arsenal, Georgia (1827–1829).

On June 25, 1829, he returned to West Point as an assistant instructor of infantry tactics (1829–1831). He served as adjutant to Superintendent Sylvanus Thayer for nearly seven years (1831–1838). The Army promoted Smith to commandant of cadets and instructor of infantry tactics (1838–1842). During his thirteen years at the Military Academy, he "won the golden opinions of all over and under him." After leaving West Point, Smith joined the Second Artillery in command of Company K.

In 1845, difficulties with Mexico, resulting from the annexation of Texas, brought Smith to the field. As an artillery battalion commander, he distinguished himself in the Mexican-American War while serving under Zachary Taylor and Winfield Scott. He led the advance across the Colorado River and won a brevet promotion to major for his gallantry at Palo Alto and Resaca-de-la-Palma. He earned a brevet promotion to lieutenant colonel for "the brilliant storming of Federation Hill, at Monterey." He was transferred to General Scott's army and took part in the various operations from Vera Cruz to Mexico City. Smith commanded the Light Infantry Battalion, "with signal ability and characteristic intrepidity" in the Capture of San Antonio, Battle of Churubusco, Storming of Chapultepec, and Assault and Capture of Mexico City. He received his third brevet to colonel for gallant and meritorious conduct in the Battles of Contreras and Churubusco. General Scott placed Smith in command of the City Guards from the end of the war until 1848. He was also an original member and officer of the Aztec Club of 1847. The citizens of Philadelphia appreciated the "value of [his] disciplined courage, military instruction, and skilled leadership" and presented him with a Sword of Honor.

After the war, Smith commanded the garrison at Fort Marion, Florida (1849). Smith was a member of a Board to devise a "Complete System of Instruction for Siege, Garrison, Seacoast, and Mountain Artillery." In November 1854, the Army promoted him to major in the First Artillery Regiment. Smith was President of the Board of Claims for supplies obtained by Colonel Frémont, in 1846 for California Volunteers (1852–1855).

When the new Tenth Infantry Regiment was formed in March 1855, the Army named Smith as the unit's lieutenant colonel. In 1856, he commanded an expedition to the Red River of the North to evaluate sites for a fort, encourage the Native Americans to make peace among their tribes, and warn Canadian hunters and trappers not to enter the United States. Colonel Smith served with the Tenth Infantry in the Utah Expedition against the Mormons. He directed the Department of Utah from February 29, 1860, to February 28, 1861.

At the beginning of the Civil War, General Scott placed Smith in command of the Department of Washington in charge of organizing defenses to protect the nation's capital. Following this temporary assignment, Smith served on recruiting duty as commander of Fort Columbus, New York. General John C. Frémont obtained a transfer Smith to the Western Theater. Frémont nominated Smith for a commission as a brigadier general of volunteers and assigned him command of the District of Western Kentucky. The district's headquarters was at the strategic city of Paducah, Kentucky at the mouth of the Tennessee River. Paducah became the base of operations against Confederate forces in the area. General Smith "put the place in a good condition of defense against any attack in front or flank."

While Smith worked day and night preparing to resist the Confederates, he was suddenly assailed by a secret and unscrupulous senior officer in his command. This person, with the support of some scurrilous newspapers, wanted to replace Smith. Fortunately, Major General Henry W. Halleck, a gentleman and a soldier in charge of the Department of the Missouri, recognized Smith's worth. He refuted the false accusations against Smith and supported the general against his "demagogic adversary." Halleck's actions "retained in command a hero soon to show his brilliant leadership against a nobler and more open foe."

He became a division commander in the Department of the Missouri under Brigadier General Ulysses S. Grant, who was one of his pupils at West Point. This potentially awkward situation was eased by Smith's loyalty to his young chief.

In early 1862, General Grant, Admiral Andrew H. Foote, and General Smith convinced Halleck to attack Fort Henry on the Tennessee River. The joint operation moved up the Tennessee and Foote forced the flooded Fort Henry to surrender. Forces under Smith captured Fort Heiman on the opposite bank. Smith and other officers encouraged Grant to attack Fort Donelson.

Grant's forces invested Fort Donelson on the Cumberland River. After several failed Union tries to seize the fort, the Confederate command decided to escape and attacked the Union right. Grant realized the forces opposing Smith on the Union left had left their earthworks[7] to support the breakout. Grant ordered Smith to seize the Confederate works. Smith led his division down the slope, across a stream at the bottom, and up the opposing slope through the thick abatis. The men captured the earthworks and Smith urged them forward. By now the Confederates had reinforced their line and stopped the Union advance. The Union forces repulsed several counterattacks by the Confederates. Smith's attack forced the fort to surrender unconditionally the following day.

Grant generously acknowledged Smith's attack and "that he owed his success at Donelson emphatically to him." Halleck immediately telegraphed General George McClellan to request Smith's promotion. Halleck said, "Brigadier General Charles F. Smith, by his coolness and bravery at Fort Donelson when the battle was against us, turned the tide and carried the enemy's outworks; make him a Major General. You can't get a better one. Honor him for this victory, and the country will applaud." The Senate unanimously confirmed the appointment. The City of Philadelphia awarded Smith another Sword of Honor.

Shortly after Fort Donelson was captured, Grant sent Smith to Clarksville and Nashville. Communication problems between Grant and Halleck forced Halleck to remove Grant from command. Plans were made to seize the critical railroad junction at Corinth, Mississippi. Halleck assigned Smith command of the expedition moving up the Tennessee River. Smith wrote his wife, "This whole force is utterly demoralized by victory. There seems to be neither head nor tail. The utter want of discipline seems to me to be something marvelous, and yet I have to go far into the bowels of the earth with these men." He closed the letter with, "You shall hear a good account of me or of my death."

When the expedition arrived at Savannah, Tennessee, Smith and General Sherman selected Pittsburg Landing to assemble forces for the advance to Corinth. Smith visited General Lew Wallace on Wallace's steamer to explain a mission. When Smith left the ship, he fell while jumping into a yawl and badly cut the lower part of his right leg to the bone. He suffered on his steamer and limped around his cabin orchestrating the disposition of troops. While his wound distressed him, he was more concerned about the effect of injury about his mobility in battle rather than the pain he had to endure. He complained, "he could not take the field soon, not being able to sit at horse, or in fact walk," which would compel him "to ride to the battlefield in an ambulance."

Despite his agony, General Smith made a reconnaissance of the Tennessee River up to Chickasaw Bluff. Before the end of March, the general had to take to his bed, where he was forced to undergo a severe operation. The surgery combined with his debility caused by a cold taken at Donelson, continued harassing exertion, bad climate, supervening erysipelas,[8] and poisonous drugs, completely drained his energy. To the last moment he hoped to be well enough "to be carried about the expected battlefield in a hand litter." Grant was forced to replace him with General W.H.L. Wallace. When the Battle of Shiloh began, Smith chafed like a caged lion as he listened to sounds from Shiloh. "Imagine," he said, "if it be possible, my feelings, but no, that is impossible lying here bedridden with my injured leg, and excessive bodily weakness, listening for two days to the sounds of battle, the roar of artillery, the rattle of musketry, without being able to take my proper part in it."

Ten days later, Smith was on his deathbed. "Although resigned to the inevitable, his soldier soul was all aglow with the anticipated success of the Union cause, in which his loyal heart was so much bound up." He died on April 25, 1862.

> The Army could boast of no better general. His stately and commanding presence inspired his soldiers with respect and almost fear. In his rigid discipline, though severe, he was always just, requiring no greater subordination from inferiors than he was ready to yield to superiors. The call of duty was to him a magic sound for which he was always ready to make every sacrifice and endure any fatigue. He was the very model of a soldier, calm, prudent, and self-poised, yet, in the hour of danger, bold almost to rashness. Had he lived he would have held a high niche in the Temple of Fame, whose doors were already opened to him.—George W. Cullum

Sherman said, "had C.F. Smith lived, Grant would have disappeared to history after Donelson."

General Halleck's Obituary Order summarized Smith's career:

> He had been in the service of his country for more than forty years, and had passed through all the military grades from Cadet to Major General. He had fought with distinction in nearly all the battles of Mexico, and by his gallantry and skill had gained imperishable laurels at the Siege of Fort Donelson. He combined the qualities of a faithful officer, an excellent disciplinarian, an able commander, and a modest, courteous gentleman. In his death, the army has lost one of its brightest ornaments, and the country a general whose place it will be difficult to supply.

General Smith's remains were taken to Philadelphia for burial at Laurel Hill Cemetery. The city paid tribute to him with the highest military and civic honors.[9]

Two forts were named in Smith's honor. The first Fort C.F. Smith was part of the perimeter defenses of Washington, D.C. during the Civil War. A second Fort C.F. Smith was in the Powder River Country in the Montana Territory during Red Cloud's War.[10]

John A. Thomas
(September 1, 1842–December 14, 1845)
Cullum Number: 721

Service at the Academy

John Addison Thomas was commandant of cadets and instructor of infantry tactics from September 1, 1842, to December 14, 1845. He spent most of his time after graduation as an instructor at the Military Academy. He was an assistant instructor of tactics (December 26, 1834, to August 30, 1837), assistant professor of geography, history, and ethics (August 30, 1837, to July 28, 1840), and principal assistant professor of geography, history, and ethics (July 28, 1840, to September 26, 1841).

Superintendents

Thomas served under Superintendent Richard Delafield who held the post from September 1, 1838, to August 15, 1845. Captain Henry Brewerton was superintendent from August 15, 1845, until September 1, 1852.

Significant Contributions

Prior to his appointment as commandant of cadets, Thomas spent a year at Fort Wolcott, Rhode Island (1833–1834) and one year as an *aide-de-camp* to General John E. Wool (September 4, 1841, to August 1, 1842). Most of his time after graduation was as an instructor at the Military Academy. He was an assistant instructor of tactics (December 26, 1834, to August 30, 1837), assistant professor of geography, history, and ethics (August 30, 1837, to July 28, 1840), and principal assistant professor of geography, history, and ethics (July 28, 1840, to September 26, 1841).

Thomas served as commandant of cadets from September 1, 1842, to December 14, 1845. Thomas brought little in the way of operating experience to this position. However, Thomas taught many cadets who became important generals in the Civil War.

U.S. Military Academy (Library of Congress).

After a summer encampment in 1842, Thomas assembled a group of plebes. "Ethical Tom," as he was called by the cadets, shouted at them.

> You are not common soldiers!" You are Gentlemen—Gentlemen of manners, of politeness & of education. The U.S. looks to you! The Country looks to you! The Army looks to you![1]

He was on a leave of absence from 1845 to 1846 and resigned his commission on May 28, 1846. He died on March 26, 1858, at Paris, France.

One former cadet taught by Thomas received the Thanks of Congress: Major General Winfield S. Hancock (Class of 1844).[2]

Notable Cadets

See "Notable West Point Graduates Who Served in the Civil War" in the Appendices for more information.

- Class of 1842 (56 Graduates)
  - Henry Eustis (1), Union, Brigadier General
  - John Newton (2), Union, Brigadier General
  - William S. Rosecrans (5), Union, Major General
  - Gustavus W. Smith (8), Confederate, Major General
  - Mansfield Lovell (9), Confederate, Major General

- Alexander P. Stewart (12), Confederate, Lieutenant General
- Martin L. Smith (16), Confederate, Major General
- John Pope (17), Union, Major General
- Seth Williams (23), Union, Brevet Brigadier General
- Abner Doubleday (24), Union, Major General
- Daniel H. Hill (28), Confederate, Lieutenant General
- Napoleon J.T. Dana (29), Union, Major General
- George Sykes (39), Union, Major General
- Richard H. Anderson (40), Confederate, Lieutenant General
- George W. Lay (41), Confederate, Colonel, Chief of Bureau of Conscription
- Lafayette McLaws (48), Confederate, Major General
- Earl van Dorn (52), Confederate, Major General
- James Longstreet (54), Confederate, Lieutenant General

- Class of 1843 (39 Graduates)
  - William B. Franklin (1), Union, Major General
  - Isaac F. Quinby (6), Union, Brigadier General
  - Roswell S. Ripley (7), Confederate, Brigadier General
  - John J. Peck (8), Union, Major General
  - Joseph J. Reynolds (10), Union, Major General
  - Samuel Gibbs French (14), Confederate, Major General
  - Christopher C. Augur (16), Union, Major General
  - Franklin K. Gardner (17), Confederate, Major General
  - Ulysses S. Grant (21), Union, Lieutenant General
  - Charles S. Hamilton (26), Union, Union, Major General
  - Frederick Steele (30), Union, Major General
  - Rufus Ingalls (32), Union, Brevet Brigadier General
  - Henry M. Judah (35), Union, Brigadier General

- Class of 1844 (25 Graduates)
  - Daniel M. Frost (4), Confederate, Brigadier General
  - Alfred Pleasonton (7), Union, Major General
  - Simon B. Buckner (11), Confederate, Lieutenant General
  - Winfield S. Hancock (18), Union, Major General
  - Alexander Hays (20), Union, Brigadier General

- Class of 1845 (41 Graduates)
  - William H.C. Whiting (1), Confederate, Major General
  - Louis Hébert (3), Confederate, Brigadier General
  - William F. Smith (4), Union, Major General
  - Thomas J. Wood (5), Union, Major General
  - Charles P. Stone (7), Union, Brigadier General
  - Fitz John Porter (8), Union, Major General
  - John P. Hatch (17), Union, Brigadier General
  - Edmund Kirby Smith (25), Confederate, General
  - John W. Davidson (27), Union, Brigadier General
  - James M. Hawes (29), Confederate, Brigadier General
  - Bernard E. Bee (33), Confederate, Brigadier General

- Gordon Granger (35), Union, Major General
- Henry B. Clitz (36), Union, Lieutenant Colonel
- David A. Russell (38), Union, Brevet Major General
- Thomas G. Pitcher (40), Union, Brigadier General
- Class of 1846 (59 Graduates)
  - George B. McClellan (2), Union, Major General
  - John G. Foster (4), Union, Major General
  - Jesse L. Reno (8), Union, Major General
  - Darius N. Couch (13), Union, Major General
  - Thomas J. Jackson (17), Confederate, Lieutenant General
  - Truman Seymour (19), Union, Brigadier General
  - Charles C. Gilbert (21), Union, Brigadier General
  - John Adams (25), Confederate, Brigadier General
  - George Stoneman (33), Union, Major General
  - William Duncan Smith (35), Confederate, Brigadier General
  - Dabney H. Maury (37), Confederate, Major General
  - Innis N. Palmer (38), Union, Brigadier General
  - David R. Jones (41), Confederate, Major General
  - Alfred Gibbs (42), Union, Brigadier General
  - George H. Gordon (43), Union, Brigadier General
  - Cadmus M. Wilcox (54), Confederate, Major General
  - William M. Gardner (55), Confederate, Brigadier General
  - Samuel B. Maxey (58), Confederate, Major General
  - George E. Pickett (59), Confederate, Major General

Promotions

- Brevet Second Lieutenant, Third Artillery Regiment, July 1, 1833,
- Second Lieutenant, Third Artillery Regiment, December 1, 1835
- First Lieutenant, Third Artillery Regiment, June 30, 1837
- Captain, Third Artillery Regiment, November 19, 1843

Assignments

- In garrison at Fort Wolcott, Rhode Island, 1833–1834
- At the Military Academy, 1831–1841
  - Assistant instructor of infantry tactics, December 26, 1834, to August 30, 1837
  - Assistant professor of geography, history, and ethics, August 30, 1837, to July 28, 1840
  - Principal assistant professor of geography, history, and ethics, July 28, 1840, to September 26, 1841
- *Aide-de-Camp* to Brigadier General John Wool, September 4, 1841, to August 1, 1842

- At the Military Academy as commandant of cadets and instructor of infantry tactics, September 1, 1842, to December 14, 1842
- On leave of absence, 1845–1846

Resigned, May 28, 1846[3]

Biographical Sketch

John Addison Thomas (1811–March 26, 1858) was an engineer and military officer who served in the U.S. Army. Following his time in the Army, he worked as United States Assistant Secretary of State.

Thomas was born in Tennessee in 1811. He graduated from the United States Military Academy in 1833, and the Army assigned Lieutenant Thomas to the Third Artillery. Thomas served in the garrison at Fort Wolcott, Rhode Island before he returned to West Point in 1831. He was an assistant instructor of infantry tactics (December 26, 1834, to August 30, 1837); assistant professor of geography, history, and ethics (August 30, 1837, to July 28, 1840); and principal assistant professor of geography, history, and ethics (July 28, 1840, to September 26, 1841). The Army promoted Thomas to second lieutenant on December 1, 1835, and to first lieutenant on June 30, 1837.

Lieutenant Thomas served as *aide-de-camp* to Brigadier General John Wool from September 1, 1842, to December 14, 1842. The Army promoted Thomas to captain on November 19, 1843. He resigned from the Army on May 28, 1846, to practice law in New York City, New York. During the Mexican War, he returned to the military when he became colonel of the Fourth New York Regiment on July 23, 1846. The unit was raised, but was not mustered into service.

Thomas was the chief engineer of New York State from 1853 to 1854. From April 19, 1853, to January 14, 1854, Colonel Thomas was advocate of the United States[4] in London, England under the convention of February 8, 1853, with Great Britain for the adjustment of American claims. From November 1, 1855, to April 3, 1857, he was United States assistant secretary of state in Washington, D.C. He gained prominence by his report of the convention with Great Britain and by other state papers. He died in Paris, France on March 26, 1858.[5]

Bradford R. Alden
(December 14, 1845–November 1, 1852)
Cullum Number: 653

Service at the Academy

Bradford Alden was an assistant professor of mathematics (January 8–September 8, 1836), an assistant instructor of infantry tactics (September 8–October 30, 1836), assistant teacher of French (August 28, 1837–August 3, 1838), assistant instructor of infantry tactics (August 13, 1838–June 24, 1839), assistant teacher of French (September 12, 1839–February 7, 1840), and assistant instructor of infantry tactics (February 7, 1840, to September 14, 1840). He served nearly seven years as commandant of cadets and instructor of infantry tactics (December 14, 1845- November 1, 1852).

Superintendent

Captain Henry Brewerton was superintendent from August 15, 1845, until September 1, 1852. Captain Robert E. Lee replaced Brewerton on September 1, 1852, and served as superintendent until March 31, 1855.

Significant Contributions

Bradford R. Alden completed seventeen years of service at the Military Academy when he left his post as commandant of cadets and instructor of infantry tactics on November 1, 1852.[1] During his tenure as commandant, 263 cadets graduated and achieved the rank of general during the Civil War. Among his notable students were Union generals George B. McClellan, John Buford, Gouverneur K. Warren, and John Gibbon, and Confederate generals Thomas J. "Stonewall" Jackson, Henry Heth, George E. Pickett, and Charles W. Field.

Two former cadets taught by Alden received the Thanks of Congress: Major General George B. McClellan (Class of 1846) and Major General Ambrose E. Burnside (Class of 1847).[2]

West Point, as seen from above Washington Valley, painted by Geo. Cooke, engraved by W.J. Bennett, ca. 1834 (Library of Congress).

Possibly due to his influence, the Corps of Cadets pledged to abstain from the use of intoxicating liquors on April 26, 1846.[3]

During Alden's term as commandant, the academy introduced new textbooks on artillery and infantry (1849), light artillery drill (1850), tactics for garrison artillery (1850), tactics for siege artillery (1850), and tactics for garrison, siege, and field artillery (1850) to replace older manuals and to provide additional reading.[4]

The graduates praised Alden for his kindness, high sense of justice, sterling character, and the moral tone he impressed upon his command.[5]

Notable Cadets

See "Notable West Point Graduates Who Served in the Civil War" in the Appendices for more information.

- Class of 1845 (41 Graduates)
  - William H.C. Whiting (1), Confederate, Major General
  - Louis Hébert (3), Confederate, Brigadier General
  - William F. Smith (4), Union, Major General
  - Thomas J. Wood (5), Union, Major General
  - Charles P. Stone (7), Union, Brigadier General
  - Fitz John Porter (8), Union, Major General

- John P. Hatch (17), Union, Brigadier General
- Edmund Kirby Smith (25), Confederate, General
- John W. Davidson (27), Union, Brigadier General
- James M. Hawes (29), Confederate, Brigadier General
- Bernard E. Bee (33), Confederate, Brigadier General
- Gordon Granger (35), Union, Major General
- Henry B. Clitz (36), Union, Lieutenant Colonel
- David A. Russell (38), Union, Brevet Major General
- Thomas G. Pitcher (40), Union, Brigadier General

- Class of 1846 (59 Graduates)
  - George B. McClellan (2), Union, Major General
  - John G. Foster (4), Union, Major General
  - Jesse L. Reno (8), Union, Major General
  - Darius N. Couch (13), Union, Major General
  - Thomas J. Jackson (17), Confederate, Lieutenant General
  - Truman Seymour (19), Union, Major General
  - Charles C. Gilbert (21), Union, Brigadier General
  - John Adams (25), Confederate, Brigadier General
  - George Stoneman (33), Union, Major General
  - William Duncan Smith (35), Confederate, Brigadier General
  - Dabney H. Maury (37), Confederate, Major General
  - Innis N. Palmer (38), Union, Brigadier General
  - David R. Jones (41), Confederate, Major General
  - Alfred Gibbs (42), Union, Brigadier General
  - George H. Gordon (43), Union, Major General
  - Cadmus M. Wilcox (54), Confederate, Major General
  - William M. Gardner (55), Confederate, Brigadier General
  - Samuel B. Maxey (58), Confederate, Major General
  - George E. Pickett (59), Confederate, Major General

- Class of 1847 (38 Graduates)
  - Orlando B. Wilcox (8), Union, Brevet Major General
  - John S. Mason (9), Union, Brigadier General
  - James B. Fry (14), Union, Brigadier General
  - Ambrose P. Hill (15), Confederate, Lieutenant General
  - Ambrose E. Burnside (18), Union, Major General
  - John Gibbon (20), Union, Major General
  - Romeyn B. Ayers (22), Union, Brevet Major General
  - Charles Griffin (23), Union, Brevet Major General
  - William W. Burns (28), Union, Major General
  - Egbert L. Viele (30), Union, Brigadier General
  - Henry Heth (38), Confederate, Major General

- Class of 1848 (38 Graduates)
  - Walter H. Stevens (4), Confederate, Brigadier General
  - William E. Jones (10), Confederate, Brigadier General
  - John C. Tidball (11), Union, Brevet Brigadier General

- John Buford (16), Union, Major General
- William Beall (30), Confederate, Brigadier General
- Nathan George Evans (36), Confederate, Brigadier General
- George H. Steuart (37), Confederate, Brigadier General
- Class of 1849 (43 Graduates)
  - Quincy A. Gilmore (1), Union, Major General
  - John C. Parke (2), Union, Major General
  - Johnson K. Duncan (5), Confederate, Brigadier General
  - Absalom Baird (9), Union, Brevet Major General
  - Richard W. Johnson (30), Union, Brigadier General
  - John Creed Moore (17), Confederate, Brigadier General
  - Rufus Saxton (18), Union, Brevet Major General
  - Beverly H. Robertson (25), Confederate, Brigadier General
  - Charles W. Field (27), Confederate, Major General
  - Seth Barton (28), Confederate, Brigadier General
  - Duff C. green (29), Confederate, Brigadier General
  - Richard W. Johnson (30), Union, Brevet Major General
  - Alfred Cumming (35), Confederate, Brigadier General
  - James M. McIntosh (43), Confederate, Brigadier General
- Class of 1850 (44 Graduates)
  - Gouverneur K. Warren (2), Union, Major General
  - Cuvier Grover (4), Union, Brevet Major General
  - Adam J. Slemmer (12), Union, Brigadier General
  - Richard Arnold (13), Union, Brigadier General
  - Lucius M. Walker (15), Confederate, Brigadier General
  - Armistead L. Long (17), Confederate, Brigadier General
  - Robert Ransom (18), Confederate, Major General
  - Eugene A. Carr (19), Union, Brigadier General
  - William P. Carlin (20), Union, Brigadier General
  - Amos Beckwith (21), Union, Brevet Brigadier General
  - Charles Sidney Winder (22), Confederate, Brigadier General
  - William Lewis Cabell (33), Confederate, Brigadier General
  - John J.A.A. Mouton (38), Confederate, Brigadier General
- Class of 1851 (42 Graduates)
  - George L. Andrews (1), Union, Brigadier General
  - James St. C. Morton (2), Union, Brevet Brigadier General
  - Kenner Garrard (8), Union, Brevet Major General
  - Benjamin Hardin Helm (9), Confederate, Brigadier General
  - Allwan C. Gillem (11), Union, Brigadier General
  - Thomas J.C. Amory (30), Union, Brevet Brigadier General
  - William D. Whipple (31), Union, Brigadier General
  - Junius Daniel (33), Confederate, Brigadier General
  - Lawrence S. Baker (42), Confederate, Brigadier General
- Class of 1852 (43 Graduates)
  - Henry W. Slocum (7), Union, Major General

- David S. Stanky (9), Union, Major General
- George B. Anderson (10), Confederate, Brigadier General
- Milo S. Hascall (14), Union, Brigadier General
- George B. Cosby (17), Confederate, Brigadier General
- George L. Hartsuff (19), Union, Major General
- Charles R. Woods (20), Union, Brevet Major General
- John H. Forney (22), Confederate, Major General
- Alexander McD. McCook (30), Union, Major General
- August V. Kautz (35), Union, Brevet Major General
- George Crook (38), Union, Major General
- John P. Hawkins (40), Union, Brigadier General
- Class of 1853 (52 Graduates)
  - James McPherson (1), Union, Major General
  - Joshua W. Sill (3), Union, Brigadier General
  - William R. Boggs (4), Confederate, Brigadier General
  - William S. Smith (6), Union, Brigadier General
  - John M. Schofield (7), Union, Brigadier General
  - John S. Bowen (13), Confederate, Major General
  - William R. Terrill (16), Union, Brigadier General
  - Robert O. Tyler (22), Union, Brevet Major General
  - John R. Chambliss (31), Confederate, Brigadier General
  - Henry B. Davidson (33), Confederate, Brigadier General
  - Philip H. Sheridan (34), Union, Major General
  - Henry Harrison Walker (41), Confederate, Brigadier General
  - Alexander Chambers (43), Union, Brigadier General
  - John B. Hood (44), Confederate, General
  - James A. Smith (45), Confederate, Brigadier General
  - Reuben R. Ross (51), Confederate, Brigadier General

Promotions

- Second Lieutenant, Fourth Infantry Regiment, July 1, 1831
- First Lieutenant, Fourth Infantry Regiment, September 13, 1836
- Captain, Fourth Infantry Regiment, June 14, 1842
- Acting Colonel, Expedition to Southern Oregon, 1853

Assignments

- In the garrisons at Fort Brooke, Florida, 1832, and Fort King, Florida, 1832–1833
- Assistant teacher of French at the U.S. Military Academy, August 13, 1833, to January 8, 1836
- *Aide-de-Camp* to Major General Winfield Scott, September 3, 1840, to June 13, 1842

- In the garrison at Jefferson Barracks, Missouri, 1842–1844
- On frontier duty at Camp Salubrity, Natchitoches, Louisiana, 1844–1845
- In the Military Occupation of Texas, 1845
- Commandant of Cadets and Instructor of Infantry Tactics at the U.S. Military Academy, December 14, 1845, to November 1, 1852
- On frontier duty at Fort Vancouver, Washington, 1853
- On the march to Scott's Valley, California, 1853
- In charge of Fort Jones, California and its dependencies, 1853
- On the Expedition to Southern Oregon against the Rogue River Indians, 1853
- Fought in battle with the Rogue River Indians near Jacksonville, Oregon, where he was severely wounded, August 24, 1853
- Resigned from the military on September 29, 1853[6]

Biographical Sketch

Colonel Bradford Ripley Alden was born on May 6, 1811, in Meadville, Pennsylvania and died on September 10, 1870, at fifty-nine years old at Newport, Rhode Island. Colonel Alden was the son of Major Roger Alden, of the Continental Army, who served under and was the friend of General Washington. Young Alden received an excellent English and Classical education and planned to enter Allegheny College in Meadville. On January 20, 1825, his father was appointed the military storekeeper at the Military Academy. The daily pomp and circumstance of drills heightened Bradford's interest in the military, and he obtained an appointment to the Academy. He entered West Point on July 1, 1827, and graduated twenty-fifth in the Class of 1831.

The Army assigned Second Lieutenant Alden to the Fourth Infantry Regiment. He served two years on garrison duty in Florida. In 1833, Alden returned to the Military Academy. He was at the Academy for seven years as assistant instructors in French (August 13, 1833, to January 8, 1836, and August 28, 1837, to August 3, 18; mathematics (January 8, 1836, to September 8, 1836); and tactics (September 8, 1836, to October 30, 1836, and August 13, 1838, to June 24, 1839). He was on recruiting service in 1839, before returning to West Point as assistant teacher of French (September 12, 1839, to February 7, 1840) and as assistant instructor of infantry tactics (February 7, 1840, to September 14, 1840).

From September 3, 1840, to January 14, 1842, he served as the *aide-de-camp* to Major General Winfield Scott. This assignment began a lifelong friendship between the two men. After the general's death, Alden was executor of Scott's estate.

The Army promoted Alden to captain on June 14, 1842, and ordered him to join the Fourth Infantry Regiment at Jefferson Barracks. The regiment traveled to the Red River and took part in the military occupation of Texas in 1845. General-in-Chief Scott recommended Alden for the appointment as commandant of cadets at the U.S. Military Academy. He held this position "with great credit to himself and advantage to the institution" from December 14, 1845, to November 1, 1852. The graduates praised Alden for the kindness of his heart, his high sense of justice, his sterling traits of character, and the moral tone he instilled in his command.

The Army transferred Alden from West Point to the Pacific Coast. In 1853, he commanded Fort Jones, in northern California, when the Rogue River Indians in southern Oregon started a "universal and formidable" uprising. Captain Alden responded to an appeal from the settlers for help and marched with his few regulars two hundred miles beyond his authorized jurisdiction. He realized his small detachment was inadequate to protect the valley against the large force of Indians. Although Alden had no orders to defend the inhabitants, he raised a battalion of volunteers at his own expense and the men chose him to be their colonel. Alden's men met the hostile Indians on August 24, 1853, near Jacksonville, Oregon. The volunteers defeated them after a severe battle. The inhabitants of the Rogue River valley praised Alden's prompt, gallant and heroic services. Alden "paid dearly for his victory." While loading a musket, he received a terrible wound through the shoulder that penetrated his spine. The wound caused partial paralysis, and forced him to resign from the Army on September 25, 1853. Alden suffered from this injury over the next seventeen years until his death on September 10, 1870.

After his resignation, Alden traveled in Europe in the hope of restoring his health. Although his body was gradually failing, his mental abilities were sound and were "continually recruited from all the surroundings of nature, from living men, and memories of those living in dead centuries." He immersed himself in study and the acquisition of new knowledge. In comparison with other travelers, he learned more, enjoyed more, and profited more from his experience and exploration of European history, art, nature, and architecture. After he returned home, he shared his experiences and knowledge with friends. He was not jealous, avoided deception, and refused to criticize his enemies.

During a visit to his home in Meadville, Pennsylvania, he investigated the oil regions in Western Pennsylvania. He learned about the petroleum deposits and was one of the first to appreciate the value of these resources. In early December 1859, he began sinking oil wells using the Artesian method.[7] He drilled forty-six wells to depths of from six to seven hundred feet.

When the Civil War began in 1861, Alden tried to re-enter the Regular Army, but his old chief and good friend General Scott refused to grant him a commission. Scott realized Alden's enthusiasm was greater than his strength to serve his country. Alden tried to raise a volunteer regiment, but became ill, and abandoned his plans. He joined the staff of a general officer, but discovered he could not ride on horseback because of his Oregon wound. Finally, he realized his wound prevented him from joining the Union forces in the field. He returned to the oil fields. His petroleum ventures allowed his to amass a "handsome fortune." This wealth allowed him to spend the rest of his life reading books, performing charitable deeds, comforting the afflicted, and delighting his friends with his brilliant conversation on art, literature, science, and current events.

General Benjamin Alvord, who knew Alden as a cadet and officer, described him:

> No man who ever lived possessed more heroic and noble traits of character. Imbued with decided religious principles from his earliest youth, his pure and genial christian character was ever exhibited in numberless acts of benevolence, many of which were unknown to mortal eyes. Real want and misfortune were ever met by him with sympathy, and he had a heart as big as the rest of the

world. Of polished manners and elegant tastes, he was highly accomplished in his knowledge of literature and art; extensive travel, with an observing mind, made him a charming companion. He has left behind him a pure, spotless fame, illustrating the brightest qualities of the true American gentleman. The only difficulties his friends encounter in writing of his qualities is how to restrain the pen within moderate limits when attempting merely to do bare and simple justice to his memory.[8]

Robert S. Garnett
(November 1, 1852–July 31, 1854)
Cullum Number: 1085

Service at the Academy

Garnett was at the Military Academy as assistant instructor of infantry tactics, from July 5, 1843, to October 17, 1844. Major Garnett was commandant of cadets from November 1, 1852, to July 31, 1854.

Superintendent

Garnett served under Brevet Colonel Robert E. Lee who was superintendent from September 1, 1852, to March 31, 1855. Following his graduation in 1829, Lee served as an engineer in the construction of forts, improvement of harbors, and enhancement of rivers. He received three brevet promotions for "gallant and meritorious conduct" in the Mexican War.[1]

Significant Contributions

Garnett was one of several commandants whose brief service was unremarkable.

Notable Cadets

See "Notable West Point Graduates Who Served in the Civil War" in the Appendices for more information.

- Class of 1852 (43 Graduates)
  - Henry W. Slocum (7), Union, Major General
  - David S. Stanky (9), Union, Major General
  - George B. Anderson (10), Confederate, Brigadier General
  - Milo S. Hascall (14), Union, Brigadier General

- George B. Cosby (17), Confederate, Brigadier General
- George L. Hartsuff (19), Union, Major General
- Charles R. Woods (20), Union, Brevet Major General
- John H. Forney (22), Confederate, Major General
- Alexander McD. McCook (30), Union, Major General
- August V. Kautz (35), Union, Brevet Major General
- George Crook (38), Union, Major General
- John P. Hawkins (40), Union, Brigadier General

- Class of 1853 (52 Graduates)
  - James McPherson (1), Union, Major General
  - Joshua W. Sill (3), Union, Brigadier General
  - William R. Boggs (4), Confederate, Brigadier General
  - William S. Smith (6), Union, Brigadier General
  - John M. Schofield (7), Union, Brigadier General
  - John S. Bowen (13), Confederate, Major General
  - William R. Terrill (16), Union, Brigadier General
  - Robert O. Tyler (22), Union, Brevet Major General
  - John R. Chambliss (31), Confederate, Brigadier General
  - Henry B. Davidson (33), Confederate, Brigadier General
  - Philip H. Sheridan (34), Union, Major General
  - Henry Harrison Walker (41), Confederate, Brigadier General
  - Alexander Chambers (43), Union, Brigadier General
  - John B. Hood (44), Confederate, General
  - James A. Smith (45), Confederate, Brigadier General
  - Reuben R. Ross (51), Confederate, Brigadier General

- Class of 1854 (46 Graduates)
  - George W. Custis Lee (1), Confederate, Major General
  - Henry L. Abbot (2), Union, Brevet Brigadier General
  - Thomas H. Ruger (3), Union, Brevet Brigadier General
  - Oliver O. Howard (4), Union, Major General
  - James Deshler (7), Confederate, Brigadier General
  - John Pegram (10), Confederate, Brigadier General
  - James E.B. Stuart (13), Confederate, Major General
  - Archibald Gracie (14), Confederate, Brigadier General
  - Stephen D. Lee (17), Confederate, Lieutenant General
  - William D. Pender (19), Confederate, Major General
  - John B. Villepique (22), Confederate, Brigadier General
  - Stephen H. Weed (27), Union, Brigadier General

- Class of 1855 (34 Graduates)
  - Cyrus B. Comstock (1), Union, Brevet Brigadier General
  - Godfrey Weitzel (2), Union, Major General
  - David McM. Gregg (8), Union, Brevet Major General
  - Francis T. Nicholls (12), Confederate, Brigadier General
  - Alexander S. Webb (13), Union, Brevet Major General
  - John W. Turner (14), Union, Brevet Major General

- Francis A. Shoup (15), Confederate, Brigadier General
- Alfred T.A. Torbert (21), Union, Brevet Major General
- William W. Averell (26), Union, Brigadier General
- William B. Hazen (28), Union, Major General

Promotions

- Brevet Second Lieutenant, Fourth Artillery Regiment, July 1, 1841
- Second Lieutenant, Fourth Artillery Regiment, January 31, 1842
- First Lieutenant, Fourth Artillery Regiment, August 18, 1846
- Brevet Captain, for gallant conduct in the Several Conflicts at Monterey, Mexico, September 23, 1846
- Brevet Major, for gallant and meritorious conduct in the Battle of Buena Vista, Mexico, February 23, 1847
- Captain, Seventh Infantry Regiment, March 9, 1851
- Captain, First Cavalry Regiment, March 3, 1855
- Major, Ninth Infantry Regiment, March 27, 1855[2]
- Brigadier General, Provisional Confederate Army, June 6, 1861[3]

Assignments

- Cadet at the Military Academy, September 1, 1837, to July 1, 1841
- On the Northern Frontier during Canada Border Disturbances in the garrisons at Buffalo, New York, 1841–1842, and Fort Ontario, New York, 1842
- In garrison at Fort Monroe, Virginia, 1842–1843
- At the Military Academy as assistant instructor of infantry tactics, July 5, 1843, to October 17, 1844
- On recruiting service, 1844
- *Aide-de Camp* to Brigadier General John E. Wool, January 1 to September 30, 1845
- In Military Occupation of Texas, 1845–1846
- Adjutant of the Artillery Battalion, October 3, 1845, to June 29, 1846
- In the War with Mexico, 1846–1848
- Battle of Palo Alto, Texas, May 8, 1846
- Battle of Resaca-de-la-Palma, Texas, May 9, 1846
- Battle of Monterey, Mexico, September 21–23, 1846
- Battle of Buena Vista, Mexico, February 22–23, 1847
- *Aide-de-Camp* to Major General Taylor, June 29, 1846, to January 31, 1849
- Transferred to Seventh Infantry Regiment, August 31, 1848
- Florida Hostilities against the Seminole Indians, 1850
- Member of Board to Revise the Uniform Dress of the Army, at Washington, D.C., 1850–1851
- On frontier duty at Corpus Christi, Texas, 1851–1852, and Ringgold Barracks, Texas, 1852

- At the Military Academy, as commandant of cadets, and instructor of infantry tactics, November 1, 1852, to July 31, 1854
- In garrison at Fort Monroe, Virginia, 1855
- On frontier duty, on Yakima Expedition and in garrison at Fort Simcoe, Washington, 1856
- In garrison at Fort Columbus, New York, 1857
- On frontier duty at Fort Simcoe, Washington, 1857–1858
- Expedition against the Puget Sound Indians, 1858
- On frontier duty at Ft. Simcoe, Washington, 1858
- On leave of absence in Europe, 1858–1861[4]
- Resigned commission and joined the Confederate Provisional Army, April 30, 1861
- At Stanton, Virginia in command in Northwestern Virginia, June 6, 1861
- Killed near Corrick's Ford on the Cheat River, Virginia, July 13, 1861[5]

Biographical Sketch

Robert Selden Garnett was born on his family's plantation in Essex County, Virginia. Robert and his cousin, Richard B. Garnett, attended the U.S. Military Academy. He graduated twenty-seventh in the Class of 1841, and the Army promoted him to second lieutenant in the Fourth U.S. Artillery Regiment. He spent a year on the Northern Frontier during the Canada Border Disturbances where he was in the garrisons at Buffalo and Fort Ontario, New York. In 1842, he performed garrison duty at Fort Monroe, Virginia. He was an assistant tactics instructor at West Point from July 5, 1843, to October 17, 1844. He was on recruiting duty in 1844. He served as an *aide-de-camp* to General John E. Wool from January 1 to September 30, 1845.

Garnett served in the Mexican-American War under General Zachary Taylor. He fought in the battles of Palo Alto and Resaca-de-la-Palma in Texas and Monterrey and Buena Vista in Mexico. He received two brevets for "distinguished service" at the Battle of Monterrey and for "gallant and meritorious conduct" in the Battle of Buena Vista.

In 1848, the Army transferred Garnett to the Seventh Infantry Regiment where he served in the Seminole Wars in Florida in 1850. He was a member of a board to revise the uniform dress of the Army in Washington, D.C. (1850–1851). He was on the Texas frontier at Corpus Christi and Ringgold Barracks. The Army promoted him to captain in the Seventh Infantry on March 9, 1851.

He received an appointment as commandant of cadets, and instructor of infantry tactics at the Military Academy on November 1, 1852.

Garnett left West Point on July 31, 1854, and he was named captain in the First Cavalry Regiment. He was sent to Fort Monroe, Virginia before moving west to serve on the frontier. The Army promoted Garnett to major of the Ninth Infantry Regiment and sent him to Fort Simcoe, Washington (1857–1858). He designed and supervised the construction of Fort Simcoe. He was on the 1856 Yakima Expedition and in the engagements against the Puget Sound Indians in 1858.

He was granted an extended leave of absence later in the year after his wife and young son died from disease and he returned east to bury their remains. He traveled in Europe when the Confederate States of America were formed.[6]

When Virginia seceded from the United States in April 1861, Garnett resigned his commission and became adjutant general for the Virginia troops commanded by Robert E. Lee. In June, he was promoted to brigadier general of the Provisional Confederate Army. At the beginning of the Civil War, Union forces crossed the Ohio River and occupied part of northwestern Virginia where they won a key victory at the Battle of Philippi on June 3, 1861. On June 15, Lee assigned Garnett to reorganize the Confederate forces in the area. Garnett positioned his forces at strategic points along the Staunton-Parkersburg Turnpike to defend the critical Confederate supply route from the federal troops. After a series of minor battles, the Union troops forced the Confederates to withdraw.

Following Brigadier General William S. Rosecrans defeat of Lieutenant Colonel John Pegram's Confederates at the Battle of Rich Mountain, General Garnett withdrew from his Laurel Hill entrenchments. He hoped to escape to northern Virginia with his 4,500 men. Unfortunately, he received mistaken information about Union troops blocking his escape route to Beverly, Virginia. This intelligence forced Garnett to march to the northeast, following ridges and valleys in a more circuitous route. His troops were pursued for several days by as many as 20,000 Federals. Garnett skirmished at several stream crossings to try to slow the Union troops. While directing his rear guard in a delaying action at Corrick's Ford, Garnett was shot and killed. A friend in the Union army recovered Garnett's body. A federal honor guard returned his remains to his family for burial in Baltimore, Maryland. He was later reinterred next to his wife in Green-Wood Cemetery in Brooklyn, New York.[7]

William H. T. Walker
(July 31, 1854–May 27, 1856)
Cullum Number: 936

Service at the Academy

Walker was commandant of cadets and instructor of tactics at the U.S. Military Academy from July 31, 1854, to May 22, 1856.

Superintendent(s)

Walker served under Brevet Colonel Robert E. Lee (September 1, 1852, to March 31, 1855) and Captain John G. Barnard (March 31, 1855–September 8, 1856). Barnard worked as an Army engineer in constructing harbor defenses and making improvements to rivers. In the War with Mexico, he constructed defenses and surveyed battlefields. After the war, he resumed assignments improving coastal forts, rivers, and harbors. Barnard returned to the Military Academy in 1855 as instructor of practical military engineering, and commandant of sappers,[1] miners, and pontoniers,[2] and Academy superintendent.[3]

Significant Contributions

Walker was a stern disciplinarian as shown by his order of July 7, 1855. Colonel Walker told fourth classmen to use their bayonets on upper classmen who interfered with them. He reminded the sentinels their muskets had bayonets on them.[4]

Two former cadets taught by Walker received the Thanks of Congress: Major General Philip H. Sheridan (Class of 1853) and Major General Oliver O. Howard (Class of 1854).[5]

Notable Cadets

See "Notable West Point Graduates Who Served in the Civil War" in the Appendices for more information.

- Class of 1854 (46 Graduates)
  - George W. Custis Lee (1), Confederate, Major General
  - Henry L. Abbot (2), Union, Brevet Brigadier General
  - Thomas H. Ruger (3), Union, Brevet Brigadier General
  - Oliver O. Howard (4), Union, Major General
  - James Deshler (7), Confederate, Brigadier General
  - John Pegram (10), Confederate, Brigadier General
  - James E.B. Stuart (13), Confederate, Major General
  - Archibald Gracie (14), Confederate, Brigadier General
  - Stephen D. Lee (17), Confederate, Lieutenant General
  - William D. Pender (19), Confederate, Major General
  - John B. Villepique (22), Confederate, Brigadier General
  - Stephen H. Weed (27), Union, Brigadier General
- Class of 1855 (34 Graduates)
  - Cyrus B. Comstock (1), Union, Brevet Brigadier General
  - Godfrey Weitzel (2), Union, Major General
  - David McM. Gregg (8), Union, Brevet Major General
  - Francis T. Nicholls (12), Confederate, Brigadier General
  - Alexander S. Webb (13), Union, Brevet Major General
  - John W. Turner (14), Union, Brevet Major General
  - Francis A. Shoup (15), Confederate, Brigadier General
  - Alfred T.A. Torbert (21), Union, Brevet Major General
  - William W. Averell (26), Union, Brigadier General
  - William B. Hazen (28), Union, Major General
- Class of 1856 (49 Graduates)
  - Orlando M. Poe (6), Union, Brigadier General
  - Francis L. Vinton (10), Union, Brigadier General
  - George D. Bayard (11), Union, Brigadier General
  - Hylan B. Lyon (19), Union, Brigadier General
  - Lunsford L. Lomax (21), Confederate, Major General
  - James P. Major (23), Confederate, Brigadier General
  - James W. Forsyth (28), Union, Brevet Brigadier General
  - William H. Jackson (38), Confederate, Brigadier General
  - William P. Sanders (41), Union, Brigadier General

William H. T. Walker.

- Samuel S. Carroll (44), Union, Brigadier General
- Fitzhugh Lee (45), Confederate, Major General
- Class of 1857 (38 Graduates)
  - E. Porter Alexander (3), Confederate, Brigadier General
  - George C. Strong (5), Union, Brigadier General
  - Charles H. Morgan (12), Union, Brevet Brigadier General
  - Samuel W. Ferguson (19), Confederate, Brigadier General
  - John S. Marmaduke (30), Confederate, Major General
  - Robert H. Anderson (35), Confederate, Brigadier General

Promotions

- Brevet Second Lieutenant, Sixth Infantry Regiment, July 1, 1847
- Second Lieutenant, Sixth Infantry Regiment, July 1, 1837
- Brevet First Lieutenant, for gallantry and good conduct in the War against the Florida Indians, December 25, 1837
- First Lieutenant, Sixth Infantry Regiment, February 1, 1838
- Combat injuries forced him to resign his commission, October 31, 1838
- Re-appointed, November 18, 1840, in the United States Army, as First Lieutenant, Sixth Infantry Regiment, his former rank, February 1, 1838
- Captain, Sixth Infantry Regiment, November 7, 1845
- Brevet Major, for gallant and meritorious conduct in the Battles of Contreras and Churubusco, Mexico, August 20, 1847
- Brevet Lieutenant Colonel, for gallant and meritorious conduct in the Battle of Molino del Rey, Mexico, where he was severely wounded, September 8, 1847
- Major, Tenth Infantry Regiment, March 3, 1855[6]
- Brigadier General, Confederate Army, May 25, 1861
- Major General, Georgia State Militia, October 1861
- Brigadier General, Confederate States Army, February 9, 1863
- Major General, Confederate States Army, May 23, 1863[7]

Assignments

- Cadet at the U.S. Military Academy, July 1, 1832, to July 1, 1837
- In the Florida War against the Seminole Indians, 1837
- Fought in the Battle of Okee-cho-bee, where he was wounded three times, December 25, 1837
- On sick leave of absence, disabled by wounds, 1838
- Resigned, October 31, 1838
- In the Florida War, 1840–1842
- On frontier duty at Fort Towson, Indian Territory, 1842, and Fort Gibson, Indian Territory, 1843–1844

- On recruiting service, 1844–1846
- On sick leave of absence, 1847–1849
- In the War with Mexico, 1846–1847
  - Siege of Vera Cruz, May 9–29, 1847
  - Battle of Cerro Gordo, April 17–18, 1847
  - Skirmish of Amazoque, May 14, 1847
  - Capture of San Antonio, August 20, 1847
  - Battle of Churubusco, August 20, 1847
  - Battle of Molino del Rey, where he was severely wounded, September 8, 1847
- On sick leave of absence, 1847–1849
- Presented with a sword of honor from the State of Georgia as a tribute to his gallantry in Florida and Mexico, 1849
- On recruiting service, 1849–1850
- On sick leave of absence in Europe, Asia, and Africa, 1850–1851
- On recruiting service, 1851–1852
- Deputy governor of East, Pascagoula Branch Military Asylum, Mississippi, December 3, 1852, to June 24, 1854
- At the Military Academy, as commandant of cadets and instructor of infantry tactics, July 31, 1854, to May 27, 1856
- On frontier duty at Fort Ripley, Minnesota, 1856
- On sick leave of absence, 1856–1860
- Resigned, December 20, 1860[8]
- Served during the Rebellion of the Seceding States, 1861–1866
- Stationed at Pensacola, Florida and Northern Virginia, May 25, 1861, to October 29, 1861
- Resigned because of health problems, October 29, 1861
- Grant's Operations against Vicksburg, March-July 1863
- Chickamauga Campaign, August-September 1863
- Atlanta Campaign, May-September 1864
- Battle of Atlanta, where he was killed during General Hardee's attack on the federal left in front of the city, July 22, 1864[9]

Biographical Sketch

William Henry Talbot Walker was born in Augusta, Georgia in 1816. He was a son of Freeman Walker, a U.S. senator and Augusta mayor, and his wife Mary Garlington Creswell. His father died in 1827 when William was eleven years old. His family sent him to Augusta's Richmond Academy for his early education. He had four children with his wife Mary Townsend, two sons and two daughters.

Walker was admitted into the U.S. Military Academy in 1832 and graduated forty-sixth in the Class of 1837. The Army promoted him to brevet second lieutenant on July 1, 1837, and assigned him to the Sixth Infantry Regiment. On July 31, 1837, he was promoted to second lieutenant. He fought in the Florida War against the Seminole

Indians and was wounded three times in the Battle of Okee-cho-bee on December 25, 1837. He received a brevet promotion to first lieutenant on December 25, 1837. He was promoted to first lieutenant on February 1, 1838. His injuries forced him to take a sick leave of absence in 1838. His health compelled him to resign his commission in the fall.

Over the next two years, Walker's health improved, and the Army reinstated him as a first lieutenant on November 18, 1840, to rank from his last promotion in early 1838. He returned to the Sixth Infantry where he received a promotion to captain on November 7, 1845.

During the Mexican-American War, he served in General Scott's campaign to Mexico City. Walker fought at the Siege of Vera Cruz (May 9–29, 1847), Battle of Cerro Gordo (April 17–18, 1847), Skirmish of Amazoque (May 14, 1847), Battle of Contreras (August 19–20, 1847), Capture of San Antonio (August 20, 1847), Battle of Churubusco (August 20, 1847), and the Battle of Molino del Rey (September 8, 1847). His performances at Churubusco, where he was wounded, and Contreras won him a brevet promotion to major. Walker fought at Molino del Rey in early September where he was again wounded. He was made a brevet lieutenant colonel for his "gallant and meritorious conduct" in the battle.

After the war with Mexico, Walker was on sick leave of absence (1847–1849), recruiting service (1849–1850), on sick leave in Europe, Asia, and Africa (1850–1851), and on recruiting duty (1851–1852).

Colonel Walker returned to the Military Academy as commandant of cadets and instructor of infantry tactics from July 31, 1854, to May 27, 1856. He was on frontier duty at Fort Ripley, Minnesota (1856) and on sick leave (1856–1860).[10]

With the outbreak of the Civil War, Walker followed his home state of Georgia and joined the Confederate cause. He resigned his U.S. Army commission on December 20, 1860, and was appointed a colonel in the Georgia State Militia on February 1, 1861. He held this rank until March 13, when he was appointed major general in the First Division of the Georgia State Militia.

Walker transferred to the Confederate Army infantry as a colonel on April 25, 1861. A month later (May 25, 1861), the Confederate command promoted him to brigadier general and assigned him to lead the first brigade in the Fourth Division of the Potomac District of the Department of Northern Virginia. He stayed in this assignment until October 29, 1861, when he resigned his commission, either due to his health or from being dissatisfied with his assignments for the Confederacy. Walker rejoined the Georgia militia as a brigadier general. He served in the militia from November 1861 to January 1863, when he resigned to re-enter the Confederate States Army.

Walker resumed his brigadier general rank in the Confederate Army on February 9, 1863, and in May the Army assigned him to command a brigade in the Confederate Department of the West. On May 21, he was assigned to direct a division in the department. He received a promotion to major general on May 23. General Joseph E. Johnston, commander of the department, strongly endorsed the advancement. Johnston considered Walker as "the only officer in his command competent to lead a division."

Walker fought in Grant's Operations against Vicksburg (March–July 1863), the

Chickamauga Campaign (August–September 1863), and the Atlanta Campaign (May–September 1864). In December 1863, Walker's division joined Lieutenant General William J. Hardee's First Corps of the Army of Tennessee. General Walker was killed on July 22, 1864, at the Battle of Atlanta during General Hardee's attack on the federal forces.[11]

William J. Hardee
(July 22, 1856–September 8, 1860)
Cullum Number: 966

Service at the Academy

William Hardee returned to West Point as an instructor of tactics instructor and served as commandant of cadets from July 22, 1856, to September 8, 1860.

Superintendent(s)

Commandant Hardee served under Captain John G. Barnard (March 31, 1855–September 8, 1856) and Major Richard Delafield (September 8, 1856–March 1, 1861).

Significant Contributions

Hardee left his mark upon West Point. He revised the practical military courses, introduced and taught the new system of tactics, and helped establish the role of commandant as second in importance only to the superintendent. Several of his cadets achieved distinction in the Civil War and provided both armies with alert, well-trained, and energetic leadership. One of Hardee's students claimed Hardee was "the best commandant the Corps of Cadets ever had…. Whatever control I have of myself I attribute to the relentless teaching of that unbending disciplinarian."

Perhaps Hardee's greatest contribution to the Military Academy was the preparation of a revised tactical manual, *Rifle and Light Infantry Tactics for the Exercise and Manoeuvres of Troops When Acting as Light Infantry or Riflemen*, popularly known as *Hardee's Tactics*. When Hardee resigned his commission and joined the Confederate States Army, his manual was withdrawn from use at the Academy. His biography in Cullum's *Register* is rather dismissive of his efforts. His work in 1854–1855 "compiling" *Rifle and Light Infantry Tactics*, was regarded as "being chiefly a translation" by Lieutenant Benét of U.S. Army Ordnance Corps from the French, textbook *L'Exercice et manoeuvres des bataillons de chasseurs à pied.* Adding insult to injury, the biography says the manual "was modified by a revising board of officers, was adopted, Mar. 29, 1855, for the use of the Army and Militia of the United States.[1]

Samuel B. McIntire's thoughts probably represented the sentiments of many of his classmates:

> [I] stood in the presence of Colonel Hardee ... as he sat at his desk, pen in hand, dressed in uniform, his handsome face turned toward me, his dark eyes seemingly full of kindness. I thought I never beheld a finer specimen of manhood: tall and slender, he looked every inch a soldier. He spoke words of encouragement, and when I passed, he was pleased, and asked me how I was "getting on," thereby showing the contrast in kindness toward me, as between the commandant and the superintendent, yet the one was from the North, the other from the South. When Colonel Hardee left the Point for other duty I felt as though I had lost my best friend.—Samuel B. McIntire[2]

William J. Hardee (Library of Congress).

On June 12, 1858, an Act of Congress "officially" recognized the Department of Tactics at the U.S. Military Academy. Tactical instruction began when the Academy opened 1802. The superintendent was commandant of cadets until 1818, when he appointed a commandant. The title of "Commandant of Cadets" was recognized in the Regulations of 1825. On December 5, 1828, the War Department designated a separate position as commandant and appointed Captain Hitchcock.[3]

Secretary of War, Jefferson Davis, wanted to combine tactical instruction into one department led by the commandant of cadets. In 1855, cavalry tactics was added to the instruction in infantry and artillery tactics.[4] This change expanded the role of the Tactics Department and increased the commandant's influence on military education.

In July 1856, Davis issued the order giving the commandant these duties. He also provided him with six junior officers as assistants. On June 12, 1856, Congress assigned the rank of colonel of engineers to the superintendent and lieutenant colonel to the commandant of cadets The act also made the commandant the instructor of tactics.[5]

On September 12, 1859, The Secretary of War assigned the commandant of cadets with instruction in strategy, grand tactics, and army organization. However, on October 20, the commandant recommended these subjects stay with the Department of Engineering.[6]

Hardee embraced his role as the Academy disciplinarian and his enforcement "remained a shivering memory for many of his cadets." Their reminiscences bear witness to his impressive bearing, his unusually stern features, and the vigor with which he sustained his demanding code. Hardee described his concept of proper discipline:

> As commandant I have the entire charge of the discipline. All reports come to and are examined by me. The system is as follows: When a cadet is reported for an offense the report is shown to me, recorded in a delinquency book, and read at evening parade; the next morning, if the young man

pleases, he may submit to me a verbal excuse. If this is satisfactory I remove the report; if not, I ask for a written excuse, which is referred to the reporting officer. If this reference is satisfactory I remove the report; if not, it is referred to the Superintendent, and passes beyond my control.

Although Hardee's administration was characterized by "forceful discipline," the cadets gained many benefits. Commandant Hardee substituted two five-week vacations in place of the one ten-week furlough. Hardee also instituted Cadet balls, held three nights a week during the summer encampment. These "hops" were usually held at Cozzen's Hotel and organized by the "more socially inclined cadets." During the winter months, Hardee suspended the rigorous military exercises and allowed the cadets to "resort to the gymnasium, or to a room where music is provided, and where those who wish can dance."

Hardee listened to the ideas offered by the cadets and impressed them with his willingness to accept their suggestions. He encouraged Lieutenant Otis Howard's to form a prayer group, where Howard could lead cadets in prayer and offer them personal guidance.[7]

Not all the cadets held Hardee in such esteem. Cadet George Custer said that when John Reynolds replaced Hardee, "It was a welcome change, as Hardee was 'disliked by all the cadets.'"[8]

Notable Cadets

See "Notable West Point Graduates Who Served in the Civil War" in the Appendices for more information.
- Class of 1857 (38 Graduates)
    - E. Porter Alexander (3), Confederate, Brigadier General
    - George C. Strong (5), Union, Brigadier General
    - Charles H. Morgan (12), Union, Brevet Brigadier General
    - Samuel W. Ferguson (19), Confederate, Brigadier General
    - John S. Marmaduke (30), Confederate, Major General
    - Robert H. Anderson (35), Confederate, Brigadier General
- Class of 1858 (27 Graduates)
    - Charles G. Harker (16), Union, Brigadier General
    - Bryan M. Thomas (22), Confederate, Brigadier General
- Class of 1859 (22 Graduates)
    - Martin D. Hardin (11), Union, Brigadier General
    - Edwin H. Stoughton (17), Union, Brigadier General
    - Joseph Wheeler (19), Confederate, Major General
- Class of 1860 (41 Graduates)
    - James H. Wilson (6), Union, Brevet Major General
    - Stephen D. Ramseur (14), Confederate, Major General
    - Wesley Merritt (22), Union, Brevet Major General
- Class of May 6, 1861, (45 Graduates)[9]
    - Adelbert Ames (5), Union, Brevet Major General
    - Emory Upton (8), Union, Brevet Major General

- Judson Kilpatrick (17), Union, Brigadier General
- Guy V. Henry (27), Union, Brevet Brigadier General
- Class of June 24, 1861, (34 Graduates)[10]
  - Arthur H. Dutton (3), Union, Brevet Brigadier General
  - George A. Custer (34), Union, Brevet Major General

Promotions

- Second Lieutenant, Second Dragoons, July 1, 1838
- First Lieutenant, Second Dragoons, December 3, 1839
- Captain, Second Dragoons, September 13, 1844
- Brevet Major, for gallant and meritorious conduct in the Affair at Medellin, near Vera Cruz, Mexico, March 25, 1847
- Brevet Lieutenant Colonel, for gallant and meritorious conduct in the Affair with the Enemy at San Agustin, Mexico, August 20, 1847
- Brevet Major, Second Cavalry, March 3, 1855
- Lieutenant Colonel, June 12, 1858
- Lieutenant Colonel, First Cavalry, June 28, 1860[11]
- Brigadier General, Confederate States Army, June 17, 1861
- Major General, Confederate States Army, October 7, 1861
- Lieutenant General, Confederate States Army, October 10, 1862[12]

Assignments

- Cadet at the Military Academy, July 1, 1834, to July 1, 1838
- In the Florida War, 1838–1840
- At the Cavalry School at Saumur, France, 1840–1842
- In the garrison at Baton Rouge, Louisiana, 1842–1843
- On frontier duty at Fort Jesup, Louisiana, 1843–1845
- Military Occupation of Texas, 1845–1846
- War with Mexico, 1846–1848
  - Skirmish at La Rosia (30 miles above Matamoras), April 25, 1846, where he was captured and held as a prisoner of war until released, May 10, 1846
  - Siege of Vera Cruz, March 9–29, 1847
  - Skirmish at Medellin, March 25, 1847
  - Skirmish of La Libya, June 20, 1847
  - Battle of Contreras, August 19, 1847
  - Skirmish at San Agustin, August 20, 1847
  - Battle of Molino del Rey, September 8, 1847
  - Operations Before and Capture of the City of Mexico, September 13–14, 1847
- On recruiting service, 1848
- At the Cavalry School for Practice, Carlisle, Pennsylvania, 1848

- On frontier duty, traveling from Fort Brown to Laredo and San Antonio, Texas, 1848–1849
- On frontier duty at Fort Inge, Texas, 1849–1850, and 1850–1851
- On the march to San Saba, 1851, and San Antonio, Texas, 1851
- Leave of absence, 1851–1852
- On frontier duty at Fort Graham, Texas, 1852
- Leave of absence, 1852–1853
- Paymaster in Florida, 1853
- On frontier duty at Fort Graham, Texas, 1853
- Compiling manual on *Rifle and Light Infantry Tactics*, which was mainly a translation, by Lieutenant Bénét, Ordnance Corps, U.S. Army, from the French, of *L'Exercice et manoeuvres des bataillons de chasseurs á pied*. The first draft was reviewed and changed by a revising board of officers. The textbook was adopted on March 29, 1855, for use by the Army and Militia of the United States
- In garrison at Jefferson Barracks, Missouri, 1855
- On frontier duty at Camp Cooper, Texas, 1856, and Fort Mason, Texas, 1856
- At the Military Academy, 1856–60, as commandant of cadets and instructor of infantry tactics from July 22, 1856, to September. 8, 1860, (with local rank of lieutenant colonel, from June 12, 1858), He also taught artillery and cavalry tactics from August 6, 1856, to September 8, 1860
- On leave of absence, 1860–1861
- Resigned, January 31, 1861[13]
- Served during the Rebellion of the Seceding States, 1861–1866
  - Federal Penetration up the Cumberland and Tennessee River—Battle of Shiloh, April 6–7, 1862
  - Confederate Heartland Offensive—Battle of Perryville, October 8, 1862
  - Stones River Campaign—Battle of Stones River, December 31, 1862, to January 2, 1863
  - Chattanooga-Ringgold Campaign—Battle of Chattanooga, November 23–25, 1863
  - Atlanta Campaign, May–September 1864—Battle of Jonesborough, August 31 to September 1, 1864
- Carolinas Campaign, February–March—Battle of Bentonville, March 19–21, 1865
- Died on November 6, 1873, at Wytheville, Virginia aged 58[14]

Biographical Sketch

William Joseph Hardee was a career Army officer, who fought in the Second Seminole War and in the Mexican-American War. He was a Confederate general in the west during the Civil War. His time as a Confederate officer was marred by sharp quarrels with Braxton Bragg and John Hood. He opposed Sherman in Georgia, escaping into Carolina, before surrendering with Joseph E. Johnston. Hardee's writings about military tactics were widely used on both sides in the conflict.

William Joseph Hardee was born on October 12, 1815, to Sarah Ellis and Major John Hardee at the "Rural Felicity" plantation in Camden County, Georgia. He graduated from the U.S. Military Academy at West Point twenty-sixth in the Class of 1838. Hardee was commissioned a second lieutenant in the Second U.S. Dragoons and sent to Florida. During the Seminole Wars (1835–1842), he became ill and was hospitalized. While in the hospital, he met and married Elizabeth Dummett. He was promoted to first lieutenant in 1839. After he recovered, the Army sent him to France to study military tactics from 1840 to 1842. The Army promoted him to captain on September 13, 1844.

In the Mexican-American War, Hardee served in the Army of Occupation under Zachary Taylor (1845–1846) and earned two brevet promotions. He was captured on April 25, 1846, in the skirmish at La Rosia, Texas, and exchanged on May 11. Colonel Hardee served under Winfield Scott in the campaign to capture Mexico City. He fought in the Skirmish at Medellin (March 25, 1847) and received a brevet promotion to major for his gallant and meritorious conduct. He fought in the Skirmish of La Hoya (June 20, 1847) and in the Battle of Contreras (August 19, 1847). Hardee earned a brevet promotion to lieutenant colonel for his performance at St. Augustin, Mexico (August 20, 1847). He fought in the Battle of Molino del Rey (September 8, 1847) and in the operations before and capture of the City of Mexico (September 13–14, 1847).

After the war, he was on recruiting service (1848); at the Cavalry School for Practice in Carlisle, Pennsylvania (1848); on the march from Fort Brown to Laredo and San Antonio, Texas (1848–1849), in the garrison at Fort Inge, Texas, (1849–1850 and 1850–1851); and on the march to San Saba and San Antonio, Texas (1851). Hardee was on a leave of absence (1851–1852) before returning to frontier duty at Fort Graham, Texas (1852). He was on another leave of absence (1852–1853); was paymaster in Florida (1853); and on frontier duty at Fort Graham, Texas (1853).

From 1854 to 1855, Hardee compiled *Rifle and Light Infantry Tactics for the Exercise and Manoeuvres* [sic] *of Troops When Acting as Light Infantry or Riflemen* which was adopted for use in the U.S. Army on March 29, 1855. The Army used *Hardee's Tactics* until the outbreak of the Civil War. During the war, the Confederate Army used the manual to train their troops.

He served as the senior major in the Second Cavalry when the regiment was formed in 1855 and the lieutenant colonel of the First Cavalry in 1860.

Colonel Hardee returned to the Military Academy on July 22, 1856, as commandant of cadets and instructor of infantry tactics. He was at West Point until September 8, 1860. He also taught artillery and cavalry tactics from August 6, 1856, to September 8, 1860.[15]

Hardee resigned his Army commission on January 31, 1861, after Georgia seceded from the Union. He joined the Confederate States Army as a colonel on March 7, 1861, and was placed in command of Fort Morgan and Fort Gaines in Alabama. The Confederate Army promoted him to brigadier general on June 17, 1861, and major general on October 7, 1861. By October 10, 1862, he was one of the first Confederate lieutenant generals. After he became a general, he organized a brigade of Arkansas regiments. Hardee impressed his men and fellow officers by solving difficult supply problems and conducting thorough training. He received his nickname, "Old Reliable," during this appointment. Hardee's brigade operated in Arkansas until he joined General Albert

Sidney Johnston's Army of Mississippi as a corps commander. He led the Third Corps of the Army of the Mississippi at the Battle of Shiloh. Hardy was wounded on the first day (April 6, 1862) of the two-day engagement. After General Johnston's death, the Army transferred Hardee's corps to General Braxton Bragg's Army of Tennessee.

At the Battle of Perryville on October 8, 1862, Hardee commanded the Left Wing of the Army of Tennessee. In the Battle of Stones River (Second Battle of Murfreesboro) from December 31, 1862, to January 2, 1863, Hardee's Corps attacked the Union's right flank. Although meeting stiff resistance, Hardee drove the Union troops back three miles until the Union commander rallied his forces. Major General William S. Rosecrans's recovered from Bragg's attack and forced the Confederates to withdraw. The 24,645 casualties at Stones River were the highest percentage of killed and wounded in any major battle in the Civil War. After the Tullahoma Campaign (Middle Tennessee Campaign), Hardee lost patience with the irritable Bragg and briefly commanded the Department of Mississippi and East Louisiana under General Joseph E. Johnston. During this period, he met Mary Foreman Lewis, an Alabama plantation owner and married her in January 1864.

Hardee returned to Bragg's army after the Battle of Chickamauga and commanded a corps in the Army of Tennessee. At the Battle of Chattanooga in November 1863, Major General George H. Thomas' Army of the Cumberland defeated Cheatham's and Hindman's divisions from Hardee's Corps and Breckinridge's and Stewart's divisions from Breckinridge's Corps at the Battle of Missionary Ridge on November 25, 1863.

Hardee joined a group of officers who finally convinced President Jefferson Davis to relieve General Bragg. Joseph E. Johnston assumed command of the Army of Tennessee for the Atlanta Campaign in May to September 1864. Johnston fought a war of maneuver and retreat against General Sherman. Jefferson Davis lost patience with Johnston and replaced him with the much more aggressive Lieutenant General John Bell Hood. Hardee could not tolerate Hood's reckless assaults and heavy casualties. After the Battle of Jonesboro (August 31–September 1, 1864), Hardee asked for a transfer and the Confederate Army sent him to command the Department of South Carolina, Georgia, and Florida. He opposed Sherman's March to the Sea as best as possible with his inadequate forces. After Union troops surrounded Savannah, Georgia, Hardee decided to escape rather than surrender. When Sherman turned north in the Carolinas Campaign, Hardee joined forces in Johnston's Army of the South in the Battle of Bentonville, North Carolina (March 19–21, 1865). Tragedy struck Hardee when his only son, sixteen-year-old Willie, was mortally wounded in a cavalry charge. Sherman's sixty-thousand-man Military Division of the Mississippi defeated Johnston's twenty-two-thousand-man army at Bentonville, North Carolina. This defeat forced Johnston's army including Hardee's troops to surrender to Sherman on April 26, 1865, at Durham Station.

After the war, Hardee settled at his wife's Alabama plantation. He returned it to "working condition," and the family moved to Selma, Alabama. In Selma, Hardee worked in the warehousing and insurance businesses. He became president of the Selma and Meridian Railroad. Hardee was the co-author of *The Irish in America*, published in 1868. He became ill at his family's summer retreat at White Sulphur Springs, West Virginia, and died in Wytheville, Virginia on November 6, 1873. He is buried in Live Oak Cemetery, Selma.[16]

John F. Reynolds
(September 8, 1860–June 25, 1861)
Cullum Number: 1084

Service at the Academy

John F. Reynolds was commandant of cadets and instructor of artillery, cavalry, and infantry tactics at West Point from September 1860 to June 1861.

Superintendent

Reynolds was commandant under superintendent Richard Delafield (September 8, 1856–March 1, 1861) and Alexander H. Bowman (March 1, 1861–July 8, 1864). Bowman graduated third in the Class of 1825 and earned an appointment to the Corps of Engineers. For the next nine years, he made engineering improvements on the facilities and defenses of Gulf Coast harbors. He built the military road between Memphis, Tennessee and Little Rock, Arkansas. He worked on the Tennessee and Cumberland River systems for the next three years. He supervised construction of the jetties and defenses of the harbor in Charleston, South Carolina. Captain Bowman worked on engineering projects in Georgetown, South Carolina and Savannah, Georgia. He was appointed to manage construction of the south wing extension of the U.S. Treasury Building. Bowman replaced P.G.T. Beauregard after Louisiana seceded from the Union on January 26, 1861. Delafield resumed the office in the interim between Beauregard's and Bowman's commands.[1]

Significant Contributions

The start of the Civil War cut short Reynolds time at West Point. On May 14, 1861, the Army promoted him to lieutenant colonel and ordered him to New London, Connecticut to recruit a regiment. He made no notable contributions to West Point, which may be partially attributed to his attitude.

I have been on duty here for a week trying to persuade myself that I shall like it but notwithstanding the kind reception I have met with on all sides from my friends here I have not made up my mind fully on the subject.... I shall try for a week or so longer the duties, which I find very disagreeable to me, so different from anything I have ever had before, and so confining, annoying, and various, that I have hardly yet had time to test them fully—then I can make up my mind as to whether I will remain or not. Of one thing I am certain, that the position to be filled is no sinecure for any one. It is a most exacting one to the patience, industry and temper of any persons and of course very different from commanding men.[2]

When Reynolds left West Point, he wrote, "I have had every expression of regret from both officers and Professors here at my leaving them, and what is more flattering, great rejoicing among the cadets at their being relieved of me."[3]

John F. Reynolds (Library of Congress).

Notable Cadets

See "Notable West Point Graduates Who Served in the Civil War" in the Appendices for more information.
- Class of May 6, 1861, (45 Graduates)[4]
  - Adelbert Ames (5), Union, Brevet Major General
  - Emory Upton (8), Union, Brevet Major General
  - Judson Kilpatrick (17), Union, Brigadier General
  - Guy V. Henry (27), Union, Brevet Brigadier General
- Class of June 24, 1861, (34 Graduates)[5]
  - Arthur H. Dutton (3), Union, Brevet Brigadier General
  - George A. Custer (34), Union, Brevet Major General

Promotions

- Brevet Second Lieutenant, Third Artillery Regiment, July 1, 1841
- Second Lieutenant, Third Artillery Regiment, October 23, 1841
- First Lieutenant, Third Artillery Regiment, June 18, 1846
- In the War with Mexico, 1846–1848
  - Brevet Captain, for gallant and meritorious conduct in the Battle of Monterrey, Mexico, September 23, 1846
  - Brevet Major, for gallant and meritorious conduct in the Battle of Buena Vista, Mexico, February 23, 1847
- Captain, Third Artillery Regiment, March 3, 1855
- Lieutenant Colonel, Fourteenth Infantry Regiment, May 14, 1861

- Brigadier General, U.S. Volunteers, August 20, 1861
- Major General, U.S. Volunteers, November 29, 1862
- Colonel, Fifth Infantry Regiment, June 1, 1863

Assignments

- Cadet at the Military Academy, July 1, 1837, to July l, 1841
- In garrison at Fort McHenry, Maryland, 1841–1842; Fort Pickens, Florida, 1842; Fort Marion, Florida., 1842, and 182–1843; and Fort Moultrie, South Carolina, 1843–1845
- In the Military Occupation of Texas, 1845–1846
- In the War with Mexico, 1846–1848
  - Defense of Fort Brown, Tex., May 3–9, 1846
  - Battle of Monterey, September 21–23, 1846
  - Battle of Buena Vista, February 22–23, 1847
- In garrisons at Fort Trumbull, Connecticut, 1848; Fort Preble, Maine, 1848–1850; and Fort Adams, Rhode Island, 1851–1852
- Quartermaster, Third Artillery Regiment, October 25, 1850, to February 14, 1852
- *Aide-de-Camp* to Major General Twigs, February 14, 1852, to November 30, 1853
- In garrisons at Fort Lafayette, New York, 1854, and Fort Wood, New York, 1854
- On frontier duty, on the march to Utah, 1854
- At Salt Lake City, Utah, 1854–1855
- In garrisons at Fort Yuma, California, 1855; Benicia, California, 1855; and Fort Orford, Oregon, 1855–1856
- Skirmishes with Oregon Indians while on the Rogue River Expedition, 1856
- In garrison at Fort Monroe, Virginia, 1856–1858
- On frontier duty at Fort Leavenworth, Kansas, 1858
- Utah Expedition, 1858–1859
- March to the Columbia River, 1859
- In garrison at Fort Vancouver, Washington, 1859–1860
- Commandant of cadets and instructor of artillery, infantry, and cavalry tactics at the U.S. Military Academy, September 8, 1860, to June 25, 1861
- Served during the Rebellion of the Seceding States, 1861–1863
  - In command of his regiment, at Fort Trumbull, Connecticut, July 6 to September 8, 1861
  - Commander of brigade of the Pennsylvania Reserve Corps posted on the right of the lines before Washington, D.C., September 16, 1861, to June 9, 1862
  - Virginia Peninsula Campaign, March-July 1862
    - Battle of Beaver Dam Creek, Virginia, June 26, 1862
    - Battle of Gaines' Mill, Virginia, June 27, 1862

- ◊ Captured at the Battle of Glendale, Virginia, June 30, 1862
- ◊ Prisoner of War, June 30, 1861, to August 8, 1862
- ❖ Northern Virginia Campaign, August 1862
  - ◊ In command of a division in the Battle of Second Manassas, August 29–30, 1862
- ❖ In command of the Pennsylvania Volunteer Militia defending the state during the Maryland Campaign, September 14–26, 1862
- ❖ In command of First Corps of the Army of the Potomac, November 29, 1862, to July 1, 1863
- ❖ On the March to Falmouth, Virginia, October-November 1862
- ❖ Maryland (Rappahannock) Campaign, November-December 1862
  - ◊ Battle of Fredericksburg, December 11–15, 1862
- ❖ Chancellorsville Campaign, April-May 1863
  - ◊ Battle of Chancellorsville, April 27–May 4, 1863
- ❖ Gettysburg Campaign, June-July 1863
  - ◊ In command of the engaged forces on day one of the Battle of Gettysburg, July 1, 1863
  - ◊ Killed at age of 42, July 1, 1863

Biographical Sketch

Major General John Fulton Reynolds was born on September 20, 1820, at Lancaster, Pennsylvania, where he received a good elementary education. Through the influence of James Buchanan, later President of the United States, he was appointed a cadet in the U.S. Military Academy. Reynolds graduated twenty-sixth in the Class of 1841 and promoted to the Artillery.

After four years of seaboard garrison duty, he was ordered to the Texas frontier. He fought in the Mexican War in the Defense of Fort Brown and at the Battles of Monterrey and Buena Vista. He received two brevets to captain and major for his "gallant and meritorious conduct." In 1852–1853, he was *aide-de-camp* to Major General David E. Twiggs. In 1856 was actively engaged against the Rogue River Indians in Oregon and in 1858–1859 took part in the Utah Expedition. All his "duties were performed with zeal, efficiency, and success."

From September 8, 1860, to June 25, 1861, Reynolds was "the soldierly, energetic, and accomplished" commandant of cadets at West Point. He "won golden opinions" from all the Military Academy's officials.

When the Civil War began, Reynolds was made lieutenant colonel of the Fourteenth Infantry Regiment on May 14, 1861. The Army promoted him to the rank of brigadier general of U.S. Volunteers on August 20, 1861. Pennsylvania Governor Curtin requested Reynolds to be assigned to command of a brigade in Pennsylvania Reserve Corps. The brigade was sent to Washington, D.C., where it held the right of the lines defending the capital. In May 1862, he was appointed military governor of Fredericksburg. In June, Reynold's brigade joined the Army of the Potomac in the Virginia Peninsula Campaign. He fought in battles of Beaver Dam Creek, Virginia (June 26, 1862);

Gaines' Mill, Virginia (June 27, 1862); and Glendale, Virginia (June 30, 1862). He was captured at Glendale and held as prisoner of war until August 8, 1862.

After his release, he commanded a division of Pennsylvania Reserves. His division played a "distinguished part" in the Battle of Second Manassas (August 29–30, 1862) in the Northern Virginia Campaign. During the threatened invasion of Pennsylvania during the Maryland Campaign (September 1862), Governor Curtin requested Reynolds help to defend Pennsylvania and the Army allowed him to be placed in command of the State Volunteer Militia.

After the Confederate invasion was rejected at Antietam, Maryland (September 16–18, 1862), Reynolds returned to the Army of the Potomac. He was appointed major general and assigned to the command of the First Corps. He led the corps in its march to Falmouth, Virginia and fought in the Battle of Fredericksburg (December 11–15, 1862). During the Chancellorsville Campaign (April-May 1863), the First Corp was held in reserve during the battle.

General Reynolds fought in the Gettysburg Campaign (June–July 1863). When the Confederate forces threatened to overrun the Union position on Cemetery Hill, Reynolds assumed command of the united forces of the First, Third, and Eleventh Corps and John Buford's Cavalry. With "animating words," he urged his men forward. A Confederate sharpshooter mortally wounded Reynolds as the general pressed his forces to stop the advance.

Colonel John Bliss praised his performance under General Zachary Taylor's command in the Mexican War. Reynolds was "greatly distinguished for his calm courage, his modest self-reliance, and his military conduct." Bliss wrote, "Your young friend has the general's high regard, and he is the idol of his men." During his "great and varied service" in Florida, Texas, Mexico, California, Oregon, and Utah, Reynolds always showed himself "without fear, without reproach, and without an enemy." His death in defense of his native state and of his country at Gettysburg was a "fitting termination of his whole life."[6]

Christopher C. Augur
(August 26, 1861–December 5, 1861)
Cullum Number: 1182

Service at the Academy

Christopher C. Augur was commandant of cadets at West Point from August 26, 1861, to December 5, 1861.

Superintendent

Augur served under Alexander H. Bowman who was superintendent from March 1, 1861, to July 8, 1864[1]

Christopher C. Augur (Library of Congress).

Significant Contributions

Christopher C. Augur was commandant for a little more than three months. This brief assignment gave little time for Augur to make a significant contribution.

Notable Cadets

See "Notable West Point Graduates Who Served in the Civil War" in the Appendices for more information.
- Class of May 6, 1861, (45 Graduates)[2]
    - Adelbert Ames (5), Union, Brevet Major General
    - Emory Upton (8), Union, Brevet Major General

- Judson Kilpatrick (17), Union, Brigadier General
- Guy V. Henry (27), Union, Brevet Brigadier General
- Class of June 24, 1861, (34 Graduates)[3]
  - Arthur H. Dutton (3), Union, Brevet Brigadier General
  - George A. Custer (34), Union, Brevet Major General

Promotions

- Brevet Second Lieutenant, Second Infantry Regiment, July 1, 1843
- Second Lieutenant, Fourth Infantry Regiment, September 12, 1845
- First Lieutenant, Fourth Infantry Regiment, February 16, 1847
- Captain, Fourth Infantry Regiment, August 1, 1852
- Major, Thirteenth Infantry Regiment, May 14, 1861
- Brigadier General, U.S. Volunteers, November 12, 1861
- Brevet Colonel, for gallant and meritorious services in the Battle of Cedar Mountain, Virginia in the Northern Virginia Campaign, August 9, 1862
- Major General, U.S. Volunteers, August 9, 1862
- Lieutenant Colonel, Twelfth Infantry Regiment, July 1, 1863
- Brevet Brigadier General, for gallant and meritorious services at the Capture of Port Hudson, Mississippi, March 13, 1865
- Brevet Major General, U.S. Army, for gallant and meritorious services in the field during the Rebellion, March 13, 1865
- Colonel, Twelfth Infantry Regiment, March 15, 1866
- Mustered out of Volunteer Service, September 1, 1866
- Brigadier General, U.S. Army, March 4, 1869

Assignments

- Cadet at the Military Academy, July 1, 1839, to July 1, 1843
- In garrison at Fort Ontario, New York, 1843–1845
- In Military Occupation of Texas, 1845–1846
- In the War with Mexico, 1846
  - Battle of Palo Alto, May 8, 1846
  - Battle of Resaca-de-la-Palma, May 9, 1846
- On recruiting service, 1846–1847
- In the War with Mexico, 1847–48
- *Aide-de-camp* to Brigadier General Hopping, March 1 to September 1, 1847
- *Aide-de-camp* to Brigadier General Cushing, September 1, 1847, to May 30, 1848
- In garrison at East Pascagoula, Mississippi, 1848, and Fort Niagara, New York, 1848–1852
- On recruiting service, 1852
- In garrison at Fort Columbus, New York, 1852, and Benicia, California, 1852

- On frontier duty at Fort Vancouver, Washington, 1852–1854
- In conducting recruits to Oregon, 1855
- In garrison at Fort Dalles, Oregon, 1855, and Fort Yakima, Washington, 1855
- On scouting duty, 1855
- Skirmish against the Yakima Indians at Two Buttes, Washington, November 9, 1855
- In garrison at Fort Vancouver, Wash. Washington, 1855–1856
- Rogue River Expedition, 1856
- Action at Big Bend of Rogue River, Oregon, May 28, 1856, and So-ho-my Creek, Oregon, June 6, 1856
- In garrison at Fort Orford, Oregon, 1856
- Oregon Hostilities, 1856
- In garrison at Fort Hoskins, Oregon, 1856–1861
- At the Military Academy, as Commandant of Cadets and Instructor of Artillery, Cavalry, and Infantry Tactics, August 26 to December 5, 1861
- Served during the Rebellion of the Seceding States, 1861–1866
  - In the advance Defenses of Washington, D.C., December 16, 1861, to March 10, 1862
  - In Operations on the Rappahannock, March to July 1862
  - Capture of Fredericksburg, April 21, 1862
  - Advance into Shenandoah Valley, May 1862
  - In command of the First Division in the Fifth Army Corps, July 9 to August 10, 1862
  - Severely wounded at the Battle of Cedar Mountain, during the Northern Virginia Campaign, August 9, 1862
  - Member of Military Court to investigate the circumstances of the Surrender of Harper's Ferry, September 23 to November 5, 1862
  - In General Banks' Expedition to New Orleans, Louisiana, November–December 1862
  - In command of the District of Baton Rouge, Louisiana, January 20 to May 20, 1863
  - In the Expedition to Port Hudson, Louisiana engaged in the Action of Port Hudson Plains, May 21, 1863
  - Siege of Port Hudson, in command of the First Division of the Nineteen Corps of the Army of the Gulf, May 22 to July 8, 1863
  - President of Military Commissions at Washington, D.C., August 31 to October 14, 1863
- In command of the Department of Washington and Twenty-Second Army Corps, October 13, 1863, to August 13, 1866
- Member of Board for the Examination of Candidates for Promotion in the Army, August 16, 1866, to June 2, 1867
- In command of the Department of the Platte, January 15, 1867, to November 13, 1871
- In command of the Department of Texas, January 29, 1872, to March 1875
- In command of the Department of the Gulf, March 27, 1875, to July 1, 1878

- In command of the Department of the South, July 1, 1878, to December 26, 1880
- In command of the Department of Texas, January 2, 1881, to October 31, 1883
- On leave of absence, September 22 to October 25, 1883
- In command of the Department of the Missouri, November 1, 1883, to July 10, 1885
- Retired from active service at the age of sixty-four, July 10, 1885[4]

Biographical Sketch

Christopher Columbus Augur (July 10, 1821–January 16, 1898) was noted for his role in the Civil War and the Army considered him an able battlefield commander.

Augur was born in Kendall, New York. He moved with his family to Michigan and entered West Point in 1839. Following his graduation in 1843, Augur served as *aide-de-camp* to Generals Hopping and Cushing during the Mexican-American War and during the 1850s took an active part in the campaigns of the western frontier against the Yakima and Rogue River tribes of Washington and, in 1856, against the Oregon Indians. In Oregon, he managed the construction of Fort Hoskins in Kings Valley.

Augur was appointed brigadier general of volunteers in 1861, he commanded a brigade under Irvin McDowell during the early part of the war. He was severely wounded at Cedar Mountain in August 1862 while leading a division under Major General Nathaniel Banks. President Abraham Lincoln named Augur a major general on November 14, 1862, to rank from August 9, 1862. President Lincoln submitted the nomination three times before the U.S. Senate finally confirmed the selection on March 10, 1863. Subsequently Augur commanded a division in the Army of the Gulf during the siege of Port Hudson. He commanded the XXII Corps and the Department of Washington (1863–1866) and ended the war with an exemplary record.

Following the war, Augur commanded the departments of the Platte (1867–1871); Texas (1871–1875, 1881–1883); Gulf (1875–1878), and South (1878–1880). He directed the Military Division of the Missouri from 1883–85. He also played a major role in negotiations of the Treaties of Medicine Lodge in 1867 and Fort Laramie in 1868. A fort in the Wyoming Territory was briefly named Fort Augur in his honor. In 1885, he retired from the Army with the rank of brigadier general.

He was a member of the Aztec Club of 1847, the Military Order of the Loyal Legion of the United States and the Military Order of Foreign Wars.

General Auger died in Georgetown, Washington, D.C., on January 16, 1898, and is buried in Arlington National Cemetery.[5]

Kenner Garrard

(December 5, 1861–September 25, 1862)
Cullum Number: 1501

Service at the Academy

On December 5, 1861, the U.S. Army appointed Kenner Garrard as commandant of cadets and instructor of artillery, cavalry, and infantry tactics of the U.S. Military Academy in West Point, New York.

Superintendent

Major Andrew H. Bowman was superintendent from March 1, 1861, to July 8, 1864.

Kenner Garrard (*Harper's Weekly*).

Significant Contributions

After graduating eighth in the West Point class of 1851, Garrard served as adjutant to Colonel Albert S. Johnston and Robert E. Lee. The military assigned him at various posts in the Southwest frontier including the New Mexico Territory. When the Civil War began in 1861, Garrard was on duty at Camp Cooper in San Antonio, Texas. He was captured at San Antonio, Texas by Texan insurgents on April 12, 1861, and put upon parole[1] until exchanged as a prisoner of war, August 27, 1862.

While awaiting a formal exchange, the Army sent him to the Military Academy. His first assignment as assistant instructor of cavalry was from September

16 to December 5, 1861. The Army appointed Garrard commandant of cadets and instructor of artillery, cavalry, and infantry tactics on December 5, 1861. He served as commandant until the Army appointed him colonel of the 146th New York Infantry on September 25, 1862. Garrard's brief, ten-month tenure as commandant did not allow him the time to make a significant impact on either the Corps of Cadets or tactical instruction.

Notable Cadets

See "Notable West Point Graduates Who Served in the Civil War" in the Appendices for more information.

Most of these graduates were too young during the Civil War to become general officers.
- Class of May 6, 1861, (45 Graduates)[2]
  - Adelbert Ames (5), Union, Brevet Major General
  - Emory Upton (8), Union, Brevet Major General
  - Judson Kilpatrick (17), Union, Brigadier General
  - Guy V. Henry (27), Union, Brevet Brigadier General
- Class of June 24, 1861, (34 Graduates)[3]
  - Arthur H. Dutton (3), Union, Brevet Brigadier General
  - George A. Custer (34), Union, Brevet Major General
- Class of 1862 (28 Graduates)
  - Ranald S. Mackenzie (1), Union, Brigadier General
  - There were only twenty-eight graduates in the Class of 1862. Most of them received promotions to first lieutenant or captain.
- Class of 1863 (25 Graduates)
  - Peter S. Michie (2), Union, Brevet Brigadier General
  - Most of the twenty-five graduates in the Class of 1863 received promotions to first lieutenant. Some received brevet promotions to captain or major.
- Class of 1864 (27 Graduates)
  - All twenty-seven graduates fought for the Union in the Civil War. Most of them served as second or first lieutenants. Some received brevet promotions to captain or major.

Promotions

- Brevet Second Lieutenant, Fourth Artillery, July 1, 1851
- Second Lieutenant, First Dragoons, October 31, 1853
- First Lieutenant, Second Cavalry, March 3, 1855
- Captain, Second Cavalry, February 27, 1861
- Captain, Fifth Cavalry, August 3, 1861
- Colonel, 146th New York Infantry Volunteers, September 23, 1862
- Brevet Lieutenant Colonel, for gallant and meritorious services at the Battle of Gettysburg, Pennsylvania, July 2, 1863

- Brigadier General, U.S. Volunteers, July 23, 1863
- Major, Third Cavalry, November 2, 1863
- Brevet Colonel, for gallant and meritorious services in the Expedition to Covington, Georgia, July 22, 1864
- Brevet Major General, U.S. Volunteers, for conspicuous gallantry and efficiency during the battle of the 15th and 16th [of December] before Nashville, Tennessee, December 15, 1864
- Brevet Brigadier General, U.S. Army, March 13, 1865, for gallant and meritorious services at the Battle of Nashville, Tennessee
- Brevet Major General, U.S. Army, March 13, 1865, for gallant and meritorious services in the field during the Rebellion
- Mustered out of volunteer service on August 24, 1865

Assignments

- Cadet at the Military Academy, July 1, 1847, to July 1, 1851
- In the garrison at Fort Mifflin, Pennsylvania, 1851–1852
- Transferred to First Dragoons on February 20, 1852
- On frontier duty at Fort Conrad, New Mexico, 1852, and Albuquerque, New Mexico, 1852–1853
- On Topographical duty on Pacific Railroad Exploration, from Doña Ana, New Mexico to Preston, Texas, 1853–1854
- In the garrison at Jefferson Barracks, Missouri, 1854–1855
- In charge of cavalry instruction at Carlisle Barracks, Pennsylvania, 1855
- Adjutant, Second Cavalry Regiment, April 20, 1855, to May 31, 1858
- At Louisville, Kentucky, 1855
- In the garrison at Jefferson Barracks, Missouri, 1855; Fort Mason, Texas, 1856: San Antonio, Texas, 1856–57 and 1857–1858; and Fort Mason, Texas, 1858
- On recruiting service, 1858–1860
- In conducting recruits to Texas, 1860–1861
- On frontier duty at Camp Cooper, Texas, 1861
- Captured at San Antonio, Texas by Texan insurgents April 12, 1861 and put upon parole until exchanged as a prisoner of war, August 27, 1862
- Served during the Rebellion of the Seceding States, 1861–1866
  - At Washington, D.C., in the Commissary-General's Office, April to September 1861
- At the Military Academy, 1861–1862
  - Assistant Instructor of Cavalry, September 16 to December 5, 1861
  - Commandant of Cadets and Instructor of Artillery, Cavalry, and Infantry Tactics, December 5, 1861, to September 25, 1862
- Served during the Rebellion of the Seceding States, 1862–1866
  - Fought in Army of the Potomac at the Battle of Fredericksburg (December 11–15, 1862) in the Fredericksburg (Rappahannock) Campaign (November–December 1862)

- In the Battle of Chancellorsville, April 27–May 4, 1863
- In the Gettysburg Campaign, June–July 1863
  - Battle of Gettysburg, July 1–3, 1863
  - Pursuit of the enemy to Warrenton, Virginia, July 1863
- In Grant's Overland (Rapidan) Campaign, October to December 1863
  - Combat of Rappahannock Station, November 7, 1863
  - Mine Run Operations, November 26 to December 6, 1863
- In charge of the Cavalry Bureau at Washington, D.C., December 1863 to January 1864
- In command of the Second Cavalry Division in the Army of the Cumberland, February to December 1864
- On detached expeditions in operations around Chattanooga
- In many engagements during the Atlanta Campaign, May–September 1864
- In command of the Second Cavalry Division (Military Division of the Mississippi) during Major General William T. Sherman's pursuit of General John B. Hood's Army of Tennessee from Dalton to Rome, Georgia, October-November 1864
- In command of the Second Division, Sixteenth Army Corps in the Frankfort-Nashville Campaign, September–December 1864
  - Battle of Nashville, Tennessee, December 15–16, 1864
- On the Mobile Campaign, March to April 1865
  - Guarding the corps train at the Siege of Spanish Fort, Alabama, March 27 to April 8, 1865
  - In command of the storming column which captured Fort Blakely, Alabama, April. 2–9, 1865
- Movement to Montgomery, Alabama and policing the area, April–August 1865
- In command of the District of Mobile, Alabama, August–September 1865
  - Assistant inspector general of the Department of the Missouri, March 2 to November 9, 1866
  - Resigned, November 9, 1866[4]

Biographical Sketch

Kenner Garrard was a brigadier general in the Union Army during the Civil War. Garrard was a member of one of Ohio's most prominent military families. General Garrard fought at the Battle of Gettysburg and led a cavalry division in Major General William T. Sherman's army during the Atlanta Campaign. He earned a reputation for personal bravery and received a brevet promotion to brigadier general for gallantry at the Battle of Nashville.

Garrard was born on September 21, 1827, at his paternal grandfather's home in Bourbon County, Kentucky. His grandfather, James Garrard, was the second Governor of Kentucky. Garrard was raised in Cincinnati, Ohio and received a private education. He brothers, Jeptha Garrard and Israel Garrard, and cousin, Theophilus T. Garrard, all became Union generals.

General Garrard briefly attended Harvard University in Cambridge, Massachusetts, but left in his sophomore year after receiving an appointment to the United States Military Academy. He graduated eighth in the Class of 1851, and the Army appointed him as a brevet second lieutenant in the Fourth U.S. Artillery Regiment. He transferred to the First U.S. Dragoons on February 20, 1852.

In 1855, the Army transferred Lieutenant Garrard to the Second U.S. Cavalry as an adjutant to Colonel Albert Sidney Johnston and Lieutenant Colonel Robert E. Lee. The Army sent him to a variety of posts in the Southwest frontier, including in the New Mexico Territory.

When the Civil War erupted in 1861, Captain Garrard was on duty in an outpost in Texas. Confederate authorities imprisoned him following the surrender of U.S. troops by Major General David E. Twiggs. The Confederates allowed him to return to the North. He reached Washington, D.C., with $20,000 of federal funds he hid from his Texas captors and returned the money to the U.S. Treasury.

After Garrard's formal exchange on August 27, 1862, the Army appointed him as colonel of the 146th New York Infantry in the Army of the Potomac. He fought in the battles of Fredericksburg, Chancellorsville, and Gettysburg. At Gettysburg, Garrard succeeded Brigadier General Stephen H. Weed, who was killed on Little Round Top, as commander of the Third Brigade of Major General George Sykes's division. In December 1863, the Army promoted him to brigadier general with an effective date of July 23, 1863.

While holding the rank of brigadier general in the U.S. Volunteers, the Army appointed him as major in the Regular Army's Third U.S. Cavalry Regiment in November 1863. In December 1863, he was appointed chief of the Cavalry Bureau in Washington. He held this post for a month when asked to be relieved from the duty to take command of the Second Division of Cavalry in the Army of the Cumberland in the Western Theater.

Garrard took part in General Sherman's Atlanta Campaign as a cavalry division commander. Unfortunately, he did not impress his superiors and returned to the infantry. His division performed well in the Battle of Nashville. Major General George H. Thomas cited Garrard for gallant conduct at Nashville. His battlefield performance was rewarded by brevet promotions to major general of volunteers and brigadier general in the Regular Army. He also received the brevet rank of major general in the Regular Army on March 13, 1865, as part of the omnibus brevet appointments at the end of the war. He ended the war in Alabama and was instrumental in the capture of Montgomery.

Garrard stayed in the Regular Army as commander of the District of Mobile, Alabama. He resigned on November 9, 1866, and returned to Cincinnati where he worked as a real estate broker. He devoted the rest of his life to civic affairs and historical studies. He served as director of the Cincinnati Music Festival for several years. He never married.

He wrote *Nolan's System for Training Cavalry Horses* (1862) New International Encyclopedia

He died in Cincinnati, Ohio on May 15, 1879, at the age of fifty-one and was interred in Spring Grove Cemetery.[5]

Henry B. Clitz
(October 23, 1862–July 4, 1864)
Cullum Number: 1266

Service at the Academy

Henry Clitz served at the Military Academy as assistant instructor of infantry tactics from September 15, 1848, to September 27, 1855. He returned to West Point on October 23, 1862, and was commandant of cadets and instructor of artillery, infantry, and cavalry tactics until July 4, 1864.

Superintendent

Major Andrew H. Bowman was superintendent from March 1, 1861, to July 8, 1864.

Significant Contributions

There were few changes in the Military Academy during Clitz's twenty months as commandant.

Notable Cadets

See "Notable West Point Graduates Who Served in the Civil War" in the Appendices for more information.
- Class of 1863 (25 Graduates)
  - Peter S. Michie (2), Union, Brevet Brigadier General
  - Most of the twenty-five graduates in the Class of 1863 received promotions to first lieutenant. Some received brevet promotions to captain or major.
- Class of 1864 (27 Graduates)
  - All twenty-seven graduates fought for the Union in the Civil War. Most of them served as second or first lieutenants. Some received brevet promotions to captain or major.

Promotions

- Brevet Second Lieutenant, Seventh Infantry Regiment, July 1, 1845
- Second Lieutenant, Third Infantry Regiment, September 21, 1846
- Brevet First Lieutenant, for Gallant and Meritorious Conduct in the Battle of Cerro Gordo, Mexico, April 18, 1847
- First Lieutenant, Third Infantry Regiment, March 5, 1851
- Captain, Third Infantry Regiment, December 6, 1858
- Major, Twelfth Infantry Regiment, May 14, 1861
- Brevet Lieutenant Colonel, for Gallant and Meritorious Services at the Battle of Gaines' Mill, Virginia, June 27, 1862
- Lieutenant Colonel, Sixth Infantry Regiment, November 4, 1863
- Brevet Colonel, for Gallant and Meritorious Services During the Rebellion, March 13, 1865
- Brevet Brigadier General, U.S. Army, for Gallant and Distinguished Services in the Field, March 13, 1865
- Colonel, Tenth Infantry Regiment, February 22, 1869

Henry B. Clitz (Library of Congress).

Assignments

- Cadet at the Military Academy, July 1, 1841, to July 1, 1845
- Military Occupation of Texas, 1845–1846
- In the War with Mexico, 1846–1848
  - Defense of Fort Brown, Texas, December 3–9, 1846
  - Battle of Monterey, Mexico, September 21–23, 1846
  - Siege of Vera Cruz, Mexico, March 9–29, 1847
  - Battle of Cerro Gordo, Mexico, April 17–18, 1847
  - Skirmish at Ocalaca, Mexico, August 16, 1847
  - Battle of Contreras, Mexico, August 19–20, 1847
  - Battle of Churubusco, Mexico, August 20, 1847
  - Storming of Chapultepec, Mexico, September 13, 1847
  - Assault and Capture of the City of Mexico, Mexico, September 13–14, 1847

- At the Military Academy, as assistant instructor of infantry tactics, September 15, 1848, to September 27, 1855
- On frontier duty at Santa Fe, New Mexico, 1856
- On frontier duty at Fort Union, New Mexico 1856
- On frontier duty at Santa Fe, New Mexico, 1856–57
- On frontier duty at Cantonment Burgwin, New Mexico, 1857
- On frontier duty at Fort Defiance, New Mexico, 1857
- On frontier duty at Albuquerque, New Mexico, 1857–1858
- On recruiting service, 1858–1859
- On leave of absence in Europe, 1859–1860
- On frontier duty at Ringgold Barracks, Texas, 1860–1861
- In the garrison at Fort Brown, Texas, 1861
- Served during the Rebellion of the Seceding States, 1861–1866
  - At Hilton Head, South Carolina, July 3 to December 9, 1865
  - At Charleston, South Carolina, December 9, 1865, to June 21, 1866
- Member of Tactics Board, June 25, 1866, to February 4, 1867
- In command of Tenth Infantry Regiment, March 21 to June 16, 1867
- At Charleston, South Carolina, March 21, 1867, to June 15, 1868, and October 24, 1868, to April 6, 1869
- On leave of absence, June 15 to October 24, 1868
- In command of regiment at Fort Brown, Texas, April 24, 1869, to May 14, 1871
- On leave of absence, May 14, 1871, to September 1872
- Member of Board for revising Army Regulations, September 1872, to May 26, 1873
- Awaiting orders, May 26 to July 1873
- In command of Tenth Infantry Regiment and Fort McKavett, Texas, July 14, 1873, to June 10, 1876, and October 23, 1876, to August 29, 1877
- On leave of absence, June 10 to October 10, 1876
- On sick leave of absence, August 29 to December 31, 1877
- In command of regiment at Fort McKavett, Texas and District of North Texas, January 22, 1878, to May 11, 1879
- At Fort Wayne, Michigan, May 11, 1879, to September 19, 1879
- On court-martial duty, September 19, 1879, to November 27, 1879
- In command of regiment at Fort Wayne, Michigan, November 27, 1879, to June 2, 1884
- On leave of absence and on delay, June 2, 1884, to July 1, 1884
- On sick leave of absence, July 1, 1884, to July 1, 1885
- Retired from active duty after forty years of service, July 1, 1885
- Died on October 30, 1888, at Niagara Falls, New York at the age of sixty-four[1]

Biographical Sketch

Brevet Brigadier General Henry B. Clitz was born on July 4, 1824, at Sackett's Harbor, New York. His father, Captain John Clitz, was adjutant for the Second Infantry, which was headquartered at Sackett's Harbor. The combination of his military parentage, birth on Independence Day, life in a military garrison, and familiarity with all the accoutrements of war, resulted in young Clitz choosing to become a soldier. At the age of seventeen, he entered the U.S. Military Academy. He graduated on July 1, 1845, fifty-sixth in the Class of 1845. The Army assigned the new brevet second lieutenant to the infantry. He immediately joined the Army of Occupation in Texas. He fought in the Defense of Fort Brown, Texas and at the Battle of Monterey, Mexico. After Monterrey was captured, he was transferred to General Winfield Scott's army. He took part in all the Army of Invasion's operations from the Siege of Vera Cruz to the Capture of the City of Mexico. He received a promotion to brevet first lieutenant for his "gallant and meritorious conduct" in the Battle of Cerro Gordo (April 18, 1847).

After the Mexican War, Clitz was sent to the U.S. Military Academy as an assistant instructor of infantry tactics (September 15, 1848, to September 27, 1845). After his service at West Point, he was on frontier duty in New Mexico, recruiting duty, and on leave of absence in Europe.

When the Civil War began, Captain Clitz accompanied an expedition to Fort Pickens, Florida. After two months at Fort Pickens, he was promoted to major and joined the Twelfth Infantry Regiment at Fort Hamilton, New York. At Fort Hamilton, he reorganized, drilled, and disciplined the regiment to prepare it for active service. The Twelfth was assigned to the Army of the Potomac and fought in the Virginia Peninsula Campaign. The regiment took part in the Siege of Yorktown and saw action at the Battle of Gaines' Mill. Clitz was wounded once at Yorktown and twice at Gaines' Mill. He was captured at Gaines' Mill and held as a prisoner of war in Libby Prison in Richmond until paroled and exchanged on July 17, 1862.

After recovering from his wounds, the military sent him to the U.S. Military Academy as the commandant of cadets (October 23, 1862, to July 4, 1864). His "soldierly bearing, devotion to duty, uniform courtesy, and kindly consideration for all," won "all hearts of both sexes and of all ages."

For the rest of the war, he served in garrisons at Bedloe's Island, New York; Savannah, Georgia; Hilton Head, South Carolina; and Charleston, South Carolina. For his "gallant and meritorious services during the Rebellion" he received a brevet promotion to colonel, and a brevet advancement to brigadier general and for "gallant and distinguished services in the field."

Following the war, he was on garrison duty at Charleston, South Carolina and Fort Brown, Texas. On February 22, 1869, the Army promoted him to colonel of the Tenth Infantry Regiment. He commanded various frontier posts and served on several important boards. He retired on July 1, 1885.

He lived in Detroit, Michigan with his aged mother. Without any clear reason, he suddenly left his home and was last seen on October 30, 1888, at Niagara Falls.

Clitz had a personal magnetism and charming character, which earned the respect and affection of "all that came within the sunshine of his genial nature." He was one of the "kindest and most affectionate of men." He was "of almost feminine gentleness," but it did not detract from his true manliness. His attention to the little amenities of life, his buoyancy of spirits, and his cheerful joyousness in conversation, always made him a welcome guest. The Michigan Commandery, Military Order of the Loyal Legion of the United States honored him for his forty years of army service "full of the most important military events in the nation's history, embracing the War with Mexico and the Rebellion of the Seceding States, in which he took an honored part without a stain upon his escutcheon, is the highest tribute we can pay to his patriotism, gallantry, and fidelity to duty."[2]

The Commandant's Role in Preparing Civil War Generals

Questions

How important was the commandant of cadets in preparing cadets to become general officers in the Civil War? The following questions must be answered before defining the commandant's contribution to military leadership:
- Did tactical training help officers become generals?
- Did the military curriculum and number of graduates meet the Army's needs?
- Did technical innovations make existing tactical instruction obsolete?
- What impact did the West Point culture have on future generals?
- Who was most responsible for tactical training at the Academy?
- Can the Civil War battlefield triumphs and failures be attributed to the U.S. Military Academy staff and faculty?
- Did the commandant equip cadets with the necessary military education, discipline, and characteristics to become general officers?

Tactical Training and Generals

Since its establishment in 1802, the U.S. Military Academy has been criticized as an elitist college which failed to produce effective general officers. Citizens and government officials wanted to abolish West Point because they objected to its exclusivity and the advantages it gave to the rich and wellborn. The U.S. Military Academy was an easy target because the federal government funded its operation. These objections had little to do with the academic curriculum or tactical training and were leveled on all institutions of higher learning.

The second complaint concerned the value of military education. After graduation, the lack of advancement gave little incentive for junior offices to increase their knowledge. In addition, their assignments were routine and lacked the required challenges to promote development. The defection of West Point graduates to the Confederate States Army and the poor performance of senior Union officers during the Civil War added to the negative opinions. Many officers and politicians questioned the Academy's ability to produce generals and they declared that generals are born, not educated, to command. Critics also questioned the Academy's mission. Was it to educate engineers who were also soldiers or to train soldiers who were also engineers?

After the defection of West Point trained officers to the Confederacy, Senator Ben Wade of Ohio questioned the purpose of West Point:

> I cannot help thinking that there is something wrong about this whole institution. I do not believe that in the history of the world you can find as many men who have proved themselves utterly faithless to their oaths, ungrateful to the Government that supported them, guilty of treason and a deliberate intention to overthrow that Government which has educated them and given them its support, as have emanated from this institution ... I believe that from the idleness of these military-educated gentlemen this great treason was hatched.[1]

The Value of Tactical Training

If military training alone cannot make a man a general, can a man become a competent general without military instruction? Among the lists of the "best" Civil War generals are two Confederate officers, Patrick Cleburne and Nathan Bedford Forrest, who were not trained at West Point. Cleburne had some military training in the British Army, but Forrest became a general without any formal military instruction. General Forrest should be considered as the exception to the requirement for military training. Most untrained politically appointed generals fared badly during the Civil War. Citizen-soldiers Gideon Pillow, Benjamin Butler, John McClernand, Franz Sigel, and Nathaniel Banks are considered among the worst generals of the war. West Point trained officers also made the list: George McClellan, Ambrose Burnside, Braxton Bragg, Don Carlos Buell, William S. Rosecrans, John Bell Hood, and Hugh Judson Kilpatrick.[2]

Some believed a West Point education was no guarantee of promotion to general or, if promoted, no guarantee of success. However, others thought an Academy education was needed for military advancement.

Cadet Martin Luther Poland in West Point uniform, 1860 (Library of Congress).

- "But military brains—a natural aptitude for arms and the best culture West Point can give him—that is what an army commander needs."—James F. Rusling, *Men and Things I Saw*, 107[3]
- "As the preacher knows his bible, as the lawyer knows his statutes, every general should know the regulations and articles of war."—Charles F. Smith[4]
- "The first quality of a good soldier is obedience and discipline. The first quality of a good officer is a sense of the indispensable [sic] need of order, and of discipline as the condition of order."—William B. Hazen, *Narrative*, 390[5]
- "Without the discipline, organization, and tactics of the old army, the new army, generals and all, would be but a loose mob."—Ethan Allen Hitchcock[6]
- "The military profession is made up of trivialities and the enforcement of trivial things is fully justified by the results produced—obedience to orders, discipline and military efficiency."—John Gibbon[7]

These comments support the belief that basic military knowledge is a prerequisite for battlefield success. A cadet needed instruction and practice in the fundamental tools of his profession to become a successful officer. Commanders needed to understand the roles of fighting units from individual soldiers to regiments to train their men and employ them effectively in battle. However, the military instruction at West Point was designed to prepare the graduate for the highest rank he was likely to reach in an army charged with controlling Indian activities. While this training was essential for military competence, it did not guarantee a successful career.

Teaching a person how to use a saw will not make him a skilled carpenter or cabinetmaker. Likewise, a cadet must master the duties of the soldier before learning and perfecting the duties of an officer. Without the basic knowledge of his profession, it is difficult if not impossible to excel in a field. To advance from second lieutenant to general required practice in the basics, battlefield experience, and a commitment to ongoing learning. Some officers recognized this deficiency and "supplemented their formal training and made their reputations by observing foreign wars or engaging in studying and translating tactical and training manuals."[8] Grant and Lee learned from their early mistakes in the Civil War to lead armies. Both men built on the fundamental military knowledge they obtained in the classroom and on the parade grounds at West Point. However, they added to their understanding and revised their strategies as battlefield conditions, technology, and the capabilities of their army and their opponents changed. The officers who learned to adapt to these dynamic forces progressed in their careers.

Some officers did not understand the West Point lessons on grand tactics were intended to be a *starting point* to plan and conduct offensive and defensive operations. In the Civil War, many West Point officers thought the method of grand tactics taught at West Point had to be rigidly obeyed. These men commanded by the manuals and were completely divorced from "tactical reality." Battlefield casualties were so shocking because "officers on both sides fought by the books, and the books were wrong."[9]

Other aspects of life at the Academy instilled in cadets the traits, which could make them good officers and, perhaps, generals. They learned self-discipline and how to enforce regulations. They learned how to obey orders and how to give them. They understood how to be gentlemen and set an example of proper behavior for their men. The Academy initiated cadets into the separate and elite society of West Point educated officers.[10]

Some regarded these traits as equal to or greater than academic studies in making outstanding generals.

- "So much of the efficiency of troops depends upon the character of those who command them, that it behooves a government to take every means to secure the best officers possible."—William B. Hazen, *A Narrative of Military Service*, p. 384[11]
- "The character of a leader is a large factor in the game of War"—William T. Sherman, *Battles and Leaders*, p. 4:253[12]

Strategic Thinking

The confusion between tactics and strategy led to criticism of the U.S. Military Academy. Some historians fault the Academy for not teaching strategy. While others erroneously believe strategy and tactics describe the same activities. As previously discussed, strategy and tactics are quite different. Generals design strategy and colonels and lower ranks employ tactics to win battles and help achieve strategic goals. The newly commissioned officers needed a thorough knowledge of company and battalion tactics to prepare them for active duty. The tactical instructors taught these skills in the classroom, on the parade grounds, and in practical field exercises. West Point's mission was to produce men who might become colonels not generals. The division of tactics into minor and grand tactics, further complicated the semantics. While the difference between minor tactics and strategy were well defined, the distinction between grand tactics and strategy is blurred.

The staff and faculty recognized their training was the first step in a lifetime study of military developments. The textbooks and manuals used at the Academy "were intended only as recipe books for basic movements: they did not pretend to tell their readers much about how to fight battles or how to behave when the enemy was close."[13]

The Antebellum Army

By the beginning of the Civil War, the United States had "created a sophisticated professional army that had successfully employed its French tactics in combat, using both regulars and volunteers." This army provided "excellent leaders for the Civil War, and American education, experience, and topography would create a distinctively American approach."[14]

The reforms instituted by Superintendent Sylvanus Thayer resulted in a high degree of uniformity in the training and socialization of American officers. By the mid-nineteenth century, the officer corps of the little United States Army was one of the world's most homogeneous and professionally educated military elites.[15]

In 1860, the Army had seventy-six forts west of the Mississippi River. For administrative purposes, the Army divided the nation into military departments. The number of departments reached seven by 1860. A brigadier general or a colonel commanded each department. Those colonels who commanded departments and were also regimental commanders, relied on a lieutenant colonel to lead their regiment. The reduction of the Army at the end of the Mexican War left the military with fifteen regiments, eight infantry, four artillery, and three mounted, to garrison the forts in the seven departments.[16]

Promotion was slow in the antebellum Army, and a West Point education did not make the process any faster. Between its founding in 1802 and the beginning of the Civil War in 1861, the U.S. Military Academy graduated 1,966 cadets, about half of whom served in the Mexican War. By 1861, 750 of the 1,063 graduates still living were on active service in the Army. However, few of them served in senior leadership positions. None of the Army's four general officers at the start of the Civil War were West Point graduates. Three of the four generals were veterans of the War of 1812. Of the nineteen regimental colonels, only six graduated from the U.S. Military Academy. The promotion system had little or no room for flexibility. It all depended on an officer's date of rank. Officers were promoted within the regiment as openings became available, usually when an officer left the Army or died. With no retirement program, officers tended to stay on active service as long as possible, regardless of age or physical infirmities. Officers spent many years as lieutenants and captains waiting for a vacancy to open ahead of them. In the years before the Civil War it took an average of forty-four years for an officer to reach the rank of colonel in the artillery. Attaining the grade took an average of thirty-seven years of service in the infantry.[17] Because promotions were based on openings not merit, officers had little incentive to improve their skills or prepare for the next level of command.

By December 1860, the Army's authorized strength totaled about 18,000 officers and men, but there were only 16,367 on the rolls. Of these, 1,108 were commissioned officers, four were general officers (one major general who served as the commanding general and three brigadier generals), and the rest were either line officers assigned to the regiments or staff officers serving in the War Department. There were 361 staff officers assigned to the nine bureaus and departments, all of which were headed by colonels, although several held staff brevets of brigadier general. The bureau chiefs were men of long service, averaging sixty-four years of age, with six over seventy. The 743-line officers served in the regiments: 351 in the infantry, 210 in the artillery, and 182 in the mounted units. Like the bureau chiefs in the War Department, the nineteen regimental colonels were mostly old men set in their ways. They ranged in age from forty-two to eighty, with an average age of sixty-three. The officers in each regimental headquarters consisted of a colonel, a lieutenant colonel, two majors, an adjutant, and a quartermaster. The adjutant and quartermaster were lieutenants.[18]

Most West Point graduates did not rise above colonels before the Civil War. Captains led companies composed of one hundred men. A regiment had ten companies or one thousand men and were commanded by colonels. Many of the promotions to captain were rewards for "Fourteen Years' Continuous Service." Therefore, of the West Point graduates who became major generals or higher (Union) and lieutenant generals or higher (Confederate), 10 percent were second lieutenants, 23 percent reached the rank of first lieutenant, 38 percent captain, 16 percent major, 6 percent lieutenant colonel, 5 percent colonel, and 2 percent brigadier general. The rank of colonel illustrates the problem of advancement in the Regular Army. Before the Civil War, regiments were the largest unit commanded by these future generals. Four of the five colonels were career officers: Samuel Cooper (46 years), Ethan A. Hitchcock (44 years), Joseph K.F. Mansfield (39 years), and Robert E. Lee (32 years). Please see "Highest Rank Prior to Civil War" in the Appendix for more information.

The slow promotion process encouraged officers to resign. This exodus reached a peak in 1837, when 117 officers including 99 West Point graduates left the Army. Joseph Johnston was one of these officers. Johnston complained, "from the rules of our service, of promotion by regiments, many of my juniors who had the luck to be assigned to regiments in which promotion was less slow than in that to which I belonged had got before me on the army list."[19]

Military Training and Army Requirements

The pre-war Army had 16,367 officers and men and was ill prepared to produce the required number of officers necessary to fight a war. The estimated 3,000 trained officers meant there was only one officer for each of the 3,050 regiments authorized during the Civil War compared to a theoretical requirement of thirty-nine officers per regiment.[20] This equates to a demand for nearly 116,000 officers to fill the vacancies. Under these conditions it is not surprising there were so many incompetent officers on both sides. However, it is unrealistic to blame the Military Academy for the lack of officers to meet Civil War demands because Congress limited the size and number of officers in the pre-war Army.

West Point was also criticized for not preparing its graduates for large scale war. This was an unfair complaint. The Academy was designed to produce civil and military engineers and officers with the potential to command regiments. The size of armies in the Mexican War (Taylor had 6,000 men at Monterrey and Scott landed with about 10,000 at Vera Cruz) were small compared to battles in the Civil War. In the Battle of First Manassas, 35,752 Union officers and men fought between 32,000 and 34,000 Confederate troops. Slightly less than a year later, 77,000 Union troops fought 50,000 Confederates at the Battle of Second Manassas. In 1860, it would be difficult for the U.S. Army to prepare for or imagine fighting battles with the sizes of opposing forces.[21]

In the 1st session of the 37th Congress of 1861, Senator Benjamin Wade of Ohio proclaimed, "I am not very much in favor of increasing the number of cadets. I do not think the experience of the country has been such as should lead us to be in any great hurry to increase the number of cadets or to add to the patronage of the Military Academy."[22]

Engineers or Soldiers

West Point authorities were committed to the technical curriculum, and they fought their critics by stressing the need in the Army and the nation for trained engineers. Cadets devoted over twice as much classroom time to mathematics, science, and engineering compared to liberal arts and strictly military subjects combined. The Military Academy faculty argued mathematics and engineering "honed the reasoning powers of cadets, resulting in tough-minded, mentally disciplined officers capable of cutting through ambiguity and making coldly logical decisions under pressure."[23]

Technical training at West Point played an important role in America's development. Military Academy graduates composed most of the Army's Corps of Engineers. Academy-trained engineers explored the country and prepared surveys, constructed lighthouses, improved rivers and harbors, and erected government buildings and monuments.[24]

Academy graduates also led soldiers in American conflicts and wars. From its founding in 1802, West Point officers served in twenty-eight conflicts including the

The Cadet Monument at West Point (Historic Structures Inventory, United States Military Academy).

Barbary Wars (1801–1805 and 1815), War of 1812 (1812–1815), Creek War (1813–1814), Tecumseh's War (1815), Seminole Wars (1817–1818, 1835–1842, and 1855–1858), Blackhawk War (1832), Mexican-American War (1846–1848), and Utah War (1857–1858).[25] Over one hundred Academy graduates died while serving their country: War of 1812 (7), Mexican-American War (50), and Indian Wars (49).[26]

In 1859, the Military Academy Board of Visitors defended the intuition's expenses:

> The Board of Visitors to West Point Military Academy in their report of the result of their examination, say the expenses of that institution are but as a drop in the ocean compared with the advantages resulting, and that have resulted, to the United States from it. All the progressive improvements in war are here tested and applied, and their uses made familiar for the time of trial. So that, on the score of strictest economy the people of the United States could not devise a better nor less expensive plan for military organization and security, in event of war, than this institution affords.[27]
>
> In spite of the prejudice of many volunteers against Regular Army men and the graduates of the U.S. Military Academy, the guidance and leadership of these experienced and educated soldiers proved essential in organizing and operating the new war machines. The military knowledge and insight of many of the regular officers would have much to do with giving the armies and the war their sophisticated character.[28]

West Point was an engineering school, which trained men to be officers.

Validation of West Point Training in the Mexican War

"The great results of the Mexican War gave the Military Academy an immense reputation."[29] General Winfield Scott said, "I give it as my fixed opinion, that but for our graduated cadets, the war between the United States and Mexico might, and probably would have lasted some four or five years, with, in its first half, more defeats than victories falling to our share; whereas, in less than two campaigns, we conquered a great country and a peace without the loss of a single battle or skirmish."[30]

> The nation is much indebted for a series of splendid victories; any one of which would more than compensate it for all the expenditures at West Point. That will be an unfortunate day for the Republic, when Congress, influenced either by motives of economy or the vile appeals of the demogogue [sic], shall Consent to abandon an Institution which has already done much to establish the reputation and extend the borders of the country.—Luther Giddings in *Campaigns in North America*[31]

Captain John Kenly noted the artillery's performance "reflected undying lustre [sic] on the Military Academy at West Point and proudly displayed the standard of its training...."[32]

The American forces showed a "fighting quality which resulted primarily from competent officers, especially West Pointers." Although Academy graduates did not dominate the high command in the Regular Army, they served brilliantly as junior officers. They were skillful troop instructors, combat leaders, and military engineers. Professionally educated officers also served with volunteer units. Many West Point graduates who had resigned from the Army received volunteer commissions. In addition, men who attended West Point, but did not graduate were appointed officers. The

General Scott's grand entry into Mexico City, lithograph by James Baillie, ca. 1848 (Library of Congress).

performance of volunteer soldiers commanded by West Pointers confirmed Scott's belief that "good leaders could quickly transform ordinary citizens into excellent soldiers."[33]

The American people appreciated the victory and graduates became heroes. Both Zachary Taylor and Winfield Scott became presidential candidates. Junior officers used their Mexican War experience to build their credentials and win promotions.

- "I came down here with high hopes, with pleasing anticipation of distinction … and acquiring a name and reputation as a stepping stone to a still greater eminence in some future and greater war."—George B. McClellan
- This was an opportunity in which he might "gain distinction & honor & therefore not to be regretted."—Robert E. Lee[34]

For a junior U.S. Army officer, the experience gained in the Mexican War "immediately" provided "practical information" to complement the valuable training he received at West Point.[35] Actual combat experience proved beneficial to the entire Army. The West Pointers had a unique opportunity to put their knowledge to the test against a professional army. This trial by combat led to commissions for Union and Confederate officers in the Civil War.

However, the junior officers learned different lessons. The knowledge gained varied depending on the officer's participation; the commander he served under; the outcomes of the battles, success and victory or failure and defeat; and the officer's ability to apply and adapt the knowledge obtained in one battle to future battles. Robert E. Lee discovered reconnaissance could be used to conduct a turning movement.[36] Ulysses Grant realized the importance of taking logistical risk. Some officers' exposure convinced them to be cautious and deliberate while other officers favored a bold and reckless approach.[37] From his commanders, the young officers learned how to manage campaigns and battles, how to use the combined assets of their army, and to employ strategies and tactics, which worked in the Mexican War to the Civil War. Unfortunately, some officers applied the lessons rigidly and did not adapt to new technology and different terrains. This was demonstrated early in the Civil War, when Union and Confederate commanders followed General Scott's Mexican War strategy of capturing the enemy capital to achieve victory, defeating a larger army, and supporting a lengthy supply line. Another lesson from the Mexican War was learning about the character of men who became their enemies in the Civil War. There were also some universal lessons learned in the war. They learned how to endure hardship, inspire the loyalty of troops, and fight and win battles.[38]

General Ulysses S. Grant stated his "experience in the Mexican war was of great advantage to me afterwards." In addition to the practical lessons he learned in the conflict, he became personally acquainted with many officers he would command and others he would fight. Grant learned about "the characters of those to whom I was afterwards opposed."[39]

The Regular Army officers formed opinions of volunteers during the War. The volunteers were undisciplined and their officers "seemed uninterested in imposing discipline." The citizen soldiers traveled back and forth across the Rio Grande to visit saloons and gambling halls. They stole and butchered local cattle and sometimes shot Mexican citizens for "sport." They quarreled with the Irish-Catholic volunteers. However, the most infuriating aspect of the regular vs. volunteer army debate was the attitude of the American people. The public considered the volunteers better and more patriotic than the regulars. They regarded the West Point officers as "a second-class bunch who served for money—mercenaries." While volunteers were "brave men willing to risk their lives out of love for their country."[40]

Technical Innovations and Tactical Instruction

Technological innovations had a significant impact on the course of the Civil War. Communication improvements included the telegraph, aerial reconnaissance, and the "wig-wag" signals developed by the signal corps. The Civil War was the first war to use railroads to transport men and supplies. Medical care moved to the battlefield with the Army ambulance corps, which moved wounded men to dressing stations and field hospitals. Other advances improved weapons and ships. Ironclad warships replaced wooden ships and the submarine entered the Confederate navy's arsenal. However, the minié ball[41] had the greatest impact on the war. Use of the minie ball and rifled muskets increased the range of fire from 300 feet to 900 feet. This invention increased the strength of defenses and had a dramatic effect on strategy and tactics. The minié ball and rifle was five times more accurate than smoothbore muskets and contributed to more than ninety percent of wounds and deaths.[42]

The minié ball originated when British Captain John Norton saw the action of blowguns used by local tribes in India. The base of their darts was made from pith, the spongy wood from the center of tree trunks. When a person blew into the blowgun's

Minié balls.

tube, the pith expanded, closed the space between the tube and the dart, produced a tight seal, and increased the dart's range.

Based on this principle, Norton developed a cylindrical bullet with a hollow base in 1832. London gunsmith William Greener improved on the design in 1836. He devised an oval-shaped bullet with a flat surface on one end. A small hole was drilled into the flat end. This hole went through most of the length of the bullet and was covered by a conical plug with a round, wooden base. When fired, the plug would expand to prevent gases from escaping.

Two French army captains, Claude-Étienne Minié and Henri-Gustave Delvigne, refined Norton and Greener's design. In 1849, they created a conical, soft-lead bullet with four rings and a rifle with a grooved barrel to go with it. Minié made the projectile smaller and longer which made the bullet easier to load. The French and English used the bullet and rifle effectively during the Crimean War against the Russians' smoothbore[43] muskets.

United States observers present during the 1853–1855 conflict were impressed, and introduced the minié in America. James Burton, an armorer at the U.S. Arsenal in Harpers Ferry, Virginia, improved the design. The American version could be mass-produced cheaply. Burton's design and the rifled musket for firing it, were adopted for use by the U.S. Army by Secretary of War Jefferson Davis in July 1855.

The federal armories at Springfield, Massachusetts and Harper's Ferry, Virginia began producing the Springfield Model 1855 rifle-musket. By the end of 1858, these arsenals had manufactured four thousand rifles.[44] Cast iron rifled cannons began to be produced during the winter of 1860–1861.[45]

When the Civil War began, most arsenals were stocked with smoothbore muskets. Both sides used smoothbore muskets until they were replaced with rifled muskets.[46] At the Battle of First Manassas in July 1861, Regular Union Army regiments used Springfield and other rifles. However most Confederate soldiers fought with smoothbore muskets. At the Battle of Shiloh in April 1862, the Union armies were well equipped with rifles, although some soldiers still had smoothbores. Most of the Confederates were armed with smoothbore muskets although some regiments had rifles. During the fighting at the Hornet's Nest, Confederates replaced their old muskets with Enfield rifles dropped by fleeing Union soldiers.

Throughout the Virginia Peninsula Campaign from March to July 1862, more than fifty percent of the Union Army of the Potomac had Enfield and Springfield rifles. Around forty percent of the Army of Northern Virginia still used smoothbore muskets. By the Battle of Antietam in September 1862, the Army of the Potomac had replaced most of the smoothbore muskets. However, forty regiments in the Army of the Potomac still carried muskets at Gettysburg and some units used muskets in Grant's Overland Campaign.

The Army of Northern Virginia added to their arsenal of rifled weapons from small arms and guns retrieved on the battlefield. The Battle of Gettysburg was the first engagement in which the Confederate forces fought with rifled muskets. In the second half of the war, the Army of Northern Virginia primarily used Enfield and Springfield rifles.

Unidentified Union soldier with Model 1855 Springfield rifle and bayonet (Library of Congress).

In the Western theater, Union armies still carried a significant number of smoothbore muskets in 1863. During the Vicksburg Campaign (March–July 1863), the Confederate Army of Tennessee and the Union Army of the Cumberland still used smoothbore muskets. By the second half of 1863, Union troops in the West were all equipped with rifles. Almost half of the Union Army of the Tennessee fought with smoothbore muskets at the Battle of Stones River at the end of 1862. The replacement of smoothbore weapons with rifles was nearly complete by the end of 1864.

To combat the arms shortage, the Union and Confederacy imported large quantities of rifles from Europe. The cash strapped South could only buy 50,000 weapons by August 1862, while the North bought 726,000. Accordingly, during the first two years of the war, soldiers from both sides used a wide variety of rifles, including many which were over fifty years old and were considered obsolete.[47]

Under these circumstances, it was nearly impossible to incorporate the potential impact of minié ball technology in the West Point curriculum. The lack of rifled bullets and muskets meant battles in the first three years of the war were conducted with tactics based on smoothbore weapons.

With the increased use of rifled weapons and minié balls, adherence to one of Professor Dennis Mahan's teachings was a huge "grand" tactical mistake. Mahan believed a "frontal attack by volunteers would fail," but an attack lead by regulars might succeed.[48]

In *The Art of War*, Baron Jomini wrote, "...the improvements in fire-arms will not introduce any important change in the manner of taking troops into battle, but that it would be useful to introduce into the tactics of infantry the formation of columns by companies, and to have a numerous body of good riflemen or skirmishers, and to exercise the troops considerably in firing."[49]

The minié ball affected "grand" tactics, but it left minor tactical training intact:

> ... troops still had to maneuver by marching erect, usually in regiments of 400 to 700 men, controlled by their captains and colonels who sought to respond to the orders of the brigade commander. Most Civil War soldiers endlessly practiced their drill. Their proficiency not only enabled them to respond promptly and maneuver quickly and easily, but also created a habit of obedience and concerted action and a feeling of cohesion even when group evolutions were inadvisable or impossible.[50]

Impact of the West Point Culture

The West Point culture had an important effect on its cadets. The school administration wanted to instill patriotic values and a commitment to public service. Superintendent Thayer "relentlessly reinforced these ideas until he transformed a socially and regionally diverse group of young into the most nationally focused professional cadre in the country." In recitations, cadets were taught to "solve problems, not just in mathematical terms but with an eye to anticipating difficulties and formulating creative responses."[51] It may seem inconsistent, in this rigidly controlled environment, cadets were encouraged to think creatively. West Point wanted their graduates to be problem solvers.

West Point created a culture in which cadets were bound by a "sacred brotherhood of arms."[52] The tight restrictions and modest enrollment forged a deep and positive sense of community. The West Point culture created a unique societal group and camaraderie that led cadets to understand they were a "band of brothers."[53]

Minor vs. Grand Tactics

> Tactics may be defined to be the art of drawing up, and moving troops systematically. It admits of a classification into two divisions. (1) Minor or elementary tactics; under which head may be placed all that refers to the drill, other preparatory instruction of troops to give them expertness in the use of their weapons, and facility of movement. (2) Grand tactics; or the art of combining, disposing, and handling troops on the field of battle.[54]

Dennis Hart Mahan and Grand Tactics

According to many historians, Professor Dennis Hart Mahan *was* military education at the U.S. Military Academy. Although some have characterized his lectures and textbooks as the art of war or strategy, his *Advanced Guard, Outpost, and Detachment Service of Troops* covered many topics including tactics, placing and handling troops, positions, advanced guards and advanced posts, detachments, convoys, and surprises and ambushes. In fact, Mahan only allocated one week in his semester long class to the art of war.[55] The book was "intended as supplement to the system of tactics." The section on tactics should be more appropriately described as grand tactics in contrast to the tactical instruction presented in the class on Infantry Tactics taught by the commandant of cadets and practiced daily during the school year and at the summer encampment.

Eighteen-year-old Mahan received an appointment to West Point in 1820. As a Third Class cadet, the Academy selected him to be acting assistant professor of mathematics. On July 1, 1824, Mahan graduated at the head of his class. The Army assigned the second lieutenant to the Corps of Engineers. He stayed at the Academy as an assistant professor of mathematics (August 29, 1824, to August 31, 1825) and as principal assistant professor of engineering (August 31, 1825, to August 1, 1826). The War Department sent him to Europe to study public works and military institutions (August 1, 1826, to June 15, 1830). On January 1, 1829, the French Minister of War allowed him to study at the celebrated Military School of Application for Engineers and Artillerists at Metz, France. Mahan examined the school's imposing architecture, the library's works and manuscripts on the art of war, its vast arsenal of trophies and arms, and its "wondrous lines of fortification."

Dennis Hart Mahan (United States Military Academy Library, Special Collections).

When he returned to the Academy on September 1, 1830, the War Department appointed him acting professor of engineering (September 1, 1830–January 1, 1832). The Army made him professor of engineering and head of the Department of Civil and Military Engineering on January 1, 1832. He held this important position over forty years until his resignation in September 1871.

Mahan taught civil and military engineering and authored nine West Point textbooks. He presented the course on Military and Civil Engineering to First Class cadets. The class in the Department of Civil and Military Engineering was divided into two parts: civil engineering was taught in the first term and military engineering and the art and science of war were presented in the second term. Military engineering covered fixed and field fortifications. The science of war included discussions on army organization and discipline, tactics, minor tactics in relation to logistics, grand tactics, minor operations, logistics, and strategy. Military engineering, which was taught in the spring semester, emphasized permanent and field fortifications and fortification drawing. Six lessons (nine hours) on "The Science of War" were included in the class.[56]

Professor Mahan only gave a few lectures during the course. His speeches included brief descriptions of campaigns and battles and comments on the tactical positions. Most of his instruction was given to the cadets during his visits to the section study room or at student recitations.

Although Mahan was an esteemed member of the faculty at West Point, the major source of his fame came from his textbooks. The following manuals were used throughout the world.

- *Treatise on Field Fortification* published in 1836 and revised six or seven times. The text was used in Mahan's class on military engineering. Military mining and siege operations were taught in the first part of "An Elementary Course of Military Engineering."
- *Permanent Fortifications* published in 1867 became the second part of Mahan's class on military engineering.
- *Advanced Guard, Outpost, and Detachment Service of Troops* was published in 1847. An expanded textbook was published in 1862. It was changed so much that it might have been renamed an "Elementary Treatise on the Art of War." The manual was adopted in many State military schools, by the National Guard of New York, and used by most volunteer and regular officers during the Civil War. Both this and Mahan's book on field fortifications were considered so indispensable that the Confederates reprinted them. Although this book was revised during the Civil War, its contents were presented in Mahan's classes from 1833 to 1862.
- *Treatise on Fortification Drawing and Stereotomy"* was published in 1865. The textbook was based on Mahan's lectures explaining how descriptive geometry could be applied to many problems of military construction.
- *Course of Civil Engineering* was published in 1837 and revised and rewritten in 1868 to incorporate engineering developments since the first edition. This manual and its many editions were extremely popular with American civil engineers. The textbook was used in engineering classes in many academies and colleges. The *Course of Civil Engineering* was translated into several foreign languages.
- Mahan revised and corrected errors in Henry Moseley's *The Mechanical Principles of Engineering and Architecture* for the American edition published in 1856.
- *Industrial Drawing* was published in 1853 and revised many times. It was specially designed for academies and common schools. It was used to teach mechanics to students who needed to understand the elements of geometrical and topographical drawing to present their ideas to others. The work was an outgrowth of Mahan's conversations and instructions for the workmen at the West Point foundry.[57]

Of all his works, *Treatise on Field Fortification* (1836) and *Advanced Guard, Outpost, and Detachment Service of Troops* (1847) probably had the greatest influence on antebellum officers. In his relationships with cadets, Mahan was not only the learned professor-teacher, but also a disciplinarian and gentleman. When he entered the cadet recitation room, the students braced themselves for the upcoming academic interrogation. The process clearly delineated the difference between superior and subordinate. Mahan strictly enforced regulations and etiquette to impress the cadets with "wholesome discipline" and to cultivate the manners and habits which should characterize an officer. However sarcastic he might have appeared; his severity was not designed to wound his pupils nor do them any injustice. If the topic was too difficult, Professor Mahan would review the subject and clarify the lesson, so the student would understand. A former cadet said Mahan had "a sovereign contempt for all knowledge that did not come through regular school channels."[58] Another student recalled Mahan as "the most particular, crabbed, exacting man I ever saw."[59]

As a member of the West Point faculty, he advanced the Academy's prosperity, preserved its reputation as America's first scientific school, helped it maintain its high standards, worked to uphold its military tradition, and graduated "honorable men, accomplished scholars, and finished soldiers."

In September 1871, the West Point Board of Visitors recommended the sixty-nine-year old professor be forced to retire from teaching. This was a sorry parting between the man who spent over forty-one years at the Academy and loved it like one of his children. A devastated Mahan committed suicide by leaping into the paddlewheel of a steamboat on the Hudson River on September 16, 1871.[60]

The Commandant's Role at West Point

The commandant of cadets was responsible for training in "minor" infantry, cavalry, and artillery tactics during drill, at the summer encampment, and in the tactics course taught to First Class cadets. Mahan's class on military and civil engineering lessons was taught to First Class cadets using *Advanced Guard, Outpost, and Detachment Service of Troops* to present the elements of grand tactics.

The West Point curriculum provided the cadets with a strong technical and military background. Additionally, life at the Academy developed future officers informally through the "general influence of the Academy as a force of professional socialization."[61] As Dennis Mahan oversaw grand tactics and classroom conduct, the commandant of cadets instructed the cadets in minor tactics, kept discipline, and served as a role model. More than any other individual, he exercised an "important influence on the military character and opinions of the junior officers of the Army."[62] Regrettably, most historians have ignored the commandant's impact. The indices of Civil War books have virtually no references to "commandant of cadets." Minor tactics was the basis of all military knowledge and teaching techniques to train and lead men in battle. The commandant handled the formal and informal education critical in producing qualified officers.

The following sixteen officers served as commandants from 1817 to 1864: George W. Gardiner (September 15, 1817, to April 2, 1818); John Bliss (April 2, 1818, to January 11, 1819); John R. Bell (February 8, 1819, to March 17, 1820); William J. Worth (March 17, 1820, to December 2, 1828); Ethan A. Hitchcock (March 13, 1829, to June 24, 1833); John Fowle (July 10, 1833, to March 31, 1838); Charles F. Smith (April 1, 1838, to September 1, 1842); J. Addison Thomas (September 1, 1842, to December 14, 1845); Bradford R. Alden (December 14, 1845, to November 1, 1852); Robert S. Garnett (November 1, 1852, to July 31, 1854); William H.T. Walker (July 31, 1854, to May 27, 1856); William J. Hardee (July 22, 1856, to September 8, 1860); John F. Reynolds (September 8, 1860, to June 25, 1861); Christopher C. Augur (August 26, 1861, to December 5, 1861); Kenner Garrard (December 5, 1861, to September 25, 1862); and Henry B. Clitz (October 23, 1862, to July 4, 1864). The officer's tenure varied from three months to eight years-eight months.[63]

The time each commandant spent at the Academy affected their impact on the West Point program. Men who served less than a year (Gardiner, Bliss, Bell, Reynolds, Augur, and Garrard) trained fewer future generals and were less influential than those whose terms were more than four years (Worth, Alden, Hitchcock, Fowle, Hardee, and Smith). There were four commandants who served between one and four years (Thomas, Garnett, Walker, and Clitz).

Answers

More than any other faculty or staff at West Point, the commandant of cadets was responsible for providing military training and leadership:

- Did tactical training help officers become generals?—This training gave the fundamental knowledge to lead troops and develop into a general officer.
- Did the military curriculum and number of graduates meet the Army's needs?—West Point was an engineering school which produced soldiers. The Army needed men who might become colonels and West Point taught the skills necessary to reach this rank. Because Congress limited the size of the pre-war Army, West Point could not graduate the number of officers needed in the Civil War
- Did technical innovations make existing tactical instruction obsolete? The introduction of the rifled bullet and rifled musket had minimal effect on military instruction. The minié ball effected grand tactics taught by Mahan, but it left intact minor tactical training taught by the commandants.
- What impact did the West Point culture have on future generals?—The West Point culture created the dedicated, "band of brothers" society of officers. Opposing generals learned about each other's personalities. The Academy's competitive environment continued in the Civil War with fights for promotions and responsibilities and battles for victories.
- Who was most responsible for tactical training at the Academy?—The commandant of cadets presented training through the four years of study. Professor Mahan allocated six lessons or nine hours on The Science of War. Minor tactical instruction began with the School of the Soldier and progressed through the Schools of the Company and Battalion to evolutions of the line. During the four-year program, cadets were drilled 204 times in artillery, 268 in equitation, and 540 in infantry.[64]
- Did the commandant equip cadets with the necessary military education, discipline, and characteristics to become general officers?—The commandant supplied the basic training in minor tactics necessary for all soldiers. The

training included opportunities for cadets to serve as commissioned and noncommissioned officers in the Corps of Cadets. The commandant taught the future officers how to efficiently move troops on the battlefield. He taught the First Class, year-long course on tactics. He administered discipline and taught the cadets how obey orders as well as giving them. The commandant presented a role model for the cadets including the necessary characteristics of an officer.

The Best Commandants at "The Best School"[65]

The commandant of cadets was more influential than the Professor of Engineering. The commandant was an integral part of a cadet's life from the first summer encampment to graduation. During a cadet's time at West Point, the commandant and his assistant tactical instructors controlled virtually every aspect of a cadet's life. They enforced discipline through the demerit system. the commandant organized their schedule and supervised their daily drill. He taught the class on infantry tactics, which was enlarged to cover artillery and cavalry tactics. He acted as a communication link to the superintendent delivering complaints about the cadet mess or suggestions for recreational activities. He made a lasting impression on cadets through his military bearing, character, and devotion to duty, honor, and country. His influence far exceeded the impact of Mahan's one-year class on military and civil engineering.

The following six commandants contributed greatly to the success of future generals in the Civil War. These officers accounted for fifty-four percent of the time of all the commandants' service at West Point. They produced 391 "notable graduates" for the Civil War.

The Most Influential Commandants of Cadets

Name	Term	Months as Commandant	Notable Graduates	Graduates per Month	Assignments at West Point
William J. Worth	March 17, 1820 to December 2, 1828	105	47	0.45	Commandant of Cadets and Instructor of Infantry Tactics
Bradford R. Alden	December 14, 1845 to November 1, 1852	82	113	1.38	Assistant Teacher of French, Assistant Teacher of Mathematics, Assistant Tactical Instructor, and Commandant of Cadets and Instructor of Infantry Tactics
John Fowle	July 10, 1833, to March 31, 1838	56	73	1.30	Commandant of Cadets and Instructor of Infantry Tactics
Charles F. Smith	April 1, 1838 to September 1, 1842	52	92	1.77	Assistant Tactical Instructor, Adjutant, and Commandant of Cadets and

Name	Term	Months as Commandant	Notable Graduates	Graduates per Month	Assignments at West Point
Ethan A. Hitchcock	March 13, 1829 to June 24, 1833	51	38	0.75	Instructor of Infantry Tactics Assistant Tactical Instructor and Commandant of Cadets and Instructor of Infantry Tactics
William J. Hardee	July 22, 1856 to September 8, 1860	49	20	0.41	Commandant of Cadets and Instructor of Infantry Tactics

The choice of the most influential commandant(s) considered (1) the number of notable graduates per month of service, (2) significant contribution(s) to tactical program, and (3) cadet evaluations.

Commandants Charles F. Smith, Bradford R. Alden, and John Fowle trained the largest number of notable graduates per month of service. William J. Worth and William J. Hardee made significant contributions to the tactical program. During Worth's term as commandant, the Army formalized the position's role and gave structure to the instruction in infantry tactics. Hardee compiled a manual on rifle and light infantry tactics and revised the practical military courses. With the support of Secretary of War, Jefferson Davis, the scope of the Department of Tactics was increased with the addition of artillery tactics and cavalry tactics. Congress formally recognized the Department of Tactics and the position of commandant of cadets.

From 1836 to 1856, West Point graduated 270 men who became generals in the Civil War. During this twenty-year period, the Academy awarded commissions to seventy-two percent of the men who became generals over the forty-six-years (1818–1864) before and during the Civil War. Three classes stand out—1837, with nineteen generals, 1841, with twenty generals, and 1846, with nineteen generals. John Fowle, Charles F. Smith, J. Addison Thomas, and Bradford Alden were commandants in these years.

Charles F. Smith, Ethan A. Hitchcock, and William J. Hardee served as general officers in the Civil War. Major General Smith and Lieutenant General Hardee served as line officers and Major General Hitchcock was a staff officer. Bradford R. Alden left the Army in September 1853, and John Fowle was killed in April 1838 enroute to an assignment. General Worth died before the war.

The four commandants taught cadets who became generals and earned the Thanks of Congress: Fowle (George G. Meade, Class of 1835 and Joseph Hooker, Class of 1837); Smith (W.T. Sherman, Class of 1840, Thomas, Class of 1840, Nathaniel Lyon, Class of 1841, William S. Rosecrans, Class of 1842, and Ulysses S. Grant, Class of 1843); Thomas (Winfield S. Hancock, Class of 1844); and Alden (George B. McClellan, Class of 1846 and Ambrose E. Burnside, Class of 1847).

The periods with the highest percent of graduates who became Civil War generals are 1837–1843, 1845–1847, 1849–1850, and 1852–1855. C.F. Smith was commandant from April 1, 1838, to September 1, 1842, Bradford R. Alden from December 14, 1845, to November 1, 1852, and Robert S. Garnett from November 1, 1852, to July 31, 1854.

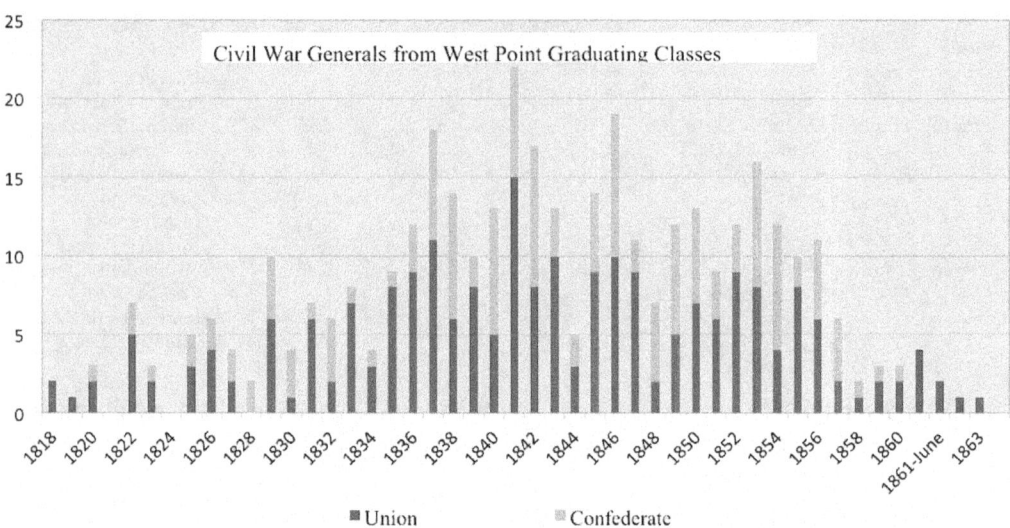

Civil War Generals from West Point graduating classes.

Was the high percentage of graduates who became Civil War generals a function of timing or training? The graduates in the Class of 1837 were forty-five years old and officers from the Class of 1855 were twenty-seven. The officers who graduated before 1847 gained military experience in the Mexican War. Their age and military experience made these graduates ideal candidates to command Civil War armies.

The combination of West Point training, Mexican War experience, and maturity catapulted these current and former officers into the ranks of general officers of the Civil War. The average age of Union generals and admirals in 1861 was 40.52 years. The average age for Confederate generals and admirals in 1861 was 42.38. Excluding the youngest and oldest officers and assuming the graduates were twenty-one indicates most officers who became Union generals graduated between 1836 and 1847, and most

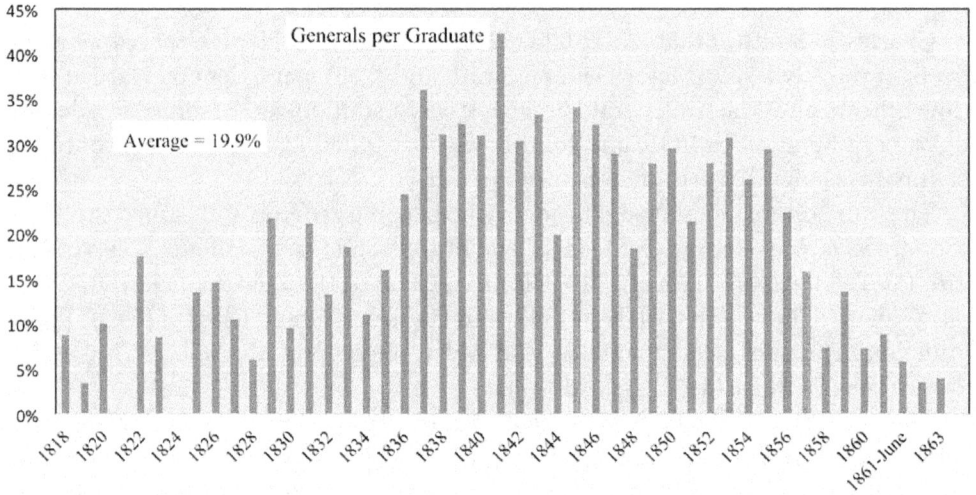

Civil War Generals per Academy Graduate.

officers who became Confederate generals graduated between 1834 and 1845.[66] Four officers served as commandants during these periods: John Fowle (July 10, 1833–March 31, 1838), C.F. Smith (April 1, 1838, to September 1, 1842), John Addison Thomas (September 1, 1842–December 14, 1845), and Bradford R. Alden (December 14, 1845-November 1, 1852).

The Best Commandants at the Military Academy

Name and Term	Months	Notable Graduates	Graduates per Month	Significant Contributions to Program	Cadet Evaluations
William J. Worth March 17, 1820 to December 2, 1828	105	47	0.45	Summer Tours; Assistant Tactical Instructors; Formalized Position	Cadets Requested Permission to Present a Sword
Bradford R. Alden December 14, 1845 to November 1, 1852	82	113	1.38	New Textbooks	Cadets Pledged to Abstain; Praised for his Kindness, Sense of Justice, Sterling Character, and the Moral Tone
John Fowle July 10, 1833 to March 31, 1838	56	73	1.30	Nothing Significant	
Charles F. Smith April 1, 1838 to September 1, 1842	52	92	1.77	Developed Many of the Senior Commanders in the Civil War	Highly Respected
Ethan A. Hitchcock March 13, 1829 to June 24, 1833	51	38	0.75	Nothing Significant	
William J. Hardee July 22, 1856 to September 8, 1860	49	20	0.41	Congressional Recognition of Program; New Tactical Manual; Grouping of all Tactical Programs	Praised by Cadets; Cadet Balls; Revised Leave Program

The Top Three Commandants

William J. Worth served the longest as commandant. He was a respected field officer in the War of 1812, highly regarded by the cadets, a tough disciplinarian, and excellent role model. He started summer tours to improve the public's opinion of the Academy. He trained several of the South's greatest leaders and West Point scholars: Military Academy Professors—Dennis Mahan (1834), Alexander D. Bache (1825), and Albert E. Church (1828); Southern leaders and generals—Albert S. Johnston (1826), Jefferson Davis (1828), Robert E. Lee (1829), and Joseph E. Johnston; and Northern Heroes—Charles F. Smith (1825) and Robert Anderson (1825).

Charles F. Smith held several posts at the Military Academy from 1829 to 1842. He was assistant instructor of infantry tactics (June 25, 1829, to September 1, 1831); adjutant to Superintendent Thayer (September 1, 1831, to April 1, 1838); and Commandant of cadets and instructor of infantry tactics (April 1, 1838, to September 1, 1842). General Smith taught an amazing number of cadets who became generals during the Civil War: Southern Commanders—P.G.T. Beauregard (1838), Richard S. Ewell (1840), Bushrod R. Johnson (1840), Josiah Gorgas (1841), Daniel H. Hill (1842), Alexander P. Stewart (1842), Richard H. Anderson (1842), James Longstreet (1842), and Daniel H. Hill (1842); Union Generals—Irvin McDowell (1838), Henry W. Halleck (1839), William T. Sherman (1840), George H. Thomas (1840), William S. Rosecrans (1842), and Ulysses S. Grant (1843); and four officers who were both commandant of cadets and Civil War generals—William J. Hardee (1838), Robert S. Garnett (1841), John F. Reynolds (1841), and Christopher C. Augur (1843). General Grant considered "General Scott and Captain C.F. Smith, the Commander of Cadets, as the two men most to be envied in the nation." Smith confirmed his credentials with three brevet promotions during the war with Mexico and national accolades for his actions at Fort Donelson.

William J. Hardee completes the list of the best commandants. He revised the practical military courses, introduced and taught the new system of tactics, and increased the commandant's responsibilities to include cavalry and artillery tactics. Several of his cadets achieved distinction in the Civil War: Confederate Generals—E. Porter Alexander (1857), John S. Marmaduke (1857), Joseph Wheeler (1859), and Stephen D. Ramseur (1860) and Northern commanders—James H. Wilson (1860), Wesley Merritt (1860), Adelbert Ames (5/6/1861), Emory Upton (5/6/1861), and George A. Custer (6/24/61). Hardee's greatest contribution to the Academy was the revised tactical manual, *Rifle and Light Infantry Tactics for the Exercise and Manoeuvres of Troops When Acting as Light Infantry or Riflemen*, popularly known as *Hardee's Tactics*. The manual was used by Southern officers and soldiers during the Civil War. His biography in Cullum's *Register* gives credit to Lieutenant Benét, labels the work as a translation of a French textbook, and explains that a board of officers changed the manual. On June 12, 1856, Congress assigned the rank of lieutenant colonel to the commandant of cadets. Hardee, like Worth and Smith was considered a tough, but highly respected, disciplinarian. Hardee made changes in cadet life including vacations, social events, and drill. If Hardee did not join the Confederacy, the Academy might have held him in greater esteem.

Appendices

Major Campaigns and Strategic Battles of the Civil War[1]

Operations in Western Virginia
    Rich Mountain, WV, July 11, 1861
    Carnifex Ferry, WV, September 10, 1861
    Cheat Mountain, WV, September 12–15, 1861

Manassas Campaign, July 1861
    First Manassas, VA, July 21, 1861

Jackson's Valley Campaign, March–June 1862
    First Kernstown, VA, March 23, 1862
    First Winchester, VA, May 25, 1862
    Cross Keys, VA, June 8, 1862
    Port Republic, VA, June 9, 1862

Virginia Peninsula Campaign, March–July 1862
    Hampton Roads, VA, March 8–9, 1862
    Yorktown, VA, April 5, May 4, 1862
    Williamsburg, VA, May 5, 1862
    Drewry's Bluff, VA, May 15, 1862
    Seven Pines, VA, May 31, June 1, 1862
    Beaver Dam Creek, VA, June 26, 1862
    Gaines' Mill, VA, June 27, 1862
    Glendale, VA, June 30, 1862
    Malvern Hill, VA, July 1, 1862

Northern Virginia Campaign, August 1862
    Cedar Mountain, VA, August 9, 1862
    Manassas Station Operations, VA, August 25–27, 1862
    Second Manassas, VA, August 28–30, 1862
    Chantilly, VA, September 1, 1862

Maryland Campaign, September 1862
    Harpers Valley, WV, September 12–15, 1862
    South Mountain, MD, September 14, 1862
    Antietam, MD, September 16–18, 1862

Fredericksburg Campaign, November–December 1862
    First Fredericksburg, VA, December 11–15, 1862

Chancellorsville Campaign, April–May 1863
    Chancellorsville, VA, April 27, May 4, 1863
    Second Fredericksburg, VA, May 3, 1863
    Salem Church, VA, May3–4, 1863

Gettysburg Campaign, June–July 1863
  Brandy Station, VA, June 9, 1863
  Second Winchester, VA, June 13–15, 1863
  Gettysburg, PA, July 1–3, 1863

Grant's Overland Campaign, May–June 1864
  Wilderness, VA, May 5–7, 1864
  Spotsylvania Court House, VA, May 8–21, 1864
  North Anna, VA, May 23–26, 1864
  Totopotomy Creek/Bethesda Church, May 28–30, 1864
  Cold Harbor, VA, June 3–12, 1864
  Trevilian Station, VA, June 11–12, 1864

Richmond-Petersburg Campaign, June–December 1864
  Second Petersburg, VA, June 15–18, 1864
  Jerusalem Plank Road, VA, June 21–24, 1864
  Crater, VA, July 30, 1864
  Second Deep Bottom, VA, August 13–20, 1864
  Globe Tavern, VA, August 18–21, 1864
  Second Ream's Station, VA, August 25, 1864
  Chaffin's Farm/New Market Heights, VA, September 29–30, 1864
  Peebles' Farm, VA, September 30, October 2, 1864
  Boydton Plank Road, VA, October 27–28, 1864

Sheridan's Valley Campaign, August–October 1864
  Opequon, VA, September 19, 1864
  Fisher's Hill, VA, September 21–22, 1864
  Cedar Creek, VA, October 19, 1864

Operations against Fort Fisher and Wilmington, January–February 1865
  Fort Fisher, NC, January 13–15, 1865

Richmond-Petersburg Campaign continued, January–March 1865
  Hatcher's Run, VA, February 5–7, 1865
  Fort Stedman, VA, March 25, 1865

Appomattox Campaign, March–April 1865
  White Oak Road, VA, March 31, 1865
  Five Forks, VA, April 1, 1865
  Third Petersburg, VA, April 2, 1865
  Sayler's Creek, VA, April 6, 1865
  Appomattox Court House, VA, April 9, 1865

Lower Seaboard Theater and Gulf Approach

Operations in Charleston Harbor, April 1861
  First Fort Sumter, SC, April 12–14, 1861

Operations against Fort Pulaski, April 1862
  Fort Pulaski, GA, April 10–11, 1862

Expedition to, and Capture of, New Orleans, April–May 1862
  Forts Jackson & Phillip, LA, April 16–28, 1862
  New Orleans, LA, April 25, May 1, 1862

Operations against Charleston, June 1862
  Secessionville, SC, June 16, 1862

Operations against Baton Rouge, July–August 1862
  Baton Rouge, LA, August 5, 1862

Operations against the Defenses of Charleston, April–September 1863
    Fort Wagner, Morris Island, SC, July 18, September 7, 1863
    Second Charleston Harbor, SC, September 7–8, 1863
Siege of Port Hudson, May–July 1863
    Port Hudson, LA, May 21, July 9, 1863
Florida Expedition, February 20, 1864
    Olustee, FL, February 20, 1864

Main Western Theater (omitting Gulf Approach)

Offensive in Eastern Kentucky, January 1862
    Mill Springs, KY, January 19, 1862
Federal Penetration up the Cumberland and Tennessee Rivers, February–June 1862
    Fort Henry, TN, February 6, 1862
    Fort Donelson, TN, February 11–16, 1862
    Shiloh, TN, April 6–7, 1862
    First Corinth, MS, April 29, June 10, 1862
Joint Operations against New Madrid, Island No. 10, and Memphis, February–June 1862
    New Madrid / Island No. 10, MO, February 28, April 8, 1862
    Memphis, TN I, June 6, 1862
Confederate Heartland Offensive, June–October 1862
    Richmond, KY, August 29–30, 1862
    Munfordville, KY, September 14–17, 1862
    Perryville, KY, October 8, 1862
Iuka and Corinth Operations, September–October 1862
    Second Corinth, MS, October 3–4, 1862
Stones River Campaign, December 1862, January 1863
    Stones River, TN, December 31, 1862, January 2, 1863
Grant's Operations against Vicksburg, March–July 1863
    Jackson, MS, May 14, 1863
    Port Gibson, MS, May 1, 1863
    Raymond, MS, May 12, 1863
    Champion Hill, MS, May 16, 1863
    Big Black River Bridge, MS, May 17, 1863
    Vicksburg, MS, May 18, July 4, 1863
    Helena, AR, July 4, 1863
Chickamauga Campaign, August–September 1863
    Chickamauga, GA, September 18–20, 1863
Meridian and Yazoo River Expeditions, February 1864
    Okolona, MS, February 22, 1864
Forrest's Expedition into West Tennessee and Kentucky, March–April 1864
    Fort Pillow, TN, April 12, 1864
Chattanooga-Ringgold Campaign, November 1863
    Third Chattanooga, TN, November 23–25, 1863
    Ringgold Gap, GA, November 27, 1863
Longstreet's Knoxville Campaign, November–December 1863
    Fort Sanders, TN, November 29, 1863
Atlanta Campaign, May–September 1864
    Pine Mountain, GA, June 9, July 3, 1864
    Marietta, GA, June 9, July 3, 1864

Kennesaw Mountain, GA, June 27, July 1, 1864
Peachtree Creek, GA, July 20, 1864
Atlanta, GA, July 22, 1864
Ezra Church, GA, July 28, 1864
Jonesborough, GA, August 31–September 1, 1864

Forrest's Defense of Mississippi, June–August 1864
    Tupelo, MS, July 14–15, 1864
    Brice's Cross Roads, MS, June 10, 1864

Operations in Mobile Bay, August 1864
    Mobile Bay, AL, August 2–23, 1864

Franklin-Nashville Campaign, September–December 1864
    Allatoona, GA, October 5, 1864
    Johnsonville, TN, November 4–5, 1864
    Spring Hill, TN, November 29, 1864
    Franklin, TN, November 30, 1864
    Nashville, TN, December 15–16, 1864

Savannah Campaign, November–December 1864
    Griswoldville, GA, November 22, 1864
    Second Fort McAllister, GA, December 13, 1864

Carolinas Campaign, February–March 1865
    Bentonville, NC, March 19–21, 1865

Mobile Campaign, March–April 1865
    Spanish Fort, AL, March 27, April 8, 1865
    Fort Blakely, AL, April 2–9, 1865

Wilson's Raid in Alabama and Georgia, April 1865
    Selma, AL, April 2, 1865

Trans-Mississippi Theater

Operations to Control Missouri, June–October 1861
    Wilson's Creek, MO, August 10, 1861

Operations in in the Indian Territory, November–December 1861
    Chustenahlah, OK, December 26, 1861

Sibley's New Mexico Campaign, February–March 1862
    Valverde, NM, February 20–21, 1862
    Glorieta Pass, NM, March 26–28, 1862

Pea Ridge Campaign, March 1862
    Pea Ridge, AR, March 7–8, 1862

Prairie Grove Campaign, November 1862
    Prairie Grove, AR, December 7, 1862

Operations Against Galveston, December 1862–January 1863
    Second Galveston, TX, January 1, 1863

Operations to Control Indian Territory, June–September 1863
    Honey Springs, OK, July 17, 1863

Operations to Blockade the Texas Coast, September 1863
    Second Sabine Pass, TX, September 8, 1863

Advance on Little Rock, September–October 1863
    Bayou Fourche or Little Rock, AR, September 10, 1863

Red River Campaign, March–April 1864
  Fort De Russy, LA, March 14, 1864
  Mansfield, LA, April 8, 1864
  Pleasant Hill, LA, April 9, 1864
Camden Expedition, April 1864
  Prairie D'Ane, AR, April 9–13, 1864
Price's Missouri Expedition, September–October 1864
  Fort Davidson, MO, September 27, 1864
  Byram's Ford, MO, October 22, 1864
  Westport, MO, October 23, 1864
  Second Newtonia, MO, October 28, 1864
Sand Creek Campaign, November 1864
  Sand Creek, CO, November 29–30, 1864[2]

U.S. Military Academy Graduating Classes

Legend

Combat Experience: BW—Black Hawk War; FW—Florida War or Seminole War; MW—Mexican War; UE—Utah Expedition.

Armies: CSA—Confederate States Army; USA—United States Army; USV—United States Volunteers; MIL—Union State Militia; VOL—Volunteers.

Units: ART—Artillery; CAV—Cavalry and Dragoons; COE—Corps of Engineers; INF—Infantry; QTR—Quartermaster; MTR—Mounted Riflemen; ORD—Ordnance; PAY—Paymaster; SIG—Signal Corps; STF—Staff; TOP—Topographical Engineers; USMA—United States Military Academy.

Rank: B—Brevet; 1LT—First Lieutenant; 2LT—Second Lieutenant; CPT—Captain; MAJ—Major; LTC—Lieutenant Colonel; COL—Colonel; BG—Brigadier General; MG—Major General; LG—Lieutenant General; G—General GEN; Unknown—Not included in officer count.

Status: D—Died or Died of Wounds; K—Killed; R—Resigned Commission; RD—Dismissed.

Class of 1818

Confederate and Union Officers based on *Biographical Register of the Officers and Graduates of the U.S. Military Academy at West Point, NY*, *Rebels from West Point* and *West Point Officers in the Civil War*.[3]

Class Rank	Last Name	First Name	Military Service Before Civil War	Civil War Service	Comments	Cullum Number
1	Delafield	Richard	U.S. COE	BG USA	Superintendent USMA	180
2	Talcott	Andrew	U.S. COE	—	R 1836	181
3	Smith	S. Stanhope	U.S. ART	—	D 1828	182
4	Webster	Horace	U.S. INF	—	R 1825	183
5	Ringgold	Samuel	FW, MW	—	D 1846	184
6	Brown	Harvey	BW, FW, MW	BG USV		185
7	Chambers	Joseph N.	U.S. ART	—	R 1823	186
8	McKenzie	Samuel	MW	—	D 1847	187
9	Porter	Giles	FW	—	R 1861	188
10	Corprew	George W.	U.S. ART	—	R 1833	189
11	Jackson	John J.	U.S. INF	—	R 1823	190
12	Harding	Edward	U.S. ART	—	D 1855	191
13	Vinning	Benjamin C.	U.S. ORD	—	D 1822	192
14	Loring	Henry H.	U.S. INF	—	R 1835	193
15	Daingerfield	Joseph F.	U.S. ART	—	D 1840	194
16	Strong	Joseph	U.S. ART	—	R 1826	195

Appendices

Class Rank	Last Name	First Name	Military Service Before Civil War	Civil War Service	Comments	Cullum Number
17	Russell	John B.F.	U.S. INF	—	R 1837	196
18	Webb	George	U.S. ART	—	D 1832	197
19	Bache	Hartman	U.S. TOP	COL U.S. COE		198
20	Newton	William S.	U.S. ART	—	D 1837	199
21	Brooke	Leonard O.	U.S. INF	—	D 1821	200
22	Giles	Henry	U.S. INF	—	R 1820	201
23	Pratt	John T.	U.S. INF	—	R 1819	202

Summary

Class	Number of Graduates	Union Civil War Officers	Confederate Civil War Officers	Union Civil War Generals	Confederate Civil War Generals	Died or Resigned Before Civil War
1818	23	3	0	2	0	20

"Graduating Song," Class of 1855 (Library of Congress).

Class of 1819

Class Rank	Last Name	First Name	Military Service Before Civil War	Civil War Service	Comments	Cullum Number
1	Elliason	William A.	U.S. COE	—	D 1839	203
2	Underhill	Frederick A.	U.S. COE	—	R 1823	204
3	Ogden	Cornelius A.	U.S. COE	—	D 1856	205
4	Mansfield	Edward D.	U.S. COE	—	R 1819	206
5	Brewerton	Henry	U.S. COE	COL U.S. COE		207
6	Bowes	John R.	U.S. ORD	—	R 1832	208
7	Thompson	Henry A.	U.S. ART	—	R 1836	209
8	Kinsley	Zebina J.D.	U.S. ART	—	R 1836	210
9	Turnbull	William	MW	—	D 1857	211
10	Baker	Joshua	U.S. ART	—	R 1820	212
11	Dimick	Justin	FW, MW	COL U.S. ART		213
12	Whistler	George A.	U.S. ART	—	R 1833	214
13	Walker	Benjamin	U.S. P	—	D 1858	215
14	Tyler	Daniel	U.S. ART	BG USV		216
15	Hamtramck	John P.	MW	—	D 1858	217
16	Sickles	Ethan C.	U.S. ART	—	D 1823	218
17	Hepburne	James S.	U.S. ART	—	R 1824	219
18	L'Engle	John	U.S. QTR	—	R 1838	220
19	Edwards	John M.	U.S. ART	—	R 1824	221
20	Brockenbrough	Austen	U.S. ART	—	R 1833	222
21	Malcolm	William	U.S. INF	—	D 1823	223
22	McKenzie	John	U.S. INF	—	K 1828	224
23	Rupp	Joseph D.	U.S. ART	—	D 1821	225
24	Dumeste	Jacob A.	U.S. ART	—	D 1831	226
25	Blaney	James R.	U.S. ART	—	RD 1826	227
26	Conant	Roswell	U.S. Rifles	—	D 1821	228
27	Strong	Jasper	U.S. INF	—	R 1823	229
28	Gilbert	Henry	U.S. ART	—	D 1827	230
29	Swift	William H.	U.S. TOP	—	R 1849	231

Summary

Class	Number of Graduates	Union Civil War Officers	Confederate Civil War Officers	Union Civil War Generals	Confederate Civil War Generals	Died or Resigned Before Civil War
1819	29	3	0	1	0	26

Class of 1820

Class Rank	Last Name	First Name	Military Service Before Civil War	Civil War Service	Comments	Cullum Number
1	Tuttle	Stephen	U.S. COE	—	D 1835	232
2	Donelson	Andrew J.	U.S. COE	—	R 1832	233
3	Sudler	Thomas E.	U.S. ORD	—	R 1821	234
4	Bell	William H.	U.S. ORD	—	R 1861	235
5	De Hart	William C.	U.S. ART	—	D 1848	236
6	Barbarin	Francis N.	U.S. ART	—	R 1836	237
7	Brooke	Robert S.	U.S. ORD	—	R 1820	238
8	Chambers	James A.	FW	—	D 1838	239
9	Butler	Edward G.W.	MW	CSA—unknown	R 1848	240
10	Tompkins	Daniel D.	FW, MW	COL USA	QTR GEN	241
11	Winder	John H.	MW	BG CSA	JAILER	242
12	Buchanan	William P.	U.S. INF	—	D 1822	243
13	Dusenberry	Samuel B.	U.S. QTR	—	D 1855	244
14	Feltus	Henry J.	U.S. ART	—	R 1827	245
15	Cruger	Nicholas	U.S. INF	—	R 1827	246
16	Lowndes	Rawlins	U.S. INF	—	R 1830	247

Class Rank	Last Name	First Name	Military Service Before Civil War	Civil War Service	Comments	Cullum Number
17	Morris	Lewis N.	MW	—	K 1846	248
18	Barney	Joshua	U.S. ART	—	R 1832	249
19	Lindsay	George F.	U.S. NAVY	—	D 1857	250
20	Tufts	John M.	U.S. ART	—	R 1822	251
21	Gorham	Benjamin	U.S. ART	—	D 1821	252
22	McRee	Samuel	FW, MW	—	D 1849	253
23	Noel	Thomas	BW, FW	—	D 1848	254
24	McArthur	Thomas	U.S. INF	—	D 1833	255
25	Guerrant	Charles	U.S. INF	—	R 1830	256
26	Ramsay	George D.	MW	BG USA	CHIEF ORD	257
27	Hawkins	Edgar S.	MW	—	R 1861	258
28	Maitland	William S.	FW	—	D 1837	259
29	Skinner	Aaron B.	U.S. INF	—	R 1821	260
30	Morris	William W.	FW, MW	BG USA		261

Summary

Class	Number of Graduates	Union Civil War Officers	Confederate Civil War Officers	Union Civil War Generals	Confederate Civil War Generals	Died or Resigned Before Civil War
1820	30	3	1	2	1	25

Class of 1821

Class Rank	Last Name	First Name	Military Service Before Civil War	Civil War Service	Comments	Cullum Number
1	Courtenay	Edward H.	USMA	—	D 1853	262
2	Burdine	Clark	U.S. ART	—	R 1825	263
3	Prescott	Jonathan	U.S. ART	—	R 1833	264
4	Wells	William W.	U.S. ART	—	R 1831	265
5	Dimmock	Charles	U.S. ART	COL ORD CSA		266
6	Holland	John C.	U.S. ART	—	D 1825	267
7	Ross	Edward C.	U.S. ART	—	R 1839	268
8	Wheelwright	Washington	U.S. ART	—	R 1833	269
9	Wallace	David	U.S. ART	—	D 1859	270
10	Allston	Robert F.W.	U.S. ART	—	R 1822	271
11	Scott	John F.	U.S. ART	—	D 1837	272
12	Grier	James	U.S. ART	—	D 1828	273
13	Scott	John B.	FW, MW	—	D 1860	274
14	Pentland	Joseph	U.S. INF	—	R 1830	275
15	Morton	Alexander H.	U.S. INF	—	R 1823	276
16	Gaillard	Wm. W.	U.S. INF	—	D 1822	277
17	Capron	Seth M.	U.S. INF	—	R 1827	278
18	Vail	Jefferson	U.S. INF	—	D 1835	279
19	Henshaw	James	U.S. INF	—	R 1821	280
20	Wheeler	Otis	FW	—	R 1844	281
21	Bainbridge	Henry	FW	—	D 1857	282
22	Rodgers	Jason	BW	—	R 1836	283
23	Porter	David M.	U.S. INF	—	R 1832	284
24	d'Lagnel	Julius A.	FW	—	D 1840	285

Summary

Class	Number of Graduates	Union Civil War Officers	Confederate Civil War Officers	Union Civil War Generals	Confederate Civil War Generals	Died or Resigned Before Civil War
1821	24	0	1	0	0	23

Class of 1822

Class Rank	Last Name	First Name	Military Service Before Civil War	Civil War Service	Comments	Cullum Number
1	Dutton	George	U.S. COE	—	D 1857	286
2	Mansfield	Joseph K.F.	MW	MG USV	D 1862	287
3	Smith	Charles G.	U.S. ART	—	D 1827	288
4	Ingalls	Thomas R.	U.S. ART	—	R 1829	289
5	Bliss	Horace	U.S. ART	—	R 1836	290
6	Cook	William	U.S. ART	—	R 1832	291
7	Rose	William	U.S. ART	—	D 1825	292
8	Gwyn	Walter	U.S. ART	BG CSA		293
9	Graham	Campbell	FW	—	R 1861	294
10	Wheelock	Thompson B.	FW	—	D 1836	295
11	Cooke	James H.	U.S. ART	—	D 1833	296
12	Young	William C.	U.S. ART	—	R 1836	297
13	Canfield	Augustus	U.S. TOP	—	D 1854	298
14	Vinton	David H.	FW, MW	COL USV		299
15	Schuler	John J.	U.S. ART	—	R 1828	300
16	Pickell	Kohn	BW, FW	COL NY VOL[4]		301
17	Trimble	Isaac R.	U.S. ART	MG CSA		302
18	Gird	Henry H.	U.S. ART	—	D 1845	303
19	Wright	Benjamin H.	U.S. INF	—	R 1823	304
20	Boyce	William M.	U.S. INF	—	R 1836	305
21	Denny	St. Clair	U.S. PAY	—	D 1858	306
22	Lacey	Westwood	U.S. INF	—	D 1829	307
23	Trenor	Eustace	U.S. CAV	—	D 1847	308
24	Wright	George	FW, MW	B BG USA		309
25	Hunter	David	MW	MG USV		310
26	McCall	George A.	MW	BG USV		311
27	Lincoln	Albert	U.S. INF	—	D 1822	312
28	Lee	Francis	MW	—	D 1859	313
29	Stephenson	James R.	FW	—	D 1841	314
30	Hopson	John D.	U.S. INF	—	D 1829	315
31	Morris	Thompson	MW	—	R 1861	316
32	Wilcox	John R.	U.S. INF	—	R 1834	317
33	Johnston	Thomas	U.S. INF	—	R 1835	318
34	Folger	George W.	U.S. INF	—	R 1826	319
35	McNamara	Thomas	U.S. INF	—	R 1830	320
36	Wright	Aaron M.	U.S. INF	—	R 1826	321
37	Abercrombie	John J.	BW, FW, MW	BG USV		322
38	Wragg	Samuel	U.S. INF	—	D 1828	323
39	Moniac	David	FW	—	K 1836	324
40	Clark	Henry	U.S. INF	—	D 1830	325

Summary

Class	Number of Graduates	Union Civil War Officers	Confederate Civil War Officers	Union Civil War Generals	Confederate Civil War Generals	Died or Resigned Before Civil War
1822	40	7	2	5	2	31

Class of 1823

Class Rank	Last Name	First Name	Military Service Before Civil War	Civil War Service	Comments	Cullum Number
1	Modecai	Alfred	MW	—	R 1861	326
2	Greene	George S.	U.S. ART	BG USV		327
3	Richards	George S.	U.S. ART	—	D 1825	328
4	Holmes	Reuben	U.S. INF	—	D 1833	329
5	Southerland	Samuel U.	U.S. ART	—	D 1836	330
6	Webster	Lucien B.	MW	—	D 1853	331

Class Rank	Last Name	First Name	Military Service Before Civil War	Civil War Service	Comments	Cullum Number
7	Guion	Frederick L.	U.S. ART	—	D 1824	332
8	Nauman	George	MW	LTC USA		333
9	Beckley	Alfred	U.S. ART	BG CSA VA VOL[5]	R 1836	334
10	Searle	Frederic	FW	—	D 1853	335
11	De Treville	Richard	U.S. ART	—	R 1825	336
12	Kinnard	Andrew	U.S. ART	—	R 1830	337
13	Waters	George W.	U.S. INF	—	R 1837	338
14	Farley	John	U.S. ART	—	R 1836	339
15	Nute	Levi M.	U.S. INF	—	R 1838	340
16	Batman	Mark W.	U.S. INF	—	D 1837	341
17	Thomas	Lorenzo	FW, MW	BG USA		342
18	Kingsbury	Julius J.B.	BW, MW	—	R 1853	343
19	Andrews	George	FW	LTC USA		344
20	Collins	Richard D.C.	U.S. INF	—	R 1841	345
21	Reynolds	William	U.S. INF	—	R 1830	346
22	Smith	Joseph R.	FW, MW	—	R 1861	347
23	Day	Hannibal	BW, FW	COL USA		348
24	Stewart	Henry R.	U.S. INF	—	R 1828	349
25	Phillips	Elias	U.S. INF	—	R 1836	350
26	Phillips	Joseph A.	U.S. INF	—	R 1840	351
27	Richardson	Asa	U.S. INF	—	D 1835	352
28	Newell	John E.	U.S. INF	—	D 1835	353
29	Nicholls	John	U.S. INF	—	R 1835	354
30	Crossman	George H.	BW, MW	COL USA		355
31	Holt	Charles	U.S. INF	—	D 1824	356
32	Cotton	John W.	U.S. INF	—	R 1845	357
33	Alexander	Edmund B.	MW	COL USA		358
34	Miller	Albert S.	FW	—	D 1852	359
35	Birdsall	Egbert B.	U.S. INF	—	D 1845	360

Summary

Class	Number of Graduates	Union Civil War Officers	Confederate Civil War Officers	Union Civil War Generals	Confederate Civil War Generals	Died or Resigned Before Civil War
1823	35	7	1	2	1	27

Class of 1824

Class Rank	Last Name	First Name	Military Service Before Civil War	Civil War Service	Comments	Cullum Number
1	Mahan	Dennis H.	U.S. COE	—	USMA	361
2	Smith	John W.A.	U.S. ART	—	RD 1828	362
3	Parrott	Robert P.	U.S. ORD	—	R 1836	363
4	Hazzard	R. Edward	U.S. ART	—	D 1831	364
5	Findlay	John King	U.S. ART	—	R 1828	365
6	Bennett	Napoleon B.	BW	—	D 1832	366
7	Dillahunty	John D.	U.S. ART	—	R 1832	367
8	Jones	Francis L.	U.S. ART	—	R 1842	368
9	Long	George W.	U.S. ART	—	R 1835	369
10	Fessenden	John M.	U.S. ART	—	R 1831	370
11	Bainbridge	William P.	FW, MW	—	D 1850	371
12	Picton	John M.W.	U.S. ART	—	R 1832	372
13	Wilson	Horatio A.	U.S. ART	—	R 1835	373
14	Tillinghast	Nicholas	BW	—	R 1836	374
15	Williams	William G.	MW	—	D 1846	375
16	Drane	Anthony	U.S. INF	—	RD 1846	376
17	Jamison	Louis T.	U.S. INF	—	RD 1838	377

Class Rank	Last Name	First Name	Military Service Before Civil War	Civil War Service	Comments	Cullum Number
18	Bickley	William	U.S. INF	—	R 1825	378
19	Low	Ephraim W.	U.S. INF	—	D 1825	379
20	Cadle	Joseph	U.S. INF	—	RD 1830	380
21	Johnston	Alexander	BW	—	D 1845	381
22	Harris	William L.	BW	—	RD 1836	382
23	Bloodgood	William	U.S. INF	—	R 1836	383
24	Eaton	William W.	U.S. INF	—	D 1828	384
25	Paige	Timothy	FW	—	R 1836	385
26	Newcomb	Francis D.	U.S. INF	—	R 1836	386
27	Miles	Dixon S.	MW	COL USA	D 1862	387
28	Backus	Electus	MW	COL USA	D 1862	388
29	Catlin	Julius	U.S. INF	—	R 1836	389
30	Van Swearingen	Joseph	FW	—	K 1837	390
31	Thompson	W. Beverhout	U.S. INF	—	R 1830	391

Summary

Class	Number of Graduates	Union Civil War Officers	Confederate Civil War Officers	Union Civil War Generals	Confederate Civil War Generals	Died or Resigned Before Civil War
1824	31	2	0	0	0	29

Class of 1825

Class Rank	Last Name	First Name	Military Service Before Civil War	Civil War Service	Comments	Cullum Number
1	Bache	Alexander D.	USMA	—	R 1829	392
2	McMartin	Peter	U.S. COE	—	R 1826	393
3	Bowman	Alexander H.	U.S. COE	LTC U.S. COE	D 1865	394
4	Brown	Thompson S.	U.S. COE	—	R 1836	395
5	Donelson	Daniel	U.S. ART	MG CSA	R 1826	396
6	Ryan	Stephen V.R.	U.S. ART	—	R 1833	397
7	Smead	Raphael C.	MW	—	D 1848	398
8	Huger	Benjamin	MW	MG CSA	R 1861	399
9	Taylor	Francis	FW, MW	—	D 1858	400
10	Brisbane	Abbott H.	FW	—	R 1828	401
11	Hopkins	William Fenn	USMA	—	R 1836	402
12	Thornton	William A.	BW	COL U.S. ORD	D 1866	403
13	Harris	Joseph W.	U.S. ART	—	D 1837	404
14	Williams	Mathew J.	U.S. ART	—	R 1837	405
15	Anderson	Robert	FW, MW	B MG USA	R 1863	406
16	Mackay	Alexander D.	USMA	—	D 1836	407
17	Irwin	James R.	FW, MW	—	D 1848	408
18	Smith	Horace	U.S. ART	—	D 1828	409
19	Smith	Charles F.	MW, UE	MG USV	D 1862	410
20	Seawell	Washington	FW, MW	COL USA	R 1862	411
21	Carter	Lawrence F.	U.S. INF	—	D 1837	412
22	Noncom	Frederick	U.S. ART	—	R 1832	413
23	Street	Nathaniel H.	U.S. INF	CSA—unknown	R 1836	414
24	Worth	Joseph S.	FW	—	D 1846	415
25	Harris	N. Sayre	U.S. INF	—	R 1835	416
26	Cross	Osborne	MW	LTC USA QTM	D 1865	417
27	Bonnell	Joseph	U.S. INF	—	D 1840	418
28	Montgomery	William R.	MW	BG USV	R 1864	419
29	Linden	H. St. James	U.S. INF	—	D 1836	420
30	Anderson	James J.	U.S. INF	—	R 1830	421
31	Burnham	James D.	U.S. ART	—	D 1828	422
32	Dorr	Gustavus	BW, FW	—	RD 1843	423

Appendices

Class Rank	Last Name	First Name	Military Service Before Civil War	Civil War Service	Comments	Cullum Number
33	Thomas	Frederick	U.S. INF	—	D 1831	424
34	Garey	George W.	BW	—	D 1834	425
35	Engle	James	U.S. INF	—	R 1834	426
36	Clay	Joseph	U.S. INF	—	D 1832	427
37	Allston	Samuel R.	U.S. INF	—	R 1836	428

Summary

Class	Number of Graduates	Union Civil War Officers	Confederate Civil War Officers	Union Civil War Generals	Confederate Civil War Generals	Died or Resigned Before Civil War
1825	37	7	2	3	2	27

Class of 1826

Class Rank	Last Name	First Name	Military Service Before Civil War	Civil War Service	Comments	Cullum Number
1	Bartlett	William H.C.	USMA	—	Professor	429
2	Twiss	Thomas S.	USMA	—	R 1829	430
3	Bryant	William	USMA	—	R 1835	431
4	Cram	Thomas Jefferson	USMA	COL U.S. STF		432
5	Ridgley	Charles G.	USMA	—	R 1827	433
6	McClellan	John	MW	—	D 1854	434
7	Henderson	Bennett H.	U.S. ART	—	R 1832	435
8	Johnston	Albert S.	BW, MW, UE	GEN CSA		436
9	White	Edward B.	BW	LTC CSA		437
10	Dancy	Francis L.	FW	CSA—unknown	R 1836	438
11	Searight	Joseph D.	U.S. INF	—	R 1845	439
12	Townsend	Joel C.	U.S. ART	—	D 1826	440
13	Herring	Daniel S.	U.S. ART	—	D 1836	441
14	Woodbridge	George	U.S. ART	—	R 1839	442
15	Clark	Michael M.	U.S. ART	—	D 1861	443
16	Ewing	Maskell C.	U.S. ART	—	R 1836	444
17	Heintzelman	Samuel P.	FW, MW	MG USV		445
18	Brown	Theophilus B.	U.S. ART	—	D 1834	446
19	Tufts	Danforth H.	FW	—	D 1840	447
20	Pleasonton	Augustus J.	U.S. ART	BG PA MIL[6]		448
21	Parks	Martin P.	U.S. ART	—	USMA D 1853	449
22	Grayson	John B.	MW	BG CSA		450
23	Williamson	John	U.S. ART	—	D 1849	451
24	Griffin	Henry J.	U.S. INF	—	D 1828	452
25	Archer	John	U.S. INF	CPT CSA	R 1834	453
26	Ridgely	Samuel H.	U.S. INF	—	D 1827	454
27	Berrien	John M.	U.S. INF	—	R 1836	455
28	Babbitt	Edwin B.	FW, MW	LTC U.S. QTR		456
29	Colcock	Richard W.	U.S. INF	—	R 1836	457
30	Minor	Charles L.C.	U.S. INF	—	D 1833	458
31	Sims	William H.	U.S. INF	—	R 1827	459
32	Brooke	Francis J.	BW, FW	—	K 1837	460
33	Macrae	Nathaniel C.	U.S. INF	MAJ USV	Recruiting	461
34	Allen	James G.	U.S. INF	—	R 1828	462
35	Baldwin	Alexander G.	U.S. INF	—	D 1835	463
36	Eaton	Amos B.	MW	BG U.S. STF		464
37	Merrill	Moses E.	MW	—	K 1847	465
38	Colerick	Charles	U.S. INF	—	D 1828	466
39	Casey	Silas	FW, MW	MG USV		467
40	Pearce	Thomas H.	U.S. INF	—	R 1839	468
41	Smith	E. Kirby	MW	—	D 1847	469

Summary

Class	Number of Graduates	Union Civil War Officers	Confederate Civil War Officers	Union Civil War Generals	Confederate Civil War Generals	Died or Resigned Before Civil War
1826	41	7	4	4	2	29

Class of 1827

Class Rank	Last Name	First Name	Military Service Before Civil War	Civil War Service	Comments	Cullum Number
1	Sibley	Ebenezer S.	U.S. ORD	LTC U.S. STF		470
2	Childe	John	U.S. ART	—	R 1835	471
3	Maynadier	William	BW	COL U.S. ORD		472
4	Bradford	James A.J.	U.S. ORD	COL CSA		473
5	Bibb	Lucien J.	U.S. ART		D 1831	474
6	Buford	Napoleon B.	U.S. ART	BG USV		475
7	Schenk	Edwin	U.S. ART	—	R 1828	476
8	Polk	Leonidas	U.S. ART	LG CSA	R 1827	477
9	Sterrett	Essex	U.S. ART	—	R 1828	478
10	Fetterman	George	U.S. ART	—	R 1836	479
11	Asquith	William E.	MW	—	RD 1838	480
12	Worthington	Thomas	MW	COL OH VOL[7]		481
13	Rains	Gabriel J.	FW	BG CSA		482
14	Furman	John G.	U.S. INF	—	D 1830	483
15	Magruder	William B.	U.S. INF	—		484
16	Stockton	Thomas B.W.	U.S. INF	COL MI VOL[8]		485
17	Hooe	Alexander S.	MW	—	D 1847	486
18	Flanagan	William	U.S. INF	—	R 1828	487
19	Prentiss	George H.	U.S. INF	—	R 1828	488
20	Perkins	David	U.S. CAV	—	R 1839	489
21	Hitchcock	Samuel	U.S. INF	—	R 1827	490
22	Center	Alexander J.	BW	—	R 1836	491
23	Cooke	Phillip St. George	BW, MW, UE	BG USA		492
24	Trask	Thomas S.	U.S. INF	—	D 1828	493
25	Hetzel	Abner R.	U.S. INF	—	D 1847	494
26	La Motte	Joseph H.	FW, MW	—	R 1856	495
27	Lacey	Edgar M.	U.S. INF	—	D 1839	496
28	Gale	Levin	BW	—	D 1832	497
29	Simonton	Isaac P.	FW	—	D 1842	498
30	Van Horne	Jefferson	MW	—	D 1857	499
31	Hood	Washington	U.S. TOP	—	D 1840	500
32	Lynde	Isaac	MW, UE	MAJ U.S. INF		501
33	Eaton	Nathaniel J.	BW	—	RD 1837	502
34	Westmore	Stephen M.	FW	—	R 1846	503
35	Greenough	Jonathan K.	U.S. INF	—	R 1836	504
36	Stilwell	William S.	U.S. INF	—	D 1837	505
37	Van Buren	Abraham	FW, MW	—	R 1854	506
38	Clarke	Nelson N.	U.S. INF	—	D 1832	507

Summary

Class	Number of Graduates	Union Civil War Officers	Confederate Civil War Officers	Union Civil War Generals	Confederate Civil War Generals	Died or Resigned Before Civil War
1827	38	7	3	2	2	28

Class of 1828

Class Rank	Last Name	First Name	Military Service Before Civil War	Civil War Service	Comments	Cullum Number
1	Church	Albert E.	USMA	—	Professor	508
2	Tilghman	Richard G.	U.S. ART	—	R 1836	509
3	Mercer	Hugh W.	U.S. ART	BG CSA		510
4	Temple	Robert E.	MW	—	D 1854	511
5	Collins	Charles O.	U.S. QTR	—	D 1846	512
6	Austin	Ivers J.	U.S. ART	—	R 1828	513
7	French	Edmund	U.S. ART	—	R 1836	514
8	Locke	Joseph L.	U.S. ART	MAJ CSA	R 1836	515
9	Chase	George E.	U.S. ART	—	R 1833	516
10	Lane	John F.	U.S. ART	—	D 1836	517
11	Palmer	William	U.S. ART	—	D 1835	518
12	Adams	Thomas B.	FW	—	D 1837	519
13	Clary	Robert E.	BW, FW	LTC U.S. STF		520
14	Sevier	Robert	BW	—	R 1837	521
15	Mather	William W.	U.S. INF	—	R 1836	522
16	Mitchell	Enos G.	BW, FW	—	D 1839	523
17	Izard	James F.	BW, FW	—	D 1836	524
18	Cutts	Thomas	U.S. INF	—	D 1838	525
19	Baker	William H.	U.S. INF	—	D 1835	526
20	Thompson	James L.	U.S. INF	—	R 1846	527
21	Rousseau	Gustave S.	MW	—		528
22	Kinsman	Benjamin W.	U.S. INF	—	D 1832	529
23	Davis	Jefferson	MW	President CSA	R 1835	530
24	Morrison	William L.E.	U.S. INF	—	R 1830	531
25	Cobb	Samuel K.	U.S. INF	—	D 1834	532
26	Torrence	Samuel	BW	—	D 1832	533
27	Foster	Amos	U.S. INF	—	K 1832	534
28	Drayton	Thomas F.	U.S. INF	BG CSA	R 1836	535
29	Brockway	Thomas C.	U.S. INF	—	D 1831	536
30	Gardenier	John R.B.	FW, MW	—	D 1850	537
31	Wright	Crafts J.	U.S. INF	COL MO VOL COL OH VOL	R 1828	538
32	Penrose	James W.	FW, MW	—	D 1849	539
33	Van Wyck	Philip R.	—	—	D 1832[9]	540

Summary

Class	Number of Graduates	Union Civil War Officers	Confederate Civil War Officers	Union Civil War Generals	Confederate Civil War Generals	Died or Resigned Before Civil War
1828	33	2	4	0	2	27

Class of 1829

Class Rank	Last Name	First Name	Military Service Before Civil War	Civil War Service	Comments	Cullum Number
1	Mason	Charles	U.S. COE	—	R 1831	541
2	Lee	Robert E.	MW	G CSA		542
3	Harford	William H.	U.S. INF	—	R 1833	543
4	Izard	J. Allen Smith	U.S. ART	—	R 1837	544
5	Barnes	James	BW	BG USV		545
6	Buckingham	Catharinus P.	U.S. ART	BG USV		546
7	Smith	Joseph Brice	U.S. ART	CPT USV		547
8	Mackay	John	U.S. COE	—	D 1848	548
9	Hackley	Charles W.	U.S. ART	—	R 1833	549
10	Knowlton	Miner	USMA	—	Professor	550
11	Casey	John C.	FW	—	D 1856	551
12	McKee	William R.	MW	—	K 1847	552

U.S. Military Academy Graduating Classes

Class Rank	Last Name	First Name	Military Service Before Civil War	Civil War Service	Comments	Cullum Number
13	Johnston	Joseph E.	BW, FW, MW	G CSA		553
14	Kennedy	John F.	U.S. ART	—	D 1837	554
15	Mitchel	O. McKnight	U.S. ART	MG USV		555
16	Brown	Gustavus	U.S. ART	—	D 1832	556
17	Burbank	Sidney	FW	COL U.S. INF		557
18	Hoffman	William	BW, MW	B BG USA		558
19	Petigru	Charles	U.S. ART	—	D 1835	559
20	Hunt	Franklin E.	BW, FW, UE	MAJ U.S. STF		560
21	Lupton	Lancaster P.	U.S. CAV	—	R 1836	561
22	Eastman	Seth	U.S. INF	LTC U.S. INF		562
23	Swords	Thomas	MW	COL U.S. STF		563
24	Cady	Albemarle	FW, MW	COL U.S. INF		564
25	Davies	Thomas A.	U.S. INF	BG USV		565
26	Blanchard	Albert G.	MW	BG CSA		566
27	Howe	Chileab S.	U.S. INF	—	R 1838	567
28	Sibley	Caleb C.	MW	COL U.S. INF		568
29	Wright	James H.	U.S. INF	—	D 1830	569
30	Sterling	George A.	U.S. INF	—	R 1831	570
31	Pawling	Joseph H.	U.S. INF	—	R 1830	571
32	Snyder	Antes	U.S. INF	—	R 1830	572
33	Warfield	William H.	U.S. INF	—	R 1832	573
34	Clark	James	U.S. INF	—	R 1830	574
35	Allen	James	MW	—	D 1846	575
36	Freeman	Jonathan	U.S. INF	—	R 1837	576
37	Davis	John P.	U.S. INF	—	RD 1845	577
38	Bowdoin	George R.J.	U.S. INF	—	R 1832	578
39	Long	Edwin R.	BW, FW	—	D 1846	579
40	Brice	W. Benjamin	MW	B BG USA		580
41	Burnet	Robert W.	U.S. INF	—	R 1833	581
42	Moore	James S.	U.S. INF	—	R 1829	582
43	May	Charles O.	U.S. INF	—	D 1830	583
44	Holmes	Theophilus H.	FW, MW	LG CSA		584
45	Williams	Edward R.	U.S. INF	—	R 1835	585
46	Screven	Richard B.	FW, MW	—	D 1851	586

Summary

Class	Number of Graduates	Union Civil War Officers	Confederate Civil War Officers	Union Civil War Generals	Confederate Civil War Generals	Died or Resigned Before Civil War
1829	46	13	4	6	4	29

Class of 1830

Class Rank	Last Name	First Name	Military Service Before Civil War	Civil War Service	Comments	Cullum Number
1	Swift	Alexander J.	U.S. COE	—	D 1847	587
2	Basinger	William E.	FW	—	D 1835	588
3	Chandler	Walter S.	U.S. ART	—	D 1835	589
4	Vinton	Francis	U.S. ART	—	R 1836	590
5	Pendleton	William N.	U.S. ART	BG CSA		591
6	Lawson	George W.	U.S. ART	—	R 1831	592
7	Lee	Thomas J.	U.S. TOP	—	R 1855	593
8	Barry	John W.	U.S. ART	—	R 1836	594
9	Linnard	Thomas B.	FW, MW	—	D 1851	595
10	Poole	Benjamin	U.S. ART	—	D 1839	596
11	Drum	Simon H.	BW, FW, MW	—	K 1847	597
12	Prentiss	James H.	BW, MW	—	D 1848	598
13	Whitely	Robert H.K.	FW	LTC U.S. ORD		599

Class Rank	Last Name	First Name	Military Service Before Civil War	Civil War Service	Comments	Cullum Number
14	Rose	Edwin	U.S. ART	COL NY VOL[10]		600
15	Magruder	John B.	FW, MW	MG CSA		601
16	Bledsoe	Albert T.	U.S. INF	COL CSA		602
17	Stoddard	John S.	U.S. NAVY	—	R 1832	603
18	Murray	John W.	U.S. INF	—	K 1831	604
19	West	James	U.S. INF	—	D 1834	605
20	Hill	James M.	FW	—	D 1849	606
21	Kinney	Samuel	U.S. INF	—	D 1835	607
22	Leavenworth	Jesse H.	U.S. INF	COL CO VOL[11]		608
23	Clark	Meriwether L.	BW, MW	BG CSA		609
24	Collinsworth	John T.	U.S. INF	—	D 1837	610
25	Beal	Lloyd J.	FW, MW	COL CSA		611
26	Heyward	William C.	U.S. INF	COL CSA	R 1832	612
27	Ritner	Joseph	U.S. INF	—	D 1834	613
28	Burgwin	John H.K.	MW	—	D 1847	614
29	Alexander	Thomas L.	FW, MW	LTC U.S. INF		615
30	Taylor	James H.	U.S. INF	—	D 1835	616
31	Buchanan	Robert C.	BW, FW, MW	B BG USV		617
32	Daviess	Camillus C.	U.S. INF	—	R 1838	618
33	Vanderveer	John S.	BW	—	R 1840	619
34	Royster	Thomas J.	BW	—	D 1832	620
35	Wilson	George	U.S. INF	—	R 1837	621
36	Patten	George W.	FW, MW	LTC U.S. INF		622
37	Eustis	William	MW	—	R 1849	623
38	Manning	David A.	U.S. INF	—	D 1835	624
39	McClure	George W.	BW	—	D 1834	625
40	Ross	Richard H.	FW, MW	—	D 1851	626
41	Clendenin	John M.	FW	—	D 1842	627
42	Legate	Stephen B.	FW, MW	—	R 1835	628

Summary

Class	Number of Graduates	Union Civil War Officers	Confederate Civil War Officers	Union Civil War Generals	Confederate Civil War Generals	Died or Resigned Before Civil War
1830	42	6	6	1	3	30

Class of 1831

Class Rank	Last Name	First Name	Military Service Before Civil War	Civil War Service	Comments	Cullum Number
1	Park	Rosewell	U.S. COE	—	R 1836	629
2	Clay	Henry	MW	—	R 1831	630
3	Allen	James	U.S. ART	—	R 1834	631
4	Prentiss	Henry E.	U.S. ART	—	R 1835	632
5	Lea	Albert Miller	U.S. INF	COL CSA	R 1836	633
6	Peyton	Richard H.	FW	—	D 1839	634
7	Norton	William A.	U.S. ART	—	R 1833	635
8	Turner	George W.	U.S. ART	—	R 1836	636
9	Ridgely	Samuel C.	MW	—	D 1859	637
10	Miller	Samuel H.	U.S. ART	—	D 1834	638
11	Talcott	George H.	BW, MW	—	D 1854	639
12	Ammen	Jacob	U.S. ART	BG USV		640
13	Humphreys	Andrew A.	U.S. ART	MG USV		641
14	Emory	William H.	MW, UE	B MG USV		642
15	Chapman	William	MW, FW, UE	B COL U.S. INF		643
16	Larnard	Charles H.	MW	—	D 1854	644
17	Eastman	Elbridge G.	U.S. INF	—	D 1834	645
18	Scott	Moses	U.S. INF	—	D 1858	646

Class Rank	Last Name	First Name	Military Service Before Civil War	Civil War Service	Comments	Cullum Number
19	McKean	Thomas J.	MW	BG USV		647
20	Van Rensselaer	Henry	U.S. INF	COL U.S. STF		648
21	Ogden	Edmund A.	BW, FW	—	D 1855	649
22	Northrop	Lucius B.	U.S. CAV	BG CSA		650
23	Covington	Erasmus F.	BW	—	R 1830	651
24	Van Cleve	Horatio P.	U.S. INF	BG USV		652
25	Alden	Bradford R.	USMA, U.S. INF	—	R 1853	653
26	Stockton	Thomas	BW	—	R 1836	654
27	Curtis	Samuel R.	MW	MG USV		655
28	Williams	James S.	BW	CSA—unknown	R 1837	656
29	Wood	Ingham	U.S. INF	—	R 1836	657
30	Wilkinson	Frederick	U.S. INF	—	R 1835	658
31	Harvey	John G.	U.S. INF	—	R 1833	659
32	Whittlesey	Charles	U.S. INF	COL OH VOL		660
33	Conrad	John	BW, FW	—	D 1838	661

Summary

Class	Number of Graduates	Union Civil War Officers	Confederate Civil War Officers	Union Civil War Generals	Confederate Civil War Generals	Died or Resigned Before Civil War
1831	33	9	2	6	1	21

Class of 1832

Class Rank	Last Name	First Name	Military Service Before Civil War	Civil War Service	Comments	Cullum Number
1	Ward	George W.	BW	—	R 1836	662
2	Smith	Robert Percy	U.S. ART	—	R 1836	663
3	Ewell	Benjamin S.	U.S. ART	COL CSA	R 1836	664
4	Cass	George W.	U.S. INF	—	R 1836	665
5	Bailey	Jacob W.	USMA	—	D 1857	666
6	Cocke	Philip St. George	U.S. ART	BG CSA		667
7	Sill	Henry G.	BW	—	D 1835	668
8	Vance	Joseph C.	BW	—	K 1840	669
9	Watson	George	BW, FW	—	R 1838	670
10	Keyes	Erasmus	U.S. ART	MG USV		671
11	McDufee	Franklin	BW	—	D 1832	672
12	Howell	Lewis	BW	—	R 1833	673
13	Wall	William	BW, FW, MW	—	D 1847	674
14	Macomb	John N.	BW	LTC U.S. COE		675
15	Deas	Edward	BW, MW	—	D 1849	676
16	Brackett	John E.	MW	—	R 1833	677
17	Burnett	Ward B.	BW, MW	—	R 1836	678
18	Simpson	James H.	FW	LTC U.S. COE		679
19	Bush	Alfred	U.S. ART	—	R 1836	680
20	Fain	Richard G.	BW	COL CSA		681
21	Yoakum	Henderson K.	U.S. ART	—	R 1833	682
22	Tilghman	Tench	BW	—	R 1833	683
23	Pettes	William H.	U.S. ART	COL NY VOL[12]		684
24	Wilkinson	Theophilus F.J.	U.S. ART	—	R 1835	685
25	Sitgreaves	Lorenzo	BW, MW	LTC U.S. COE		686
26	Crittenden	George B.	BW, MW	MG CSA		687
27	Brown	Jacob	BW	—	R 1836	688
28	Whiting	Daniel P.	FW, MW	LTC U.S. INF		689
29	Marcy	Randolph B.	BW, MW, UE	BG USV		690

Class Rank	Last Name	First Name	Military Service Before Civil War	Civil War Service	Comments	Cullum Number
30	Hardin	James P.	U.S. INF	—	R 1832	691
31	Hill	Thomas M.	U.S. INF	—	D 1838	692
32	Dix	Roger S.	BW, MW	—	D 1849	693
33	Archer	Robert H.	U.S. ART	CPT CSA	R 1837	694
34	Bomford	James V.	BW, FW, MW	COL U.S. INF		695
35	Gatlin	Richard C.	BW, MW, UE	BG CSA		696
36	Storer	William H.	FW	—	R 1839	697
37	Griffin	George H.	BW, FW	—	D 1839	698
38	Beach	John	U.S. INF	—	R 1838	699
39	Kello	William O.	FW	—	D 1848	700
40	Swartwout	Henry	BW, FW	—	D 1852	701
41	Kingsbury	Gaines P.	U.S. CAV	—	R 1836	702
42	Marshall	Humphrey	MW	BG CSA		703
43	Bowman	James M.	BW	—	D 1839	704
44	Ury	Asbury	U.S. CAV	—	D 1838	705
45	Edwards	Albert G.	BW	—	R 1835	706

Summary

Class	Number of Graduates	Union Civil War Officers	Confederate Civil War Officers	Union Civil War Generals	Confederate Civil War Generals	Died or Resigned Before Civil War
1832	45	8	7	2	4	30

Class of 1833

Class Rank	Last Name	First Name	Military Service Before Civil War	Civil War Service	Comments	Cullum Number
1	Smith	Frederick A.	U.S. COE	—	D 1852	707
2	Barnard	John G.	MW	B MG USV		708
3	Cullum	George W.	U.S. COE	BG USV		709
4	King	Rufus	U.S. COE	BG USV		710
5	Smith	Francis H.	U.S. ART	COL CSA		711
6	Sidell	William H.	U.S. ART	LTC U.S. INF		712
7	Harris	David B.	U.S. ART	COL CSA		713
8	Lee	Roswell W.	FW	—	RD 1838	714
9	Bliss	William W.S.	FW, MW	—	D 1853	715
10	Capron	Eratus A.	FW, MW	—	D 1847	716
11	Garrett	Isaiah	U.S. ART	—	R 1833	717
12	Miller	John H.	FW, MW	—	D 1850	718
13	Hale	David E.	FW	—	D 1839	719
14	Mudge	Robert R.	FW	—	K 1835	720
15	Thomas	John A.	USMA	—	R 1846	721
16	Davis	J. Lucius	U.S. ART	COL CSA		722
17	Schriver	Edmund	FW	B BG USA	IN G USA	723
18	Waller	Henry	U.S. ART	—	R 1833	724
19	Allen	John H.	FW	—	R 1836	725
20	Shiras	Alexander E.	FW	B BG USA		726
21	DuPont	Henry	U.S. ART	—	R 1834	727
22	Alvord	Benjamin	FW, MW	BG USV		728
23	Dimon	George D.	U.S. INF	—	D 1834	729
24	Burnett	Isaac R.D.	U.S. INF	—	D 1846	730
25	Blake	Jacob E.	FW, MW	—	K 1846	731
26	Hooper	John L.	FW	—	R 1840	732
27	Riggs	Joel	U.S. INF	—	R 1833	733
28	McCrabb	John W.	FW	—	D 1839	734
29	Wessells	Henry W.	FW, MW	BG USV		735
30	Center	John P.	FW	—	K 1837	736
31	Pegram	George H.	FW	—	D 1854	737

Class Rank	Last Name	First Name	Military Service Before Civil War	Civil War Service	Comments	Cullum Number
32	Myers	Abraham C.	FW, MW	COL CSA		738
33	Ringgold	George H.	MW	LTC U.S. STF		739
34	Ruggles	Daniel	MW, UE	BG CSA		740
35	Anderson	James W.	FW, MW	—	D 1847	741
36	McClure	James	U.S. INF	—	D 1838	742
37	Reid	J. Chester	U.S. INF	—	D 1845	743
38	Johns	Thomas	U.S. INF	COL MD VOL[13]	R 1841	744
39	Du Bose	Benjamin	U.S. INF	CSA—unknown	RD 1833	745
40	Harrison	Joseph P.	FW	—	R 1839	746
41	Scott	Henry L.	FW, MW	COL U.S. STF		747
42	Seaton	Augustine F.	U.S. INF	—	D 1835	748
43	Hunter	Nathaniel W.	FW, MW	—	D 1849	749

Summary

Class	Number of Graduates	Union Civil War Officers	Confederate Civil War Officers	Union Civil War Generals	Confederate Civil War Generals	Died or Resigned Before Civil War
1833	43	11	4	7	1	26

Class of 1834

Class Rank	Last Name	First Name	Military Service Before Civil War	Civil War Service	Comments	Cullum Number
1	Fraser	William D.	MW	—	D 1856	750
2	Sanders	John	MW	—	D 1858	751
3	Loughborough	Harrison	U.S. ART	—	D 1836	752
4	Morris	Thomas A.	U.S. ART	BG IN VOL[14]	R 1836	753
5	Allen	Robert T.P.	U.S. ART	COL CSA		754
6	Duncan	James	MW	—	D 1849	755
7	Kirby	Epaphras	U.S. ART	—	D 1839	756
8	Stockton	William T.	U.S. ART	LTC CSA	R 1836	757
9	Lee	John F.	FW	B MAJ U.S. STF	Judge Adv	758
10	Fuller	Charles A.	FW	COL CSA		759
11	Pope	Curran	U.S. ART	COL KY VOL[15]		760
12	Chalmers	Charles B.	U.S. ART	—	RD 1838	761
13	Henderson	John E.	U.S. ART	—	D 1836	762
14	Miller	Morris S.	MW	MAJ U.S. QTR		763
15	Freeman	William G.	FW, MW	—	R 1856	764
16	Walbach	Louis A.B.	FW	—	D 1853	765
17	Cooper	James F.	U.S. INF	LTC CSA	R 1837	766
18	Paul	Gabriel R.	FW, MW, UE	BG USV		767
19	Field	George P.	FW, MW	—	K 1846	768
20	Fry	Cary H.	MW	MAJ U.S. STF		769
21	Turner	Henry S.	MW	—	R 1848	770
22	Simmons	Seneca G.	FW	MAJ U.S. INF		771
23	Barnwell	Thomas O.	U.S. INF	CSA—unknown		772
24	McKavett	Henry	FW, MW	—	K 1846	773
25	Bryan	Goode	MW	BG CSA		774
26	Coburn	Joseph L.	U.S. INF	CPT U.S. STF		775
27	Reed	James G.	U.S. INF	—	D 1856	776
28	Barbour	Philip N.	FW, MW	—	K 1846	777
29	Harris	Arnold	U.S. INF	—	R 1837	778
30	Smith	Richard S.	USMA	MAJ U.S. INF		779
31	Robinson	Eustace	U.S. INF	—	unknown	780
32	Ketchum	William Scott	UE	BG USV		781
33	Britton	Forbes	FW, MW	—	R 1850	782
34	Graham	John	FW	—	R 1838	783

Class Rank	Last Name	First Name	Military Service Before Civil War	Civil War Service	Comments	Cullum Number
35	Price	William H.	U.S. INF	—	R 1836	784
36	Montgomery	Alexander	FW	MAJ U.S. STF		785

Summary

Class	Number of Graduates	Union Civil War Officers	Confederate Civil War Officers	Union Civil War Generals	Confederate Civil War Generals	Died or Resigned Before Civil War
1834	36	11	5	3	1	19

Class of 1835

Class Rank	Last Name	First Name	Military Service Before Civil War	Civil War Service	Comments	Cullum Number
1	Morell	George W.	U.S. COE	BG USV		786
2	Bigelow	Charles H.	U.S. COE	—	R 1846	787
3	Martindale	John H.	U.S. CAV	BG USV	R 1836	788
4	Whiting	Charles J.	FW	MAJ U.S. CAV		789
5	Legate	George M.	U.S. ART	—	R 1836	790
6	Herbert	Alfred	FW	—	R 1837	791
7	Brumby	Arnoldus V.	FW	—	R 1836	792
8	Roberts	Joseph	FW	LTC U.S. ART		793
9	Brooks	Horace	FW, MW	COL U.S. ART		794
10	Morgan	James M.	FW, MW	—	D 1853	795
11	Renick	Robert M.	U.S. ART	—	R 1836	796
12	Henderson	Richard	FW	—	K 1835	797
13	Ellis	James N.	U.S. ART	—	R 1835	798
14	Keais	John L.	FW	—	K 1835	799
15	Brown	William Spencer	U.S. ART	—	R 1835	800
16	Kendrick	Henry L.	MW, USMA	—		801
17	Stokes	James H.	FW	LTC USV		802
18	Blair	Montgomery	FW	U.S. PM G[16]	R 1836	803
19	Meade	George G.	FW	MG USA		804
20	Betts	William H.	FW	—	R 1839	805
21	Waggaman	George G.	MW	—	R 1861	806
22	Hanson	Weightman K.	FW	—	D 1844	807
23	Naglee	Henry M.	MW	BG USV		808
24	Campbell	Archibald	U.S. INF	—	R 1836	809
25	Macomb	Alexander S.	U.S. CAV	—	R 1841	810
26	Hanley	John H.	U.S. CAV	—	K 1836	811
27	Griffin	William H.	U.S. INF	COL CSA	R 1837	812
28	Johnston	Abraham R.	MW	—	K 1846	813
29	Gaillard	Peter C.	U.S. INF	COL CSA		814
30	Prince	Henry	FW, MW	BG USV		815
31	Haupt	Herman	U.S. INF	BG USV		816
32	Plummer	Samuel M.	MW	—	D 1851	817
33	Mitchell	Alexander M.	FW, MW	—	D 1861	818
34	Tappan	Alexander H.	U.S. INF	—	D 1852	819
35	De Forest	William H.	FW	CPT U.S. INF		820
36	Thompson	Philip R.	MW	—	RD 1855	821
37	McKissack	William M.D.	FW	—	D 1849	822
38	Tibbats	S. Theodore	FW	—	D 1838	823
39	Wells	James M.	FW, MW	COL CSA		824
40	Henry	William S.	FW, MW	—	D 1851	825
41	Scott	John M.	FW, MW	—	D 1850	826
42	Shaw	George W.	U.S. INF	—	D 1854	827
43	Eaton	Joseph H.	MW	MAJ U.S. STF		828

Class Rank	Last Name	First Name	Military Service Before Civil War	Civil War Service	Comments	Cullum Number
44	Withers	John M.	MW	MG CSA		829
45	Reeve	Isaac V.D.	FW, MW	—	R 1860	830
46	Scott	John W.	U.S. INF	—	D 1859	831
47	Smith	Larkin	FW, MW	BG CSA		832
48	Patrick	Marsena R.	MW	BG USV		833
49	Arden	Thomas B.	FW	—	R 1842	834
50	Whipple	Joseph H.	MW	—	D 1847	835
51	Bradbury	Lucius	U.S. INF	—	R 1835	836
52	Wainwright	Robert A.	U.S. ORD	LTC U.S. ORD		837
53	Roberts	Benjamin S.	MW	BG USV		838
54	Grier	William N.	MW	B COL USA		839
55	Brent	Thomas L.	FW, MW	—	D 1858	840
56	McLeod	Hugh	U.S. INF	COL CSA		841

Summary

Class	Number of Graduates	Union Civil War Officers	Confederate Civil War Officers	Union Civil War Generals	Confederate Civil War Generals	Died or Resigned Before Civil War
1835	56	16	6	8	2	34

Class of 1836

Class Rank	Last Name	First Name	Military Service Before Civil War	Civil War Service	Comments	Cullum Number
1	Welker	George L.	U.S. COE	—	D 1848	842
2	Mason	James L.	MW	—	D 1853	843
3	Leadbetter	Danville	U.S. COE	BG CSA		844
4	Anderson	Joseph R.	U.S. ART	BG CSA		845
5	Meigs	Montgomery C	U.S. COE	B MG USA		846
6	Woodbury	Daniel P.	U.S. COE	B MG USA		847
7	Lewis	Fisher A.	FW	—	R 1838	848
8	Bransford	Samuel J.	FW	—	K 1840	849
9	Allen	Augustus P.	FW	—	D 1841	850
10	Warner	William H.	FW, MW	—	K 1849	851
11	Conkling	Barnabas	FW	—	D 1839	852
12	Wallace	William B.	U.S. ART	—	D 1841	853
13	Churchill	Marlborough	U.S. ART	—	R 1836	854
14	De Witt	David P.	U.S. ART	COL VRC[17]	R 1836	855
15	Donaldson	James Lowry	FW, MW	B BG USA		856
16	O'Brien	John P.J.	FW, MW	—	D 1850	857
17	Luther	Roland A.	FW, MW	—	D 1853	858
18	Sherman	Thomas W.	FW, MW	BG USV		859
19	Roland	John F.	FW, MW	—	D 1852	860
20	Sing	Charles B.	FW	—	R 1837	861
21	Crittenden	Alexander P.	U.S. ART	—	R 1836	862
22	Lockwood	Henry H.	FW	BG USV		863
23	Greene	Christopher A.	U.S. ART	—	R 1837	864
24	Phelps	John W.	FW, MW, UE	BG USV		865
25	Hagner	Peter V.	FW, MW	LTC U.S. ORD		866
26	Shackleford	Muscoe L.	FW, MW	—	D 1847	867
27	Tompkins	Christopher Q.	FW, MW	COL WV MIL CSA[18]		868
28	Burke	Martin J.	FW, MW	—	K 1847	869
29	Judson	John W.	U.S. ART	—	R 1836	870
30	Woodruff	I. Carle	U.S. TOP	LTC U.S. COE		871
31	Arven	William B.	FW	—	R 1836	872

Class Rank	Last Name	First Name	Military Service Before Civil War	Civil War Service	Comments	Cullum Number
32	Hatheway	John S.	FW, MW	—	D 1853	873
33	Allen	Robert	FW, MW	B BG USA		874
34	Frazer	William	FW	—	D 1844	875
35	Thomas	George C.	FW	MG DC MIL[19]		876
36	Lansing	Arthur B.	MW	—	R 1851	877
37	Daniels	Charles B.	FW, MW	—	D 1847	878
38	Mock	William	FW	—	R 1841	879
39	Baker	Robert F.	U.S. INF	—	RD 1844	880
40	Hoskins	Charles	FW, MW	—	K 1846	881
41	Whitehorn	Samuel	U.S. INF	—	D 1850	882
42	Gates	Collinson R.	FW, MW	—	D 1849	883
43	Hammond	Marcus C.M.	FW, MW	—	R 1847	884
44	Stockton	Richard G.	U.S. CAV	BG MO MIL[20]		885
45	Chiffelle	Thomas P.	U.S. INF	—	R 1836	886
46	Tilghman	Lloyd	MW	BG CSA		887
47	McCrate	Thomas	U.S. CAV	—	D 1845	888
48	Moorhead	Henry C.	U.S. CAV	—	R 1836	889
49	Spoor	Charles H.E.	FW	—	D 1838	890

Summary

Class	Number of Graduates	Union Civil War Officers	Confederate Civil War Officers	Union Civil War Generals	Confederate Civil War Generals	Died or Resigned Before Civil War
1836	49	12	4	9	3	36

Class of 1837

Class Rank	Last Name	First Name	Military Service Before Civil War	Civil War Service	Comments	Cullum Number
1	Benham	Henry W.	MW	BG USV		891
2	Gunnison	John W.	FW	—	K 1853	892
3	Morgan	Edwin W.	FW, MW	—	R 1848	893
4	Bratt	John	U.S. ART	—	R 1837	894
5	Bragg	Braxton	FW, MW	GEN CSA		895
6	Dyer	Alexander B.	FW	BG U.S. ORD		896
7	Chapman	William W.	FW, MW	—	D 1859	897
8	Mackall	William W.	FW, MW	BG CSA		898
9	Scammon	E. Parker	FW	BG USV		899
10	Arnold	Lewis G.	FW, MW	BG USV		900
11	Vogdes	Israel	FW	BG USV		901
12	Williams	Thomas	FW, MW, UE	BG USV		902
13	Jones	Robert T.	FW	COL CSA		903
14	Woodbridge	Francis	FW, MW	—	D 1855	904
15	Gregory	A. Park	FW	—	R 1838	905
16	Townsend	Edward D.	FW	B BG USA		906
17	Martin	William T.	FW	—	R 1838	907
18	Early	Jubal A.	FW, MW	LG CSA		908
19	Bradford	Edmund	FW, MW	IG CSA[21]		909
20	Pratt	Henry C.	FW, MW	MAJ U.S. STF		910
21	Hill	Bennett H.	FW, MW	LTC U.S. ART		911
22	French	William H.	FW, MW	MG USV		912
23	Taylor	George	FW, MW	—	D 1853	913
24	Sedgwick	John	FW, MW, UE	MG USV		914
25	Bates	Joshua H.	FW	BG OH VOL[22]		915
26	Rodney	George C.	FW	—	D 1839	916
27	Pemberton	John C.	FW, MW, UE	LG CSA		917
28	Armstrong	William	FW, MW	—	K 1847	918
29	Hooker	Joseph	FW, MW	MG USV		919

U.S. Military Academy Graduating Classes

Class Rank	Last Name	First Name	Military Service Before Civil War	Civil War Service	Comments	Cullum Number
30	Harvie	John M.	FW	—	D 1841	920
31	Wooster	Charles F.	FW, MW	—	D 1856	921
32	Rutledge	Arthur M.	FW	MAJ CSA		922
33	Elzey (Jones)	Arnold	FW, MW	MG CSA		923
34	Steptoe	Edward J.	FW, MW	—	R 1861	924
35	Fowler	William H.	FW, MW	—	D 1851	925
36	Woods	Samuel	FW, MW	—		926
37	McLane	Robert M.	FW	—	R 1843	927
38	Sherwood	Walter	FW	—	K 1840	928
39	Todd	John B.S.	FW, MW	BG USV		929
40	Soley	James R.	FW	—	D 1845	930
41	Moore	Samuel D.J.	—	—	R 1837[23]	931
42	Ridgley	Randolph	FW, MW	—	K 1846	932
43	Wyse	Francis O.	FW, MW	LTC U.S. ART		933
44	Grandin	William G.	FW	CPT U.S. STF		934
45	Hopson	Nevil	FW, MW	—	D 1847	935
46	Walker	William H.T.	FW, MW	MG CSA		936
47	Davidson	Levi	U.S. CAV	—	D 1842	937
48	Chilton	Robert H.	MW	BG CSA		938
49	Hardia	William	FW	—	RD 1840	939
50	Saunders	Franklin	FW, MW	—	R 1847	940

Summary

Class	Number of Graduates	Union Civil War Officers	Confederate Civil War Officers	Union Civil War Generals	Confederate Civil War Generals	Died or Resigned Before Civil War
1837	50	16	10	11	7	24

Class of 1838

Class Rank	Last Name	First Name	Military Service Before Civil War	Civil War Service	Comments	Cullum Number
1	Wright	William H.	U.S. COE	—	D 1845	941
2	Beauregard	P.G.T.	MW	G CSA		942
3	Trapier	James H.	MW	BG CSA		943
4	Campbell	Stephen H.	U.S. COE	—	D 1845	944
5	Scarritt	Jeremiah M.	FW, MW	—	D 1854	945
6	Dearborn	Alexander H.	U.S. ORD	—	D 1853	946
7	Metcalfe	John T.	U.S. ART	—	R 1840	947
8	Casey	Thomas	FW	—	R 1839	948
9	Reeves	Isaac S.K.	U.S. ART	—	D 1851	949
10	Board	Buckner	U.S. ART	COL KY VOL[24]		950
11	Blair	William B.	MW	MAJ CSA		951
12	Ringgold	Thomas Lee	FW	—	D 154	952
13	Ketchum	James M.	FW	—	R 1844	953
14	Wayne	Henry C.	MW	BG CSA		954
15	Pitkin	Lucius	U.S. ART	—	R 1844	955
16	Shover	William H.	FW, MW	—	D 1850	956
17	Barry	William F.	FW, MW	B MG USV		957
18	Haynes	Milton A.	FW	LTC CSA		958
19	Nichols	William A.	MW	COL U.S. STF		959
20	Fletcher	John C.	FW	—	R 1840	960
21	Chase	Leslie	MW	—	D 1849	961
22	Easton	Langdon C.	FW	B BG USA		962
23	McDowell	Irvin	MW	MG USV		963
24	Jennings	Rowley S.	U.S. ART	—	D 1839	964
25	Austine	William	MW	MAJ U.S. ART		965
26	Hardee	William J.	FW, MW	LG CSA		966

Class Rank	Last Name	First Name	Military Service Before Civil War	Civil War Service	Comments	Cullum Number
27	Merrill	Hamilton W.	FW, MW	—	R 1857	967
28	Granger	Robert S.	FW, MW	BG USV		968
29	Ransom	Owen P.	FW	COL OH VOL[25]	RD 1845	969
30	Mathews	John H.	U.S. INF	—	D 1838	970
31	Sibley	Henry H.	FW, MW, UE	MG CSA		971
32	Johnson	Edward	FW, MW, UE	MG CSA		972
33	Arnold	Ripley A.	FW, MW	—	K 1853	973
34	Freeman	Constant	U.S. INF	—	D 1839	974
35	Reynolds	Alexander W.	FW	BG CSA		975
36	Smith	Andrew J.	U.S. CAV	MG USV		976
37	Hughes	Charles S.	FW	—	D 1839	977
38	Hulbert	William	FW	—	K 1839	978
39	Cochran	Robert M.	FW	—	RD 1844	979
40	McKinstry	Justus	FW, MW	BG USV	RD 1863	980
41	Mumford	Ferdinand S.	FW, MW	—	R 1849	981
42	Stevenson	Carter L.	FW, MW, UE	MG CSA		982
43	Graham	Richard H.	MW	—	D 1846	983
44	Ruff	Charles F.	MW	LTC U.S. CAV		984
45	Inge	Zebulon M.P.	FW	—	K 1846	985

Summary

Class	Number of Graduates	Union Civil War Officers	Confederate Civil War Officers	Union Civil War Generals	Confederate Civil War Generals	Died or Resigned Before Civil War
1838	45	11	10	6	8	24

Class of 1839

Class Rank	Last Name	First Name	Military Service Before Civil War	Civil War Service	Comments	Cullum Number
1	Stevens	Isaac I.	MW	MG USV		986
2	Butler	Robert Q.	U.S. COE	—	D 1843	987
3	Halleck	Henry C.	MW	MG USA	Gen-in-Chief	988
4	Gilmer	Jeremy F.	U.S. COE	MG CSA		989
5	Smith	Henry L.	U.S. COE	—	D 1853	990
6	Culbertson	Michael S.	U.S. ART	—	R 1841	991
7	Thom	George	U.S. TOP	LTC U.S. COE		992
8	Callender	Franklin D.	FW, MW	MAJ U.S. ORD		993
9	Burton	Henry S.	MW	COL U.S. ART		994
10	Haskin	Joseph A.	MW	BG USV		995
11	Grafton	Henry D.	FW, MW	—	D 1855	996
12	Rankin	James L.	FW	—	K 1845	997
13	Lawton	Alexander R.	U.S. ART	BG CSA		998
14	Judd	Henry B.	FW, MW	MAJ U.S. ART		999
15	Allen	Lucius H.	U.S. ART	—	R 1846	1000
16	Ricketts	James B.	FW, MW	B MG USV		1001
17	Ord	Edward C.	FW, MW	MG USV		1002
18	Boyd	Joseph B.	FW	—	R 1841	1003
19	Hunt	Henry L.	MW	B MG USV		1004
20	Irvin	William	MW	—	R 1841	1005
21	Smith	William S.	U.S. ART	—	D 1849	1006
22	Dawson	Samuel K.	MW, FW	LTC U.S. INF		1007
23	Gibson	Augustus A.	MW	MAJ U.S. ART		1008
24	Paine	Eleazer A.	FW	BG USV		1009
25	Barry	Garrett	FW	—	D 1860	1010
26	Wickliffe	Charles	MW	COL CSA		1011
27	Hunton	Thomas	U.S. CAV	—	R 1839	1012
28	Gaither	Edgar B.	MW	—	R 1839	1013

Class Rank	Last Name	First Name	Military Service Before Civil War	Civil War Service	Comments	Cullum Number
29	Korn	William H.	FW	—	R 1840	1014
30	Canby	Edward R.S.	MW, UE	MG USV		1015
31	Hill	John H.	FW, MW	—	D 1847	1016

Summary

Class	Number of Graduates	Union Civil War Officers	Confederate Civil War Officers	Union Civil War Generals	Confederate Civil War Generals	Died or Resigned Before Civil War
1839	31	14	3	8	2	14

Class of 1840

Class Rank	Last Name	First Name	Military Service Before Civil War	Civil War Service	Comments	Cullum Number
1	Hébert	Paul O.	MW	BG CSA		1017
2	Kingsbury	Charles P.	MW	MAJ U.S. ORD		1018
3	McNutt	John	MW	MAJ U.S. ORD		1019
4	Jones	William P.	U.S. ART	—	K 1841	1020
5	Gilham	William	FW, MW	COL CSA	R 1846	1021
6	Sherman	William T.	MW	MG USA		1022
7	Lancaster	Job R.H.	FW	—	K 1841	1023
8	Churchill	William H.	FW, MW	—	D 1847	1024
9	Van Vliet	Stewart	FW, MW	BG USV		1025
10	McCown	John P.	FW, MW, UE	MG CSA		1026
11	Clarke	Francis N.	FW, UE	B COL U.S. ART		1027
12	Thomas	George H.	FW, MW	MG USA		1028
13	Ewell	Richard S.	MW	LG CSA		1029
14	Martin	James G.	MW	BG CSA		1030
15	Getty	George W.	MW	B MG USV		1031
16	Field	Horace B.	FW, MW	—	D 1853	1032
17	Whiting	Henry	U.S. INF	COL VT VOL[26]		1033
18	Hays	William	MW	BG USV		1034
19	Hamilton	Fowler	MW	—	D 1851	1035
20	Tilden	Bryant P.	FW, MW	—	D 1859	1036
21	Higgins	Thaddeus	U.S. INF	—	K 1845	1037
22	Winship	Oscar F.	FW, MW	—	D 1855	1038
23	Johnson	Bushrod R.	FW	MG CSA		1039
24	Humber	Charles H.	MW	—	D 1858	1040
25	Caldwell	James N.	FW	B LTC U.S. INF		1041
26	Gardiner	John W.T.	U.S. CAV	MAJ U.S. CAV		1042
27	Campbell	Reuben P.	FW, MW, UE	COL CSA		1043
28	Lugenbeel	Pinckney	FW, MW	MAJ U.S. INF		1044
29	Wardwell	Henry	U.S. INF	—	D 1841	1045
30	Robertson	William	FW	—	R 1843	1046
31	Steele	William	MW, UE	BG CSA		1047
32	Maclay	Robert P.	FW, MW	BG CSA		1048
33	Shepherd	Oliver L.	FW, MW	COL U.S. INF		1049
34	Wallen	Henry D.	FW, MW	B COL U.S. INF		1050
35	Carpenter	Stephen D.	FW	M U.S. INF		1051
36	Folsom	Joseph L.	FW	—	D 1855	1052
37	Torrey	William G.	FW	—	RD 1844	1053
38	Rogers	Daniel G.	FW, MW	—	D 1848	1054
39	Johns	William B.	FW, MW	—	RD 1861	1055
40	Irwin	Douglass S.	FW, MW	—	K 1846	1056
41	Jordan	Thomas	FW, MW	BG CSA		1057
42	Bacon	John D.	FW, MW	—	D 1847	1058

Summary

Class	Number of Graduates	Union Civil War Officers	Confederate Civil War Officers	Union Civil War Generals	Confederate Civil War Generals	Died or Resigned Before Civil War
1840	42	15	10	5	8	17

Class of 1841

Class Rank	Last Name	First Name	Military Service Before Civil War	Civil War Service	Comments	Cullum Number
1	Tower	Zealous B.	MW	BG USV		1059
2	Wright	Horatio G.	U.S. COE	MG USV		1060
3	Harrison	Masillon	U.S. COE	—	D 1854	1061
4	Stansbury	Smith	U.S. ORD	MAJ CSA	R 1844	1062
5	Whipple	Amiel W.	U.S. TOP	B MG USA		1063
6	Gorgas	Josiah	MW	BG CSA	Chief-of-Ordnance	1064
7	Rodman	Thomas J.	MW	MAJ U.S. ORD		1065
8	Howe	Albion P.	MW	BG USV		1066
9	MacDonald	Philip W.	MW	—	D 1851	1067
10	Ayers	George W.	MW	—	K 1847	1068
11	Lyon	Nathaniel	FW, MW	BG USV		1069
12	Irons	Joseph F.	MW	—	D 1847	1070
13	Jenkins	Leonidas	MW	—	D 1847	1071
14	Love	John	MW	MG IN VOL[27]		1072
15	Allen	Harvey A.	MW	MAJ U.S. ART		1073
16	Garesche	Julius P.	MW	LTC USA		1074
17	Fremont	Sewall L.	MW	LTC CSA		1075
18	Anderson	Samuel S.	FW, MW	COL CSA		1076
19	Jones	Samuel	U.S. ART	MG CSA		1077
20	Fahnestock	Simon S.	MW	—	R 1850	1078
21	Hammond	Richard P.	MW	—	R 1851	1079
22	Plummer	Joseph B.	MW	BG USV		1080
23	Brannan	John M.	MW	B MG USV		1081
24	Hamilton	Schuyler	MW	MG USV		1082
25	Totten	James	U.S. ART	BG MO MIL[28]		1083
26	Reynolds	John F.	MW	MG USV		1084
27	Garnett	Robert S.	MW	BG CSA		1085
28	Parker	Robert B.	FW	—	D 1842	1086
29	Garnett	Richard B.	FW, MW, UE	BG CSA		1087
30	Bacot	Richard H.	FW	—	D 1861	1088
31	Sears	Claudius W.	FW	BG CSA	R 1842	1089
32	Buell	Don Carlos	MW	MG USV		1090
33	Burbank	John G.	MW	—	D 1847	1091
34	Sully	Alfred	FW	B MG USV		1092
35	Flint	Franklin F.	FW	LTC U.S. INF		1093
36	Beardsley	John	MW	COL U.S. CAV		1094
37	Calhoun	Patrick	FW	—	D 1858	1095
38	Richardson	Israel	MW	MG USV		1096
39	Jones	John M.	UE	BG CSA		1097
40	Bowman	Andrew W.	MW	MAJ U.S. INF		1098
41	Murray	Edward	FW, MW	LTC CSA	R 1855	1099
42	Page	Francis N.	MW	—	D 1860	1100
43	Nelson	Anderson D.	MW	MAJ U.S. INF		1101
44	Berry	Benjamin A.	FW	—	K 1845	1102
45	Darne	Alexander C.H.	FW	—	R 1845	1103
46	Brooks	William T.H.	MW	BG USV		1104
47	Kane	Elias K.	MW	—	D 1853	1105
48	Gantt	Levi	FW	—	D 1847	1106

Class Rank	Last Name	First Name	Military Service Before Civil War	Civil War Service	Comments	Cullum Number
49	Rosecrants	Mortimer	MW	—	D 1848	1107
50	Ernst	Rudolph F.	FW, MW	—	D 1847	1108
51	Buford	Abraham	MW F	BG CSA		1109
52	Morris	Charles F.	MW, FW	—	D 1847	1110

Summary

Class	Number of Graduates	Union Civil War Officers	Confederate Civil War Officers	Union Civil War Generals	Confederate Civil War Generals	Died or Resigned Before Civil War
1841	52	22	11	15	7	19

Class of 1842

Class Rank	Last Name	First Name	Military Service Before Civil War	Civil War Service	Comments	Cullum Number
1	Eustis	Henry L.	U.S. COE	BG USV		1111
2	Newton	John	U.S. COE	BG USV		1112
3	Rains	George W.	MW	COL CSA		1113
4	Kurtz	John D.	U.S. COE	MAJ U.S. COE		1114
5	Rosecrans	William S.	U.S. COE	MG USV		1115
6	Laidley	Theodore T.S.	MW	MAJ U.S. ORD		1116
7	Alexander	Barton S.	U.S. COE	MAJ U.S. COE		1117
8	Smith	Gustavus W.	MW	MG CSA		1118
9	Lovell	Mansfield	MW	MG CSA		1119
10	Benjamin	Calvin	MW	—	K 1847	1120
11	Benton	James G.	U.S. ORD	MAJ U.S. ORD		1121
12	Stewart	Alexander P.	U.S. ART	LG CSA		1122
13	Beckwith	Edward G.	MW	MAJ U.S. ART		1123
14	Whiting	Henry M.	MW	—	D 1853	1124
15	Bowen	Isaac	MW	—	D 1858	1125
16	Smith	Martin L.	MW	MG CSA		1126
17	Pope	John	MW	MG USA		1127
18	Stewart	Joseph	MW	CPT U.S. ART		1128
19	Johnston	Richard W.	MW	—	R 1847	1129
20	Hillhouse	John	U.S. ART	CPT U.S. STF		1130
21	Gibson	David	MW	—	D 1847	1131
22	Kilburn	Charles L.	MW	COL U.S. STF		1132
23	Williams	Seth	MW	B MG USV		1133
24	Doubleday	Abner	MW	MG USV		1134
25	Brown	Hachalliah	MW	—	D 1853	1135
26	Loeser	Lucien	U.S. ART	—	R 1858	1136
27	Denman	Frederick J.	MW	—	D 1853	1137
28	Hill	Daniel H.	MW	LG CSA		1138
29	Dana	Napoleon J.T.	MW	MG USV		1139
30	Norton	Allen H.	U.S. INF	—	D 1846	1140
31	Rust	Armistead T.M.	U.S. CAV	COL CSA		1141
32	McCalmont	John S.	U.S. INF	COL PA VOL[29]		1142
33	Noble	Patrick	U.S. CAV	—	D 1848	1143
34	Story	Henry C.	U.S. INF	—	R 1844	1144
35	Beaman	Jenks	MW	—	D 1848	1145
36	Clark	John D.	MW	—	D 1848	1146
37	Kirkham	Ralph W.	MW	MAJ U.S. QTR		1147
38	Hall	Cyrus	U.S. INF	—	D 1849	1148
39	Sykes	George	FW, MW	MG USV		1149
40	Anderson	Richard H.	MW, UE	LG CSA		1150
41	Lay	George W.	MW	LTC CSA		1151
42	Schureman	James W.	MW	—	D 1852	1152

Class Rank	Last Name	First Name	Military Service Before Civil War	Civil War Service	Comments	Cullum Number
43	Mason	George T.	MW	—	K 1846	1153
44	Jordan	Charles D.	MW	MAJ U.S. INF		1154
45	Stanton	Henry W.	MW	—	K 1855	1155
46	Williamson	Andrew J.	MW	—	R 1851	1156
47	McLean	Eugene E.	MW	LTC CSA		1157
48	McLaws	Lafayette	MW, UE	MG CSA		1158
49	Hammond	Thomas C.	MW	—	K 1846	1159
50	Baker	Charles T.	FW	—	R 1851	1160
51	Hayman	Samuel B.	MW, UE	B COL U.S. INF		1161
52	Van Dorn	Earl	MW	MG CSA		1162
53	Perry	Christopher R.	MW	—	D 1848	1163
54	Longstreet	James	MW	LG CSA		1164
55	Abert	James W.	FW	MAJ U.S. COE		1165
56	Handy	James O.	U.S. INF	—	D 1845	1166

Summary

Class	Number of Graduates	Union Civil War Officers	Confederate Civil War Officers	Union Civil War Generals	Confederate Civil War Generals	Died or Resigned Before Civil War
1842	56	21	13	8	9	22

Class of 1843

Class Rank	Last Name	First Name	Military Service Before Civil War	Civil War Service	Comments	Cullum Number
1	Franklin	William B.	MW	MG USV		1167
2	Deshon	George	U.S. ORD	—	R 1851	1168
3	Bereton	Thomas J.	MW	—	R 1858	1169
4	Grelaud	John H.	U.S. ART	—	R 1857	1170
5	Raynolds	William F.	U.S. TOP	MAJ U.S. COE		1171
6	Quinby	Isaac F.	U.S. ART	BG USV		1172
7	Ripley	Rosewell S.	MW	BG CSA		1173
8	Peck	John J.	MW	MG USV		1174
9	Johnstone	John P.	MW	—	K 1847	1175
10	Reynolds	Joseph J.	U.S. ART	MG USV		1176
11	Hardie	James A.	U.S. ART	COL U.S. STF		1177
12	Clarke	Henry F.	MW, UE	LTC U.S. STF		1178
13	Booker	Jacob J.	MW	—	D 1849	1179
14	French	Samuel G.	MW	MG CSA		1180
15	Chadbourne	Theodore L.	MW	—	K 1846	1181
16	Augur	Christopher C.	MW	MG USV		1182
17	Gardner	Franklin K.	MW, UE	MG CSA		1183
18	Stevens	George	MW	—	D 1846	1184
19	Holloway	Edmunds B.	MW	COL CSA		1185
20	Neill	Lewis	MW	—	D 1850	1186
21	Grant	Ulysses S.	MW	LG USA		1187
22	Potter	Joseph H.	MW, UE	B COL U.S. INF		1188
23	Hazlitt	Robert	MW	—	K 1846	1189
24	Howe	Edwin	MW	—	D 1850	1190
25	Wood	Lafayette B.	MW	—	D 1858	1191
26	Hamilton	Charles S.	MW	MG USV		1192
27	Van Bokkelen	William K.	MW	—	RD 1861	1193
28	Crozet	A. St. Amand	MW	—	D 1855	1194
29	Jarvis	Charles E.	MW	—	D 1849	1195
30	Steele	Frederick	MW	MG USV		1196
31	Selden	Henry R.	MW, UE	COL NM VOL[30]		1197

Class Rank	Last Name	First Name	Military Service Before Civil War	Civil War Service	Comments	Cullum Number
32	Ingalls	Rufus	MW	B BG USA		1198
33	Dent	Frederick T.	MW	LTC U.S. STF		1199
34	McFerran	John C.	MW	COL U.S. STF		1200
35	Judah	Henry M.	MW	BG USV		1201
36	Elting	Norman	U.S. INF	—	R 1846	1202
37	Couts	Cave J.	MW	—	R 1851	1203
38	Merchant	Charles G.	MW	—	D 1855	1204
39	McClelland	George C.	MW	—	RD 1847	1205

Summary

Class	Number of Graduates	Union Civil War Officers	Confederate Civil War Officers	Union Civil War Generals	Confederate Civil War Generals	Died or Resigned Before Civil War
1843	39	17	4	10	3	18

Class of 1844

Class Rank	Last Name	First Name	Military Service Before Civil War	Civil War Service	Comments	Cullum Number
1	Peck	William G.	U.S. TOP	—	R 1855	1206
2	Whittlesey	Joseph H.	MW	MAJ U.S. CAV		1207
3	Gill	Samuel	MW	—	R 1847	1208
4	Frost	Daniel M.	MW, UE	BG CSA		1209
5	Eddy	Asher R.	U.S. ART	COL U.S. STF		1210
6	Thomas	Francis J.	MW	COL CSA		1211
7	Pleasanton	Alfred	MW, FW	MG USV		1212
8	Curd	Thomas J.	MW	—	R 1847	1213
9	Cook	Augustus	U.S. CAV	—	D 1845	1214
10	Bicknell	John Y.	MW	—	D 1849	1215
11	Buckner	Simon B.	MW	LG CSA		1216
12	Trevitt	John	MW, UE	—	R 1861	1217
13	Dilworth	Rankin	MW	—	D 1846	1218
14	Strong	Erastus B.	MW	—	K 1847	1219
15	Burwell	William T.	MW	—	K 1847	1220
16	Read	William	MW	—	R 1850	1221
17	Woods	James S.	MW	—	K 1846	1222
18	Hancock	Winfield S.	MW, FW	MG USV		1223
19	Henry	James M. Lake	MW	—	R 1852	1224
20	Hays	Alexander	MW	BG USV		1225
21	Wainwright	George	MW	—	D 1848	1226
22	Schroeder	Henry B.	MW	—	R 1861	1227
23	Smith	Joseph P.	MW	—	K 1847	1228
24	Bibb	John J.C.	MW	—	R 1846	1229
25	Hawkins	George W.	MW	—	RD 1853	1230

Summary

Class	Number of Graduates	Union Civil War Officers	Confederate Civil War Officers	Union Civil War Generals	Confederate Civil War Generals	Died or Resigned Before Civil War
1844	25	5	3	3	2	17

Class of 1845

Class Rank	Last Name	First Name	Military Service Before Civil War	Civil War Service	Comments	Cullum Number
1	Whiting	William H.C.	U.S. COE	MG CSA		1231
2	Hunt	Edward B.	U.S. COE	M U.S. COE		1232

Class Rank	Last Name	First Name	Military Service Before Civil War	Civil War Service	Comments	Cullum Number
3	Hébert	Louis	U.S. COE	BG CSA		1233
4	Smith	William F.	U.S. TOP	MG USV		1234
5	Wood	Thomas J.	MW, UE	MG USV		1235
6	Rhett	Thomas G.	U.S. MTR	M CSA		1236
7	Stone	Charles P.	MW	BG USV		1237
8	Porter	Fitz-John	MW, UE	MG USV		1238
9	Carlisle	Josiah H.	MW, FW	B MAJ U.S. ART		1239
10	Edwards	George	MW, FW	—	R 1851	1240
11	Coppeé	Henry	MW	Prof at U of PA	R 1855	1241
12	Collins	Francis	MW, FW	—	R 1850	1242
13	Farry	Joseph F.	MW	—	K 1847	1243
14	Welch	Louis D.	MW	—	D 1848	1244
15	Andrews	George P.	MW	COL U.S. ART		1245
16	Weld	Thomas B.J.	MW	—	D 1850	1246
17	Hatch	John P.	MW	BG USV		1247
18	Richey	John A.	MW	—	K 1847	1248
19	Merrill	Henry	U.S. INF	—	K 1845	1249
20	Farrelly	Patrick A.	MW	—	K 1851	1250
21	Lincoln	Abram B.	MW	—	D 1852	1251
22	Armstrong	Bezaleel W.	MW	—	D 1849	1252
23	Allen	William T.	U.S. CAV	—	D 1845	1253
24	Snelling	James G.S.	MW	—	D 1855	1254
25	Smith	Edmund K.	MW	G CSA		1255
26	Montgomery	Thomas J.	MW	—	D 1854	1256
27	Davidson	John W.	MW	BG USV		1257
28	Ward	James N.	MW	—	D 1858	1258
29	Hawes	James M.	MW, UE	BG CSA		1259
30	Givens	Newton C.	MW	—	D 1859	1260
31	Radford	Richard C.W.	MW	COL CSA		1261
32	Sacket	Delos B.	MW, UE	COL U.S. STF IG[31]		1262
33	Bee	Bernard E.	MW, UE	BG CSA		1263
34	Rhea	William	MW	—	D 1847	1264
35	Granger	George	MW	MG USV		1265
36	Clitz	Henry B.	MW, USMA	LTC U.S. INF		1266
37	Wood	William H.	MW	LTC U.S. INF		1267
38	Russell	David A.	MW	B MG USV		1268
39	McElvain	Joseph	MW	—	K 1847	1269
40	Pitcher	Thomas G.	MW	BG USV		1270
41	Crittenden	William L.	MW	—	R 1849	1271

Summary

Class	Number of Graduates	Union Civil War Officers	Confederate Civil War Officers	Union Civil War Generals	Confederate Civil War Generals	Died or Resigned Before Civil War
1845	41	15	7	9	5	19

Class of 1846

Class Rank	Last Name	First Name	Military Service Before Civil War	Civil War Service	Comments	Cullum Number
1	Stewart	C. Seaforth	U.S. COE	B LTC U.S. COE		1272
2	McClellan	George B.	MW	MG USA		1273
3	Blunt	Charles E.	U.S. COE	MAJ U.S. COE		1274
4	Foster	John G.	MW	MG USV		1275

U.S. Military Academy Graduating Classes

Class Rank	Last Name	First Name	Military Service Before Civil War	Civil War Service	Comments	Cullum Number
5	Hardcastle	Edmund L.F.	MW	—	R 1856	1276
6	Bryan	Francis T.	MW	—	R 1861	1277
7	Derby	George H.	MW	—	D 1861	1278
8	Reno	Jesse L.	MW, UE	MG USV		1279
9	Wilson	Clarendon J.L.	MW	—	D 1853	1280
10	Whedbee	Thomas M.	U.S. ORD	—	D 1849	1281
11	Hayes	Edmund	U.S. ART	—	D 1853	1282
12	Boyton	Edward C.	MW, FW	CPT U.S. INF		1283
13	Couch	Darius N.	MW, FW	MG USV		1284
14	Sears	Henry B.	MW	—	R 1849	1285
15	Dutton	William	U.S. ART	COL NY VOL[32]		1286
16	Brown	John A.	MW, FW	LTC CSA		1287
17	Jackson	Thomas J.	MW	LG CSA		1288
18	Magilton	Albert L.	MW	—	R 1857	1289
19	Seymour	Truman	MW, FW	BG USV		1290
20	Minor	Colville J.	MW	—	D 1847	1291
21	Gilbert	Charles C.	MW	BG USV	Invalid Corps	1292
22	Simpson	Marcus D.L.	MW	LTC U.S. STF		1293
23	Bacon	Rufus	U.S. ART	—	D 1846	1294
24	Shields	Hamilton L.	MW	—	R 1854	1295
25	Adams	John	MW	BG CSA		1296
26	Rush	Richard H.	U.S. ART	COL PA VOL[33]		1297
27	Ehninger	Henry A.	MW	—	R 1849	1298
28	Castor	Thomas F.	MW	—	D 1855	1299
29	Chapman	Orren	MW	—	D 1859	1300
30	Rodgers	Alexander P.	MW	—	K 1847	1301
31	Taylor	Oliver H.P.	MW	—	K 1858	1302
32	Sturgis	Samuel D.	MW	LTC U.S. CAV		1303
33	Stoneman	George	MW	MG USV		1304
34	Oakes	James	MW	LTC U.S. CAV		1305
35	Smith	William D.	MW, UE	BG CSA		1306
36	Evans	George F.	MW	—	D 1859	1307
37	Maury	Dabney H.	MW	MG CSA		1308
38	Palmer	Innis N.	MW	BG USV		1309
39	Stuart	James	MW	—	D 1851	1310
40	Turnley	Parmenas T.	MW	CPT U.S. STF		1311
41	Jones	David R.	MW	MG CSA		1312
42	Gibbs	Alfred	MW	BG USV		1313
43	Gordon	George H.	MW	BG USV		1314
44	Myers	Frederick	MW	MAJ U.S. QTR		1315
45	Floyd-Jones	DeLancey	MW	LTC U.S. INF		1316
46	Wilkens	John D.	MW	MAJ U.S. INF		1317
47	Whistler	Joseph N.G.	MW	B LTC U.S. INF		1318
48	Easley	Thomas	MW	—	K 1847	1319
49	Davis	Nelson H.	MW	B COL U.S. INF		1320
50	McConnell	Thomas R.	MW	—	R 1856	1321
51	Stevenson	Matthew R.	MW	CPT U.S. INF		1322
52	Humphreys	George S.	U.S. CAV	—	D 1847	1323
53	Tyler	William H.	MW	—	D 1853	1324
54	Wilcox	Cadmus M.	MW	MG CSA		1325
55	Gardner	William M.	MW	BG CSA		1326
56	Russell	Edmund	MW	—	K 1853	1327
57	Botts	Archibald B.	U.S. INF	—	D 1847	1328
58	Maxey	Samuel B.	MW	MG CSA		1329
59	Pickett	George E.	MW	MG CSA		1330

Summary

Class	Number of Graduates	Union Civil War Officers	Confederate Civil War Officers	Union Civil War Generals	Confederate Civil War Generals	Died or Resigned Before Civil War
1846	59	25	10	10	9	24

Class of 1847

Class Rank	Last Name	First Name	Military Service Before Civil War	Civil War Service	Comments	Cullum Number
1	Symmes	John C.	U.S. ORD	—	R 1861	1331
2	Hamilton	John	U.S. ART	B COL U.S. ART		1332
3	Woods	Joseph J.	U.S. ART	COL IA VOL[34]		1333
4	McAllister	Julian	MW	CPT U.S. ORD		1334
5	Hazzard	George W.	MW, FW	COL IN VOL[35]		1335
6	Van Buren	Daniel T.	MW	COL U.S. STF		1336
7	Chalfin	Samuel F.	MW, FW	B LTC U.S. STF		1337
8	Willcox	Orlando B.	MW, FW	B MG USV		1338
9	Mason	John S.	MW	BG USV		1339
10	Patten	George	MW, FW	—	R 1851	1340
11	Dickerson	John H.	MW, FW	CPT U.S. STF		1341
12	Beltzhoover	Daniel M.	MW	LTC CSA		1342
13	Tillinghast	Otis H.	MW, FW	CPT U.S. STF		1343
14	Fry	James B.	MW	BG USA PM[36]		1344
15	Hill	Ambrose P.	MW, FW	LG CSA		1345
16	Cook	Anson J.	MW, FW	—	D 1853	1346
17	Gibson	Horatio G.	MW	COL OH VOL[37]		1347
18	Burnside	Ambrose E.	MW	MG USV		1348
19	Long	Richard H.	MW	—	D 1849	1349
20	Gibbon	John	MW	MG USV		1350
21	Best	Clermont L.	MW, UE	B LTC U.S. ART		1351
22	Ayers	Romeyn B.	MW	B MG USV		1352
23	Griffin	Charles	MW	B MG USV		1353
24	Black	Henry M.	MW, FW	MAJ U.S. INF		1354
25	Hendershott	Henry B.	MW	CPT U.S. ART		1355
26	Moore	Tredwell	MW	CPT U.S. STF		1356
27	Neill	Thomas H.	MW, UE	B COL U.S. INF		1357
28	Burns	William W.	MW, FW	MG USV		1358
29	Abbott	Edward F.	MW	—	R 1854	1359
30	Viele	Egbert L.	MW	BG USV		1360
31	Street	Washington P.	MW	—	D 1852	1361
32	Harrison	Mont. P.	MW	—	K 1849	1362
33	Hunt	Lewis C.	MW	B LTC U.S. INF		1363
34	Seward	Augustus H.	MW, UE	MAJ U.S. STF		1364
35	Plympton	Peter W.L.	MW, UE	B LTC U.S. INF		1365
36	De Russy	John	MW	—	D 1850	1366
37	Blake	Edward D.	MW	LTC CSA		1367
38	Heth	Henry	MW, UE	MG CSA		1368

Summary

Class	Number of Graduates	Union Civil War Officers	Confederate Civil War Officers	Union Civil War Generals	Confederate Civil War Generals	Died or Resigned Before Civil War
1847	38	26	4	9	2	8

Class of 1848

Class Rank	Last Name	First Name	Military Service Before Civil War	Civil War Service	Comments	Cullum Number
1	Trowbridge	William P.	U.S. COE	—	R 1856	1369
2	Donelson, Jr.	Andrew J.	U.S. COE	—	D 1859	1370
3	Duane	James C.	UE	MAJ U.S. COE		1371
4	Stevens	Walter H.	U.S. COE	BG CSA		1372
5	Williamson	Robert S.	U.S. COE	B LTC U.S. COE		1373
6	Roys	Rufus A.	U.S. COE	—	D 1850	1374
7	Michler	Nathaniel	U.S. TOP	B LTC U.S. COE		1375
8	Haynes	James M.	U.S. ART	—	D 1850	1376
9	Clark	Joseph C.	U.S. ART	B LTC U.S. ART		1377
10	Jones	William E.	U.S. MTR	BG CSA		1378
11	Tidball	John C.	U.S. ART	B BG USV		1379
12	Gill	William G.	FW	COL CSA		1380
13	Forsythe	Benjamin D.	U.S. INF	—	D 1861	1381
14	Rhett	Thomas S.	FW	COL CSA		1382
15	Holmes	James	U.S. ART	—	D 1854	1383
16	Buford	John	U.S. CAV	MG USV		1384
17	Walbridge	Truman K.	FW	—	D 1856	1385
18	Bryan	Edward B.	U.S. ART	LTC CSA		1386
19	Dodge	Richard I.	U.S. INF	LTC U.S. STF		1387
20	Tallmadge	Grier	U.S. ART	CPT U.S. STF		1388
21	Slaughter	William A.	U.S. INF	—	K 1855	1389
22	Russell	Robert M.	U.S. INF	—	R 1850	1390
23	Tyler	Charles H.	UE	LTC CSA		1391
24	Booth	John C.	FW	MAJ CSA		1392
25	Jackson	Thomas K.	U.S. INF	MAJ CSA		1393
26	Paige	George H.	U.S. INF	—	D 1859	1394
27	McLean	Nathaniel H.	U.S. INF	MAJ U.S. STF		1395
28	Miller	A. Galbraith	U.S. INF	LTC MD VOL[38]		1396
29	Ogle	Charles H.	U.S. CAV	MAJ NY VOL[39]		1397
30	Beall	William N.R.	U.S. INF	BG CSA		1398
31	Paine	Ferdinand	U.S. INF	—	D 1854	1399
32	Johns	Thomas D.	U.S. INF	COL MA VOL[40]		1400
33	Mechling	William T.	U.S. INF	MAJ CSA		1401
34	Barber	George C.	U.S. INF	—	D 1853	1402
35	Huston	Daniel	U.S. INF	B LTC U.S. INF		1403
36	Evans	N. George	U.S. CAV	BG CSA		1404
37	Steuart	George H.	U.S. CAV	BG CSA		1405
38	Howland	George W.	U.S. MTR	B MAJ U.S. MTR		1406

Summary

Class	Number of Graduates	Union Civil War Officers	Confederate Civil War Officers	Union Civil War Generals	Confederate Civil War Generals	Died or Resigned Before Civil War
1848	38	14	12	2	5	12

Class of 1849

Class Rank	Last Name	First Name	Military Service Before Civil War	Civil War Service	Comments	Cullum Number
1	Gilmore	Quincy A.	U.S. COE	MG USV		1407
2	Parke	John G.	U.S. TOP	MG USV		1408
3	Benét	Stephen V.	U.S. ORD	CPT U.S. ORD		1409

Class Rank	Last Name	First Name	Military Service Before Civil War	Civil War Service	Comments	Cullum Number
4	Haines	Thomas J.	FW	MAJ U.S. STF		1410
5	Duncan	Johnson K.	FW	BG CSA		1411
6	Silvey	William	FW	CPT U.S. ART		1412
7	Du Barry	Beekman	FW	MAJ U.S. STF		1413
8	Perkins	Delvan D.	FW, UE	MAJ U.S. STF		1414
9	Baird	Absalom	FW	B MG USV		1415
10	Nimmo	William A.	U.S. ART	—	D 1856	1416
11	Gogswell	Milton	U.S. INF	B LTC USA		1417
12	Stockton	Edward D.	FW	—	D 1857	1418
13	Platt	Edward R.	FW	MAJ U.S. STF JAG[41]		1419
14	McKeever	Chauncey	FW, UE	LTC U.S. STF		1420
15	Lewis	William H.	FW, UE	MAJ U.S. INF		1421
16	Kellogg	John	U.S. ART	MAJ U.S. STF		1422
17	Moore	John C.	FW	BG CSA		1423
18	Saxton	Rufus	FW	B MG USV		1424
19	Wright	Thomas	FW	—	D 1857	1425
20	De Lano	Horace F.	U.S. CAV	—	D 1854	1426
21	McClure	Daniel	U.S. MTR	MAJ U.S. STF		1427
22	Hudson	Edward McK.	FW	LTC U.S. STF		1428
23	Withers	John	U.S. INF	LTC CSA		1429
24	Tevis	Washington C.	U.S. MTR	COL MD VOL[42]		1430
25	Robertson	Beverly H.	U.S. CAV	BG CSA		1431
26	Tidball	Joseph L.	UE	—	R 1861	1432
27	Field	Charles W.	U.S. CAV	MG CSA		1433
28	Barton	Seth M.	U.S. INF	BG CSA		1434
29	Green	Duff C.	U.S. INF	BG AL MIL[43]		1435
30	Johnson	Richard W.	U.S. CAV	B MG USV		1436
31	Holabird	Samuel B.	U.S. INF	COL U.S. STF		1437
32	Williams	Thomas G.	U.S. INF	LTC CSA		1438
33	Washington	Thornton A.	U.S. INF	LTC CSA		1439
34	Frazer	John W.	U.S. INF	COL CSA		1440
35	Cumming	Alfred	UE	BG CSA		1441
36	English	Thomas C.	U.S. INF	MAJ U.S. INF		1442
37	McArthur	Joseph H.	U.S. CAV	MAJ U.S. CAV		1443
38	Roy	James P.	U.S. INF	MAJ U.S. INF		1444
39	Alvord	Charles B.	U.S. INF	—	D 1860	1445
40	Clark	Darius D.	U.S. INF	—	D 1859	1446
41	Marshall	Louis H.	U.S. INF	MAJ U.S. INF		1447
42	Reynolds	Samuel H.	U.S. INF	COL CSA		1448
43	McIntosh	James McQ.	U.S. CAV	BG CSA		1449

Summary

Class	Number of Graduates	Union Civil War Officers	Confederate Civil War Officers	Union Civil War Generals	Confederate Civil War Generals	Died or Resigned Before Civil War
1849	43	23	13	5	7	7

Class of 1850

Class Rank	Last Name	First Name	Military Service Before Civil War	Civil War Service	Comments	Cullum Number
1	Prime	Frederick E.	U.S. COE	MAJ U.S. COE		1450
2	Warren	Gouverneur K.	U.S. TOP	MG USV		1451
3	Crispin	Silas	U.S. ORD	CPT U.S. ORD		1452
4	Grover	Cuvier	U.S. INF	B MG USV		1453

Class Rank	Last Name	First Name	Military Service Before Civil War	Civil War Service	Comments	Cullum Number
5	Wyman	Powell T.	FW	COL MA VOL[44]		1454
6	Wheelock	Joseph H.	FW	COL MA VOL[45]		1455
7	Culbertson	Jacob	U.S. ART	CPT CSA		1456
8	Mack	Oscar A.	FW	MAJ U.S. STF		1457
9	Dungan	Hugh E.	U.S. ART	—	D 1853	1458
10	Bowen	Achilles	U.S. ART	MAJ CSA COE	R 1850	1459
11	Magruder	William T.	U.S. CAV	CPT CSA		1460
12	Slemmer	Adam J.	FW	BG USV		1461
13	Arnold	Richard	U.S. ART	BG USV		1462
14	Flewellen	James P.	U.S. ART	MAJ CSA	R 1854	1463
15	Walker	Lucius M.	U.S. CAV	BG CSA		1464
16	Mebane	John A.	FW	—	D 1854	1465
17	Long	Armistead L.	U.S. ART	BG CSA		1466
18	Ransom	Robert	U.S. CAV	MG CSA		1467
19	Carr	Eugene A.	U.S. CAV	BG USV		1468
20	Carlin	William P.	UE	BG USV		1469
21	Beckwith	Amos	FW	B BG USV		1470
22	Winder	Charles S.	U.S. INF	BG CSA		1471
23	Bates	Francis H.	U.S. INF	B MAJ U.S. INF		1472
24	Holliday	Jonas P.	UE	COL VT VOL[46]		1473
25	Marshall	Elisha G.	UE	B COL NY VOL[47]		1474
26	Pearce	N. Bartlett	U.S. INF	MAJ CSA		1475
27	Calhoun	William R.	U.S. CAV	COL CSA		1476
28	Johnston	Robert	UE	COL CSA		1477
29	Bingham	Thomas	U.S. CAV	CSA—unknown		1478
30	Colcord	Austin N.	U.S. CAV	—	R 1854	1479
31	MacFeely	Robert	U.S. INF	MAJ U.S. STF		1480
32	Alley	John W.	U.S. INF	CPT U.S. INF		1481
33	Cabell	William L.	U.S. INF	BG CSA	Mayor of Dallas	1482
34	Wilson	James H.	U.S. INF	LTC CSA	R 1851	1483
35	Bankhead	Henry C.	U.S. INF	B COL USV		1484
36	Sargent	Alden	U.S. INF	—	R 1856	1485
37	Cole	Robert G.	U.S. INF	LTC CSA		1486
38	Mouton	John J.A.A.	U.S. INF	BG CSA		1487
39	Haile	Joseph T.	U.S. INF	—	D 1853	1488
40	Corley	James L.	UE	LTC CSA		1489
41	Searle	Zetus S.	U.S. INF	—	R 1850	1490
42	Maxwell	J. Edward	U.S. INF	—	K 1854	1491
43	Follett	Frederick M.	U.S. INF	B MAJ USA		1492
44	Stith	Donald C.	UE	COL USA		1493

Summary

Class	Number of Graduates	Union Civil War Officers	Confederate Civil War Officers	Union Civil War Generals	Confederate Civil War Generals	Died or Resigned Before Civil War
1850	44	20	16	7	6	7

Class of 1851

Class Rank	Last Name	First Name	Military Service Before Civil War	Civil War Service	Comments	Cullum Number
1	Andrews	George L.	U.S. COE	BG USV		1494
2	Morton	James St. C.	U.S. COE	B BG USA		1495
3	Balch	George T.	U.S. ORD	CPT U.S. ORD		1496

Class Rank	Last Name	First Name	Military Service Before Civil War	Civil War Service	Comments	Cullum Number
4	Welcker	William T.	U.S. ORD	MAJ CSA		1497
5	Piper	Alexander	U.S. ART	B LTC U.S. ART		1498
6	Thompson	James	U.S. ART	B MAJ U.S. ART		1499
7	Huse	Caleb	U.S. ART	MAJ CSA		1500
8	Garrard	Kenner	U.S. CAV	B MG USV		1501
9	Helm	Ben Hardin	U.S. CAV	BG CSA	Orphan Brigade	1502
10	Day	Edward H.	U.S. ART	—	D 1860	1503
11	Gillem	Alvan C.	U.S. ART	BG USV		1504
12	Root	De Witt N.	U.S. ART	—	D 1851	1505
13	Perry	Alexander J.	U.S. ART	COL U.S. STF		1506
14	Moore	Isaiah N.	U.S. CAV	COL U.S. CAV		1507
15	Edwards	John	U.S. ART	B LTC U.S. ART		1508
16	Molinard	Albert J.S.	FW	CPT U.S. ART		1509
17	Maynadier	Henry E.	UE	MAJ U.S. INF		1510
18	Bell	David	U.S. CAV	—	D 1860	1511
19	Williams	Robert	U.S. CAV	B LTC U.S. CAV		1512
20	Mendenhall	John	U.S. ART	B LTC USA		1513
21	Parks	Martin P. Jr.	U.S. INF	—	D 1852	1514
22	Ransom	Hyatt C.	U.S. MTR	LTC U.S. STF		1515
23	McRae	Alexander	U.S. MTR	CPT U.S. MTR		1516
24	Norris	Charles E.	U.S. CAV	B MAJ U.S. CAV		1517
25	Chapin	Gurden	UE	MAJ U.S. INF		1518
26	Kelton	John C.	U.S. INF	MAJ U.S. STF		1519
27	Morris	William H.	U.S. INF	CPT USV		1520
28	Curtiss	James	U.S. INF	B MAJ U.S. INF		1521
29	Patterson	Robert E.	U.S. INF	COL PA VOL[48]		1522
30	Amory	Thomas J.C.	UE	B BG USV		1523
31	Whipple	William D.	U.S. INF	BG USV		1524
32	Hodges	Henry C.	U.S. INF	CPT U.S. STF		1545
33	Daniel	Junius	U.S. INF	BG CSA		1526
34	Jones	Roger	U.S. MTR	MAJ U.S. STF		1527
35	Bond	Adolphus F.	U.S. INF	CPT U.S. INF		1528
36	Smith	Melancthon	U.S. INF	COL CSA		1529
37	Palfrey	Edward A.	U.S. INF	LTC CSA		1530
38	Shaaf	John T.	U.S. INF	CPT CSA		1531
39	Witter	Henry C.	U.S. INF	—	R 1855	1532
40	Tilford	Joseph G.	UE	B MAJ U.S. MTR		1533
41	Greene	James B.	U.S. INF	CPT CSA	POW	1534
42	Baker	Lawrence S.	U.S. MTR	BG CSA		1535

Summary

Class	Number of Graduates	Union Civil War Officers	Confederate Civil War Officers	Union Civil War Generals	Confederate Civil War Generals	Died or Resigned Before Civil War
1851	42	28	9	6	3	5

Class of 1852

Class Rank	Last Name	First Name	Military Service Before Civil War	Civil War Service	Comments	Cullum Number
1	Casey	Thomas L.	U.S. COE	MAJ U.S. COE		1536
2	Alexander	Newton F.	U.S. COE	—	D 1858	1537
3	Mendell	George H.	U.S. TOP	B COL U.S. COE		1538
4	Rose	George W.	U.S. TOP	—	R 1856	1539
5	Ives	Joseph C.	U.S. TOP	COL CSA		1540
6	Todd	John W.	U.S. ORD	CPT U.S. ORD		1541
7	Slocum	Henry W.	U.S. ART	MG USV		1542
8	Voast	James van	U.S. INF	MAJ U.S. INF		1543
9	Stanky	David S.	U.S. CAV	MG USV		1544
10	Anderson	George B.	U.S. CAV	BG CSA		1545
11	Bonaparte	Jerome N.	U.S. MTR	—	R 1854 French Military	1546
12	DeVeue	Henry	U.S. ART	CPT CSA		1547
13	Robinson	James W.	FW	1LT U.S. ART		1548
14	Hascall	Milo S.	U.S. ART	BG USV		1549
15	Mullan	John	U.S. ART	CPT U.S. ART		1550
16	Mowry	Sylvester	U.S. ART	—	R 1858	1551
17	Cosby	George B.	U.S. CAV	BG CSA		1552
18	Thomas	Robert B.	FW	COL CSA		1553
19	Hartsuff	George L.	U.S. ART	MG USV		1554
20	Woods	Charles R.	U.S. INF	B MG USV		1555
21	Davis	Matthew L.	U.S. INF	COL CSA		1556
22	Forney	John H.	UE	MG CSA		1557
23	Polk	Marshall T.	U.S. INF	LTC CSA		1578
24	Swaine	Peter T.	UE	B LTC U.S. INF		1559
25	Rundell	Charles H.	U.S. INF	MAJ CSA		1560
26	Evans	Andrew W.	U.S. INF	B LTC U.S. CAV		1561
27	O'Connell	John D.	U.S. INF	B LTC U.S. INF		1562
28	Nugen	John	U.S. INF	—	D 1857	1563
29	Fleming	Hugh B.	U.S. INF	CPT U.S. INF		1564
30	McCook	Alexander McD.	U.S. INF	MG USV		1565
31	Douglass	Henry	U.S. INF	B MAJ U.S. INF		1566
32	Myers	William	U.S. INF	COL U.S. STF		1567
33	Stockton	Philip	U.S. INF	COL CSA		1568
34	Williams	George A.	U.S. INF	B LTC U.S. INF		1569
35	Kautz	August V.	U.S. INF	B MG USV		1570
36	Williams	Lawrence A.	UE	MAJ U.S. CAV		1571
37	Kellogg	Lyman M.	U.S. ART	B MAJ U.S. INF		1572
38	Crook	George	U.S. INF	MG USV		1573
39	Bagby	Arthur P.	U.S. INF	COL CSA		1574
40	Hawkins	John P.	U.S. INF	BG USV		1575
41	Phillips	Edwin D.	U.S. INF	CPT U.S. INF		1576
42	Bonneau	Richard V.	U.S. INF	MAJ CSA		1577
43	Garber	Hezekiah H.	U.S. INF	—	D 1859	1578

Summary

Class	Number of Graduates	Union Civil War Officers	Confederate Civil War Officers	Union Civil War Generals	Confederate Civil War Generals	Died or Resigned Before Civil War
1852	43	25	12	9	3	6

Class of 1853

Class Rank	Last Name	First Name	Military Service Before Civil War	Civil War Service	Comments	Cullum Number
1	McPherson	James B.	U.S. COE	MG USV		1579
2	Craighill	William P.	U.S. COE	CPT U.S. COE		1580
3	Sill	Joshua W.	U.S. ORD	BG USV		1581
4	Boggs	William R.	U.S. ORD	BG CSA		1582
5	Shunk	Francis J.	UE	CPT U.S. ORD		1583
6	Smith	William S.	U.S. ART	BG USV		1584
7	Schofield	John M.	U.S. ART	BG USA		1585
8	Blunt	Matthew M.	U.S. ART	B LTC U.S. INF		1586
9	Hight	Thomas	U.S. CAV	COL ME VOL[49]		1587
10	Bissell	George R.	U.S. ART	—	R 1856	1588
11	Vincent	Thomas M.	FW	MAJ U.S. STF		1589
12	Symonds	Henry C.	U.S. ART	MAJ U.S. STF		1590
13	Bowen	John S.	U.S. MTR	MG CSA		1591
14	Bell	George	U.S. ART	LTC USV		1592
15	Burns	James D.	U.S. ART	—	D 1854	1593
16	Terrill	William R.	FW	BG USV		1594
17	Pelouze	Louis H.	FW, UE	B LTC USA		1595
18	Solomon	Owen F.	FW	—	D 1859	1596
19	Livingston	La Rhett L.	U.S. ART	B LTC U.S. ART		1597
20	Duryea	Richard C.	FW	COL NY VOL[50]		1598
21	Chandler	John G.	U.S. ART	CPT U.S. STF		1599
22	Tyler	Robert O.	U.S. ART	B MG USV		1600
23	Jenkins	Walworth	U.S. ART	CPT U.S. STF		1601
24	Sweitzer	N. Bowman	U.S. CAV	COL NY VOL[51]		1602
25	White	James L.	U.S. ART	MAJ CSA		1603
26	Allston	Benjamin	U.S. CAV	COL CSA		1604
27	Chamberlain	Benjamin F.	U.S. INF	MAJ WV VOL[52]		1605
28	Edson	John H.	U.S. MTR	MAJ MA VOL[53]		1606
29	Wilson	Thomas	FW	B COL USV		1607
30	Lowe	William W.	U.S. CAV	B LTC USV		1608
31	Chambliss	John R.	U.S. MTR	BG CSA		1609
32	Dye	William McE.	U.S. INF	B LTC USV		1610
33	Davidson	Henry B.	MW	BG CSA		1611
34	Sheridan	Philip H.	U.S. INF	MG USA		1612
35	Webb	William A.	FW	CPT U.S. INF		1613
36	Grattan	John L.	U.S. INF	—	K 1854	1614
37	Otis	Elmer	U.S. CAV	B LTC USA		1615
38	Latimer	Alfred E.	U.S. INF	CPT USA		1616
39	Smith	Benjamin F.	U.S. INF	COL OH VOL[54]		1617
40	Higgins	Silas P.	U.S. INF	—	D 1860	1618
41	Walker	Henry H.	U.S. INF	BG CSA		1619
42	Jones	Edmund C.	U.S. INF	CPT U.S. INF		1620
43	Chambers	Alexander	FW, UE	BG USV		1621
44	Hood	John B.	U.S. CAV	G CSA		1622
45	Smith	James A.	UE	BG CSA		1623
46	Hunter	Robert F.	U.S. INF	—	RD 1861	1624
47	Jones	Thomas M.	U.S. INF	COL CSA		1625
48	Plummer	Augustus H.	UE	CPT U.S. INF		1626
49	McIntyre	James B.	UE	B LTC U.S. CAV		1627
50	Rich	Lucius L.	UE	COL CSA		1628
51	Ross	Reuben R.	U.S. INF	BG CSA		1629
52	Craig	William	U.S. INF	CPT U.S. QTR		1630

U.S. Military Academy Graduating Classes

Summary

Class	Number of Graduates	Union Civil War Officers	Confederate Civil War Officers	Union Civil War Generals	Confederate Civil War Generals	Died or Resigned Before Civil War
1853	52	34	12	8	8	6

Class of 1854

Class Rank	Last Name	First Name	Military Service Before Civil War	Civil War Service	Comments	Cullum Number
1	Lee	G.W. Custis	U.S. COE	MG CSA		1631
2	Abbot	Henry L.	U.S. TOP	B BG USV		1632
3	Ruger	Thomas H.	U.S. COE	B MG USV		1633
4	Howard	Oliver O.	FW	MG USA		1634
5	Treadwell	Thomas J.	U.S. ORD	CPT U.S. ORD		1635
6	Turnbull	Charles N.	U.S. TOP	B MAJ U.S. COE		1636
7	Deshler	James	U.S. INF	BG CSA		1637
8	Closson	Henry W.	U.S. ART	B LTC U.S. INF		1638
9	Bingham	Judson D.	U.S. ART	CPT U.S. STF		1639
10	Pegram	John	UE	BG CSA		1640
11	Rogers	Charles G.	U.S. CAV	LTC CSA		1641
12	Wright	Thomas J.	U.S. CAV	—	D 1857	1642
13	Stuart	James E.B.	UE	MG CSA		1643
14	Gracie	Archibald	U.S. INF	BG CSA		1644
15	Smead	John R.	U.S. ART	CPT U.S. ART		1645
16	Morgan	Michael R.	U.S. ART	B LTC U.S. STF		1646
17	Lee	Stephen D.	FW	LG CSA		1647
18	Carr	Milton T.	U.S. CAV	CPT U.S. CAV		1648
19	Pender	William D.	U.S. CAV	MG CSA		1649
20	Langdon	Loomis L.	U.S. ART	B LTC U.S. ART		1650
21	Greble	John T.	U.S. ART	B LTC U.S. ART		1651
22	Villepigue	John B.	UE	BG CSA		1652
23	Smalley	Henry A.	U.S. ART	CPT U.S. ART		1653
24	Kinsey	Samuel	U.S. ART	—	D 1855	1654
25	Smead	Abner	U.S. CAV	COL CSA	RD 1861	1655
26	Greene	Oliver D.	UE	CPT U.S. ART		1656
27	Weed	Stephen H.	UE	BG USV		1657
28	Townsend	E. Franklin	U.S. ART	B MAJ U.S. ART		1658
29	Chapman	Alfred B.	U.S. CAV	—	R 1861	1659
30	Gordon	George A.	UE	B LTC U.S. CAV		1660
31	Long	John O.	U.S. INF	LTC CSA		1661
32	Davis	Benjamin F.	U.S. CAV	COL NY VOL[55]		1662
33	Wright	James	U.S. MTR	—	D 1857	1663
34	Waterman	Palmer	U.S. INF	—	D 1855	1664
35	Hancock	David P.	UE	B MAJ U.S. INF		1665
36	Sheppard	Samuel T.	U.S. INF	—	D 1855	1666
37	Davant	William M.	U.S. MTR	—	D 1855	1667
38	Sawtelle	Charles G.	UE	LTC USV		1668
39	Wade	Levi L.	—	—	D 1854	1669
40	Mercer	John T.	U.S. CAV	COL CSA		1670
41	Bliss	Zenas R.	U.S. INF	B LTC USV		1671
42	O'Connor	Edgar	U.S. INF	COL WI VOL[56]		1672
43	Mullins	John	UE	COL CSA		1673
44	Brotherton	David H.	FW, UE	B MAJ U.S. INF		1674
45	Randal	Horace	U.S. INF	COL CSA		1675
46	McCleary	John	UE	B MAJ U.S. INF		1676

Summary

Class	Number of Graduates	Union Civil War Officers	Confederate Civil War Officers	Union Civil War Generals	Confederate Civil War Generals	Died or Resigned Before Civil War
1854	46	24	14	4	8	8

Class of 1855

Class Rank	Last Name	First Name	Military Service Before Civil War	Civil War Service	Comments	Cullum Number
1	Comstock	Cyrus B.	U.S. COE	B BG USV		1677
2	Weitzel	Godfrey	U.S. COE	MG USV		1678
3	Van Camp	Cornelius	U.S. CAV	—	K 1858	1679
4	Elliot	George H.	U.S. COE	CPT U.S. COE		1680
5	Wheeler	Junius B.	U.S. TOP	B MAJ U.S. COE		1681
6	Gay	Ebenezer	U.S. CAV	B LTC U.S. INF		1682
7	Breck	Samuel	U.S. ART	B LTC U.S. STF		1683
8	Gregg	David McM.	U.S. CAV	B MG USV		1684
9	Childs	Frederick L.	U.S. ART	LTC CSA		1685
10	Du Bois	John V.D.	U.S. MTR	B MAJ U.S. CAV		1686
11	Small	Michael P.	U.S. ART	B COL USV		1687
12	Nicholls	Francis R.T.	U.S. ART	BG CSA		1688
13	Webb	Alexander S.	U.S. ART	B MG USV		1689
14	Turner	John W.	U.S. ART	B MG USV		1690
15	Shoup	Francis A.	U.S. ART	BG CSA		1691
16	Church	John R.	UE	CSA—unknown		1692
17	Colburn	Albert V.	UE	MAJ U.S. STF		1693
18	Wheeler	James	U.S. CAV	CPT U.S. CAV		1694
19	Ruggles	George D.	U.S. INF	MAJ U.S. STF		1695
20	Merrill	Lewis	UE	B MAJ U.S. CAV		1696
21	Torbert	Alfred T.A.	UE	B MG USV		1697
22	Thomas	Charles W.	U.S. INF	LTC USV		1698
23	Hill	James H.	UE	MAJ CSA		1699
24	Hartz	Edward L.	U.S. INF	CPT U.S. STF		1700
25	Bennett	Clarence E.	UE	LTC CA VOL[57]		1701
26	Averell	William W.	U.S. MTR	BG USV		1702
27	Bryan	Timothy M.	U.S. INF	COL PA VOL[58]		1703
28	Hazen	William B.	U.S. INF	MG USV		1704
29	Freedley	Henry W.	U.S. INF	B LTC U.S. INF		1705
30	Lazelle	Henry M.	U.S. INF	B MAJ U.S. INF		1706
31	Pease	William R.	UE	COL NY VOL[59]		1707
32	Allen	Jesse K.	U.S. INF	—	K 1858	1708
33	Hill	Robert C.	FW, UE	COL CSA		1709
34	Dick	George McGunigle	U.S. INF	—	D 1856	1710

Summary

Class	Number of Graduates	Union Civil War Officers	Confederate Civil War Officers	Union Civil War Generals	Confederate Civil War Generals	Died or Resigned Before Civil War
1855	34	25	6	8	2	3

Class of 1856

Class Rank	Last Name	First Name	Military Service Before Civil War	Civil War Service	Comments	Cullum Number
1	Snyder	George W.	U.S. COE	B MAJ U.S. COE		1711
2	Houston	David C.	U.S. COE	B LTC U.S. COE		1712
3	McAlester	Miles D.	U.S. COE	B COL U.S. COE		1713
4	Lee	Charles C.	U.S. ORD	COL CSA		1714
5	De Hart	Henry V.	U.S. ART	CPT U.S. ART		1715
6	Poe	Orlando M.	U.S. TOP	BG USV		1716
7	Tipton	John	U.S. ART	1L U.S. ART		1717
8	Hascall	Herbert A.	U.S. ART	CPT U.S. ART		1718
9	Porter	A. Parker	U.S. CAV	LTC USV		1719
10	Vinton	Francis L.	U.S. CAV	BG USV	Mining Engineer	1720
11	Bayard	George D.	U.S. CAV	BG USV		1721
12	Sullivan	Thomas C.	U.S. ART	LTC U.S. STF		1722
13	Barriger	John C.	U.S. ART	LTC USV		1723
14	Lorain	Lorenzo	U.S. ART	CPT U.S. ART		1724
15	Bennett	John	U.S. ART	—	D 1859	1725
16	Owens	Wesley	U.S. CAV	LTC U.S. STF		1726
17	Bailey	Guilford	U.S. ART	COL NY VOL[60]		1727
18	Shinn	John B.	U.S. ART	CPT U.S. ART		1728
19	Lyon	Hylan B.	FW	BG CSA		1729
20	Bainbridge	Edmund C.	FW	MAJ U.S. STF		1730
21	Lomax	Lunsford L.	U.S. CAV	MG CSA		1731
22	Lodor	Richard	U.S. ART	LTC USV		1732
23	Major	James P.	U.S. CAV	BG CSA		1733
24	Gilman	Jeremiah H.	U.S. ART	B LTC U.S. INF		1734
25	Miller	Thomas E.	U.S. ART	1L U.S. ART		1735
26	Stivers	Charles B.	UE	CPT U.S. INF		1736
27	Gaston	William	U.S. CAV	—	K 1858	1737
28	Forsyth	James W.	U.S. INF	B BG USV		1738
29	Walker	Thomas W.	U.S. INF	B MAJ U.S. INF		1739
30	Jackson	George	U.S. CAV	COL CSA		1740
31	Taylor	Joseph H.	U.S. CAV	LTC USV		1741
32	Ritter	John F.	U.S. INF	B LTC U.S. INF		1742
33	Mizner	John K.	U.S. CAV	B LTC USV		1743
34	Armistead	Frank S.	UE	COL CSA		1744
35	Biggs	Herman	U.S. INF	LTC USV		1745
36	Gentry	William T.	U.S. INF	B MAJ U.S. INF		1746
37	Alexander	James B.S.	U.S. INF	—	R 1861	1747
38	Jackson	William H.	U.S. MTR	BG CSA		1748
39	McLemore	Owen K.	U.S. INF	LTC CSA		1749
40	Lord	Richard S.C.	U.S. INF	B MAJ U.S. INF		1750
41	Sanders	William P.	U.S. CAV	BG USV		1751
42	McMillan	James	U.S. INF	CPT U.S. INF		1752
43	Hughes	William B.	U.S. INF	CPT U.S. STF		1753
44	Carrol	Samuel S.	UE	BG USV		1754
45	Lee	Fitzhugh	U.S. CAV	MG CSA		1755
46	Hildt	J. McLean	U.S. INF	B MAJ U.S. INF		1756
47	Ives	Brayton C.	U.S. INF	—	D 1857	1757
48	Enos	Herbert M.	U.S. INF	MAJ U.S. STF		1758
49	Cunningham	Arthur S.	UE	LTC CSA		1759

Summary

Class	Number of Graduates	Union Civil War Officers	Confederate Civil War Officers	Union Civil War Generals	Confederate Civil War Generals	Died or Resigned Before Civil War
1856	49	35	10	6	5	4

Class of 1857

Class Rank	Last Name	First Name	Military Service Before Civil War	Civil War Service	Comments	Cullum Number
1	Palfrey	John C.	U.S. COE	B MAJ U.S. COE		1760
2	Meade	Richard K.	U.S. COE	MAJ CSA		1761
3	Alexander	E. Porter	U.S. COE	BG CSA		1762
4	Robert	Henry M.	U.S. COE	CPT U.S. COE		1763
5	Strong	George C.	U.S. ORD	BG USV		1764
6	Smith	J.L. Kirby	U.S. TOP	B COL U.S. TOP		1765
7	Baylor	Thomas G.	U.S. ORD	B LTC U.S. ORD		1766
8	Putnam	Haldiman S.	U.S. TOP	B COL U.S. TOP		1767
9	Smith	William P.	U.S. TOP	COL CSA		1768
10	Kensel	George A.	U.S. ART	LTC USV		1769
11	Berry	Thomas J.	U.S. CAV	LTC CSA		1770
12	Morgan	Charles H.	U.S. ART	B BG USV		1771
13	Fish	Oliver H.	UE	CSA—none		1772
14	Wildrick	Abram C.	UE	B MAJ U.S. ART		1773
15	Walker	Charles J.	UE	COL KY VOL[61]		1774
16	Beach	Francis	U.S. ART	B LTC U.S. ART		1775
17	Sinclair	William	U.S. ART	LTC USV		1776
18	Robinson	Augustus G.	U.S. ART	CPT U.S. STF		1777
19	Ferguson	Samuel W.	UE	BG CSA		1778
20	Reno	Marcus A.	U.S. CAV	B LTC U.S. CAV		1779
21	Warner	Edward R.	U.S. ART	B COL USV		1780
22	Kimmel	Manning M.	U.S. CAV	MAJ CSA		1781
23	Weeks	George H.	U.S. ART	CPT U.S. STF		1782
24	Magruder	John T.	U.S. CAV	—	D 1858	1783
25	Cunningham	George A.	UE	COL CSA		1784
26	McNeill	Henry C.	U.S. MTR	COL CSA		1785
27	Claflin	Ira W.	U.S. MTR	B MAJ U.S. CAV		1786
28	Cone	Aurelius F.	U.S. INF	LTC CSA		1787
29	Quattlebaum	Paul J.	U.S. INF	MAJ CSA		1788
30	Marmaduke	John S.	UE	MG CSA		1789
31	Holt	George W.	U.S. INF	LTC CSA		1790
32	Conrad	Joseph S.	U.S. INF	B LTC U.S. STF		1791
33	Conner	Edward J.	U.S. INF	CPT U.S. INF		1792
34	Ryan	George	UE	COL NY VOL[62]		1793
35	Anderson	Robert H.	U.S. INF	BG CSA		1794
36	Farrand	Charles E	U.S. INF	CPT U.S. INF		1795
37	Lee	Thomas J.	U.S. INF	IN VOL[63]	Private	1796
38	Peck	Lafayette	U.S. INF	LT CSA		1797

Summary

Class	Number of Graduates	Union Civil War Officers	Confederate Civil War Officers	Union Civil War Generals	Confederate Civil War Generals	Died or Resigned Before Civil War
1857	38	21	15	2	4	2

Class of 1858

Class Rank	Last Name	First Name	Military Service Before Civil War	Civil War Service	Comments	Cullum Number
1	Paine	William C.	U.S. COE	CPT U.S. COE		1798
2	White	Moses J.	U.S. ORD	COL CSA		1799
3	Dixon	Joseph	U.S. TOP	CPT CSA		1800
4	Echols	William H.	U.S. TOP	MAJ CSA		1801
5	Saunders	John C.	U.S. ORD	LTC CSA		1802
6	Hallonquist	James H.	U.S. ART	COL CSA		1803
7	Tannatt	Thomas R.	U.S. ART	COL USV		1804
8	Miller	Marcus	U.S. ART	CPT U.S. ART		1805
9	Ingraham	Charles H.	U.S. INF	CPT U.S. INF		1806
10	Napier	Leroy	U.S. CAV	LTC CSA		1807
11	Williams	Solomon	U.S. CAV	COL CSA		1808
12	Brewer	Richard H.	U.S. CAV	COL CSA		1809
13	McKee	Samuel	U.S. CAV	CPT U.S. CAV		1810
14	Van Horn	James J.	U.S. INF	B MAJ U.S. INF		1811
15	Jackson	Andrew	U.S. CAV	COL CSA		1812
16	Harker	Charles G.	U.S. INF	BG USV		1813
17	Reed	Sardine P.	U.S. INF	—	D 1859	1814
18	Frank	Royal T.	U.S. INF	B LTC U.S. INF		1815
19	Cressey	Edward B.	U.S. MTR	CPT U.S. CAV		1816
20	Carey	Asa B.	UE	B MAJ U.S. INF		1817
21	Bell	William H.	U.S. INF	CPT U.S. STF		1818
22	Thomas	Bryan M.	UE	BG CSA		1819
23	Nicodemus	William J.L.	UE	LTC U.S. SIG		1820
24	Gooding	Oliver P.	UE	CPT U.S. INF		1821
25	Robinson	William G.	U.S. INF	COL CSA		1822
26	Bascom	George N.	UE	CPT U.S. INF		1823
27	Jesup	Charles E.	U.S. INF	—	R 1860	1824

Summary

Class	Number of Graduates	Union Civil War Officers	Confederate Civil War Officers	Union Civil War Generals	Confederate Civil War Generals	Died or Resigned Before Civil War
1858	27	14	11	1	1	2

Class of 1859

Class Rank	Last Name	First Name	Military Service Before Civil War	Civil War Service	Comments	Cullum Number
1	Merrill	William E.	U.S. COE	COL USV		1825
2	Lockett	Samuel H.	U.S. COE	MAJ CSA		1826
3	Collins	Charles R.	U.S. TOP	COL CSA		1827
4	Reese	Chauncey B.	U.S. COE	LTC USV		1828
5	Wagner	Orlando G.	U.S. TOP	B MAJ U.S. TOP		1829
6	Beckham	Robert F.	U.S. TOP	COL CSA		1830
7	Wright	Moses H.	U.S. ORD	COL CSA		1831
8	Bush	Edward G.	U.S. INF	B MAJ U.S. INF		1832
9	Guenther	Francis L.	U.S. ART	B MAJ U.S. ART		1833

Class Rank	Last Name	First Name	Military Service Before Civil War	Civil War Service	Comments	Cullum Number
10	Carling	Elias B.	U.S. ART	CPT U.S. STF		1834
11	Hardin	Michael D.	U.S. ART	BG USV		1835
12	Baker	Eugene M.	U.S. CAV	B LTC U.S. CAV		1836
13	Hall	Norman J.	U.S. ART	B LTC U.S. ART		1837
14	Stone	Roderic	U.S. INF	B MAJ U.S. INF		1838
15	Crilly	Francis J.	U.S. INF	CPT U.S. STF		1839
16	Anderson	Allen L.	U.S. INF	COL CA VOL[64]		1840
17	Stoughton	Edwin H.	U.S. INF	BG USV		1841
18	Carlton	Caleb H.	U.S. INF	COL OH VOL[65]		1842
19	Wheeler	Joseph	U.S. MTR	MG CSA		1843
20	Upham	John J.	U.S. INF	B MAJ U.S. INF		1844
21	Arnold	Abraham K.	U.S. CAV	B MAJ U.S. CAV		1845
22	Worth	Henry A.F.	U.S. INF	CPT U.S. INF		1846

Summary

Class	Number of Graduates	Union Civil War Officers	Confederate Civil War Officers	Union Civil War Generals	Confederate Civil War Generals	Died or Resigned Before Civil War
1859	22	17	5	2	1	0

Class of 1860

Class Rank	Last Name	First Name	Military Service Before Civil War	Civil War Service	Comments	Cullum Number
1	McFarland	Walter	U.S. COE	CPT U.S. COE		1847
2	Tardy	John A.	U.S. COE	CPT U.S. COE		1848
3	Porter	Horace	U.S. ORD	B LTC USV		1849
4	Bowen	Nicholas	U.S. TOP	LTC U.S. STF		1850
5	Edson	Theodore	U.S. ORD	CPT U.S. ORD		1851
6	Wilson	James H.	U.S. TOP	B MG USV		1852
7	Sloan	Benjamin F.	U.S. CAV	MAJ CSA		1853
8	Whittemore	James M.	U.S. ORD	CPT U.S. ORD		1854
9	Randol	Alanson M.	U.S. ART	B LTC U.S. ART		1855
10	Hook	Cornelius	U.S. ART	CPT U.S. ART		1856
11	McCreery	William W.	U.S. ART	CPT CSA		1857
12	Wilson	John M.	U.S. ART	CPT U.S. COE		1858
13	Kellogg	Josiah H.	U.S. CAV	COL PA VOL[66]		1859
14	Ramseur	Stephen D.	U.S. ART	MG CSA		1860
15	Hopkins	Edward R.	U.S. INF	CPT U.S. STF		1861
16	Lynn	Daniel D.	U.S. INF	CPT U.S. INF		1862
17	Foster	Sam A.	U.S. INF	COL MO VOL[67]		1863
18	Pennington	Alex. C.M.	U.S. ART	COL NJ VOL[68]		1864
19	Kerr	John M.	U.S. MTR	2LT CSA		1865
20	Powell	Albert M.	U.S. INF	B LTC U.S. INF		1866
21	Smith	Alfred T.	U.S. INF	CPT U.S. INF		1867
22	Merritt	Wesley	U.S. CAV	B MG USV		1868
23	Martin	James P.	U.S. INF	B MAJ U.S. INF		1869
24	Burtwell	John R.B.	U.S. CAV	COL CSA		1870
25	Jones	William G.	U.S. INF	COL OH VOL[69]		1871
26	Lewis	Martin V.B.	U.S. INF	1LT U.S. INF		1872
27	Marsh	Salem S.	U.S. INF	B LTC U.S. INF		1873
28	Gibbes	Wade E.	U.S. CAV	MAJ CSA		1874
29	Bowman	Charles S.	U.S. CAV	B MAJ U.S. CAV		1875

U.S. Military Academy Graduating Classes

Class Rank	Last Name	First Name	Military Service Before Civil War	Civil War Service	Comments	Cullum Number
30	Cushing	Samuel T.	U.S. INF	CPT U.S. STF		1876
31	Huger	Frank	U.S. INF	COL CSA		1877
32	Hall	Robert H.	U.S. INF	B LTC U.S. INF		1878
33	Andrews	John N.	U.S. INF	B MAJ U.S. INF		1879
34	Riley	Edward B.D.	U.S. INF	LTC CSA		1880
35	Jordan	William H.	U.S. INF	M CA VOL[70]		1881
36	Sweet	John J.	U.S. CAV	1LT U.S. CAV		1882
37	Mishler	Lyman	U.S. INF	B CPT U.S. INF		1883
38	Hollister	George S.	U.S. INF	LTC NY VOL[71]		1884
39	Vanderbilt	George W.	U.S. INF	CPT U.S. INF		1885
40	Warner	James W.	U.S. INF	CPT U.S. INF		1886
41	Borland	Harold	U.S. INF	MAJ CSA		1887

Summary

Class	Number of Graduates	Union Civil War Officers	Confederate Civil War Officers	Union Civil War Generals	Confederate Civil War Generals	Died or Resigned Before Civil War
1860	41	32	9	2	1	0

Class of May 6, 1861

Class Rank	Last Name	First Name	Military Service Before Civil War	Civil War Service	Comments	Cullum Number
1	Du Pont	Henry A.	U.S. COE	B LTC U.S. ART		1888
2	Cross	Charles E.	U.S. COE	B COL U.S. COE		1889
3	Babcock	Orville E.	U.S. COE	B COL U.S. COE		1890
4	Kingsbury	Henry W.	U.S. ORD	COL CT VOL[72]		1891
5	Ames	Albert	U.S. ART	B MG USV		1892
6	Hoxton	Llewellyn G.	U.S. ORD	LTC CSA		1893
7	Buffington	Adelbert R.	U.S. ORD	CPT U.S. ORD		1894
8	Upton	Emory	U.S. ART	B MG USV		1895
9	Chambliss	Nathaniel R.	U.S. ART	MAJ CSA		1896
10	Kirby	Edmund	U.S. ART	1LT U.S. ART		1897
11	Rodgers	John I.	U.S. ART	CPT U.S. ART		1898
12	Benjamin	Samuel N.	U.S. ART	CPT U.S. ART		1899
13	Adair	John	U.S. CAV	—	RD 1861	1900
14	Barlow	John W.	U.S. ART	B MAJ U.S. COE		1901
15	Hazlett	Charles E.	U.S. ART	1LT U.S. ART		1902
16	Patterson	Charles E.	U.S. INF	LTC CSA		1903
17	Kilpatrick	Judson	U.S. ART	BG USV		1904
18	Harwood	Franklin	U.S. ART	B MAJ U.S. COE		1905
19	Dresser	George W.	U.S. ART	B CPT U.S. ART		1906
20	Leoser	Charles McK.	U.S. CAV	CPT U.S. CAV		1907
21	Hasbrouck	Henry C.	U.S. ART	B CPT U.S. ART		1908
22	Elderkin	William A.	U.S. ART	CPT U.S. STF		1909
23	Davies	Francis A.	U.S. ART	B MAJ U.S. INF		1910
24	Campbell	Charles C.	U.S. CAV	MAJ CSA		1911
25	Watson	Malbone F.	U.S. CAV	B MAJ U.S. ART		1912
26	Williams	John B.	U.S. INF	1LT U.S. INF	RD 1863	1913
27	Henry	Guy V.	U.S. ART	B BG USV		1914

Class Rank	Last Name	First Name	Military Service Before Civil War	Civil War Service	Comments	Cullum Number
28	Smyser	Jacob H.	U.S. ART	1LT U.S. ORD		1915
29	Rawles	Jacob B.	U.S. ART	B CPT U.S. ART		1916
30	Gittings	Erskine	U.S. ART	B MAJ U.S. ART		1917
31	Kent	J. Ford	U.S. INF	B COL USV		1918
32	Beaumont	Eugene B.	U.S. CAV	B LTC USA		1919
33	Martin	Leonard	U.S. ART	COL WI VOL		1920
34	Poland	John S.	U.S. INF	B LTC U.S. INF		1921
35	Eastman	Robert L.	U.S. INF	B MAJ U.S. INF		1922
36	Noble	Henry B.	U.S. INF	B CPT U.S. INF		1923
37	Janes	Leroy L.	U.S. ART	CPT U.S. ART		1924
38	Emory	Campbell D.	U.S. INF	B LTC U.S. INF		1925
39	McQuesten	James F.	U.S. CAV	CPT U.S. CAV		1926
40	Sokalski	George O.	U.S. CAV	LTC USV		1927
41	Rice	Olin F.	U.S. INF	COL CSA		1928
42	Rives	Wright	U.S. INF	CPT U.S. INF		1929
43	Gibson	Charles H.	U.S. CAV	1LT U.S. CAV		1930
44	Henry	Mathis W.	U.S. MTR	MAJ CSA		1931
45	Sturgeon	Sheldon	U.S. INF	CPT U.S. INF		1932

Summary

Class	Number of Graduates	Union Civil War Officers	Confederate Civil War Officers	Union Civil War Generals	Confederate Civil War Generals	Died or Resigned Before Civil War
1861—May	45	38	6	4	0	1

Class of June 24, 1861

Class Rank	Last Name	First Name	Military Service Before Civil War	Civil War Service	Comments	Cullum Number
1	O'Rorke	Patrick H.	U.S. COE	B COL U.S. COE		1933
2	Farquhar	Francis U.	U.S. COE	B MAJ COE		1934
3	Dutton	Arthur H.	U.S. COE	B BG USV		1935
4	Derrick	Clarence	U.S. COE	LTC CSA		1936
5	Flagler	Daniel W.	U.S. ORD	B MAJ U.S. ORD		1937
6	Bradford	Thomas C.	U.S. ORD	CPT U.S. ORD		1938
7	Hill	Richard M.	U.S. ORD	CPT U.S. ORD		1939
8	Harris	William H.	U.S. ORD	B LTC U.S. ORD		1940
9	Modecai	Alfred	U.S. TOP	B MAJ U.S. ORD		1941
10	Buel	David H.	U.S. CAV	B MAJ U.S. ORD		1942
11	Lyford	Stephen C.	U.S. CAV	CPT U.S. ORD		1943
12	Cushing	Alonzo H.	U.S. ART	1LT U.S. ART		1944
13	Parsons	Charles C.	U.S. ART	B MAJ U.S. ART		1945
14	Edie	John R.	U.S. CAV	CPT U.S. ORD		1946
15	Babbitt	Lawrence S.	U.S. ART	1LT U.S. ORD		1947
16	Woodruff	George A.	U.S. ART	1LT U.S. ART		1948
17	Audenried	Joseph C.	U.S. CAV	B MAJ U.S. CAV		1949
18	Adams	Julius W.	U.S. INF	CPT U.S. INF		1950
19	Hains	Peter C.	U.S. ART	1LT U.S. ORD		1951
20	Parker	Francis H.	U.S. CAV	1LT U.S. ORD		1952

U.S. Military Academy Graduating Classes

Class Rank	Last Name	First Name	Military Service Before Civil War	Civil War Service	Comments	Cullum Number
21	Farley	Joseph P.	U.S. ART	1LT U.S. ORD		1953
22	Campbell	Joseph B.	U.S. ART	B MAJ U.S. STF		1954
23	Noyes	Henry E.	U.S. CAV	CPT U.S. CAV		1955
24	Remington	Philip H.	U.S. INF	1LT U.S. INF		1956
25	Fuller	William D.	U.S. ART	B MAJ U.S. ART		1957
26	Dimick	Justin E.	U.S. ART	1LT U.S. ART		1958
27	Drouillard	James P.	U.S. INF	CPT U.S. STF		1959
28	Elbert	Leroy S.	U.S. MTR	CPT U.S. CAV		1961
29	Brightly	Charles H.	U.S. INF	B LTC U.S. INF		1962
30	Carter	Eugene	U.S. INF	B MAJ U.S. INF		1963
31	Ferris	Samuel P.	U.S. INF	B MAJ U.S. INF		1964
32	Watts	George O.	U.S. MTR	MAJ CSA		1965
33	Reynolds	Frank A.	U.S. CAV	LTC CSA		1966
34	Custer	George A.	U.S. CAV	B MG USV		1966

Summary

Class	Number of Graduates	Union Civil War Officers	Confederate Civil War Officers	Union Civil War Generals	Confederate Civil War Generals	Died or Resigned Before Civil War
1861—June	34	31	3	2	0	0

Class of 1862

Class Rank	Last Name	First Name	Military Service Before Civil War	Civil War Service	Comments	Cullum Number
1	Mackenzie	Ranald S.	U.S. COE	BG USV		1967
2	Gillespie	George L.	U.S. COE	B LTC COE		1968
3	Burroughs	George	U.S. COE	CPT U.S. COE		1969
4	Suter	Charles R.	U.S. COE	CPT U.S. COE		1970
5	Smith	Jared A.	U.S. COE	CPT U.S. COE		1971
6	Mansfield	Samuel M.	U.S. COE	CPT U.S. COE		1972
7	Wharton	Henry C.	U.S. COE	B CPT U.S. COE		1973
8	Chaffee	Clemens C.	U.S. ORD	—	D 1857	1974
9	Schaff	Morris	U.S. ORD	B CPT U.S. ORD		1975
10	Myers	Jasper	U.S. ORD	1LT U.S. ORD		1976
11	Marye	William A.	U.S. ORD	1LT U.S. ORD		1977
12	Hamilton	Frank B.	U.S. ART	B CPT U.S. ART		1978
13	Arnold	Isaac	U.S. ART	1LT U.S. ORD		1979
14	McCrea	Tully	U.S. ART	B MAJ U.S. ART		1980
15	Lancaster	James M.	U.S. ART	1LT U.S. ART		1981
16	Egan	John	U.S. ART	B MAJ U.S. ART		1982
17	Bolles	Asa	U.S. ART	2LT U.S. ART		1983
18	Sanderson	James A.	U.S. ART	2LT U.S. ART		1984
19	Comly	Clifton	U.S. CAV	1LT U.S. ORD		1985
20	Bartlett	William C.	U.S. ART	LTC NC VOL[73]		1986
21	Wilson	J. Eveleth	U.S. ART	1LT U.S. ART		1987
22	Calef	John H.	U.S. ART	B CPT U.S. ART		1988
23	McIntire	Samuel B.	U.S. ART	B CPT U.S. ART		1989
24	Murray	Albert N.	U.S. ART	B MAJ U.S. ART		1990

Class Rank	Last Name	First Name	Military Service Before Civil War	Civil War Service	Comments	Cullum Number
25	Rollins	James H.	U.S. ART	1LT U.S. ORD		1991
26	Lord	James H.	U.S. ART	B MAJ U.S. ART		1992
27	James	Frederick J.	U.S. CAV	1LT U.S. CAV		1993
28	Warner	Charles N.	U.S. ART	B CPT U.S. ART		1994

Summary

Class	Number of Graduates	Union Civil War Officers	Confederate Civil War Officers	Union Civil War Generals	Confederate Civil War Generals	Died or Resigned Before Civil War
1862	28	27	0	1	0	1

Class of 1863

Class Rank	Last Name	First Name	Military Service Before Civil War	Civil War Service	Comments	Cullum Number
1	Meigs	John R.	U.S. COE	B MAJ U.S. COE		1995
2	Mitchie	Peter S.	U.S. COE	B BG U.S. COE		1996
3	Rabb	James D.	U.S. COE	1LT U.S. COE		1997
4	Twinning	William J.	U.S. COE	B LTC USV		1998
5	King	William R.	U.S. COE	B MAJ U.S. COE		1999
6	Benyaurd	William H.H.	U.S. COE	B MAJ U.S. COE		2000
7	Howell	Charles W.	U.S. COE	B MAJ U.S. COE		2001
8	Holgate	Asa H.	U.S. COE	1LT U.S. COE		2002
9	McGinness	John R.	U.S. ORD	B CPT U.S. ORD		2003
10	McKee	George W.	U.S. ORD	1LT U.S. ORD		2004
11	Phipps	Frank H.	U.S. ORD	1LT U.S. ORD		2005
12	Reilly	James W.	U.S. ORD	1LT U.S. ORD		2006
13	Field	Josiah H.V.	U.S. ORD	1LT U.S. ORD		2007
14	Rockwell	Charles F.	U.S. ORD	1LT U.S. ORD		2008
15	Beebe	William S.	U.S. ORD	B MAJ U.S. ORD		2009
16	Ward	Thomas	U.S. ART	1LT U.S. ART		2010
17	Counselman	Jacob H.	U.S. ART	LTC MD VOL[74]		2011
18	Ramsay	George D. Jr.	U.S. ART	1LT U.S. ART		2012
19	Dodge	Henry C.	U.S. ART	1LT U.S. ART		2013
20	Butler	John G.	U.S. ART	1LT U.S. ART		2014
21	Catlin	Robert	U.S. ART	B CPT U.S. ART		2015
22	Lester	Charles H.	U.S. CAV	B CPT U.S. CAV		2016
23	Robbins	Kenelm	U.S. CAV	B CPT U.S. CAV		2017
24	Sano	James M.J.	U.S. INF	1LT U.S. INF		2018
25	Reid	James R.	U.S. INF	1LT U.S. INF		2019

Summary

Class	Number of Graduates	Union Civil War Officers	Confederate Civil War Officers	Union Civil War Generals	Confederate Civil War Generals	Died or Resigned Before Civil War
1863	25	25	0	1	0	0

Class of 1864

Class Rank	Last Name	First Name	Military Service Before Civil War	Civil War Service	Comments	Cullum Number
1	Lydecker	Garrett J.	U.S. COE	B CPT U.S. COE		2020
2	Burnham	Arthur H.	U.S. COE	B MAJ U.S. COE		2021
3	Stickney	Amos	U.S. COE	B CPT U.S. COE		2022
4	Cuyler	James W.	U.S. COE	1LT U.S. COE		2023
5	Mackenzie	Alexander	U.S. COE	1LT U.S. COE		2024
6	Ernst	Oswald H.	U.S. COE	1LT U.S. COE		2025
7	Heap	David P.	U.S. COE	B CPT U.S. COE		2026
8	Ludlow	William	U.S. COE	B MAJ U.S. COE		2027
9	Phillips	Charles B.	U.S. COE	B CPT U.S. COE		2028
10	Jones	William A.	U.S. COE	1LT U.S. COE		2029
11	Cantwell	John T.	U.S. COE	1LT U.S. COE		2030
12	Damrell	Andrew N.	U.S. COE	1LT U.S. COE		2031
13	Waterman	C. Douglas	U.S. COE	1LT U.S. COE		2032
14	Allen	Vanderbilt	U.S. COE	1LT U.S. COE		2033
15	Allen	Charles J.	U.S. COE	B CPT U.S. COE		2034
16	Bryant	Cullen	U.S. ORD	2LT U.S. ORD		2035
17	Poland	Martin L.	U.S. ORD	2LT U.S. ORD		2036
18	Clarke	Alexander S.	U.S. ART	B CPT U.S. CAV		2037
19	Andruss	E. van Arsdale	U.S. ART	B 1LT U.S. ART		2038
20	Ennis	William	U.S. ART	B 1LT U.S. ART		2039
21	Elliott	John	U.S. ART	B 1LT U.S. ART		2040
22	Loucks	Melville R.	U.S. ART	1LT U.S. ART		2041
23	Maclay	Isaac W.	U.S. ART	2LT U.S. ORD		2042
24	Howell	Rezin G.	U.S. ART	1LT U.S. ART		2043
25	Vose	William P.	U.S. ART	1LT U.S. ART		2044
26	Wheeler	Edward D.	U.S. ART	1LT U.S. ART		2045
27	Kinney	Samuel H.	U.S. ART	B CPT U.S. ART		2046

Summary

Class	Number of Graduates	Union Civil War Officers	Confederate Civil War Officers	Union Civil War Generals	Confederate Civil War Generals	Died or Resigned Before Civil War
1864	27	27	0	0	0	0

Overall Summary

Class	Number of Graduates	Union Civil War Officers	Confederate Civil War Officers	Union Civil War Generals	Confederate Civil War Generals	Died Before Civil War	Union and Confederate Generals
1818	23	3	0	2	0	20	2
1819	29	3	0	1	0	26	1
1820	30	3	1	2	1	25	3
1821	24	0	1	0	0	23	0
1822	40	7	2	5	2	31	7
1823	35	7	1	2	1	27	3
1824	31	2	0	0	0	29	0
1825	37	7	2	3	2	27	5

Class	Number of Graduates	Union Civil War Officers	Confederate Civil War Officers	Union Civil War Generals	Confederate Civil War Generals	Died Before Civil War	Union and Confederate Generals
1826	41	7	4	4	2	29	6
1827	38	7	3	2	2	28	4
1828	33	2	4	0	2	27	2
1829	46	13	4	6	4	29	10
1830	42	6	6	1	3	30	4
1831	33	9	2	6	1	21	7
1832	45	8	7	2	4	30	6
1833	43	11	4	7	1	26	8
1834	36	11	5	3	1	19	4
1835	56	16	6	8	2	34	9
1836	49	12	4	9	3	36	12
1837	50	16	10	11	7	24	18
1838	45	11	10	6	8	24	14
1839	29	14	3	8	2	14	10
1840	42	15	10	5	8	17	13
1841	52	22	11	15	7	19	22
1842	56	21	13	8	9	22	17
1843	39	17	4	10	3	18	13
1844	25	5	3	3	2	17	5
1845	41	15	7	9	5	19	14
1846	59	25	10	10	9	24	19
1847	38	26	4	9	2	8	11
1848	38	14	12	2	5	12	7
1849	43	23	13	5	7	7	12
1850	44	20	16	7	6	7	13
1851	42	28	9	6	3	5	9
1852	43	25	12	9	3	6	12
1853	52	34	12	8	8	6	16
1854	46	24	14	4	8	8	12
1855	34	25	6	8	2	3	10
1856	49	35	10	6	5	4	11
1857	38	21	15	2	4	2	6
1858	27	14	11	1	1	2	2
1859	22	17	5	2	1	0	3
1860	41	32	9	2	1	0	3
1861 May	45	38	6	4	0	1	4
1861 June	34	31	3	2	0	0	2
1862	28	27	0	1	0	1	1
1863	25	25	0	1	0	0	1
1864	27	27	0	0	0	0	0
TOTAL	1,867	781	294	227	146	782	373

Notable Valedictorians: First in Class

Class	Last Name	First Name	Branch of Service After Graduation	Combat Service Before Civil War	Civil War Service	Comments	Cullum Number
1818	Delafield	Richard	U.S. COE	—	BG USA	USMA[75]	180
1819	Elliason	William A.	U.S. COE	—	—	D 1839	203
1820	Tuttle	Stephen	U.S. COE	—	—	D 1835	232
1821	Courtenay	Edward H.	U.S. COE	—	—	USMA, D 1857	262
1822	Dutton	George	U.S. COE	—	—	R 1861	286
1823	Mordecai	Alfred	U.S. COE	MW	—	—	326

Class	Last Name	First Name	Branch of Service After Graduation	Combat Service Before Civil War	Civil War Service	Comments	Cullum Number
1824	Mahan	Dennis H.	U.S. COE	—	—	USMA, R 1829	361
1825	Bache	Alexander D.	U.S. COE	—	—	USMA	392
1826	Bartlett	William H.C.	U.S. COE	—	—	USMA	429
1827	Sibley	Ebenezer S.	U.S. ART	FW, MW	—	R 1854	470
1828	Church	Albert E.	U.S. ART	—	—	USMA	508
1829	Mason	Charles	U.S. COE	—	—	R 1831	541
1830	Swift	Alexander J.	U.S. COE	MW	—	D 1847	587
1831	Park	Rosewell	U.S. COE	—	—	R 1836	629
1832	Ward	George W.	U.S. ART	BW, FW	—	R 1836	662
1833	Smith	Frederick A.	U.S. COE	—	—	D 1852	707
1834	Fraser	William D.	U.S. COE	MW	—	D 1856	750
1835	Morell	George W.	U.S. COE	—	BG USV	—	786
1836	Welcker	George L.	U.S. COE	—	—	D 1848	842
1837	Behan	Henry W.	U.S. COE	MW	BG USV	—	891
1838	Wright	William H.	U.S. COE	—	—	D 1845	941
1839	Stephens	Isaac I.	U.S. COE	MW	MG USV	—	986
1840	Herbert	Paul O.	U.S. COE	MW	BG CSA	—	1017
1841	Tower	Zealous B.	U.S. COE	MW	BG USV	—	1059
1842	Eustis	Henry L.	U.S. COE	—	BG USV	USMA	1111
1843	Franklin	William B.	U.S. TOP	MW	MG USV	—	1167
1844	Peck	William G.	U.S. TOP	MW	—	USMA, R 1855	1206
1845	Whiting	William H.C.	U.S. COE	—	MG CSA	—	1231
1846	Stewart	C. Seaforth	U.S. COE	—	B LTC U.S. COE	USMA	1272
1847	Symmes	John C.	U.S. ART	—	—	USMA, R 1861	1331
1848	Trowbridge	William P.	U.S. COE	—	—	USMA, R 1856	1369
1849	Gilmore	Quincy A.	U.S. COE	—	MG USV	USMA	1407
1850	Prime	Frederick E.	U.S. COE	—	MAJ U.S. COE	—	1450
1851	Andrews	George L.	U.S. COE	—	BG USV	—	1494
1852	Casey	Thomas L.	U.S. COE	—	MAJ U.S. COE	USMA	1536
1853	McPherson	James B.	U.S. COE	—	MG USV	USMA	1579
1854	Lee	G.W. Custis	U.S. COE	—	MG CSA	—	1631
1855	Comstock	Cyrus B.	U.S. COE	—	B BG USV	USMA	1677
1856	Snyder	George W.	U.S. COE	—	B MAJ U.S. COE	USMA	1711
1857	Palfrey	John C.	U.S. COE	—	B MAJ U.S. COE	—	1760
1858	Paine	William C.	U.S. COE	—	CPT U.S. COE	USMA	1798
1859	Merrill	William E.	U.S. COE	—	COL USV	USMA	1825
1860	McFarland	Walter	U.S. COE	—	CPT U.S. COE	—	1847
1861 May	DuPont	Henry A.	U.S. COE	—	B LTC U.S. ART	—	1888
1861 June	O'Rorke	Patrick H.	U.S. COE	—	B COL U.S. COE	—	1933
1862	Mackenzie	Ranald S.	U.S. COE	—	BG USV	—	1967
1863	Meigs	John R.	U.S. COE	—	BG U.S. COE	—	1995
1864	Lydecker	Garrett J.	U.S. COE	—	B CPT U.S. COE	—	2020

Notable Class Goats: Last in Class

Class	Last Name	First Name	Branch of Service After Graduation	Combat Service Before Civil War	Civil War Service	Comments	Cullum Number
1818	Pratt	John T.	U.S. INF	—	—	R 1819	202
1819	Swift	William H.	U.S. TOP	—	—	R 1849	231
1820	Morris	William W.	U.S. INF	FW, MW	B BG USA	—	261
1821	D'Lagnel	Julius A.	U.S. INF	FW	—	D 1840	285
1822	Clark	Henry	U.S. INF	—	—	D 1830	325
1823	Birdsall	Egbert	U.S. INF	FW	—	D 1845	360
1824	Thompson	W. Beverhout	U.S. INF	—	—	R 1830	391
1825	Allston	Samuel R.	U.S. INF	—	—	R 1836	428
1826	Smith	E. Kirby	U.S. INF	MW	—	D 1847	469
1827	Clarke	Nelson N.	U.S. INF	—	—	D 1832	507
1828	Van Wyck	Philip R.	—	—	—	D 1833	540
1829	Screven	Richard B.	U.S. INF	FW, MW	—	D 1851	586
1830	Legate	Stephen B.	U.S. INF	—	—	R 1835	628
1831	Conrad	John	U.S. INF	BW, MW	—	D 1838	661
1832	Edwards	Albert G.	U.S. CAV	BW	—	R 1835	706
1833	Hunter	Nathaniel W.	U.S. INF	FW, MW	—	D 1849	749
1834	Montgomery	Alexander	U.S. INF	FW, MW	MAJ U.S. STF	—	785
1835	McLeod	Hugh	U.S. INF	—	COL CSA	—	841
1836	Spoor	Charles H.E.	U.S. INF	FW	—	D 1838	890
1837	Saunders	Franklin	U.S. CAV	FW, MW	—	R 1847	940
1838	Inge	Zebulan M.P.	U.S. CAV	FW	—	K 1846	985
1839	Hill	John H.	U.S. CAV	FW, MW	—	D 1847	1016
1840	Bacon	John D.	U.S. INF	FW, MW	—	D 1847	1058
1841	Morris	Charles F.	U.S. INF	FW, MW	—	D 1847	1110
1842	Handy	James O.	U.S. INF	—	—	D 1845	1166
1843	McClelland	George C.	U.S. INF	MW	—	RD 1847	1205
1844	Hawkins	George W.	U.S. INF	MW	—	RD 1853	1230
1845	Crittenden	William	U.S. INF	MW	—	R 1849	1271
1846	Pickett	George E.	U.S. INF	MW	MG CSA	—	1330
1847	Heth	Henry	U.S. INF	MW, UE	MG CSA	—	1368
1848	Howland	George W.	U.S. MTR	—	B MAJ U.S. MTR	—	1406
1849	McIntosh	James	U.S. CAV	—	BG CSA	—	1449
1850	Stith	Donald C.	U.S. INF	UE	COL USA	—	1493
1851	Baker	Lawrence S.	U.S. MTR	—	BG CSA	—	1535
1852	Garber	Hezekiah H.	U.S. INF	—	—	D 1859	1578
1853	Craig	William	U.S. INF	—	CPT U.S. QTR	—	1630
1854	McCleary	John	U.S. INF	UE	B MAJ U.S. INF	—	1676
1855	Dick	George McGunnegle	U.S. INF	—	—	D 1856	1710
1856	Cunningham	Arthur S.	U.S. INF	UE	LTC CSA	—	1759
1857	Peck	Lafayette	U.S. INF	—	LT CSA	—	1796
1858	Jesup	Charles E.	U.S. INF	—	—	R 1860	1824
1859	Worth	Henry A.F.	U.S. INF	—	CPT U.S. INF	—	1846
1860	Borland	Harold	U.S. INF	—	MAJ CSA	—	1887
1861 May	Sturgeon	Sheldon	U.S. INF	—	CPT U.S. INF	—	1932
1861 June	Custer	George A.	U.S. CAV	—	B MG USV	—	1996

Class	Last Name	First Name	Branch of Service After Graduation	Combat Service Before Civil War	Civil War Service	Comments	Cullum Number
1862	Warner	Charles N.	U.S. ART	—	B CPT U.S. ART	—	1994
1863	Reid	James R.	U.S. INF	—	1LT U.S. INF	—	2019
1864	Kinney	Samuel H.	U.S. ART	—	B CPT U.S. ART	—	2046

Notable West Point Graduates Who Served in the Civil War

Class of 1818 (23 Graduates)

- Richard Delafield (1), Union, BG, Chief of Engineers, Corps of Engineers, Engineer Bureau, Superintendent of U.S. Military Academy[76]
- Harvey Brown (6), Union, BG, Defense of Fort Pickens, Suppression of New York Draft Riots[77]
- Hartman Bache (19), Union, COL, Bureau of Topographical Engineers[78]

Class of 1819 (29 Graduates)

- Daniel Tyler (14), Union, BG, Army of Northeastern Virginia and Army of the Mississippi, Manassas Campaign (First Manassas), Iuka and Corinth Operations (Second Corinth), Commandant at Camp Douglas for Union Parolees[79]

Members of the class of 1860, U.S. Military Academy, at Harrison's Landing, Virginia (Library of Congress).

Class of 1820 (30 Graduates)

- Andrew J. Donelson (2), Diplomat, Publisher, *chargé d'affaires* to Texas, Know Nothing Party Vice Presidential Candidate[80]
- John H. Winder (11), Confederate, BG, Provisional Confederate Army, Provost Marshall of Richmond, Bureau of Prison Camps[81]
- George D. Ramsay (26), Union, BG, Ordnance Bureau, Inspector of Arsenals[82]
- William W. Morris (30), Union, BG, Middle Department, Harbor Defenses of Baltimore[83]

Class of 1821 (24 Graduates)

- Charles Dimmock (5), Confederate, BG, Ordnance, Fortifications at Roanoke Island and Petersburg[84]

Class of 1822 (40 Graduates)

- Joseph K.F. Mansfield (2), Union, MG, Army of the Potomac, Maryland Campaign (Antietam),[85] Took off hat to reveal long white hair while riding among his men[86]
- Walter Gwyn (8), Confederate, BG, Virginia Provisional Army and North Carolina and Virginia Militias, Operations in Charleston Harbor (Fort Sumter)[87]
- Isaac R. Trimble (17), Confederate, MG, Provisional Confederate Army and Army of Northern Virginia, Virginia Peninsula Campaign (Malvern Hill and Gaines' Mill), Jackson's Valley Campaign (Cross Keys), Northern Virginia Campaign (Cedar Mountain and Second Manassas), Gettysburg Campaign (Gettysburg)[88]
- George Wright (24), Union, Brevet BG, Department of the Pacific[89]
- David Hunter (25), Union, MG, Departments of Kansas, the South, and West Virginia, Manassas Campaign (First Manassas), Operations against Fort Pulaski (Fort Pulaski), Destruction of the Lexington Military Institute, Military Commission for the trial of the conspirators in the assassination of President Lincoln[90]
- George A. McCall (26), Union, BG, Pennsylvania Reserve, Pennsylvania Volunteers, and Army of the Potomac, Virginia Peninsula Campaign (Beaver Dam Creek, and Gaines' Mill), Prisoner at Libby Prison[91]
- John J. Abercrombie (37), Union, BG, Army of the Potomac, Virginia Peninsula Campaign (Malvern Hill), Captured at New Market Cross Roads[92]

Class of 1823 (35 Graduates)

- George S. Greene (2), Union, BG, Army of the Potomac and Army of the Cumberland, Northern Virginia Campaign (Cedar Mountain), Maryland Campaign (Antietam), Fredericksburg Campaign (First Fredericksburg), Chancellorsville Campaign (Chancellorsville), Gettysburg Campaign (Gettysburg)[93]
- Alfred Beckley (9), Confederate, BG, Virginia Militia, Resigned commission and surrendered to Union troops[94]
- Lorenzo Thomas (17), Union, BG, U.S. Army, Adjutant General, Organization of USCT[95]

Class of 1824 (31 Graduates)

- Dennis H. Mahan (1), Union, Professor of Engineering, Corps of Engineers, U.S. Military Academy, Department of Civil and Military Engineering[96]
- Robert P. Parrott (3), Union, CPT, Rifled Ordnance, Inventor of the Parrott Guns and Projectiles, Superintendent of the West Point Iron and Cannon Foundry[97]

Class of 1825 (37 Graduates)

- Alexander D. Bache (1), Union, 2LT, Corps of Engineers, U.S. Military Academy, Superintendent of the Geodetic and Hydrographic Survey of the United States

Coasts and of the Office of Weights and Measures, Vice-President of the U.S. Sanitary Commission[98]
- Daniel S. Donelson (5), Confederate, MG, Department of East Tennessee, Stones River Campaign (Stones River)[99]
- Benjamin Huger (8), Confederate, MG, Department of Southern Virginia and North Carolina, Army of Northern Virginia, Trans-Mississippi Department, and Bureau of Ordnance, Virginia Peninsula Campaign (Seven Pines), Relieved of field command, Inspector of Artillery and Ordnance[100]
- Robert Anderson (15), Union, Brevet MG, Departments of Kentucky and the Cumberland, Operations in Charleston Harbor (Fort Sumter), Retired on October 27, 1863[101]
- Charles F. Smith (19), Union, MG, Department of Washington and District of Western Kentucky, Federal Penetration up the Cumberland and Tennessee Rivers (Fort Donelson), Died on April 25, 1862[102]
- William R. Montgomery (28), Union, BG, New Jersey Volunteers and U.S. Volunteers, Resigned on April 4, 1864[103]

Class of 1826 (41 Graduates)
- Albert S. Johnston (8), Confederate, GEN, Western Department and Army of Central Kentucky, Federal Penetration up the Cumberland and Tennessee Rivers (Shiloh), Killed at Shiloh, Highest-ranking fatality of the war, Davis considered him the country's best general[104]
- Samuel P. Heintzelman (17), Union, MG, Army of Northeastern Virginia, Army of the Potomac, Army of Virginia, Northern Department, and Department of Washington, Manassas Campaign (First Manassas), Virginia Peninsula Campaign (Yorktown, Williamsburg, Glendale, and Malvern Hill), Northern Virginia Campaign (Second Manassas)[105]
- Augustus J. Pleasonton (20), Union, BG, Pennsylvania Militia[106]
- John B. Grayson (22), Confederate, BG, Confederate Provisional Army and Department of Middle and Eastern Florida, Died on October 21, 1861[107]
- Amos Eaton (36), Union, BG, Bureau of Washington, DC, Commissary General of Subsistence[108]
- Silas Casey (39), Union, MG, Army of the Potomac, Virginia Peninsula Campaign, Board for the Examination of Candidates for Officers of Colored Troops[109]

Class of 1827 (38 Graduates)
- Napoleon H. Buford (6), Union, BG, Army of the Mississippi, Joint Operations against New Madrid, Island No. 10, and Memphis (New Madrid/Island No. 10), Iuka and Corinth Operations (Second Corinth), Grant's Operations against Vicksburg (Vicksburg and Helena)[110]
- Leonidas Polk (8), Confederate, Lieutenant General, Department No. 2, Army of Tennessee, Department of Mississippi and East Louisiana, Federal Penetration up the Cumberland and Tennessee Rivers (Shiloh), Confederate Heartland Offensive (Perryville), Stones River Campaign (Stones River), Chickamauga Campaign (Chickamauga), Atlanta Campaign, Episcopal minister, Killed in the Atlanta Campaign[111]
- Gabriel J. Rains (13), Confederate, BG, Provisional Confederate Army, Torpedo Bureau, Virginia Peninsula Campaign (Seven Pines), Developed anti-personnel mine[112]
- Philip St. George Cooke (23), Union, BG, Army of the Potomac, Virginia Peninsula Campaign (Yorktown, Williamsburg, Gaines' Mill, and Glendale)[113]

Class of 1828 (33 Graduates)

- Albert E. Church (1), Union, Professor of Mathematics, U.S. Military Academy[114]
- Hugh W. Mercer (3), Confederate, BG, District of Georgia and Army of Tennessee, Atlanta Campaign (Jonesborough)[115]
- Jefferson Davis (23), Confederate, President of the Confederate States of America[116]
- Thomas F. Drayton (28), Confederate, BG, Army of Northern Virginia and Trans-Mississippi Department, Jackson's Valley Campaign (Port Royal), Northern Virginia Campaign (Second Manassas), Maryland Campaign (South Mountain and Antietam)[117]

Class of 1829 (46 Graduates)

- Robert E. Lee (2), Confederate, GEN, Army of Northern Virginia and Armies of the Confederate States, Operations in Western Virginia (Cheat Mountain), Virginia Peninsula Campaign (Seven Days), Northern Virginia Campaign (Second Manassas), Maryland Campaign (South Mountain and Antietam), Fredericksburg Campaign (First Fredericksburg), Chancellorsville Campaign (Chancellorsville), Gettysburg Campaign (Gettysburg), Grant's Overland Campaign (Wilderness, Spotsylvania, Totopotomoy Creek, North Anna, and Cold Harbor), Richmond-Petersburg Campaign (Second Petersburg, Crater, and Fort Stedman), Appomattox Campaign (Five Forks, Third Petersburg, and Lee's surrender at Appomattox Court House), Greatly respected Confederate officer[118]
- James Barnes (5), Union, BG, Army of the Potomac, Virginia Peninsula Campaign, Northern Virginia Campaign, Maryland Campaign (Antietam), Fredericksburg Campaign (First Fredericksburg), Chancellorsville Campaign (Chancellorsville), Gettysburg Campaign (Gettysburg)[119]
- Cathanarinus P. Buckingham (6), Union, BG, State of Ohio and War Department[120]
- Joseph E. Johnston (13), Confederate, GEN, Army of Northern Virginia, Army of the West, and Army of Tennessee, Manassas Campaign (First Manassas), Virginia Peninsula Campaign (Seven Pines), Atlanta Campaign, Carolinas Campaign (Bentonville), Johnston's surrender at Durham Station[121]
- O. McKnight Mitchell (15), Union, MG, Army of the Ohio and Department of the South, Tennessee and North Alabama Operations[122]
- William Hoffman (18), Union, Brevet BG, Commissary General of Prisoners[123]
- Thomas A. Davies (25), Union, BG, Army of the Potomac, Manassas Campaign (First Manassas), Federal Penetration up the Cumberland and Tennessee Rivers (First Corinth), Iuka and Corinth Operations (Second Corinth)[124]
- Albert G. Blanchard (26), Confederate, BG, Trans-Mississippi Department and Army of Northern Virginia, Camps of instruction and conscript duty[125]
- Benjamin W. Brice (40), Union, Brevet BG, Paymaster General[126]
- Theodolphilus H. Holmes (44), Confederate, LG, Army of Northern Virginia, Trans-Mississippi Department, Virginia Peninsula Campaign (Seven Days)[127]

Class of 1830 (42 Graduates)

- William N. Pendleton (5), Confederate, BG, Army of Northern Virginia, Artillery Operations, Manassas Campaign (First Manassas), Virginia Peninsula Campaign (Seven Days), Northern Virginia Campaign (Second Manassas), Maryland Campaign (South Mountain and Antietam), Fredericksburg Campaign (First Fredericksburg), Chancellorsville Campaign (Chancellorsville), Gettysburg Campaign (Gettysburg), Grant's Overland Campaign (Wilderness, Spotsylvania, Totopotomoy Creek, North Anna, and Cold Harbor), Richmond-Petersburg Campaign

(Second Petersburg, Crater, and Fort Stedman), Appomattox Campaign (Five Forks, Third Petersburg and Lee's surrender at Appomattox Court House), Episcopal Minister[128]
- John B. Magruder (15), Confederate, MG, Army of Northern Virginia, Virginia Peninsula Campaign (Yorktown and Seven Days), Operations against Galveston (Second Galveston)[129]
- Albert Taylor Bledsoe (16), Confederate, COL, Assistant Secretary of War and Chief of the Bureau of War, Principal architect of the "Lost Cause" mythology[130]
- Meriwether L. Clark (23), Confederate, BG, Missouri State Guard, Ordnance Department, and Army of Northern Virginia, Appomattox Campaign (Sayler's Creek), Captured at Sayler's Creek, Commandant of Cadets at Kentucky Military Institute[131]
- Robert C. Buchanan (31), Union, Brevet BG, Army of the Potomac, Virginia Peninsula Campaign (Yorktown, Gaines' Mill, Glendale, and Malvern Hill), Northern Virginia Campaign (Second Manassas), Maryland Campaign (Antietam), Fredericksburg Campaign (First Fredericksburg)[132]

Class of 1831 (33 Graduates)

- Jacob Ammen (12), Union, BG, Army of the Ohio, West Virginia Campaign (Cheat Mountain), Federal Penetration up the Cumberland and Tennessee Rivers (Shiloh and First Corinth)[133]
- Andrew A. Humphreys (13), Union, MG, Army of the Potomac, Virginia Peninsula Campaign (Yorktown, Williamsburg, and Malvern Hill), Maryland Campaign (Antietam), Fredericksburg Campaign (First Fredericksburg), Chancellorsville Campaign (Chancellorsville), Gettysburg Campaign (Gettysburg), Grant's Overland Campaign (Wilderness, Spotsylvania, North Anna, Totopotomy Creek, and Cold Harbor), Richmond-Petersburg Campaign (Second Petersburg and Peebles' Farm), Appomattox Campaign (Sayler's Creek and Lee's surrender at Appomattox Court House)[134]
- William H. Emory (14), Union, Brevet MG, Army of the Potomac and Department of the Gulf, Virginia Peninsular Campaign (Yorktown and Williamsburg), Siege of Port Hudson (Port Hudson), Red River Campaign (Pleasant Hill), Sheridan's Valley Campaign (Opequon, Fisher's Hill, and Cedar Creek)[135]
- Thomas J. McKean (19), Union, BG, Department of the Gulf, Federal Penetration up the Cumberland and Tennessee River (First Corinth), Iuka and Corinth Operations (Second Corinth)[136]
- Lucius B. Northrop (22), Confederate, BG, Commissary Services, Supplied food for Confederate armies and Union Prisoners[137]
- Horatio P. van Cleve (24), Union, BG, Army of the Ohio, Federal Penetration up the Cumberland and Tennessee River (First Corinth), Iuka and Corinth Operations (Second Corinth), Stones River Campaign (Stones River), Wounded at Stones River, Chickamauga Campaign (Chickamauga), Offensive in Eastern Kentucky (Mill Springs), Chattanooga-Ringgold Campaign (Ringgold)[138]
- Samuel R. Curtis (27), Union, MG, Army of the Southwest and Department of the Missouri, Camp of Instruction at Jefferson Barracks, Pea Ridge Campaign (Pea Ridge), Grant's Operations against Vicksburg (Helena)[139]

Class of 1832 (45 Graduates)

- Philip St. George Cocke (6), Confederate, BG, Provisional Confederate Army and Army of Northern Virginia, Manassas Campaign (First Manassas[140]
- Erasmus D. Keyes (10), Union, MG, Army of the Potomac, Manassas Campaign (First Manassas), Virginia Peninsula Campaign (Yorktown and Malvern Hill), Board for Retiring Disabled Officers, Resigned in May 1864[141]

- George B. Crittenden (26), Confederate, MG, Department of East Tennessee, Offensive in Eastern Kentucky (Mill Springs), Resigned in October 1862[142]
- Randolph B. Marcy (29), Union, BG, Army of the Potomac and Departments of the Northwest, Western Virginia Campaign, Virginia Peninsular Campaign, Maryland Campaign, Inspector General of U.S. Army[143]
- Richard C. Gatlin (35), Confederate, BG, Department of North Carolina, Blamed for loss of Fort Hatteras and surrender of New Bern, Resigned in March 1862[144]
- Humphrey Marshall (42), Confederate, BG, Confederate Heartland Offensive, Resigned on June 17, 1863, Member of Second Confederate Congress[145]

Class of 1833 (43 Graduates)

- John G. Barnard (2), Union, Brevet MG, Army of the Potomac, Chief Engineer of the U.S. Army, Manassas Campaign (First Manassas), Virginia Peninsular Campaign (Yorktown, Williamsburg, Gaines' Mill, and Malvern Hill), Richmond-Petersburg Campaign (Second Petersburg and Hatcher's Run), Appomattox Campaign (Lee's surrender at Appomattox Court House), Corporator of the National Military and Naval Asylum[146]
- George W. Cullum (3), Union, BG, Corps of Engineers and Department of Missouri, U.S. Sanitary Commission, Chief of Staff for General-in-Chief Halleck, Iuka and Corinth Operations (Second Corinth)[147]
- Rufus King (4), Union, BG, Army of the Potomac, Northern Virginia Campaign (Second Manassas), Maryland Campaign, Resigned October 20, 1863, Medal of Honor for Actions at White Oak Swamp[148]
- Francis Smith (5), Confederate, COL CSA, Virginia Militia, Led VMI cadets at the Battle of New Market, Superintendent Virginia Military Institute[149]
- Edmund Schriver (17), Union, Brevet BG, Army of the Potomac, Northern Virginia Campaign (Cedar Mountain and Second Manassas), Chancellorsville Campaign (Chancellorsville), Gettysburg Campaign (Gettysburg), Richmond-Petersburg Campaign (Second Petersburg), Inspector General of the U.S. Army[150]
- Alexander E. Shiras (20), Union, Brevet BG, U.S. Commissary of Subsistence and U.S. Sanitary Commission[151]
- Benjamin Alvord (22), Union, BG, District of Oregon[152]
- Henry W. Wessells (29), Union, BG, Army of the Potomac, Virginia Peninsular Campaign (Yorktown), Wounded at Fair Oaks, Captured in the Defense of Plymouth, Commissary of Prisoners[153]
- Abraham C. Myers (32), Confederate, COL, Quartermaster General of the Confederate States Army, Jewish-American army officer[154]
- Daniel Ruggles (34), Confederate, BG, Army of Potomac and Army of the West, Federal Penetration up the Cumberland and Tennessee Rivers (Shiloh), Commissary General of Prisons[155]

Class of 1834 (36 Graduates)

- Thomas A. Morris (4), Union, BG, Indiana Volunteers, Western Virginia Campaign, Mustered out of service on July 27, 1861[156]
- Robert T.P. Allen (5), Confederate, COL, Superintendent of the Kentucky Military Institute, Commander of the Fourth and Seventeenth Texas Infantries[157]
- Gabriel R. Paul (18), Union, BG, Department of New Mexico and Army of the Potomac, Fredericksburg Campaign (First Fredericksburg), Chancellorsville Campaign (Chancellorsville), Gettysburg Campaign (Gettysburg), Blinded and disabled at Gettysburg[158]
- Goode Bryan (25), Confederate, BG, Army of Northern Virginia, Virginia Peninsula Campaign (Seven Days), Maryland Campaign, Fredericksburg Campaign, Chancellorsville Campaign, Gettysburg Campaign Grant's Overland Campaign (Wilderness), Resigned September 20, 1864[159]

- William Scott Ketchum (32), Union, BG, Departments of the Missouri and Mississippi, Commission to inspect and report on the Quartermaster Department[160]

Class of 1835 (56 Graduates)

- George W. Morrell (1), Union, BG, Army of the Potomac, Virginia Peninsula Campaign (Yorktown, Beaver Dam Creek, Gaines' Mill, and Malvern Hill), Northern Virginia Campaign (Second Manassas), Maryland Campaign (Antietam)[161]
- John H. Martindale (3), Union, BG, Army of the Potomac and Army of the James, Virginia Peninsula Campaign (Yorktown, Beaver Dam Creek, Gaines' Mill, and Malvern Hill), Richmond-Petersburg Campaign (Second Petersburg and Cold Harbor), Resigned on September 13, 1864[162]
- Montgomery Blair (18), Union, U.S. Postmaster General of the United States[163]
- George G. Meade (19), Union, MG, Army of the Potomac, Virginia Peninsula Campaign (Beaver Dam Creek, Gaines' Mill, and Glendale), Wounded and disabled at Glendale, Northern Virginia Campaign (Second Manassas), Maryland Campaign (South Mountain and Antietam), Fredericksburg Campaign (First Fredericksburg), Chancellorsville Campaign (Chancellorsville), Gettysburg Campaign (Gettysburg), Grant's Overland Campaign (Wilderness, Spotsylvania, North Anna, Totopotomy, and Cold Harbor), Richmond-Petersburg Campaign (Second Petersburg, Crater, Peebles' Farm, Hatcher's Run, and Fort Stedman), Appomattox Campaign (Third Petersburg, Sayler's Creek, and Lee's surrender at Appomattox Court House)[164]
- Henry M. Naglee (23), Union, BG, Army of the Potomac, Virginia Peninsula Campaign (Yorktown and Williamsburg), Wounded at Fair Oaks, Mustered out of service on April 4, 1864[165]
- Henry Prince (30), Union, BG, Army of the Potomac, Northern Virginia Campaign (Cedar Mountain), Captured at Cedar Mountain[166]
- Herman Haupt (31), Union, COL, Chief of Construction and Transportation of U.S. Military Railroads, Declined appointment as BG[167]
- John M. Withers (44), Confederate, MG, Army of Mississippi, Army of Tennessee, and Alabama Reserve Forces, Federal Penetration up the Cumberland and Tennessee Rivers (Shiloh), Stones River Campaign (Stones River)[168]
- Larkin Smith (47), Confederate, BG, Confederate States Army, Assistant Quartermaster General[169]
- Marsena R. Patrick (48), Union, BG, Army of the Potomac, Northern Virginia Campaign (Second Manassas and Chantilly), Maryland Campaign (South Mountain and Antietam)[170]
- Benjamin S. Roberts (53), Union, BG, Army of the Potomac and Army of Virginia, Sibley's New Mexico Campaign (Valverde), Northern Virginia Campaign (Cedar Mountain and Second Manassas)[171]

Class of 1836 (49 Graduates)

- Danville Leadbetter (3), Confederate, BG, Army of Tennessee and District of the Gulf, Engineering Operations, Longstreet's Knoxville Campaign (Fort Sanders), Chief Engineer of the Army of Tennessee[172]
- Joseph R. Anderson (4), Confederate, BG, Army of Northern Virginia, Ordnance Operations, Virginia Peninsula Campaign (Seven Days), Superintendent of the Tredegar Iron Works[173]
- Montgomery C. Meigs (5), Union, Brevet MG, Quartermaster General, Transported equipment and supplies for the Union armies, Chattanooga-Ringgold Campaign (Chattanooga), Supplied and refitted Sherman's army at Savannah and Goldsborough[174]

- Daniel P. Woodbury (6), Union, Brevet MG, Army of the Potomac, Engineering Operations, Manassas Campaign (First Manassas), Virginia Peninsula Campaign (Yorktown), Fredericksburg Campaign (First Fredericksburg)[175]
- James Lowry Donaldson (15), Union, Brevet BG, Middle Department and Army of the Cumberland, Quartermaster Services, Sibley's New Mexico Campaign (Valverde), Franklin-Nashville Campaign (Nashville)[176]
- Thomas W. Sherman (18), Union, BG, Army of the Tennessee, Army of Mississippi, Department of the Gulf, Federal Penetration up the Cumberland and Tennessee Rivers (First Corinth), Siege of Port Hudson (Port Hudson), Wounded and disabled at Port Hudson[177]
- Henry H. Lockwood (22), Union, BG, Army of the Potomac, Gettysburg Campaign (Gettysburg) and Richmond-Petersburg Campaign[178]
- John W. Phelps (24), Union, BG, Expedition to, and Capture of, New Orleans (Fort Jackson and Fort St. Philip and New Orleans), Organized the first Negro Troops at Camp Parapet, Louisiana, Resigned August 21, 1862[179]
- Robert Allen (33), Union, BG, Department of Missouri, Quartermaster Operations, Chief Quartermaster, Transportation and supplies for operations in Kentucky, Tennessee, and Virginia, Federal Penetration up the Cumberland and Tennessee Rivers (First Corinth), Grant's Operations against Vicksburg (Vicksburg)[180]
- George C. Thomas (35), Union, MG, Washington, DC Militia and Volunteers[181]
- Richard G. Stockton (44), Union, BG, Missouri Militia, Resigned January 1863[182]
- Lloyd Tilghman (46), Confederate, BG, Army of Tennessee and Army of the West, Federal Penetration up the Cumberland and Tennessee Rivers (Fort Henry), Iuka and Corinth Operations (Second Corinth), Grant's Operations against Vicksburg (Champion Hill), Killed at Champion Hill[183]

Class of 1837 (50 Graduates)

- Henry W. Benham (1), Union, BG, Department of the Ohio and Army of the Potomac, Engineering Operations, Operations in Western Virginia (Carnifex Ferry), Operations against Fort Pulaski (Fort Pulaski), Operations against Charleston (Secessionville), Chancellorsville Campaign (Chancellorsville)[184]
- Braxton Bragg (5), Confederate, GEN, Provisional Army of the Confederate States, Army of Mississippi, Army of the West, and Army of Tennessee, Federal Penetration up the Cumberland and Tennessee Rivers (Shiloh), Confederate Heartland Offensive (Perryville), Stones River Campaign (Stones River), Chickamauga Campaign (Chickamauga), Chattanooga-Ringgold Campaign (Chattanooga)[185]
- Alexander B. Dyer (6), Union, BG, U.S. Army Ordnance Bureau, Springfield Armory, Chief of Ordnance of the U.S. Army[186]
- William W. Mackall (8), Confederate, BG, Army of Tennessee, Department of West, and Department of the Gulf, Joint Operations against New/Madrid, Island No. 10, and Memphis (Island No. 10), Captured at Island No. 10), Chickamauga Campaign (Chickamauga), Atlanta Campaign[187]
- E. Parker Scammon (9), Union, BG, Operations in Western Virginia (Carnifex Ferry), Maryland Campaign (South Mountain and Antietam), Prisoner of War, Operations against the Defenses of Charleston (Fort Wagner/Morris Island)[188]
- Lewis G. Arnold (10), Union, BG, Department of Florida, Defense of Fort Pickens, Defense of Santa Rosa Island, Retired on February 8, 1864[189]
- Israel Vogdes (11), Union, BG, Department of Florida, Defense of Fort Pickens, Captured during Confederate attack on Santa Rosa Island, Maryland Campaign, Operations against the Defenses of Charleston (Fort Wagner and Charleston Harbor)[190]

- Thomas Williams (12), Union, BG, Department of Virginia and Department of the Gulf, Operations against Baton Rouge (Baton Rouge), Killed at Baton Rouge on August 5, 1862[191]
- Edward D. Townsend (16), Union, Brevet BG, U.S. Army and Department of the Pacific, Chief of Staff for Winfield Scott, Adjutant General's Office[192]
- Jubal Early (18), Confederate, LG, Virginia Infantry, Army of Northern Virginia, and Department of the Valley, Manassas Campaign (First Manassas), Virginia Peninsula Campaign, Northern Virginia Campaign, Maryland Campaign, Fredericksburg Campaign, Chancellorsville Campaign (Salem Church), Gettysburg Campaign, Grant's Overland Campaign (Wilderness), Sheridan's Valley Campaign (Opequon, Fisher's Hill, and Cedar Creek), Never surrendered, Escaped to Mexico, Author of the "Lost Cause"[193]
- Bennett H. Hill (21), brevet BG, U.S. Army and District of Michigan, Recruiting operations in West Virginia and Michigan[194]
- William H. French (22), Union, MG, Army of the Potomac, Virginia Peninsula Campaign (Yorktown, Gaines' Mill, Glendale, and Malvern Hill), Maryland Campaign (Antietam), Fredericksburg Campaign (First Fredericksburg), Chancellorsville Campaign (Chancellorsville), Gettysburg Campaign[195]
- John Sedgwick (24), Union, MG, Army of the Potomac, Virginia Peninsula Campaign (Yorktown and Glendale), Maryland Campaign (Antietam), Gettysburg Campaign (Gettysburg), Richmond-Petersburg Campaign, Grant's Overland Campaign (Wilderness and Spotsylvania), Killed at Spotsylvania[196]
- Joshua H. Bates (25), Union, BG, Ohio Volunteers, Member of Sanitary Commission[197]
- John C. Pemberton (27), Confederate, LG, Department of Mississippi and Eastern Louisiana and Confederate States Army, Grant's Operations against Vicksburg (Vicksburg), Resigned in 1864, Davis commissioned him as a LTC of artillery[198]
- Joseph Hooker (29), Union, MG, Army of the Potomac and Army of the Cumberland, Virginia Peninsula Campaign (Yorktown, Williamsburg, Glendale, and Malvern Hill), Northern Virginia Campaign (Second Manassas and Chantilly), Maryland Campaign (South Mountain and Antietam), Fredericksburg Campaign (First Fredericksburg), Chancellorsville Campaign (Chancellorsville), Gettysburg Campaign (Brandy Station), Chattanooga-Ringgold Campaign (Chattanooga and Ringgold), Atlanta Campaign (Pine Mountain, Peach Tree Creek and Atlanta)[199]
- Arnold Elzey (Jones) (33), Confederate, MG, First Maryland Infantry, Army of Northern Virginia, and Army of Tennessee, Manassas Campaign (First Manassas), Jackson's Valley Campaign, Virginia Peninsula Campaign (Seven Days), Wounded and disabled in Seven Days Battles[200]
- John B.S. Todd (39), Union, BG, North Missouri District and Army of the Tennessee, Delegate from North Dakota[201]
- William H.T. Walker (46), Confederate, MG, Army of Tennessee, U.S. Military Academy, Grant's Operations against Vicksburg, Chickamauga Campaign, Atlanta Campaign, Killed at Atlanta on July 22, 1864, Commandant of Cadets at U.S. Military Academy[202]
- Robert H. Chilton (48), Confederate, BG, Army of Northern Virginia, Inspector General, Lee's Chief of Staff[203]

Class of 1838 (45 Graduates)

- P.G.T. Beauregard (2), Confederate, GEN, Confederate States Army, Army of Mississippi, Department of Georgia, South Carolina, and Florida, and Army of Northern Virginia, Operations in Charleston Harbor (Fort Sumter), Manassas Campaign (First Manassas), Federal Penetration up the Cumberland and Tennessee Rivers (Shiloh and First Corinth), Operations Against the Defenses of

Charleston (Fort Wagner, Morris Island and Second Fort Sumter), Richmond-Petersburg Campaign (Second Petersburg), Carolinas Campaign (Bentonville),[204] Superintendent at West Point for five days, beginning on January 23, 1861[205]
- James H. Trapier (3), Confederate, BG, Eastern and Middle Florida, Iuka and Corinth Operations (Second Corinth), Considered unfit for command[206]
- Henry C. Wayne (14), Confederate, BG, Georgia Militia[207]
- William F. Barry (17), Union, Brevet MG, Army of the Potomac, Artillery Operations, Manassas Campaign (First Manassas), Virginia Peninsula Campaign (Yorktown, Gaines' Mill, and Malvern Hill), Atlanta Campaign (Kennesaw Mountain, Peach Tree Creek, Atlanta, and Jonesborough), Carolinas Campaign[208]
- Milton A. Haynes (18), Confederate, LTC, Army of Tennessee, Artillery Operations, Federal Penetration up the Cumberland and Tennessee Rivers (Fort Donelson), Author of *The Confederate Artillerist Instructions in Artillery, Horse & Foot*[209]
- Langdon C. Easton (22), Union, Brevet BG, Army of the Cumberland and Department of the Missouri, Quartermaster Operations, Chattanooga-Ringgold Campaign, Atlanta Campaign, Carolinas Campaign[210]
- Irvin McDowell (23), Union, MG, Department of North East Virginia, Army of the Potomac, and Army of Virginia, Manassas Campaign (First Manassas), Northern Virginia Campaign (Cedar Mountain and Second Manassas)[211]
- William J. Hardee (26), Confederate, LG, Army of Tennessee, U.S. Military Academy, Commandant of Cadets, Author of *Rifle and Light Infantry Tactics*, Federal Penetration up the Cumberland and Tennessee Rivers (Shiloh), Stones River Campaign (Stones River), Chattanooga-Ringgold Campaign (Chattanooga), Atlanta Campaign (Jonesborough), Carolinas Campaign, Johnston's surrender at Durham Station[212]
- Robert S. Granger (28), Union, BG, Army of the Cumberland, District of Middle Tennessee, District of Northern Alabama, Captured by Sibley's command on the Texas coast and paroled, Confederate Heartland Offensive, Operations in Tennessee, Expulsion of General Wheeler from Middle Tennessee, Defense against Forrest's Raid in Middle Tennessee, Defense of Decatur against General Hood's Army[213]
- Henry S. Sibley (31), Confederate, MG, Sibley's New Mexico Campaign (Valverde and Glorieta Pass), Invented the Sibley Tent[214]
- Edward Johnson (32), Confederate, MG, Army of Tennessee, Jackson's Valley Campaign, Gettysburg Campaign (Gettysburg), Grant's Overland Campaign (Wilderness and Spotsylvania), Franklin-Nashville Campaign (Spring Hill, Franklin, and Nashville), Captured at Nashville[215]
- Alexander W. Reynolds (35), Confederate, BG, Fiftieth Virginia Infantry and Army of Tennessee, Grant's Operations against Vicksburg (Vicksburg), Chattanooga-Ringgold Campaign (Chattanooga), Captured at Vicksburg, Atlanta Campaign, Wounded at the Battle of New Hope Church, Assistant Inspector General of the District of Georgia[216]
- Andrew J. Smith (36), Union, MG, Department of the Ohio and Army of the Tennessee, Iuka and Corinth Operations (Second Corinth), Grant's Operations against Vicksburg (Jackson, Port Gibson, Champion Hill, Big Black River Bridge, and Vicksburg), Red River Campaign (Fort De Russy and Pleasant Hill), Forrest's Defense of Mississippi (Tupelo), Franklin-Nashville Campaign (Nashville), Mobile Campaign (Spanish Fort and Fort Blakely)[217]
- Justus McKinstry (40), Union, BG, Military Operations in Missouri, Dismissed on January 28, 1863, for neglect and violation of duty[218]
- Carter L. Stevenson (42), Confederate, MG, Army of Tennessee, Confederate Heartland Offensive (Perryville and Munfordville), Chattanooga-Ringgold Cam-

paign (Chattanooga), Grant's Operations against Vicksburg (Vicksburg and Champion Hill), Captured at Vicksburg, Atlanta Campaign (Kennesaw Mountain and Peachtree Creek), Franklin-Nashville Campaign (Nashville), Carolinas Campaign (Bentonville)[219]

Class of 1839 (31 Graduates)

- Isaac I. Stevens (1), Union, MG, Department of the South and Port Royal Expeditionary Corps, Operations against Charleston (Secessionville), Northern Virginia Campaign (Second Manassas and Chantilly), Killed at Chantilly[220]
- Henry W. Halleck (3), Union, MG, Armies of the United States, Department of the Missouri, Missouri Militia, Department of the Mississippi, Military Division of the Pacific, and Military Division of the James, Federal Penetration up the Cumberland and Tennessee Rivers (First Corinth), General-in-Chief of Armies of the United States, Chief of Staff, U.S. Army,[221] Lincoln characterized him as "little more than a first-rate clerk"[222]
- Jeremy F. Gilmer (4), Confederate, MG, Army of Mississippi, Army of Northern Virginia, and Confederate States Army, Engineering Operations, Federal Penetration up the Cumberland and Tennessee Rivers (Shiloh), Chief Engineer of the Confederate States Army[223]
- Joseph A. Haskin (10), Union, BG, Department of Washington, Defense of Washington, DC, Chief of Artillery in the Department of Washington[224]
- Alexander R. Lawton (13), Confederate, BG, Army of Northern Virginia, Virginia Peninsula Campaign (Seven Days), Maryland Campaign (Antietam), Wounded at Antietam, Quartermaster-General of the Confederate States Army[225]
- James B. Ricketts (16), Union, MG, Army of the Potomac, Manassas Campaign (First Manassas), Wounded and captured at First Manassas, Northern Virginia Campaign (Cedar Mountain, Second Manassas, and Chantilly), Maryland Campaign (South Mountain and Antietam), Grant's Overland Campaign (Wilderness, Spotsylvania, North Anna, and Cold Harbor), Richmond-Petersburg Campaign (Second Petersburg), Sheridan's Valley Campaign (Opequon, Fisher's Hill, and Cedar Creek)[226]
- Edward O.C. Ord (17), Union, MG, Department of the Gulf, Federal Penetration up the Cumberland and Tennessee Rivers (First Corinth), Iuka and Corinth Operations (Second Corinth), Grant's Operations against Vicksburg (Vicksburg and Jackson), Richmond-Petersburg Campaign (Second Petersburg), Appomattox Campaign (Lee's surrender at Appomattox Court House)[227]
- Henry J. Hunt (19), Union, Brevet MG, Army of the Potomac, Chief of Artillery, Manassas Campaign (First Manassas), Virginia Peninsula Campaign (Yorktown, Gaines' Mill, and Malvern Hill), Maryland Campaign (South Mountain and Antietam), Fredericksburg Campaign (First Fredericksburg), Chancellorsville Campaign (Chancellorsville), Gettysburg Campaign (Gettysburg), Richmond-Petersburg Campaign (Second Petersburg and Fort Stedman), Grant's Overland Campaign (Wilderness, Spotsylvania, and Cold Harbor), Appomattox Campaign (Lee's surrender at Appomattox Court House)[228]
- Eleazer A. Paine (24), Union, BG, Army of the Mississippi, Joint Operations against New Madrid, Island No. 10, and Memphis (New Madrid/Island No. 10), Iuka and Corinth Operations (Second Corinth)[229]
- Edward R.S. Canby (30), Union, MG, Department of New Mexico, City and Harbor of New York, Military Division of West Mississippi, and Department of the Gulf, Sibley's New Mexico Campaign (Valverde), Suppressed Draft Riots in New York City, Wounded by Rebel guerrillas on White River, Mobile Campaign (Spanish Fort and Fort Blakely), Surrender of LG R. Taylor's Confederate Army and other Confederate Forces in the Trans-Mississippi[230]

Class of 1840 (42 Graduates)

- Paul O. Hebert (1), Confederate, BG, Louisiana Artillery, Trans-Mississippi Department, and Department of Texas, Grant's Operations against Vicksburg[231]
- William T. Sherman (6), Union, MG, Army of the Potomac, Army of the Cumberland, Army of the Ohio, and Army of the Tennessee, Manassas Campaign (First Manassas), Federal Penetration up the Cumberland and Tennessee Rivers (Shiloh), Wounded at Shiloh, Iuka and Corinth Operations (Second Corinth), Grant's Operations against Vicksburg (Vicksburg and Jackson), Chattanooga-Ringgold Campaign (Chattanooga), Atlanta Campaign (Marietta, Kennesaw Mountain, Peach Tree Creek, Atlanta, and Jonesborough), Savannah Campaign (Fort McAlister), Carolinas Campaign (Bentonville), Johnston's surrender at Durham Station[232]
- Stewart van Vliet (9), Union, BG, Army of the Potomac, Quartermaster Operations, Virginia Peninsula Campaign, Stationed at New York City where he oversaw furnishing supplies and transportation to Union forces[233]
- John P. McCown (10), Confederate, MG, Army of the West and Army of Tennessee, Stones River Campaign (Stones River), Bragg preferred charges against him for disobedience of orders[234]
- George H. Thomas (12), Union, MG, Army of the Cumberland, Army of the Ohio, and Army of the Tennessee, Offensive in Eastern Kentucky (Mill Springs), Iuka and Corinth Operations (Second Corinth), Confederate Heartland Offensive (Perryville), Stones River Campaign (Stones River), Chickamauga Campaign (Chickamauga), Chattanooga-Ringgold Campaign (Chattanooga and Ringgold), Atlanta Campaign (Pine Mountain, Kennesaw Mountain, Peach Tree Creek, Atlanta, and Jonesborough), Franklin-Nashville Campaign (Franklin and Nashville)[235]
- Richard S. Ewell (13), Confederate, LG, Army of Northern Virginia, Manassas Campaign (First Manassas), Jackson's Valley Campaign, Virginia Peninsula Campaign (Seven Days), Northern Virginia Campaign (Second Manassas), Lost left leg at Second Manassas, Gettysburg Campaign (Gettysburg), Grant's Overland Campaign (Spotsylvania), Appomattox Campaign (Sayler's Creek)[236]
- James G. Martin (14), Confederate, BG, North Carolina Militia, Adjutant General of North Carolina, Richmond-Petersburg Campaign (Second Petersburg)[237]
- George W. Getty (15), Union, Brevet MG, Army of the Potomac, Virginia Peninsula Campaign (Yorktown, Gaines' Mill, and Malvern Hill), Maryland Campaign (South Mountain and Antietam), Fredericksburg Campaign (First Fredericksburg), Grant's Overland Campaign (Wilderness), Severely wounded at the Wilderness, Sheridan's Valley Campaign (Opequon, Fisher's Hill, and Cedar Creek), Richmond-Petersburg Campaign (Second Petersburg), Appomattox Campaign (Sayler's Creek and Lee's surrender at Appomattox Court House)[238]
- William Hays (18), Union, BG, Army of the Potomac, Virginia Peninsula Campaign (Yorktown, Williamsburg, Beaver Dam Creek, and Malvern Hill), Maryland Campaign (Antietam), Fredericksburg Campaign (First Fredericksburg), Chancellorsville Campaign (Chancellorsville), Captured at Chancellorsville, Gettysburg Campaign, Richmond-Petersburg Campaign (Second Petersburg), Appomattox Campaign (Lee's surrender at Appomattox Court House)[239]
- Bushrod R. Johnson (23), Confederate, MG, Army of the Mississippi and Army of Northern Virginia, Federal Penetration up the Cumberland and Tennessee Rivers (Fort Donelson and Shiloh), Stones River Campaign (Stones River), Chickamauga Campaign (Chickamauga), Longstreet's Knoxville Campaign, Richmond-Petersburg Campaign (Second Petersburg), Appomattox Campaign (Sayler's Creek)[240]
- William Steele (31), Confederate, BG, Seventh Texas Cavalry, Trans-Mississippi

Department, and Indian Territory, Sibley's New Mexico Campaign, Red River Campaign (Pleasant Hill)[241]
- Robert Plunket Maclay (32), Confederate, BG, Sixth Louisiana Military Brigade, Trans-Mississippi Department, Red River Campaign[242]
- James Green Martin (39), Confederate, BG, North Carolina Militia, Appomattox Campaign (Third Petersburg)[243]
- Thomas Jordan (41), Confederate, BG, Army of Northern Virginia and Army of Mississippi, Manassas Campaign (First Manassas), Adjutant General and Chief of Staff, Federal Penetration up the Cumberland and Tennessee Rivers (Shiloh), Operations against the Defenses of Charleston[244]

Class of 1841 (52 Graduates)

- Zealous B. Tower (1), Union, BG, Army of Tennessee and Army of Mississippi, Chief Engineer, Northern Virginia Campaign (Cedar Mountain and Second Manassas), Wounded and disabled at Second Manassas, Franklin-Nashville Campaign (Nashville)[245]
- Horatio G. Wright (2), Union, MG, Army of the Potomac and Army of the Ohio, Manassas Campaign (First Manassas), Jackson's Valley Campaign, Gettysburg Campaign (Gettysburg), Grant's Overland Campaign (Wilderness, Spotsylvania, North Anna, Totopotomoy and Cold Harbor), Operations against Charleston (Secessionville), Richmond-Petersburg Campaign (Second Petersburg), Sheridan's Valley Campaign (Opequon, Fisher's Hill, and Cedar Creek), Appomattox Campaign (Sayler's Creek and Lee's surrender at Appomattox Court House)[246]
- Amiel W. Whipple (5), Union, Brevet MG, Army of the Potomac and Corps of Engineers, Manassas Campaign (First Manassas), Fredericksburg Campaign (First Fredericksburg), Chancellorsville Campaign (Chancellorsville)[247]
- Josiah Gorgas (6), Confederate, BG, Chief of Ordnance, Authorized blockade running[248]
- Albion Powell Howe (8), Union, BG, Army of the Potomac, Operations in Western Virginia (Rich Mountain), Virginia Peninsula Campaign (Yorktown, Williamsburg and Seven Days), Northern Virginia Campaign (Second Manassas), Fredericksburg Campaign (First Fredericksburg), Maryland Campaign (South Mountain and Antietam), Gettysburg Campaign (Gettysburg)[249]
- Nathaniel Lyon (11), Union, BG, Operations to Control Missouri (Wilson's Creek), Killed at Wilson's Creek[250]
- John Love (14), Union, MG, Indiana Volunteers, Chief of Staff, Western Virginia Campaign, Pursuit of John Morgan's Raiders in Indiana, Resigned January 1, 1863[251]
- Samuel Jones (19), Confederate, MG, Western Department and Department of South Carolina, Georgia, and Florida, Artillery Operations, Manassas Campaign (First Manassas), Iuka and Corinth Operations (Second Corinth)[252]
- Joseph B. Plummer (22), Union, BG, Eleventh Missouri Volunteers, Operations to Control Missouri (Wilson's Creek), Severely wounded at Wilson's Creek, Federal Penetration up the Cumberland and Tennessee Rivers (First Corinth), Died on August 9, 1862, near Corinth[253]
- John M. Brannan (23), Union, Brevet MG, Army of the Cumberland and Army of the Tennessee, Artillery Operations, Chickamauga Campaign (Chickamauga), Chattanooga-Ringgold Campaign (Chattanooga), Atlanta Campaign (Kennesaw Mountain, Peach Tree Creek, Atlanta, and Jonesborough)[254]
- Schuyler Hamilton (24), Union, MG, Department of the Missouri, Joint Operations against New Madrid, Island No. 10, and Memphis (New Madrid/Island No. 10), Iuka and Corinth Operations (Second Corinth)[255]
- James Totten (25), Union, BG, Missouri Militia, Department of Missouri, Military

- Division of West Mississippi, Artillery and Ordnance Operations, Operations to Control Missouri (Wilson Creek), Mobile Campaign[256]
- John F. Reynolds (26), Union, MG, Army of the Potomac, Virginia Peninsula Campaign (Beaver Dam Creek, Gaines' Mill, and Glendale), Captured at Gaines' Mill, Commandant of Cadets at U.S. Military Academy, Northern Virginia Campaign (Second Manassas), Fredericksburg Campaign (First Fredericksburg), Chancellorsville Campaign (Chancellorsville), Gettysburg Campaign (Gettysburg), Mortally wounded at Gettysburg[257]
- Robert S. Garnett (27), Confederate, BG, Provisional Confederate Army, Commandant of Cadets at U.S. Military Academy, First general killed in Civil War, Killed on July 13, 1861, at Carrick's Ford[258]
- Richard B. Garnett (29), Confederate, BG, Provisional Confederate Army and Army of Northern Virginia, Jackson's Valley Campaign (First Kernstown), Maryland Campaign (South Mountain and Antietam), Gettysburg Campaign (Gettysburg), Killed during Pickett's Charge at Gettysburg[259]
- Claudius W. Sears (31), Confederate, BG, Army of Mississippi and Army of Tennessee, Grant's Operations against Vicksburg (Port Gibson and Vicksburg), Atlanta Campaign, Franklin-Nashville (Allatoona and Nashville), Wounded and captured at Nashville[260]
- Don Carlos Buell (32), Union, MG, Army of the Ohio, Federal Penetration up the Cumberland and Tennessee Rivers (Shiloh and First Corinth), Investigated by a military commission, Mustered out of volunteer service on May 23, 1864[261]
- Alfred Sully (34), Union, Brevet MG, Army of the Potomac, Virginia Peninsula Campaign (Yorktown, Glendale, and Malvern Hill), Northern Virginia Campaign (Chantilly), Maryland Campaign (South Mountain and Antietam), Fredericksburg Campaign (First Fredericksburg), Chancellorsville Campaign (Chancellorsville)[262]
- Israel B. Richardson (38), Union, MG, Army of the Potomac, Manassas Campaign (First Manassas), Virginia Peninsula Campaign (Yorktown, Williamsburg, Richmond, and Seven Days), Maryland Campaign (South Mountain and Antietam), Mortally wounded at Antietam[263]
- John M. Jones (39), Confederate, BG, Army of Northern Virginia, Chancellorsville Campaign (Chancellorsville), Gettysburg Campaign (Gettysburg), Grant's Overland Campaign (Wilderness), Killed at the Wilderness[264]
- William T.H. Brooks (46), Union, BG, Army of the Potomac and Army of the James, Virginia Peninsula Campaign (Glendale and Yorktown), Maryland Campaign (Antietam), Wounded at Antietam, Fredericksburg Campaign, Grant's Overland Campaign (Cold Harbor), Richmond-Petersburg Campaign (Second Petersburg)[265]
- Abraham Buford (51), Confederate, BG, Army of Tennessee, Grant's Operations against Vicksburg, Stones River Campaign (Stones River), Chickamauga Campaign (Chickamauga), Forrest's Expedition into Western Tennessee and Kentucky (Fort Pillow), Forrest's Defense of Mississippi (Brice's Crossroads and Tupelo), Franklin-Nashville Campaign (Nashville), Wilson's Raid in Alabama and Georgia[266]

Class of 1842 (56 Graduates)

- Henry Eustis (1), Union, BG, Army of the Potomac, Maryland Campaign, Fredericksburg Campaign (First Fredericksburg), Gettysburg Campaign (Gettysburg), Grant's Overland Campaign (Wilderness, Spotsylvania, Cold Harbor), Resigned June 27, 1864[267]
- John Newton (2), Union, BG, Army of the Potomac and Army of the Cumberland, Chief Engineer, Virginia Peninsula Campaign (Gaines' Mill and Glendale), Maryland Campaign (South Mountain and Antietam), Fredericksburg Campaign (First

Fredericksburg), Gettysburg Campaign (Gettysburg), Grant's Overland Campaign (Wilderness, Spotsylvania Court House, and Cold Harbor), Atlanta Campaign (Pine Mountain, Kennesaw, Peach Tree Creek, Atlanta, and Jonesborough)[268]
- William S. Rosecrans (5), Union, MG, Army of the Mississippi and Army of the Cumberland, Operations in Western Virginia (Rich Mountain and Carnifex Ferry), Federal Penetration up the Cumberland and Tennessee Rivers (First Corinth), Iuka and Corinth Operations (Second Corinth), Stones River Campaign (Stones River), Chickamauga Campaign (Chickamauga)[269]
- Gustavus W. Smith (8), Confederate, MG, Army of Northern Virginia, Army of the Potomac, and Army of Virginia, Virginia Peninsula Campaign, Acting Secretary of War in 1862, Resigned February 17, 1863, superintendent of the Etowah Iron Works, Atlanta Campaign[270]
- Mansfield Lovell (9), Confederate, MG, Army of District of Mississippi and Department of Georgia, South Carolina, and Florida, Expedition to, and Capture of, New Orleans (Forts Jackson and Phillip), Iuka and Corinth Operations (Second Corinth)[271]
- Alexander P. Stewart (12), Confederate, LG, Army of Tennessee and Army of the Mississippi, Camps of Instruction, Federal Penetration up the Cumberland and Tennessee Rivers (Shiloh), Confederate Heartland Offensive (Perryville), Stones River Campaign (Stones River), Chickamauga Campaign (Chickamauga), Chattanooga-Ringgold Campaign (Chattanooga), Atlanta Campaign (Peach Tree Creek and Ezra Church), Franklin-Nashville Campaign (Franklin and Nashville), Carolinas Campaign[272]
- Martin L. Smith (16), Confederate, MG, Twenty-first Louisiana Infantry, Army of Northern Virginia, Army of Tennessee, and Department of Gulf, Engineering Operations, Grant's Operations against Vicksburg (Vicksburg)[273]
- John Pope (17), Union, MG, Army of the Mississippi and Army of Virginia, Northern Virginia Campaign (Cedar Mountain, Second Manassas, and Chantilly), Joint Operations against New Madrid, Island No. 10, and Memphis (New Madrid/Island No. 10), Iuka and Corinth Operations (Second Corinth)[274]
- Seth Williams (23), Union, Brevet MG, Army of the Potomac, Inspector General, Adjutant General, Virginia Peninsula Campaign, Maryland Campaign, Fredericksburg Campaign, Gettysburg Campaign, Richmond-Petersburg Campaign[275]
- Abner Doubleday (24), Union, MG, Army of the Potomac, Operations in Charleston Harbor (Fort Sumter), Northern Virginia Campaign (Second Manassas), Maryland Campaign (South Mountain and Antietam), Fredericksburg Campaign (First Fredericksburg), Chancellorsville Campaign (Chancellorsville), Gettysburg Campaign (Gettysburg)[276]
- Daniel H. Hill (28), Confederate, LG, First North Carolina Infantry, Army of Northern Virginia, Department of North Carolina, and Army of Tennessee, Superintendent of North Carolina Military Institute, Virginia Peninsula Campaign (Yorktown, Williamsburg, Seven Pines, and Seven Days), Northern Virginia Campaign (Second Manassas, South Mountain, and Antietam), Chickamauga Campaign (Chickamauga), Carolinas Campaign (Bentonville), Outspoken critic of Braxton Bragg[277]
- Napoleon J.T. Dana (29), Union, MG, Army of the Potomac and Army of Mississippi, Virginia Peninsula Campaign (Yorktown, Glendale, and Malvern Hill), Maryland Campaign (Harper's Ferry, South Mountain, and Antietam), Wounded and disabled at Antietam[278]
- George Sykes (39), Union, MG, Army of the Potomac, Manassas Campaign (First Manassas), Virginia Peninsula Campaign (Yorktown, Gaines' Mill, and Malvern Hill), Northern Virginia Campaign (Second Manassas), Maryland Campaign (Antietam), Fredericksburg Campaign (First Fredericksburg), Chancellorsville

Campaign (Chancellorsville), Gettysburg Campaign (Gettysburg), Grant's Overland Campaign[279]
- Richard H. Anderson (40), Confederate, LG, Army of Northern Virginia, Operations in Charleston Harbor (Fort Sumter), Virginia Peninsula Campaign, Maryland Campaign (Antietam), Chancellorsville Campaign (Chancellorsville), Richmond-Petersburg Campaign, Appomattox Campaign (Sayler's Creek)[280]
- George W. Lay (41), Confederate, LTC, Acting Chief of Bureau of Conscription[281]
- Lafayette McLaws (48), Confederate, MG, Tenth Georgia Infantry, Army of Northern Virginia and Army of Tennessee, Virginia Peninsula Campaign, Carolinas Campaign (Bentonville)[282]
- Earl van Dorn (52), Confederate, MG, Mississippi Militia, Confederate Department of Texas, Confederate Army of the Potomac, Army of the West, Army of Mississippi, and Army of Tennessee, Pea Ridge Campaign (Pea Ridge), Iuka and Corinth Operations (Second Corinth), Grant's Operations against Vicksburg (Holly Springs), Murdered on May 7, 1863[283]
- James Longstreet (54), Confederate, LG, Army of Northern Virginia, Army of Tennessee, and Department of East Tennessee, Virginia Peninsula Campaign, Northern Virginia Campaign (Second Manassas), Maryland Campaign (Antietam), Fredericksburg Campaign (First Fredericksburg), Gettysburg Campaign (Gettysburg), Chickamauga Campaign (Chickamauga), Longstreet's Tidewater Campaign, Longstreet's Knoxville Campaign (Fort Sanders), Grant's Overland Campaign (Wilderness), Wounded at the Battle of the Wilderness, Appomattox Campaign (Appomattox Court House)[284]

Class of 1843 (39 Graduates)

- William B. Franklin (1), Union, MG, Army of the Potomac and Department of the Gulf, Manassas Campaign (First Manassas), Virginia Peninsula Campaign (Yorktown and Malvern Hill), Maryland Campaign (South Mountain and Antietam), Fredericksburg Campaign (First Fredericksburg), Operations against Baton Rouge (Baton Rouge), Operations to Blockade the Texas Coast (Second Sabine Pass), Red River Campaign (Pleasant Hill), Wounded at Sabine Cross Roads, President of the Board for Retiring Disabled Officers[285]
- Isaac F. Quinby (6), Union, BG, District of Mississippi, Manassas Campaign (First Manassas), Forrest's Expedition into Western Tennessee and Kentucky (Fort Pillow), Grant's Operations against Vicksburg (Champion Hill and Vicksburg), Forced to resign in December 1863 because of failing health[286]
- Roswell S. Ripley (7), Confederate, BG, Department of South Carolina, Army of Northern Virginia, and Army of Tennessee, Occupied Fort Moultrie after evacuation of Union forces, Virginia Peninsula Campaign (Seven Days), Maryland Campaign (Antietam), Wounded at the Battle of Antietam, Carolinas Campaign (Bentonville)[287]
- John J. Peck (8), Union, MG, Army of the Potomac and Department of the East, Virginia Peninsula Campaign (Yorktown, Williamsburg, Malvern Hill, and Seven Days), Longstreet's Tidewater Campaign (Suffolk and Hill's Point), Injured at Suffolk[288]
- Joseph J. Reynolds (10), Union, MG, Army of the Cumberland, Operations in Western Virginia (Cheat Mountain), Chickamauga Campaign (Chickamauga), Chattanooga-Ringgold Campaign (Chattanooga)[289]
- Samuel Gibbs French (14), Confederate, MG, Provisional Confederate Army, Army of Tennessee, and Confederate forces in Mobile, Alabama, Grant's Operations against Vicksburg (Jackson and Vicksburg), Franklin-Nashville Campaign[290]
- Christopher C. Augur (16), Union, MG, Commandant of Cadets at U.S. Military Academy, Fredericksburg Campaign, Northern Virginia Campaign (Cedar Mountain), Wounded at Cedar Mountain, Siege of Port Hudson (Port Hudson)[291]

- Franklin K. Gardner (17), Confederate, MG, Confederate States Army and Army of Mississippi, Federal Penetration up the Cumberland and Tennessee Rivers (Shiloh), Confederate Heartland Offensive (Perryville), Siege of Port Hudson (Port Hudson)[292]
- Ulysses S. Grant (21), Union, LG, Army of the Tennessee, Army of the Mississippi, Army of the Cumberland, and Armies of the United States, Federal Penetration up the Cumberland and Tennessee Rivers (Fort Henry, Fort Donelson, and Shiloh), Iuka and Corinth Operations (Second Corinth), Grant's Operations against Vicksburg (Raymond, Jackson, Big Black River Bridge, Port Gibson, Champion's Hill, and Vicksburg), Chattanooga-Ringgold Campaign (Chattanooga), Grant's Overland Campaign (Wilderness, Spotsylvania, North Anna, Totopotomoy and Cold Harbor), Richmond-Petersburg Campaign (Second Petersburg), Appomattox Campaign (Sayler's Creek and Lee's surrender at Appomattox Court House)[293]
- Charles S. Hamilton (26), Union, MG, Army of the Potomac and Army of the Tennessee, Virginia Peninsula Campaign (Yorktown), Iuka and Corinth Operations (Second Corinth), Resigned in April 1863[294]
- Frederick Steele (30), Union, MG, Army of the Southwest and Army of Arkansas, Operations to Control Missouri (Wilson's Creek), Grant's Operations against Vicksburg (Helena, Jackson, and Vicksburg), Advance on Little Rock (Little Rock), Mobile Campaign (Fort Blakely)[295]
- Rufus Ingalls (32), Union, Brevet BG, Army of the Potomac, Chief Quartermaster, Virginia Peninsula Campaign (Yorktown), Maryland Campaign (South Mountain and Antietam), Fredericksburg Campaign (First Fredericksburg), Chancellorsville Campaign (Chancellorsville), Gettysburg Campaign (Gettysburg), Grant's Overland Campaign (Wilderness, Spotsylvania, and Cold Harbor), Richmond-Petersburg Campaign (Second Petersburg)[296]
- Henry M. Judah (35), Union, BG, Army of the Tennessee, Army of the Ohio, and Army of the Cumberland, Federal Penetration up the Cumberland and Tennessee (First Corinth)[297]

Class of 1844 (25 Graduates)

- Daniel M. Frost (4), Confederate, BG, Trans-Mississippi Department, Prairie Grove Campaign (Prairie Grove), Frost's family moved to Canada and Frost deserted and joined his family, Stayed in Canada for the rest of the war[298]
- Alfred Pleasonton (7), Union, MG, Army of the Potomac and Department of the Missouri, Virginia Peninsula Campaign (Yorktown and Seven Days), Maryland Campaign (South Mountain and Antietam), Fredericksburg Campaign (First Fredericksburg), Chancellorsville Campaign (Chancellorsville), Gettysburg Campaign (Gettysburg and Brandy Station)[299]
- Simon B. Buckner (11), Confederate, LG, Confederate States Army, Army of Tennessee, and Department of East Tennessee, Federal Penetration up the Cumberland and Tennessee Rivers (Fort Donelson), Captured at Fort Donelson, Confederate Heartland Offensive (Perryville), Chickamauga Campaign (Chickamauga)[300]
- Winfield S. Hancock (18), Union, MG, Army of the Potomac and Army of the Shenandoah, Virginia Peninsula Campaign (Yorktown and Williamsburg), Maryland Campaign (South Mountain and Antietam), Fredericksburg Campaign (First Fredericksburg), Chancellorsville Campaign (Chancellorsville), Gettysburg Campaign (Gettysburg), Wounded and disabled at Gettysburg, Grant's Overland Campaign (Wilderness, Spotsylvania, North Anna, Totopotomy, and Cold Harbor), Richmond-Petersburg Campaign (Second Petersburg, Second Deep Bottom, Reams's Station, and Boydton Plank Road)[301]

- Alexander Hays (20), Union, BG, Army of the Potomac, Virginia Peninsula Campaign (Yorktown, Williamsburg, Peach Orchard, Glendale, and Malvern Hill), Northern Virginia Campaign (Second Manassas), Wounded and disabled at Second Manassas, Gettysburg Campaign (Gettysburg), Grant's Overland Campaign (Wilderness), Killed at the Wilderness[302]

Class of 1845 (41 Graduates)

- William H.C. Whiting (1), Confederate, MG, Army of Northern Virginia, Manassas Campaign (First Manassas), Jackson's Valley Campaign, Virginia Peninsula Campaign (Seven Days), Constructed Fort Fisher, North Carolina[303]
- Louis Hébert (3), Confederate, BG, Iuka and Corinth Operations (Second Corinth), Grant's Operations against Vicksburg (Vicksburg), Captured at Vicksburg, Operations against Fort Fisher and Wilmington (Fort Fisher)[304]
- William F. Smith (4), Union, MG, Army of the Potomac, Department of the Susquehanna, Army of the Cumberland, Department of West Virginia, and Military Division of the Mississippi, Manassas Campaign (First Manassas), Virginia Peninsula Campaign (Yorktown, Williamsburg, Glendale, and Malvern Hill), Maryland Campaign (South Mountain and Antietam), Fredericksburg Campaign (First Fredericksburg), Chattanooga-Ringgold Campaign (Chattanooga), Grant's Overland Campaign (Cold Harbor), Richmond-Petersburg Campaign (Second Petersburg)[305]
- Thomas J. Wood (5), Union, MG, Army of the Ohio and Army of the Cumberland, Federal Penetration up the Cumberland and Tennessee Rivers (Shiloh and First Corinth), Confederate Heartland Offensive (Perryville), Stones River Campaign (Stones River), Wounded and disabled at Stones River, Chickamauga Campaign (Chickamauga), Chattanooga-Ringgold Campaign (Chattanooga), Atlanta Campaign (Kennesaw Mountain, Peach Tree Creek, Atlanta, and Jonesborough), Franklin-Nashville Campaign (Franklin and Nashville)[306]
- Charles P. Stone (7), Union, BG, Army of the Shenandoah, Army of the Potomac, and Department of the Gulf, Battle of Ball's Bluff, Virginia, Accused of disloyalty and treason, Held without charges in prisons at Fort Lafayette, Pennsylvania and Fort Hamilton, New York, Siege of Port Hudson (Port Hudson), Red River Campaign (Pleasant Hill), Richmond-Petersburg Campaign (Second Petersburg)[307]
- Fitz John Porter (8), Union, MG, Army of the Potomac, Virginia Peninsula Campaign (Yorktown, Beaver Dam Creek, Gaines' Mill, and Malvern Hill), Northern Virginia Campaign (Second Manassas), Maryland Campaign (Antietam), Dismissed on January 21, 1863, and "forever disqualified from holding any office of trust or profit under, the Government of the United States, for violation of the 9th and 52nd Articles of War"[308]
- John P. Hatch (17), Union, BG, Department of the South District of Florida, Medal of Honor for actions at South Mountain, Commanded the "Iron Brigade", Jackson's Valley Campaign (Winchester), Maryland Campaign (South Mountain), Northern Virginia Campaign (Second Manassas and Chantilly), Wounded at Second Manassas, Maryland Campaign (South Mountain)[309]
- Edmund Kirby Smith (25), Confederate, LG, Provisional Confederate Army, Army of the Shenandoah, Trans-Mississippi Department, Army of Kentucky, Manassas Campaign (First Manassas), Confederate Heartland Offensive (Perryville), Red River Campaign (Mansfield)[310]
- John W. Davidson (27), Union, BG, Army of the Potomac and Army of Southeast Missouri, Virginia Peninsula Campaign (Gaines' Mill and Glendale), Advance on Little Rock (Little Rock)[311]
- James M. Hawes (29), Confederate, BG, Second Kentucky Cavalry, Trans-Mississippi Department, and Western Department, Federal Penetration up the

Cumberland and Tennessee Rivers (Shiloh), Grant's Operations against Vicksburg[312]
- Bernard E. Bee (33), Confederate, BG, First Carolina Regulars, Provisional Confederate Army, and Army of Shenandoah, Manassas Campaign (First Manassas), Killed at First Manassas, Gave Jackson his sobriquet of "Stonewall"[313]
- Gordon Granger (35), Union, MG, Army of the Mississippi, Army of Kentucky, Army of the Cumberland, and Department of the Gulf, Operations to Control Missouri (Wilson's Creek), Federal Penetration up the Cumberland and Tennessee Rivers (First Corinth), Joint Operations against New Madrid, Island No. 10, and Memphis (New Madrid/Island No. 10), Chickamauga Campaign (Chickamauga), Chattanooga-Ringgold Campaign (Chattanooga), Mobile Campaign (Spanish Fort and Fort Blakely)[314]
- Henry B. Clitz (36), Union, LTC, Army of the Potomac, Virginia Peninsula Campaign (Yorktown and Gaines' Mill), Wounded at Yorktown and Gaines' Mill, Captured at Gaines' Mill, Commandant of Cadets at U.S. Military Academy[315]
- David A. Russell (38), Union, Brevet MG, Army of the Potomac, Virginia Peninsula Campaign (Yorktown, Williamsburg, and the Seven Days), Maryland Campaign (Antietam), Fredericksburg Campaign (First Fredericksburg), Gettysburg Campaign (Gettysburg), Grant's Overland Campaign (Wilderness, Spotsylvania, North Anna, Totopotomy Creek, and Cold Harbor), Richmond-Petersburg Campaign (Second Petersburg), Sheridan's Valley Campaign (Opequon), Killed at Opequon[316]
- Thomas G. Pitcher (40), Union, BG, Northern Virginia Campaign (Cedar Mountain), Severely wounded at Cedar Mountain[317]

Class of 1846 (59 Graduates)

- George B. McClellan (2), Union, MG, Department of the Ohio, Army of Potomac, and Armies of the United States, Operations in Western Virginia (Rich Mountain), Virginia Peninsula Campaign (Yorktown and Seven Days), Maryland Campaign (South Mountain and Antietam), Relieved of command, Democratic Party Presidential Candidate, Resigned on November 8, 1864[318]
- John G. Foster (4), Union, MG, Army of the Ohio and Department of the South, Operations in Charleston Harbor (Fort Sumter), Burnside's North Carolina Expedition (Roanoke Island and New Bern), Appointed Horace James as "Superintendent of Negro Affairs for the North Carolina District" to develop Freedmen's colonies,[319] During expedition against Roanoke Island was part of "The Four Horsemen of the Point"[320]
- Jesse L. Reno (8), Union, MG, Army of the Potomac and Department of North Carolina, Burnside's Expedition to North Carolina (Roanoke Island and New Bern), Northern Virginia Campaign (Second Manassas and Chantilly), Maryland Campaign (South Mountain), Killed at South Mountain,[321] During expedition against Roanoke Island was part of "The Four Horsemen of the Point"[322]
- Darius N. Couch (13), Union, MG, Army of the Potomac and Army of the Cumberland, Virginia Peninsula Campaign (Yorktown, Williamsburg, and Malvern Hill), Northern Virginia Campaign (Second Manassas), Maryland Campaign (Harper's Ferry), Fredericksburg Campaign (First Fredericksburg), Chancellorsville Campaign (Chancellorsville), Gettysburg Campaign, Franklin-Nashville Campaign (Nashville)[323]
- Thomas J. Jackson (17), Confederate, LG, Army of Northern Virginia, Jackson's Valley Campaign, Manassas Campaign (First Manassas), Chancellorsville Campaign (Chancellorsville), Mortally wounded by his own troops at Chancellorsville[324]
- Truman Seymour (19), Union, BG, Army of the Potomac and Department of the

South, Operations in Charleston Harbor (First Fort Sumter), Virginia Peninsula Campaign (Beaver Dam Creek, Gaines' Mill, Glendale, and Malvern Hill), Northern Virginia Campaign (Second Manassas), Maryland Campaign (South Mountain and Antietam), Operations against the Defenses of Charleston (Fort Wagner/Morris Island), Severely wounded at Fort Wagner, Florida Expedition (Olustee), Richmond-Petersburg Campaign, Grant's Overland Campaign (Wilderness), Captured at the Wilderness, Operations in Shenandoah Valley, Richmond-Petersburg Campaign (Second Petersburg), Appomattox Campaign (Third Petersburg, Sayler's Creek and Lee's surrender at Appomattox Court House)[325]

- Charles C. Gilbert (21), Union, BG, Army of the Cumberland, Army of the Ohio, and Army of Kentucky, Operations to Control Missouri (Wilson's Creek), Sibley's New Mexico Campaign (Valverde), Wounded and disabled at Valverde, Federal Penetration up the Cumberland and Tennessee Rivers (Shiloh), Iuka and Corinth Operations (Second Corinth), Confederate Heartland Offensive (Perryville), Helped organize Invalid Corps[326]
- John Adams (25), Confederate, BG, Army of Tennessee, Grant's Operations against Vicksburg (Vicksburg), Atlanta Campaign, Franklin-Nashville Campaign (Franklin), Killed at Franklin[327]
- George Stoneman (33), Union, MG, Army of the Potomac and Army of the Ohio, Virginia Peninsula Campaign (Yorktown, Williamsburg, and Seven Days), Fredericksburg Campaign (First Fredericksburg), Atlanta Campaign, Captured at Clinton, Georgia[328]
- William Duncan Smith (35), Confederate, BG, Twentieth Georgia Infantry and Department of South Carolina, Operations against Charleston (Secessionville), Died from disease on October 4, 1862[329]
- Dabney H. Maury (37), Confederate, MG, Army of the West, Department of the Gulf, and Department of Alabama, Mississippi, and East Tennessee, Pea Ridge Campaign (Pea Ridge), Iuka and Corinth Operations (Second Corinth), Grant's Operations against Vicksburg (Vicksburg)[330]
- Innis N. Palmer (38), Union, BG, Army of the Potomac, Manassas Campaign (First Manassas), Virginia Peninsula Campaign (Yorktown, Williamsburg, Glendale, and Malvern Hill)[331]
- David R. Jones (41), Confederate, MG, Army of Northern Virginia, Operations in Charleston Harbor (First Fort Sumter), Manassas Campaign (First Manassas), Virginia Peninsula Campaign (Seven Days), Northern Virginia Campaign (Second Manassas), Maryland Campaign (South Mountain and Antietam), Died from heart disease in January 1863[332]
- Alfred Gibbs (42), Union, BG, Army of the Potomac, Jackson's Valley Campaign, Virginia Peninsula Campaign (Beaver Dam Creek), Grant's Overland Campaign (Spotsylvania, Cold Harbor, and Trevilian Station), Richmond-Petersburg Campaign, Sheridan's Valley Campaign (Opequon and Cedar Creek), Appomattox Campaign (Five Forks, Sayler's Creek and Lee's surrender at Appomattox Court House)[333]
- George H. Gordon (43), Union, BG, Army of the Potomac, Jackson's Valley Campaign (First Winchester), Northern Virginia Campaign (Cedar Mountain and Chantilly), Maryland Campaign (South Mountain and Antietam), Operations against the Defenses of Charleston, Mobile Campaign[334]
- Cadmus M. Wilcox (54), Confederate, MG, Army of Northern Virginia, Manassas Campaign (First Manassas), Virginia Peninsula Campaign (Seven Days), Northern Virginia Campaign, Maryland Campaign, Fredericksburg Campaign, Chancellorsville Campaign, Gettysburg Campaign (Gettysburg), Grant's Overland Campaign, Richmond-Petersburg Campaign, Appomattox Campaign[335]
- William M. Gardner (55), Confederate, BG, Army of Northern Virginia, Bureau of

Prisons, Manassas Campaign (First Manassas), Wounded at First Manassas, Florida Expedition (Olustee)[336]
- Samuel B. Maxey (58), Confederate, MG, Ninth Texas Infantry, Army of Mississippi and Trans-Mississippi Department, Grant's Operations against Vicksburg, Siege of Port Hudson (Port Hudson), Red River Campaign[337]
- George E. Pickett (59), Confederate, MG, Army of Northern Virginia and Department of Virginia and North Carolina, Virginia Peninsula Campaign (Gaines' Mill), Fredericksburg Campaign, Gettysburg Campaign (Gettysburg), Appomattox Campaign (Five Forks and Sayler's Creek)[338]

Class of 1847 (38 Graduates)

- Orlando B. Wilcox (8), Union, Brevet MG, Manassas Campaign (First Manassas), Wounded and captured at First Manassas, Maryland Campaign (South Mountain and Antietam), Fredericksburg Campaign (First Fredericksburg), Indiana Draft Riots, Longstreet's Knoxville Campaign, Grant's Overland Campaign (Wilderness, Spotsylvania, and Totopotomoy), Richmond-Petersburg Campaign (Hatcher's Run and Second Petersburg)[339]
- John S. Mason (9), Union, BG, Army of the Potomac and Department of the Pacific, Operations in Western Virginia, Jackson's Valley Campaign (First Winchester), Virginia Peninsula Campaign, Fredericksburg Campaign (First Fredericksburg)[340]
- James B. Fry (14), Union, BG, Department of Northeastern Virginia and Army of the Ohio, Manassas Campaign (First Manassas), Federal Penetration up the Cumberland and Tennessee Rivers (Shiloh and First Corinth), Confederate Heartland Offensive (Perryville), Provost Marshall General of the U.S. Army[341]
- Ambrose P. Hill (15), Confederate, LG, Army of Northern Virginia, Virginia Peninsula Campaign (Williamsburg and Seven Days), Northern Virginia Campaign (Cedar Mountain), Maryland Campaign (Antietam), Chancellorsville Campaign, Gettysburg Campaign, Richmond-Ringgold Campaign (Second Petersburg), Killed at Petersburg[342]
- Ambrose E. Burnside (18), Union, MG, Army of the Potomac, Army of the Ohio, and Department of North Carolina, Manassas Campaign (First Manassas), Operations in North Carolina (Roanoke Island, Newbern, and Fort Macon), Maryland Campaign (South Mountain and Antietam), Fredericksburg Campaign (First Fredericksburg), Longstreet's Knoxville Campaign, Grant's Overland Campaign (Wilderness, Spotsylvania, North Anna, and Totopotomy Creek), Richmond-Petersburg Campaign (Second Petersburg and the Crater),[343] During expedition against Roanoke Island was part of "The Four Horsemen of the Point"[344]
- John Gibbon (20), Union, MG, Department of the Rappahannock and Army of the Potomac, Northern Virginia Campaign (Second Manassas), Maryland Campaign (South Mountain and Antietam), Fredericksburg Campaign (First Fredericksburg), Gettysburg Campaign (Gettysburg), Grant's Overland Campaign (Wilderness, Spotsylvania, Cold Harbor, and Totopotomy Creek), Richmond-Petersburg Campaign (Second Petersburg), Appomattox Campaign (Lee's surrender at Appomattox Court House)[345]
- Romeyn B. Ayers (22), Union, Brevet MG, Army of the Potomac, Manassas Campaign (First Manassas), Virginia Peninsula Campaign (Yorktown, Williamsburg, Gaines' Mill, and Glendale), Maryland Campaign (South Mountain and Antietam), Fredericksburg Campaign (First Fredericksburg), Chancellorsville Campaign (Chancellorsville), Gettysburg Campaign (Gettysburg), Grant's Overland Campaign (Wilderness, Spotsylvania, and Totopotomoy Creek), Richmond-Petersburg Campaign (Second Petersburg), Wounded at Second Petersburg, Appomattox Campaign (Five Forks, White Oak Road and Lee's surrender at Appomattox Court House[346]

- Charles Griffin (23), Union, Brevet MG, Army of the Potomac, Manassas Campaign (First Manassas), Virginia Peninsula Campaign (Yorktown, Gaines' Mill and Malvern Hill), Northern Virginia Campaign (Second Manassas), Maryland Campaign (Antietam), Fredericksburg Campaign (First Fredericksburg), Chancellorsville Campaign (Chancellorsville), Gettysburg Campaign (Gettysburg), Richmond-Petersburg Campaign, Grant's Overland Campaign (Wilderness and Spotsylvania), Appomattox Campaign (Third Petersburg and Five Forks and Lee's surrender at Appomattox Court House)[347]
- William W. Burns (28), Union, MG, Army of the Ohio, Commissary Services, Operations in Western Virginia, Virginia Peninsula Campaign (Yorktown, Glendale and Malvern Hill), Wounded at Savage Station, Fredericksburg Campaign (First Fredericksburg)[348]
- Egbert L. Viele (30), Union, BG, Department of Virginia, Resigned on October 20, 1863[349]
- Henry Heth (38), Confederate, MG, Army of Northern Virginia, Prepared Army's first marksmanship manual in 1858, Offensive in Eastern Kentucky, Chancellorsville Campaign (Chancellorsville), Gettysburg Campaign (Gettysburg), Grant's Overland Campaign, Richmond-Petersburg Campaign, Appomattox Campaign[350]

Class of 1848 (38 Graduates)

- Walter H. Stevens (4), Confederate, BG, Regular Confederate Army, Army of Virginia, Army of Northern Virginia, Virginia Peninsula Campaign, Northern Virginia Campaign, Richmond-Ringgold Campaign, Appomattox Campaign, Chief Engineer of Richmond defenses[351]
- William E. Jones (10), Confederate, BG, Washington Mounted Rifles, Army of Northern Virginia, and Department of Southwest Virginia and East Tennessee, Manassas Campaign (First Manassas), Gettysburg Campaign (Gettysburg and Brandy Station), Longstreet's Knoxville Campaign, Killed at the Battle of Piedmont on June 5, 1864[352]
- John C. Tidball (11), Union, Brevet BG, Army of the Potomac, Manassas Campaign (First Manassas), Virginia Peninsula Campaign (Yorktown, Williamsburg, Gaines' Mill, and Malvern Hill), Maryland Campaign (Antietam), Fredericksburg Campaign (First Fredericksburg), Chancellorsville Campaign (Chancellorsville), Gettysburg Campaign (Gettysburg), Grant's Overland Campaign (Wilderness, Spotsylvania, North Anna, Totopotomy Creek, and Cold Harbor), Richmond-Petersburg Campaign (Second Petersburg and Fort Stedman), Appomattox Campaign (Lee's surrender at Appomattox Court House)[353]
- John Buford (16), Union, MG, Army of the Potomac, Northern Virginia Campaign (Second Manassas), Wounded and disabled at Second Manassas, Maryland Campaign (South Mountain and Antietam), Fredericksburg Campaign (First Fredericksburg), Gettysburg Campaign, (Gettysburg), Died on December 16, 1863, in Washington[354]
- William Beall (30), Confederate, BG, Army of West and Department of Mississippi and East Louisiana, Siege of Port Hudson (Port Hudson), Captured at Port Hudson, Served as Confederate Agent to supply Confederate POWs[355]
- Nathan George Evans (36), Confederate, BG, Army of Potomac and Army of Northern Virginia, Manassas Campaign (First Manassas), Northern Virginia Campaign (Second Manassas), Maryland Campaign (South Mountain and Antietam), Grant's Operations against Vicksburg, Behavior caused difficulties[356]
- George H. Steuart (37), Confederate, BG, First Maryland Regiment and Army of Northern Virginia, Manassas Campaign (First Manassas), Jackson's Valley Campaign (Cross Keyes), Wounded at Cross Keyes, Gettysburg Campaign (Gettysburg), Grant's Overland Campaign (Spotsylvania), Appomattox Campaign (Five Forks)[357]

Class of 1849 (43 Graduates)

- Quincy A. Gilmore (1), Union, MG, Department of the South, District of Western Virginia, Army of Kentucky, and District of Central Kentucky, Chief Engineer of the Port Royal Expedition, Operations against Fort Pulaski (Fort Pulaski), Operations against the Defenses of Charleston (Fort Wagner/Morris Island and Second Charleston Harbor), Richmond-Petersburg Campaign, Severely injured from fall off horse, Resigned July 14, 1864.[358]
- John G. Parke (2), Union, MG, Department of the Ohio, Department of North Carolina, and Army of the Potomac, Operations in North Carolina (Roanoke Island, Newbern, and Fort Macon), Maryland Campaign (South Mountain and Antietam), Chief of Staff of MG Burnside, Fredericksburg Campaign (First Fredericksburg), Grant's Operations against Vicksburg (Vicksburg), East Tennessee Campaign, Grant's Overland Campaign (Wilderness and Spotsylvania), Richmond-Petersburg Campaign (Second Petersburg, Hatcher's Run, Peebles' Farm, and Fort Stedman), Appomattox Campaign (Third Petersburg and Lee's surrender at Appomattox Court House),[359] During expedition against Roanoke Island was part of "The Four Horsemen of the Point"[360]
- Johnson K. Duncan (5), Confederate, BG, New Orleans Coastal Defenses, Expedition to, and Capture of, New Orleans (Forts Jackson and St. Philip), Died on December 18, 1862[361]
- Absalom Baird (9), Union, Brevet MG, Army of the Potomac, Army of the Ohio, and Army of Kentucky, Manassas Campaign (First Manassas), Virginia Peninsula Campaign (Yorktown and Williamsburg), Chickamauga Campaign (Chickamauga), Chattanooga-Ringgold Campaign (Chatttanooga), Atlanta Campaign (Pine Mountain, Kennesaw Mountain, Peach Tree Creek, Atlanta, and Jonesborough), Carolinas Campaign (Bentonville), Johnston's surrender at Durham Station[362]
- John Creed Moore (17), Confederate, BG, Army of Tennessee, Western Theater, and Army of the West, Grant's Operations against Vicksburg (Vicksburg), Captured at Vicksburg, Resigned February 3, 1864[363]
- Rufus Saxton (18), Union, Brevet MG, Department of the South, Operations to Control Missouri, Operations in Western Virginia, Organizing and Recruiting Colored troops, Bureau of Refugees, Freedmen, and Abandoned Lands, Inspection Duty in Freedmen's Bureau[364]
- Beverly H. Robertson (25), Confederate, BG, Army of Northern Virginia, Fredericksburg Campaign (First Fredericksburg), Gettysburg Campaign (Gettysburg)[365]
- Charles W. Field (27), Confederate, MG, Army of Northern Virginia, Jackson's Valley Campaign, Virginia Peninsula Campaign, Northern Virginia Campaign (Second Manassas), Severely wounded at Second Manassas, Grant's Overland Campaign (Cold Harbor)[366]
- Seth M. Barton (28), Confederate, BG, Army of Northern Virginia and Department of East Tennessee, Jackson's Valley Campaign, Virginia Peninsula Campaign (Drewry's Bluff), Grant's Operations against Vicksburg (Vicksburg), Captured at Vicksburg, Richmond-Petersburg Campaign, Appomattox Campaign[367]
- Duff C. Greene (29), Confederate, BG, Alabama Militia[368]
- Richard W. Johnson (30), Union, Brevet MG, Army of the Cumberland, Army of the Ohio, and Division of the Mississippi, Federal Penetration up the Cumberland and Tennessee Rivers (First Corinth), Stones River Campaign (Stones River), Chickamauga Campaign (Chickamauga), Chattanooga-Ringgold Campaign (Chattanooga), Wounded and disabled at New Hope Church, Franklin-Nashville Campaign (Nashville)[369]
- Alfred Cumming (35), Confederate, BG, First Georgia Infantry and Tenth Georgia Infantry, Virginia Peninsula Campaign (Yorktown, Savage's Station, and

Malvern Hill), Maryland Campaign, Grant's Operations against Vicksburg (Champion Hill and Vicksburg), Chattanooga-Ringgold Campaign (Missionary Ridge), Atlanta Campaign (Jonesborough)[370]
- James M. McIntosh (43), Confederate, BG, Provisional Army of the Confederacy, Pea Ridge Campaign (Pea Ridge), Killed at Pea Ridge[371]

Class of 1850 (44 Graduates)

- Gouverneur K. Warren (2), Union, MG, Department of Virginia and Army of the Potomac, Virginia Peninsula Campaign (Yorktown, Gaines' Mill, and Malvern Hill), Wounded at Gaines' Mill, Northern Virginia Campaign (Second Manassas), Maryland Campaign (Antietam), Fredericksburg Campaign (First Fredericksburg), Gettysburg Campaign (Gettysburg), Wounded at Gettysburg, Grant's Overland Campaign (Wilderness, Spotsylvania, North Anna, Totopotomy Creek, and Cold Harbor), Richmond-Petersburgh Campaign (Second Petersburg, Peebles' Farm, and Hatcher's Run), Appomattox Campaign (Five Forks),[372] Saw importance of Little Round Top at Gettysburg[373]
- Cuvier Grover (4), Union, Brevet MG, Army of the Potomac and Department of the Gulf, Virginia Peninsula Campaign (Yorktown, Williamsburg, Glendale, and Malvern Hill), Northern Virginia Campaign (Second Manassas), Operations against Baton Rouge (Baton Rouge), Siege of Port Hudson (Port Hudson), Sheridan's Valley Campaign (Opequon, Fisher's Hill, and Cedar Creek), Wounded at Cedar Creek[374]
- Adam J. Slemmer (12), Union, BG, Army of the Ohio and Army of the Cumberland, Federal Penetration up the Cumberland and Tennessee Rivers (First Corinth), Stones River Campaign (Stones River), Wounded and disabled at Stones River[375]
- Richard Arnold (13), Union, BG, Army of the Potomac and Department of the Gulf, Manassas Campaign (First Manassas), Virginia Peninsula Campaign (Glendale and Malvern Hill), Siege of Port Hudson (Port Hudson), Red River Campaign (Pleasant Hill), Operations in Mobile Bay (Mobile Bay)[376]
- Lucius M. Walker (15), Confederate, BG, Western Theater and the Trans-Mississippi Department, Mortally wounded in a duel with John S. Marmaduke[377]
- Armistead L. Long (17), Confederate, BG, Army of Northern Virginia, Chief of Artillery[378]
- Robert Ransom (18), Confederate, MG, U.S. Military Academy, Army of Northern Virginia, Fredericksburg Campaign (First Fredericksburg)[379]
- Eugene A. Carr (19), Union, BG, Army of Arkansas, Operations to Control Missouri (Wilson's Creek), Pea Ridge Campaign (Pea Ridge), Wounded at Pea Ridge, Grant's Operations against Vicksburg (Vicksburg, Champion Hill, Port Gibson, and Big Black River Bridge), Advance on Little Rock (Little Rock), Mobile Campaign (Spanish Fort)[380]
- William P. Carlin (20), Union, BG, Army of the Ohio and Army of the Cumberland, Federal Penetration up the Cumberland and Tennessee Rivers (First Corinth), Confederate Heartland Offensive (Perryville), Stones River Campaign (Stones River), Chickamauga Campaign (Chickamauga), Chattanooga-Ringgold Campaign (Chattanooga and Ringgold), Atlanta Campaign (Kennesaw Mountain, Atlanta, and Jonesborough), Carolinas Campaign (Bentonville)[381]
- Amos Beckwith (21), Union, Brevet BG, Commissary Services, Atlanta Campaign, Carolinas Campaign, Johnston's surrender at Durham Station[382]
- Charles Sidney Winder (22), Confederate, BG, Army of Northern Virginia, Northern Virginia Campaign (Cedar Mountain), Killed at Cedar Mountain[383]
- William Lewis Cabell (33), Confederate, BG, Army of the West, Captured by Union forces during Price's Raid[384]

- John J.A.A. Mouton (38), Confederate, BG, Western Theater and the Trans-Mississippi Department, Red River Campaign (Mansfield), Killed at Mansfield[385]

Class of 1851 (42 Graduates)

- George L. Andrews (1), Union, BG, Army of the Gulf, Jackson's Valley Campaign (Winchester), Northern Virginia Campaign (Cedar Mountain), Maryland Campaign (Antietam), Siege of Port Hudson (Port Hudson), Operations in Mobile Bay (Mobile Bay)[386]
- James St. C. Morton (2), Union, Brevet BG, Army of the Ohio and Army of the Cumberland, Stones River Campaign (Stones River), Chickamauga Campaign (Chickamauga), Wounded at Chickamauga, Grant's Overland Campaign (North Anna, and Totopotomy), Richmond-Petersburg Campaign (Second Petersburg), Killed at Second Petersburg[387]
- Kenner Garrard (8), Union, Brevet MG, Army of the Potomac, Army of the Cumberland, and Military Division of the Mississippi, Commandant of Cadets at U.S. Military Academy, Fredericksburg Campaign (First Fredericksburg), Chancellorsville Campaign (Chancellorsville), Gettysburg Campaign (Gettysburg), Chattanooga-Ringgold Campaign, Atlanta Campaign Franklin-Nashville Campaign (Nashville), Mobile Campaign (Spanish Fort and Blakely)[388]
- Benjamin Hardin Helm (9), Confederate, BG, Commanded the Kentucky Orphan Brigade, Chickamauga Campaign (Chickamauga), Killed at Chickamauga, Brother-in-law of Abraham Lincoln[389]
- Alvan C. Gillem (11), Union, BG, Army of the Ohio, Offensive in Eastern Kentucky (Mill Springs), Federal Penetration up the Cumberland and Tennessee Rivers (Shiloh and First Corinth), Member of convention to revise the Constitution and reorganize the State Government of Tennessee[390]
- Thomas J.C. Amory (30), Union, Brevet BG, Department of North Carolina, Commissary Services[391]
- William D. Whipple (31), Union, BG, Department of Pennsylvania, Department of Virginia, Army of the Tennessee, and Army of the Cumberland, Manassas Campaign (First Manassas), Chattanooga-Ringgold Campaign (Chattanooga), Atlanta Campaign (Kennesaw Mountain, Peach Tree Creek, Atlanta, and Jonesborough), Franklin-Nashville Campaign (Nashville)[392]
- Junius Daniel (33), Confederate, BG, Gettysburg Campaign (Gettysburg), Grant's Overland Campaign (Spotsylvania), Killed at Spotsylvania[393]
- Laurence S. Baker (42), Confederate, BG, Gettysburg Campaign (Gettysburg), Wounded at Gettysburg[394]

Class of 1852 (43 Graduates)

- Henry W. Slocum (7), Union, MG, Army of the Potomac and Department of the Mississippi, Manassas Campaign (First Manassas), Wounded and disabled at First Manassas, Virginia Peninsula Campaign (Yorktown, Gaines' Mill, Glendale, and Malvern Hill), Northern Virginia Campaign (Second Manassas), Maryland Campaign (Harpers Ferry, South Mountain, and Antietam), Fredericksburg Campaign (First Fredericksburg), Chancellorsville Campaign (Chancellorsville), Gettysburg Campaign (Gettysburg), Atlanta Campaign, Carolinas Campaign (Bentonville), Johnston's surrender at Durham Station[395]
- David S. Stanky (9), Union, MG, Army of the Mississippi and Army of the Cumberland, Operations to Control Missouri (Wilson's Creek), Joint Operations against New Madrid, Island No. 10, and Memphis (New Madrid/Island No. 10), Federal Penetration up the Cumberland and Tennessee Rivers (First Corinth), Iuka and Corinth Operations (Second Corinth), Stones River Campaign (Stones River), Atlanta Campaign (Pine Mountain, Kennesaw Mountain, Peach Tree

Creek, Atlanta, and Jonesborough), Wounded at Jonesborough, Franklin-Nashville Campaign (Spring Hill and Franklin), Wounded and disabled at Franklin[396]
- George B. Anderson (10), Confederate, BG, Fourth North Carolina and Army of Northern Virginia, Virginia Peninsula Campaign (Seven Days), Northern Virginia Campaign (Second Manassas), Maryland Campaign (South Mountain Antietam), Mortally wounded at Antietam[397]
- Milo S. Hascall (14), Union, BG, Army of the Ohio and Army of the Cumberland, Operations in Western Virginia, Stones River Campaign (Stones River), Atlanta Campaign (Atlanta)[398]
- George B. Cosby (17), Confederate, BG, Army of Central Kentucky and Confederate Department of the West, Federal Penetration up the Cumberland and Tennessee Rivers (Fort Donelson), Grant's Vicksburg Campaign (Jackson)[399]
- George L. Hartsuff (19), Union, MG, Army of the Potomac, Department of West Virginia, and Army of the Gulf, Operations in Western Virginia (Carnifex Ferry), Northern Virginia Campaign (Cedar Mountain and Second Manassas), Maryland Campaign (South Mountain and Antietam), Severely wounded at Antietam, Board to Revise Rules and Articles of War, Richmond-Petersburg Campaign (Second Petersburg)[400]
- Charles R. Woods (20), Union, Brevet MG, Operations in Charleston Harbor (Fort Sumter), Federal Penetration up the Cumberland and Tennessee Rivers (Fort Donelson, Shiloh, and First Corinth), Grant's Operations against Vicksburg (Jackson and Vicksburg), Chattanooga-Ringgold Campaign (Chattanooga and Ringgold), Atlanta Campaign (Kennesaw Mountain, Atlanta, and Jonesborough), Savannah Campaign (Griswoldville), Carolinas Campaign (Bentonville)[401]
- John Horace Forney (22), Confederate, MG, Army of Northern, Virginia, Army of Mississippi, and Trans-Mississippi Department, Manassas Campaign (First Manassas), Grant's Operations against Vicksburg[402]
- Alexander McD. McCook (30), Union, MG, Army of the Ohio and Army of the Cumberland, Manassas Campaign (First Manassas), Operations in Kentucky, Federal Penetration up the Cumberland and Tennessee Rivers (Shiloh and First Corinth), Confederate Heartland Offensive (Perryville), Stones River Campaign (Stones River), Chickamauga Campaign (Chickamauga)[403]
- August V. Kautz (35), Union, Brevet MG, Army of the Potomac, Army of the Ohio, and Army of the James, Virginia Peninsula Campaign (Yorktown, Beaver Dam Creek, and Malvern Hill), Richmond-Petersburg Campaign (Second Petersburg), Military Commission for the trial of Lincoln's assassins[404]
- George Crook (38), Union, MG, Army of the Cumberland, Army of the Potomac, and Department of West Virginia, Operations in West Virginia, Wounded at Lewisburg, Jackson's Valley Campaign (Kernstown), Northern Virginia Campaign, Maryland Campaign (South Mountain and Antietam), Chickamauga Campaign (Chickamauga), Captured at Cumberland, Maryland in Action of Berryville, Sheridan's Valley Campaign (Opequon, Fisher's Hill, and Cedar Creek), Appomattox Campaign (Sayler's Creek and Lee's surrender at Appomattox Court House)[405]
- John P. Hawkins (40), Union, BG, Army of the Tennessee, Commissary Services, Mobile Campaign (Fort Blakely)[406]

Class of 1853 (52 Graduates)
- James B. McPherson (1), Union, MG, Army of the Tennessee, Federal Penetration up the Cumberland and Tennessee Rivers (Fort Henry, Fort Donelson, Shiloh and First Corinth), Iuka and Corinth Operations, Grant's Operations against Vicksburg (Jackson, Port Gibson, Raymond, Champion Hills, and Vicksburg), Atlanta Campaign (Kennesaw Mountain and Atlanta), Killed during reconnaissance at Atlanta[407]

- Joshua W. Sill (3), Union, BG, Army of the Ohio and Army of the Cumberland, Operations in Western Virginia (Rich Mountain), Confederate Heartland Offensive (Perryville), Stones River Campaign (Stones River), Killed at Stones River[408]
- William R. Boggs (4), Confederate, BG, Trans-Mississippi Department, Chief Engineer of Georgia[409]
- William S. Smith (6), Union, BG, Army of the Ohio and Military Division of the Mississippi, Operations in Western Virginia (Carnifex Ferry), Federal Penetration up the Cumberland and Tennessee Rivers (Shiloh and First Corinth), Iuka and Corinth Operations (Second Corinth), Confederate Heartland Offensive (Perryville), Grant's Operations against Vicksburg, Meridian and Yazoo River Expeditions (Okolona)[410]
- John M. Schofield (7), Union, BG, Militia of Missouri, Army of the Cumberland, and Army of the Ohio, Operations to Control Missouri (Wilson's Creek), Atlanta Campaign (Kennesaw Mountain and Atlanta), Franklin-Nashville Campaign (Franklin and Nashville), Johnston's surrender at Durham Station[411]
- John S. Bowen (13), Confederate, MG, Army of Mississippi, Federal Penetration up the Cumberland and Tennessee Rivers (Shiloh), Grant's Operations against Vicksburg (Vicksburg and Port Gibson), Died of disease on July 13, 1863[412]
- William R. Terrill (16), Union, BG, Department of Washington and Army of the Ohio, Federal Penetration up the Cumberland and Tennessee Rivers (Shiloh and First Corinth), Confederate Heartland Offensive (Perryville), Killed at Perryville[413]
- Robert O. Tyler (22), Union, Brevet MG, Army of the Potomac, Operations in Charleston Harbor (Fort Sumter), Virginia Peninsula Campaign (Yorktown, Gaines' Mill, and Malvern Hill), Fredericksburg Campaign (First Fredericksburg), Chancellorsville Campaign (Chancellorsville), Gettysburg Campaign (Gettysburg), Grant's Overland Campaign (Spotsylvania, North Anna, Totopotomy, and Cold Harbor), Wounded and disabled at Cold Harbor[414]
- John R. Chambliss (31), Confederate, BG, Army of Northern Virginia and Cavalry Corps., Maryland Campaign, Gettysburg Campaign (Brandy Station), Killed in cavalry battle on Charles River Road[415]
- Henry B. Davidson (33), Confederate, BG, Army of Tennessee and Army of the Valley, Adjunct and Inspector General's Department, Garrison of Island No. 10, Joint Operations against New Madrid, Island No. 10, and Memphis (New Madrid/Island No. 10), Sheridan's Valley Campaign[416]
- Philip H. Sheridan (34), Union, MG, Army of Southwest Missouri, Army of the Potomac, Army of the Shenandoah, Army of the Ohio, and Army of the Cumberland, Confederate Heartland Offensive (Perryville), Stones River Campaign (Stones River), Chickamauga Campaign (Chickamauga), Chattanooga-Ringgold Campaign, Richmond-Petersburg Campaign, Grant's Overland Campaign (Wilderness, Spotsylvania, Totopotomy Creek, Cold Harbor, and Trevilian Station), Sheridan's Valley Campaign (Opequon, Fisher's Hill, and Cedar Creek), Richmond-Petersburg Campaign, Appomattox Campaign (Five Forks, Sayler's Creek and Lee's surrender at Appomattox Court House)[417]
- Henry Harrison Walker (41), Confederate, BG, Confederate States Army and Army of Northern Virginia, Virginia Peninsula Campaign (Seven Days), Grant's Overland Campaign (Spotsylvania), Wounded at Spotsylvania[418]
- Alexander Chambers (43), Union, BG, 16th Iowa Volunteer Regiment, Federal Penetration up the Cumberland and Tennessee Rivers (Shiloh and First Corinth), Wounded at Shiloh, Iuka and Corinth Operations (Iuka), Wounded and disabled at Iuka, Grant's Operations against Vicksburg (Vicksburg, Black River Bridge, and Champion Hill)[419]
- John B. Hood (44), Confederate, GEN, Army of Northern Virginia and Army of Tennessee, Virginia Peninsula Campaign (Gaines' Mill and Seven Days), Northern Virginia Campaign (Second Manassas), Maryland Campaign (Antietam),

Fredericksburg Campaign (First Fredericksburg), Gettysburg Campaign (Gettysburg), Chickamauga Campaign (Chickamauga), Atlanta Campaign (Peachtree Creek, Atlanta, and Ezra Church), Franklin-Nashville Campaign (Spring Hill, Franklin, and Nashville), Carolinas Campaign, Severely wounded arm at Gettysburg and leg at Chickamauga[420]
- James A. Smith (45), Confederate, BG, Confederate States Army, Army of Mississippi, and Army of Tennessee, Federal Penetration up the Cumberland and Tennessee Rivers (Shiloh), Confederate Heartland Offensive (Perryville), Stones River Campaign (Stones River), Chickamauga Campaign (Chickamauga), Atlanta Campaign, Franklin-Nashville Campaign (Franklin and Nashville)[421]
- Reuben R. Ross (51), Confederate, BG, Army of Mississippi, Federal Penetration up the Cumberland and Tennessee Rivers (Fort Donelson), Captured at Fort Donelson, Died December 16, 1864[422]

Class of 1854 (46 Graduates)

- George W. Custis Lee (1), Confederate, MG, Richmond-Petersburg Campaign, Appomattox Campaign (Sayler's Creek), Captured at Sayler's Creek, Robert E. Lee's son[423]
- Henry L. Abbott (2), Union, Brevet BG, Army of the Potomac, Manassas Campaign (First Manassas), Wounded at First Manassas, Virginia Peninsula Campaign (Yorktown and Seven Days), Richmond-Petersburg Campaign (Second Petersburg, the Crater and Fort Stedman), Operations against Fort Fisher and Wilmington (Fort Fisher)[424]
- Thomas H. Ruger (3), Union, Brevet MG, Army of the Potomac, Jackson's Valley Campaign (Winchester), Northern Virginia Campaign (Cedar Mountain), Maryland Campaign (Antietam), Fredericksburg Campaign (First Fredericksburg), Chancellorsville Campaign (Chancellorsville), Gettysburg Campaign (Gettysburg), Suppressing the Draft Riots in New York City, Atlanta Campaign (Peach Tree Creek and Atlanta), Franklin-Nashville Campaign (Franklin and Nashville), Johnston's surrender at Durham Station[425]
- Oliver O. Howard (4), Union, MG, Army of the Potomac, Army of the Cumberland, and Army of the Tennessee, Manassas Campaign (First Manassas), Virginia Peninsula Campaign (Yorktown), Wounded and disabled at Fair Oaks, Northern Virginia Campaign, Maryland Campaign (Antietam), Fredericksburg Campaign (First Fredericksburg), Chancellorsville Campaign (Chancellorsville), Gettysburg Campaign (Gettysburg), Chattanooga-Ringgold Campaign (Chattanooga), Atlanta Campaign (Peach Tree Creek, Ezra Church, Kennesaw Mountain, Atlanta, and Jonesborough), Savannah Campaign (Griswoldville), Carolinas Campaign (Bentonville), Johnston's surrender at Durham Station, Commissioner of the Bureau of Refugees, Freedmen, and Abandoned Lands[426]
- James Deshler (7), Confederate, BG, Army of the Northwest and Army of Tennessee, Virginia Peninsula Campaign (Seven Days), Chickamauga Campaign (Chickamauga), Killed at Chickamauga on September 20, 1863[427]
- John Pegram (10), Confederate, BG, Army of Northern Virginia, Operations in Western Virginia (Rich Mountain), Captured at Rich Mountain, Stones River Campaign (Stones River), Chickamauga Campaign (Chickamauga), Grant's Overland Campaign (Wilderness), Richmond-Petersburg Campaign (Hatcher's Run), Killed at Hatcher's Run[428]
- James E.B. Stuart (13), Confederate, MG, Army of Northern Virginia, Manassas Campaign (First Manassas), Virginia Peninsula Campaign (Seven Days), Northern Virginia Campaign (Second Manassas), Maryland Campaign (South Mountain and Antietam), Fredericksburg Campaign (First Fredericksburg), Chancellorsville Campaign (Chancellorsville), Richmond-Petersburg Campaign (Second Peters-

burg), Grant's Overland Campaign (Wilderness, Spotsylvania, and Cold Harbor), Gettysburg Campaign (Brandy Station and Gettysburg), Mortally wounded at Yellow Tavern[429]
- Archibald Gracie (14), Confederate, BG, Army of Northern Virginia (Second Manassas), Chickamauga Campaign (Chickamauga), Richmond-Petersburg Campaign (Second Petersburg), Killed at Petersburg[430]
- Stephen D. Lee (17), Confederate, LG, Army of Northern Virginia and Army of Tennessee, Manassas Campaign, Virginia Peninsula Campaign, Northern Virginia Campaign, Fredericksburg Campaign (First Fredericksburg), Chancellorsville Campaign, Grant's Operations against Vicksburg (Vicksburg), Youngest LG in Confederate States Army[431]
- William D. Pender (19), Confederate, MG, Army of Northern Virginia, Virginia Peninsula Campaign (Seven Pines and Seven Days), Northern Virginia Campaign (Cedar Mountain, Second Manassas), Maryland Campaign (Harpers Valley, Antietam), Fredericksburg Campaign (First Fredericksburg), Chancellorsville Campaign (Chancellorsville), Gettysburg Campaign (Gettysburg), Mortally wounded at Gettysburg[432]
- John Bordenave Villepigue (22), Confederate, BG, Died of pneumonia in 1862[433]
- Steven H. Weed (27), Union, BG, Army of the Potomac, Virginia Peninsula Campaign (Yorktown, Gaines' Mill, and Malvern Hill), Northern Virginia Campaign (Second Manassas), Maryland Campaign (Antietam), Chancellorsville Campaign (Chancellorsville), Gettysburg Campaign (Gettysburg), Killed at Gettysburg[434]

Class of 1855 (34 Graduates)

- Cyrus B. Comstock (1), Union, Brevet BG, Army of the Potomac, Army of the Tennessee, and Military Division of the Mississippi, Engineering Operations, Virginia Peninsula Campaign (Yorktown), Maryland Campaign (South Mountain and Antietam), Fredericksburg Campaign (First Fredericksburg), Chancellorsville Campaign (Chancellorsville), Grant's Operations against Vicksburg (Vicksburg), Richmond-Petersburg Campaign (Second Petersburg), Grant's Overland Campaign (Wilderness, Spotsylvania, and Cold Harbor), Operations against Fort Fisher and Wilmington, (Fort Fisher), Mobile Campaign (Spanish Fort and Fort Blakely)[435]
- Godfrey Weitzel (2), Union, MG, Department of the Gulf and Army of the James, Engineering Operations, Virginia Peninsular Campaign (Drewry's Bluff and Williamsburg), Expedition to, and Capture of, New Orleans (Capture of New Orleans), Siege of Port Hudson (Port Hudson), Operations to Blockade the Texas Coast (Second Sabine Pass), Appomattox Campaign[436]
- David McM. Gregg (8), Union, Brevet MG, Army of the Potomac, Virginia Peninsula Campaign (Seven Pines, Glendale, and Malvern Hill), Maryland Campaign, Fredericksburg Campaign (First Fredericksburg), Gettysburg Campaign (Gettysburg), Grant's Overland Campaign (Trevilian Station), Richmond-Petersburg Campaign (Ream's Station, Second Deep Bottom, Peebles' Farm, and Boydton Plank Road)[437]
- Francis T. Nicholls (12), Confederate, BG, Army of the Potomac, Army of the Shenandoah, Army of Northern Virginia, Manassas Campaign (First Manassas), Jackson's Valley Campaign (Winchester), Lost arm at Winchester, Chancellorsville Campaign (Chancellorsville), Lost leg at Chancellorsville[438]
- Alexander S. Webb (13), Union, Brevet MG, Army of the Potomac, Manassas Campaign (First Manassas), Virginia Peninsular Campaign (Yorktown, Beaver Dam Creek, Gaines' Mill, and Malvern Hill), Maryland Campaign (Antietam), Fredericksburg Campaign, Chancellorsville Campaign (Chancellorsville), Gettysburg Campaign (Gettysburg), Wounded at Gettysburg, Grant's Overland Cam-

paign (Wilderness and Spotsylvania), Wounded and disabled at Spotsylvania, Richmond-Petersburg Campaign (Hatcher's Run and Second Petersburg)[439]
- John W. Turner (14), Union, Brevet MG, Army of the James, Department of the Gulf, Department of the South, and Department of Kansas, Operations against Fort Pulaski (Fort Pulaski), Operations against the Defenses of Charleston (Fort Wagner), Richmond-Petersburg Campaign (Second Petersburg), Appomattox Campaign (Third Petersburg and Lee's surrender at Appomattox Court House)[440]
- Francis A. Shoup (15), Confederate, BG, Army of the Trans-Mississippi, Army of Mississippi, Federal Penetration up the Cumberland and Tennessee Rivers (Shiloh), Prairie Grove Campaign (Prairie Grove), Grant's Operations against Vicksburg (Vicksburg), Captured at Vicksburg, Atlanta Campaign[441]
- Alfred T.A. Torbert (21), Union, Brevet MG, Army of the Potomac and Army of the Shenandoah, Virginia Peninsula Campaign (Yorktown and Gaines' Mill), Northern Virginia Campaign (Second Manassas), Maryland Campaign (South Mountain and Antietam), Wounded at Antietam, Fredericksburg Campaign, Gettysburg Campaign (Gettysburg), Grant's Overland Campaign (North Anna, Cold Harbor, and Trevilian Station), Jackson's Valley Campaign (Winchester), Sheridan's Valley Campaign (Opequon and Cedar Creek)[442]
- William W. Averell (26), Union, BG, Army of the Potomac, Operations in Western Virginia, Manassas Campaign (First Manassas), Virginia Peninsula Campaign (Yorktown, Williamsburg, and Seven Days), Maryland Campaign, Fredericksburg Campaign (First Fredericksburg), Wounded at Cove Gap, Jackson's Valley Campaign (Winchester), Sheridan's Valley Campaign (Opequon and Fisher's Hill)[443]
- William B. Hazen (28), Union, MG, Army of the Ohio, Army of the Cumberland, and Army of the Tennessee, Federal Penetration up the Cumberland and Tennessee Rivers (Shiloh and First Corinth), Stones River Campaign (Stone's River), Confederate Heartland Offensive (Perryville), Chickamauga Campaign (Chickamauga), Chattanooga-Ringgold Campaign (Chattanooga), Atlanta Campaign (Kennesaw Mountain, Peach Tree Creek, Atlanta, and Jonesborough), Savannah Campaign (Fort McAllister), Carolinas Campaign (Bentonville), Johnston's surrender at Durham Station[444]

Class of 1856 (49 Graduates)

- Orlando M. Poe (6), Union, BG, Army of the Potomac and Army of the Ohio, Topographical Engineering, Operations in Western Virginia (Rich Mountain), Virginia Peninsula Campaign (Yorktown and Williamsburg), Northern Virginia Campaign (Second Manassas), Maryland Campaign, Fredericksburg Campaign (First Fredericksburg), Atlanta Campaign (Kennesaw Mountain, Atlanta, and Jonesborough), Savannah Campaign, Carolinas Campaign (Bentonville), Johnston's surrender at Durham Station[445]
- Francis L. Vinton (10), Union, BG, Army of the Potomac, Virginia Peninsula Campaign (Yorktown, Williamsburg, Gaines' Mill, and Glendale), Maryland Campaign, Fredericksburg Campaign (First Fredericksburg), Wounded and disabled at Fredericksburg, Resigned May 5, 1863[446]
- George D. Bayard (11), Union, BG, Pennsylvania Reserve Corps, Jackson's Valley Campaign (Port Republic), Northern Virginia Campaign (Cedar Mountain and Second Manassas), Fredericksburg Campaign (First Fredericksburg), Mortally wounded at Fredericksburg[447]
- Hylan B. Lyon (19), Confederate, BG, Army of Tennessee and Army of Mississippi, Federal Penetration up the Cumberland and Tennessee Rivers (Fort Donelson), Captured at Fort Donelson, Grant's Operations against Vicksburg (Vicksburg), Escaped from Siege of Vicksburg, Chattanooga-Ringgold Campaign (Chattanooga)[448]

- Lunsford L. Lomax (21), Confederate, MG, Virginia Militia, Army of West Tennessee, and Army of Northern Virginia, Gettysburg Campaign (Gettysburg), Grant's Overland Campaign, Sheridan's Valley Campaign (Opequon and Cedar Creek)[449]
- James P. Major (23), Confederate, BG, Missouri State Guard and Trans-Mississippi Department, Operations to Control Missouri (Wilson's Creek), Grant's Operations against Vicksburg (Vicksburg), Red River Campaign (Mansfield and Pleasant Hill)[450]
- James W. Forsyth (28), Union, Brevet BG, Army of the Potomac and Military Division of the Gulf, Virginia Peninsula Campaign, Maryland Campaign, Stones River Campaign, Chickamauga Campaign (Chickamauga), Richmond-Petersburg Campaign, Shenandoah Campaign, Sheridan's Valley Campaign (Opequon, Fisher's Hill, and Cedar Creek), Appomattox Campaign (Five Forks)[451]
- William H. Jackson (38), Confederate, BG, Army of Mississippi and Army of Tennessee, Grant's Operations against Vicksburg, Atlanta Campaign, Franklin-Nashville Campaign[452]
- William P. Sanders (41), Union, BG, Army of the Potomac and Army of the Ohio, Virginia Peninsula Campaign (Yorktown, Williamsburg, and Beaver Dam Creek), Maryland Campaign, Offensive in Eastern Kentucky, Mortally wounded in the Combat of Campbell's Station[453]
- Samuel S. Carroll (44), Union, BG, Army of the Potomac and Army of the Shenandoah, Jackson's Valley Campaign (Kernstown and Port Republic), Northern Virginia Campaign (Cedar Mountain), Wounded in Skirmish on the Rapidan River, Maryland Campaign, Fredericksburg Campaign (First Fredericksburg), Chancellorsville Campaign (Chancellorsville), Gettysburg Campaign (Gettysburg), Grant's Overland Campaign (Wilderness and Spotsylvania), Wounded twice at Spotsylvania, Disabled by wounds[454]
- Fitzhugh Lee (45), Confederate, MG, Army of Northern Virginia, Manassas Campaign (First Manassas), Virginia Peninsula Campaign, Northern Virginia Campaign, Maryland Campaign (Antietam), Chancellorsville Campaign (Chancellorsville), Gettysburg Campaign (Gettysburg), Grant's Overland Campaign (Spotsylvania), Richmond-Petersburg Campaign, Sheridan's Valley Campaign (Opequon), Appomattox Campaign[455]

Class of 1857 (38 Graduates)

- E. Porter Alexander (3), Confederate, BG, Confederate Army of the Potomac and Army of Northern Virginia, Fredericksburg Campaign (First Fredericksburg), Chancellorsville Campaign (Chancellorsville), Gettysburg Campaign (Gettysburg), Richmond-Petersburg Campaign (Second Petersburg), Conducted massive artillery bombardment preceding Pickett's Charge at Gettysburg,[456] Helped develop semaphore[457] system[458]
- George C. Strong (5), Union, BG, Department of the Gulf, Manassas Campaign (First Manassas), Expedition and Capture of New Orleans (New Orleans), Operations against Charleston (Fort Wagner), Mortally wounded at Fort Wagner[459]
- Charles H. Morgan (12), Union, Brevet BG, Army of the Potomac, Western Virginia Operations, Virginia Peninsula Campaign (Yorktown), Maryland Campaign, Fredericksburg Campaign (First Fredericksburg), Chancellorsville Campaign (Chancellorsville), Gettysburg Campaign (Gettysburg), Grant's Overland Campaign (Wilderness, Spotsylvania, North Anna, Totopotomy, and Cold Harbor), Richmond-Petersburg Campaign (Second Petersburg, Second Deep Bottom, Ream's Station, and Boydton Plank Road), Board for the Examination of Candidates for Appointment for Officers of Colored Troops[460]
- Samuel W. Ferguson (19), Confederate, BG, South Carolina Militia, Operations in

Charleston Harbor (Fort Sumter), Federal Penetration up the Cumberland and Tennessee Rivers (Shiloh), Escorted Jefferson Davis into Georgia[461]
- John S. Marmaduke (30), Confederate, MG, Army of Mississippi and Army of the Trans-Mississippi, Federal Penetration up the Cumberland and Tennessee Rivers (Shiloh), Prairie Grove Campaign (Prairie Grove), Red River Campaign, Captured at Mine Creek[462]
- Robert H. Anderson (35), Confederate, BG, Army of Northern Virginia, Virginia Peninsula Campaign, Chancellorsville Campaign, Grant's Overland Campaign (Wilderness), Appomattox Campaign (Sayler's Creek)[463]

Class of 1858 (27 Graduates)

- Charles G. Harker (16), Union, BG, U.S. Volunteers, Federal Penetration up the Cumberland and Tennessee Rivers (Shiloh), Iuka and Corinth Operations (Second Corinth), Confederate Heartland Offensive (Perryville), Stones River Campaign (Stones River), Chickamauga Campaign (Chickamauga), Chattanooga-Ringgold Campaign (Chattanooga), Atlanta Campaign (Kennesaw Mountain), Killed at Kennesaw Mountain[464]
- Bryan M. Thomas (22), Confederate, BG, Army of Mississippi and Department of the Gulf, Federal Penetration up the Cumberland and Tennessee Rivers (Shiloh), Stones River Campaign (Stones River), Mobile Campaign (Spanish Fort and Fort Blakely), Captured at Fort Blakely[465]

Class of 1859 (22 Graduates)

- Martin D. Hardin (11), Union, BG, Army of the Potomac, Virginia Peninsula Campaign (Yorktown and Seven Days), Northern Virginia Campaign (Second Manassas), Wounded and disabled at Second Manassas, Gettysburg Campaign (Gettysburg), Wounded and disabled in Mine Run Operations, Grant's Overland Campaign (Spotsylvania, North Anna, and Totopotomy Creek), Wounded and disabled at Bethesda Church[466]
- Edwin H. Stoughton (17), Union, BG, Senate did not confirm appointment and it expired, Captured by John S. Mosby at Fairfax Court House, Resigned when Army refused his reappointment as a BG[467]
- Joseph Wheeler (19), Confederate, MG, Army of Tennessee and Army of Mississippi, Federal Penetration up the Cumberland and Tennessee Rivers (Shiloh), Iuka and Corinth Operations (Second Corinth), Confederate Heartland Offensive (Perryville), Stones River Campaign (Stones River), Chickamauga Campaign (Chickamauga), Chattanooga-Ringgold Campaign (Chattanooga), Atlanta Campaign, Carolinas Campaign, Captured in Georgia[468]

Class of 1860 (41 Graduates)

- James H. Wilson (6), Union, Brevet MG, Army of the Potomac, Army of the Tennessee, and Department of Georgia, Topographical Engineering, Maryland Campaign (South Mountain and Antietam), Grant's Operations against Vicksburg (Jackson, Port Gibson, Champion Hill, Big Black River Bridge, and Vicksburg), Grant's Overland Campaign (Wilderness, Spotsylvania, and Totopotomy), Richmond-Petersburg Campaign (Second Petersburg), Sheridan's Valley Campaign (Opequon), Franklin-Nashville Campaign (Franklin and Nashville), Operations against Fort Pulaski (Fort Pulaski), Chattanooga-Ringgold Campaign (Chattanooga), Wilson's Raid in Alabama and Georgia (Selma), Capture of Jefferson Davis[469]
- Stephen D. Ramseur (14), Confederate, MG, Tenth North Carolina Militia, Army of North Virginia and Army of Northern Virginia, Peninsula Campaign (Malvern Hill), Chancellorsville Campaign (Chancellorsville), Gettysburg Campaign (Get-

tysburg), Grant's Overland Campaign (Wilderness, Spotsylvania Court House, and Cold Harbor), Sheridan's Valley Campaign (Opequon and Cedar Creek), Mortally wounded at Cedar Creek[470]
- Wesley Merritt (22), Union, Brevet MG, Army of the Potomac and Military Division of the Gulf, Gettysburg Campaign (Gettysburg), Grant's Overland Campaign (Cold Harbor and Trevilian Station), Richmond-Petersburg Campaign, Sheridan's Valley Campaign (Opequon, Fisher's Hill, and Cedar Creek), Appomattox Campaign (Five Forks, Sayler's Creek and Lee's surrender at Appomattox Court House)[471]

Class of May 6, 1861 (45 Graduates)[472]

- Adelbert Ames (5), Union, Brevet MG, Army of the Potomac, Manassas Campaign (First Manassas), Wounded and disabled at First Manassas, Virginia Peninsula Campaign (Yorktown, Gaines' Mill, and Malvern Hill), Maryland Campaign (Antietam), Fredericksburg Campaign (First Fredericksburg), Chancellorsville Campaign (Chancellorsville), Gettysburg Campaign (Gettysburg), Grant's Overland Campaign (Cold Harbor), Richmond-Petersburg Campaign (Second Petersburg), Operations against Fort Fisher and Wilmington (Fort Fisher)[473]
- Emory Upton (8), Union, Brevet MG, Army of the Potomac, Manassas Campaign (First Manassas), Wounded and disabled at First Manassas, Virginia Peninsula Campaign (Yorktown, Gaines' Mill, and Glendale), Northern Virginia Campaign (Second Manassas), Maryland Campaign (South Mountain and Antietam), Fredericksburg Campaign (First Fredericksburg), Gettysburg Campaign (Gettysburg), Grant's Overland Campaign (Wilderness, Spotsylvania, and Cold Harbor), Wounded at Spotsylvania, Richmond-Petersburg Campaign (Second Petersburg), Sheridan's Valley Campaign (Opequon), Wounded and disabled at Opequon, Wilson's Raid in Alabama and Georgia (Selma)[474]
- Judson Kilpatrick (17), Union, BG, Military Division of the Mississippi, Army of the Potomac, and Army of the Cumberland, Wounded and disabled at Big Bethel, Northern Virginia Campaign (Second Manassas), Fredericksburg Campaign, Chattanooga-Ringgold Campaign (Ringgold Gap), Gettysburg Campaign (Brandy Station and Gettysburg), Florida Expedition (Olustee), Carolinas Campaign[475]
- Guy V. Henry (27), Union, Brevet BG, Army of the Potomac and Army of the James, Manassas Campaign (First Manassas), Operations against the Defenses of Charleston (Fort Wagner), Florida Expedition (Olustee), Grant's Overland Campaign (Cold Harbor), Richmond-Petersburg Campaign (Second Petersburg), Sheridan's Valley Campaign (Cedar Creek)[476]

Class of June 24, 1861 (34 Graduates)[477]

- Arthur H. Dutton (3), Union, Brevet BG, Army of the Potomac, Army of the James, and Army of North Carolina, Engineering Operations, Maryland Campaign, Fredericksburg Campaign (First Fredericksburg), Mortally wounded at Bermuda Hundred[478]
- George A. Custer (34), Union, Brevet MG, Army of the Potomac, Military Division of the Southwest, and Military Division of the Gulf, Manassas Campaign (First Manassas), Virginia Peninsula Campaign (Yorktown), Maryland Campaign (South Mountain and Antietam), Gettysburg Campaign (Brandy Station and Gettysburg), Wounded at Culpeper, Grant's Overland Campaign (Wilderness, Cold Harbor, and Trevilian Station), Richmond-Petersburg Campaign, Sheridan's Valley Campaign (Opequon, Fisher's Hill, and Cedar Creek), Appomattox Campaign (Five Forks, Sayler's Creek and Lee's surrender at Appomattox Court House)[479]

Class of 1862 (28 Graduates)[480]

- Ranald S. Mackenzie (1), Union, BG, Army of the Potomac and Army of the James, Engineering Operations, Northern Virginia Campaign (Second Manassas), Wounded at Second Manassas, Maryland Campaign, Fredericksburg Campaign (First Fredericksburg), Chancellorsville Campaign (Chancellorsville), Gettysburg Campaign (Gettysburg), Grant's Overland Campaign (Wilderness and Spotsylvania), Richmond-Petersburg Campaign (Second Petersburg), Wounded at Petersburg, Sheridan's Valley Campaign (Opequon, Fisher's Hill, and Cedar Creek), Wounded at Cedar Creek, Appomattox Campaign (Five Forks and Lee's surrender at Appomattox Court House)[481]
- Most of the twenty-eight graduates in the Class of 1862 received promotions to first lieutenant. Some received brevet promotions to captain (10), major (4) or lieutenant colonel (1 brevet and 1 regular).

Class of 1863 (25 Graduates)[482]

- Peter S. Michie (2), Union, Brevet BG, Army of the Potomac, Army of the James, and Department of the South, Engineering Operations, Operations against the Defense of Charleston (Fort Wagner and Charleston Harbor), Florida Expedition (Olustee), Grant's Overland Campaign, Richmond-Petersburg Campaign (The Crater and Hatcher's Run), Lee's surrender at Appomattox Court House[483]
- Most of the twenty-five graduates in the Class of 1863 received promotions to first lieutenant. Some received brevet promotions to captain (4), major (5) or lieutenant colonel (1 brevet and 1 regular).

Detail of windows with figures at West Point (Library of Congress).

Class of 1864 (27 Graduates)[484]

- All twenty-seven graduates fought for the Union in the Civil War. Most of them served as second or first lieutenants. Some received brevet promotions to captain (7) or major (2).

Highest Rank Prior to the Civil War

Confederate Officers

Name	Highest Rank Prior to Civil War	Highest Rank in Civil War	Class
Beauregard, P.G.T.	CPT	GEN	1838
Bragg, Braxton	MAJ	GEN	1837
Cooper, Samuel	COL	GEN	1815
Hood, John B.	1LT	GEN	1853
Johnston, Albert S.	Brevet BG	GEN	1826
Johnston, Joseph E.	BG	GEN	1829
Lee, Robert E.	COL	GEN	1829
Smith, Edmund K.	MAJ	GEN	1845
Anderson, Richard H	CPT	LG	1842
Buckner, Simon B.	CPT	LG	1844
Early, Jubal A.	MAJ	LG	1837
Ewell, Richard S.	CPT	LG	1840
Hardee, William J.	LTC	LG	1838
Hill, Ambrose P.	1LT	LG	1847
Hill, Daniel H.	Brevet MAJ	LG	1842
Holmes, Theophilus H.	MAJ	LG	1829
Jackson, Thomas J.	Brevet MAJ	LG	1846
Lee, Stephen D.	1LT	LG	1854
Longstreet, James	MAJ	LG	1842
Pemberton, John C.	CPT	LG	1837
Polk, Leonidas	Brevet 2LT	LG	1827
Stewart, Alexander P.	2LT	LG	1842
Wheeler, Joseph	1LT	LG	1859

Union Officers

Name	Highest Rank Prior to Civil War	Highest Rank in Civil War	Class
Grant, Ulysses S.	CPT	GEN	1843
Sheridan, Philip H.	Brevet 2LT	GEN	1853
Sherman, William T.	CPT	GEN	1840
Schofield, John M.	1LT	LG	1853
Augur, Christopher C.	MAJ	MG	1843
Bliss, Zenas R.	1LT	MG	1854
Buell, Don Carlos	LTC	MG	1841
Buford, John	CPT	MG	1848
Burns, William W.	CPT	MG	1847
Burnside, Ambrose E.	1LT	MG	1847
Canby, Edward R.S.	MAJ	MG	1839
Casey, Silas	LTC	MG	1826
Couch, Darius N.	1LT	MG	1846
Crook, George	1LT	MG	1852
Curtis, Samuel R.	COL	MG	1831
Custer, George A.	2LT	Brevet MG	June 1861
Dana, Napoleon J.T.	CPT	MG	1842
Doubleday, Abner	CPT	MG	1842
Emory, William H.	LTC	MG	1831
Forsyth, James W.	1LT	MG	1856

Name	Highest Rank Prior to Civil War	Highest Rank in Civil War	Class
Foster, John G.	CPT	MG	1846
Franklin, William B.	CPT	MG	1843
French, William H.	CPT	MG	1837
Gibbon, John	CPT	MG	1847
Gillespie, George L.	2LT	MG	1862
Gillmore, Quincy A.	1LT	MG	1847
Granger, Gordon	1LT	MG	1845
Greene, George S.	1LT	MG	1823
Griffin, Charles	1LT	Brevet MG	1847
Halleck, Henry W.	CPT	MG	1839
Hamilton, Charles S.	Brevet CPT	MG	1843
Hamilton, Schuyler	1LT	MG	1841
Hancock, Winfield S.	CPT	MG	1844
Hartsuff, George L.	Brevet CPT	MG	1852
Hazen, William B.	CPT	MG	1855
Heintzelman, Samuel P.	MAJ	MG	1826
Hitchcock, Ethan A.	COL	MG	1817
Hooker, Joseph	CPT	MG	1837
Howard, Oliver O.	1LT	MG	1854
Humphreys, Andrew A.	CPT	MG	1831
Hunter, David	MAJ	MG	1822
Kent, J. Ford	2LT	MG	May 1861
Keyes, Erasmus D.	LTC	MG	1832
Kilpatrick, Judson	2LT	MG	May 1861
Mansfield, Joseph K.F.	COL	MG	1822
McClellan, George B.	CPT	MG	1846
McCook, Alexander	1LT	MG	1852
McDowell, Irvin	Brevet MAJ	MG	1838
McPherson, James B.	CPT	MG	1853
Meade, George G.	CPT	MG	1835
Merritt, Wesley	2LT	MG	1860
Mitchel, Ormsby Mc-Knight	2LT	MG	1829
Morell, George W.	2LT	MG	1835
Newton, John	CPT	MG	1842
Ord, Edward O.C.	CPT	MG	1839
Parke, John G.	1LT	MG	1849
Peck, John J.	Brevet MAJ	MG	1843
Pleasonton, Alfred	CPT	MG	1844
Pope, John	CPT	MG	1842
Porter, Fitz-John	Brevet CPT	MG	1845
Reno, Jesse L.	CPT	MG	1846
Reynolds, John F.	CPT	MG	1841
Reynolds, Joseph J.	1LT	MG	1843
Richardson, Israel B.	CPT	MG	1841
Rosecrans, William S.	1LT	MG	1842
Ruger, Thomas H.	Brevet 1LT	MG	1854
Sedgwick, John	MAJ	MG	1837
Slocum, Henry W.	1LT	MG	1852
Smith, Andrew J.	MAJ	MG	1838
Smith, Charles F.	LTC	MG	1825
Smith, William F.	CPT	MG	1845
Stanley, David S.	CPT	MG	1852
Steele, Frederick	CPT	MG	1843
Stevens, Isaac I.	Brevet MAJ	MG	1839
Stoneman, George	CPT	MG	1846
Strong, George C.	1LT	MG	1857
Sykes, George	CPT	MG	1842
Thomas, George H.	MAJ	MG	1836
Warren, Gouverneur K.	1LT	MG	1850

Highest Rank Prior to the Civil War

"Prominent Union and Confederate Generals and Statesmen as They Appeared During the Great Civil War, 1861–5," lithograph by Kurz & Allison, 1885 (Library of Congress).

Weitzel, Godfrey	1LT	MG	1855
Whipple, Amiel V.	CPT	MG	1841
Wilson, James H.	Brevet 2LT	Brevet MG	1860
Wood, Thomas J.	CPT	MG	1845
Wright, Horatio G.	CPT	MG	1841

Notes

Preface

1. *The Centennial of United States Military Academy* (Washington: Government Printing Office, 1904), vol. I, 469.
2. *Centennial*, vol. I, 470.
3. *Centennial*, vol. I, 470.
4. *Centennial*, vol. I, 474–475.
5. *Centennial*, vol. I, 470–471.
6. *Centennial*, vol. I, 476.
7. *Centennial*, vol. I, 478.
8. *Centennial*, vol. I, 479–480.
9. Porter, Horace (late U.S. Army), Ambassador of the United States to France (U.S. Military Academy, 1860). *Centennial*, vol. I, 43.
10. A musket is a smoothbore firearm fired from the shoulder. Mark M. Boatner III, *Civil War Dictionary* (New York: David Key Company, Inc., 1988), 576.
11. *Centennial*, vol. I, 43.

The United States Military Academy

1. James L. Morrison, Jr., *"The Best School"—West Point, 1833–1866* (Kent: Kent State University Press, 1998), 11.
2. Rodger L. Geiger, ed., *The American College in the 19th Century* (Nashville: Vanderbilt University Press, 2000), 82.
3. United States War Department, *Annual Report of the Secretary of War* (Washington: Government Printing Office, 1896), 233.
4. Artillery describes the guns used to fire heavy rounds (6, 12, 18 and 24 caliber rounds). Based on its success in the Mexican War, the term mostly applied highly mobile field artillery designed to operate in batteries on the battlefield. The guns included the 12-pound howitzer (commonly called a Napoleon), the 3-inch ordinance rifle, and 10-pound Parrott gun. Phillip Katcher and Tony Bryan, *American Civil War Artillery—1861–1865 Field Artillery* (Botley: Osprey Publishing, 2001), 3–6.
5. James M. Volvo and Dorothy Dennen Volvo, *The Antebellum Period* (Westport: Greenwood Press, 2004), 93.
6. *Official Register of the Officers and Cadets of the U.S. Military Academy*, June 1850, Digital Archives, U.S. Military Academy Library.
7. The classes at the Military Academy correspond to the following traditional college grade levels: First Class—senior—fourth year, Second Class—junior—third year, Third Class—sophomore—second year, and Fourth Class—plebe—freshman—first year.
8. Artillery Tactics deals with the organization and composition of an artillery company, artillery movements, commands, and bugle calls. Other topics described the School of the Piece, School of the Section, School of the Battery, and Evolutions of Batteries. The Artillery Tactics manual explained in detail all the operations of the gun and battery. William H. French, William F. Barry, and H. J. Hunt, *The 1864 Field Artillery Tactics* (Mechanicsburg: Stackpole Books, 2005), Table of Contents.
9. Ordinance covers several subjects including a battery or group of guns, vehicles used in combat, ammunition, and equipment. Webb Garrison, *The Encyclopedia of Civil War Usage* (New York: Castle Books, 2001), 182.
10. Gunnery is the science concerned with use and performance of projectiles. Priscilla S. Taylor and John M. Taylor, *Dictionary of Military Terms* (New York: The H. W. Wilson Company, 2003), 122.
11. Morrison, 91.
12. "VMI Civil War Generals," Virginia Military Institute, accessed November 25, 2017, http://www.vmi.edu/archives/civil-war-and-new-market/vmi-civil-war-generals/.
13. The Citadel Alumni Association, accessed November 30, 2017, http://www.citadelalumni.org/s/1674/alumni/index.aspx?sid=1674&gid=1001&pgid=535.
14. Lynwood Mathis Holland, *Pierce M.B. Young: The Warwick of the South* (Athens: University of Georgia Press, 1964).
15. Robert F. Hoke, Civil War Trust, accessed December 22, 2017, https://www.civilwar.org/learn/biographies/robert-f-hoke.
16. Stephen G. Burbridge, Stephen Gano Burbridge, Arlington National Cemetery Website, accessed December 18, 2017, http://www.arlingtoncemetery.net/sgburb.htm.
17. Thomas Benton Smith, Wikipedia, accessed December 21, 2017, https://en.wikipedia.org/wiki/Thomas_Benton_Smith.
18. George Gordon (Civil War general), Wikipedia, accessed December 21, 2017, https://en.wikipedia.org/wiki/George_Gordon_(Civil_War_General).
19. William Arba Ellis, *Norwich University 1819–*

1911—*Her History, Her Graduates, Her Roll of Honor* (Montpelier: The Capital City Press, 1911), 184.

20. Ellis, 253.

21. Thomas E. G. Ransom, Ransom, Thomas Edward Greenfield, Vermont in the Civil War, accessed December 18, 2017, http://www.vermontcivilwar.org/get.php?input=4869.

22. Ellis, 97.

23. Edmund Rice, #92 Edmund Rice Received the Medal of Honor for Bravery at Gettysburg, Norwich University, accessed December 18, 2017, http://bicentennial.norwich.edu/92-0/.

24. Jacksonian democracy was a United States political movement from the 1820s to the 1850s. It refers to the democratic reforms symbolized by Andrew Jackson and his followers during the Second Party System. This democratic movement was dedicated to powerful and egalitarian ideals. The Jacksonian democracy promoted the powers of the executive and the presidency at the expense of the Congress. It also sought to broaden and influence public participation in government. The Jacksonians rewrote many state constitutions and demanded elected judges, instead of appointed officials, to reflect their new values. Jacksonian democracy was mainly limited to Americans of European descent. Voting rights were only extended to white, male adults. There was little progress for Native Americans and African Americans. Jackson's presidency also promoted racist legislation, including the Indian Removal Act. This democracy adhered to the following general principles: manifest destiny, strict constructionism, expanded suffrage, patronage and laissez-faire economics. What is Jacksonian Democracy? Reference.com, accessed December 18, 2017, https://www.reference.com/government-politics/jacksonian-democracy-6194d7e044d1cd33#.

25. Mary Beth Norton; et al. *A People and a Nation: A History of the United States, Volume I: To 1877* (New York: Houghton-Mifflin Company, 2007), 327.

26. Stephen E. Ambrose, *Duty, Honor, Country: A History of West Point* (Baltimore: Johns Hopkins University Press, 1996), 107–108.

27. Geiger, 41.

28. Richard Hofstadter, *Anti-Intellectualism in American Life* (New York: Vintage, Alfred A. Knopf, 1963), 164.

29. Geiger, 3.

30. "Congress—House of Representatives," *The Hillsborough Recorder*, March 29, 1820, 2.

31. "Congress—House of Representatives," *Buffalo Journal*, December 25, 1821, 2.

32. Sylvanus Thayer is regarded as the "Father of West Point." George W. Cullum, *Biographical Register Officers and Graduates of the U.S. Military Academy at West Point, N. Y. from Its Establishment in 1802 to 1890 with the Early History of the United States Military Academy* (Cambridge: The Riverside Press, 1891), Third Edition, vol. I, 83–87.

33. Ambrose, 110–111.

34. "Congress—House of Representatives," *Hartford Courant*, December 15, 1834, 2.

35. *Centennial*, vol. II, 92.

36. "Legislative," *Buffalo Daily Gazette*, March 13, 1843, 3.

37. "Congressional Proceedings," *New York Tribune*, January 13, 1844, 2.

38. "Congressional Proceedings," *New York Tribune*, February 28, 1844, 2.

39. Craig Symonds, *Joseph E. Johnston—A Civil War Biography* (New York: W. W. Norton & Company, 1992), 35.

40. "West-Point Military Academy," *The People's Press*, January 9, 1835, 3.

41. Rosewell Park, *A Sketch of the History and Topography of West Point and the U.S. Military Academy* (Philadelphia: Henry Perkins, 1840), 119.

42. Allen H. Mesch, *Teacher of Civil War Generals* (Jefferson: McFarland, 2015), 18.

43. Ambrose, 512.

44. Ethan S. Rafuse, *George Gordon Meade and the War in the East* (Abilene: McWhiney Foundation Press, 2003), 18.

45. Freeman Cleaves, *Rock of Chickamauga—The Life of General George H. Thomas* (Norman: University of Oklahoma Press, 1948), 12.

Military Training

1. Lithography is the art or process of producing a picture and/or writing on a flat, specially prepared stone or some other substance, with some greasy or oily substance, and of taking ink impressions from this as in ordinary printing. Dictionary.com, accessed December 16, 2017, http://www.dictionary.com/browse/lithography.

2. *Centennial*, vol. I, 275–279.

3. *Centennial*, vol. I, 415.

4. *Centennial*, vol. I, 416.

5. *Centennial*, vol. I, 421. Colonel S. M. Mills prepared the historical sketch of the department of tactics in 1896 for the report of the superintendent for 1896.

6. *Centennial*, vol. I, 422.

7. *Centennial*, vol. I, 423.

8. On duty at West Point June 30, 1841, to November 19, 1841; duty not known, but probably organizing department of practical engineering.

9. John B. Barnard was superintendent of the U.S. Military Academy from March 31, 1855 to September 8, 1856.

10. Initial velocity is the speed a projectile leaves the piece. It is measured as the length in feet the projectile covers in a second. Other measures of velocity are the remaining velocity, space passed over in a second at any succeeding point of the trajectory, and the terminal velocity which is the velocity with which it strikes the object. H. L. Scott, *Military Dictionary* (New York: D. Van Nostrand, 1861), 349–350.

11. Proving the strength of gunpowder is done using the service charges, in the arms for which it is designed. The measurement is done using an *Eprouvette*. Alfred Mordecai, *Report on Experiments in Gunpowder Made at Washington Arsenal in 1843 and 1844* (Washington: J. and G. S. Gideon, 1845), 320.

12. Originally gunpowder was an explosive combination of sulfur, saltpeter, and charcoal. It is more broadly any explosive mixture used as a propelling charge in a gun. Taylor, 122.

13. Taylor, 211.

14. Deviation in Firing—In artillery, an accidental phenomenon not allowed for in the laws of dispersion, by which shells (bullets) veer away from the mean trajectory expected under the given firing conditions. Causes of deviation may be the mechanical disruption of the movement of the shell in the bore (for example, separation of the shell from the rifling

grooves) or in the air (for example, defect in the stabilizer fins or other parts), as well as a chance sharp change in weather conditions during the flight of the shell. Deviation, accessed November 10, 2017, http://encyclopedia2.thefreedictionary.com/deviations.

15. *Centennial*, vol. 1, 427.

16. Heinrich Otto Scheel, *De Scheel's Treatise on Artillery* (Bloomfield: Museum Restoration Service, 1984).

17. Pyrotechny refers to the preparation and use of ammunition containing chemicals for producing smoke or light for signaling, illuminating, or screening. Pyrotechnics, accessed November 16, 2017, http://www.dictionary.com/browse/pyrotechnics.

18. A mortar is a muzzle-loading weapon, which fires shells at relatively short range with a high trajectory. Taylor, 174.

19. *Centennial*, vol. 1, 425.

20. A projectile is an object fired from a gun with an explosive propelling charge, such as a bullet, shell, rocket, or grenade. Projectile, accessed November 14, 2017, http://www.dictionary.com/browse/projectile.

21. *Centennial*, vol. 1, 428.

22. *Centennial*, vol. 1, 425

23. *Centennial*, vol. I, 426.

24. A slow match is a length of three-strand rope used to ignite an explosive. The rate of burning varied from flax to hemp to cotton and the treatments with which the material was soaked. Garrison, *Civil War Usage*, 231–232.

25. "Black match" is simply a cotton string covered with Black Powder. When a small piece of Black Match is inserted in a length of Japanese Time Fuse, it's then called "crossmatch." If Black Match is covered in a thin paper tube, it burns hundreds of times faster than normal and is called "quickmatch." "Pyrotechnic Projects: Black Match Fuse & Quickmatch," accessed November 13, 2017, https://www.cannonfuse.com/store/pc/Pyrotechnic-Projects-Black-Match-Fuse-Quickmatch-d6.htm.

26. Portfire is a case of strong paper filled with a composition of nitre, sulphur, and mealed powder, used principally to ignite the priming in proving guns, and as an incendiary material in shells. Portfire, Wikipedia, accessed April 15, 2017, https://en.wiktionary.org/wiki/portfire#English.

27. Priming tubes are small pipes, filled with a combustible composition for firing cannon. Priming tube, accessed November 10, 2017, https://www.thefreedictionary.com/Priming+tube.

28. The rifle is a firearm whose bore is constructed with spiral grooves to spin its projectile and give it more accurate flight. Boatner, 700.

29. A cartridge is a cylindrical case containing the charge, primer, and projectile for use in a firearm. Taylor, 51.

30. Canister is an artillery projectile consisting of a tin can filled with small cast iron or lead balls or long slugs, set in dry sawdust, which scattered immediately on leaving the muzzle. Boatner, 119.

31. A fuse is any device which ignites an explosive charge. The three types were concussion, percussion, and time fuse. Boatner, 320.

32. Fireballs are projectiles discharged from guns or mortars, for the purpose either of setting fire to, or of merely illuminating some work, against which hostile operations are directed. The usual ingredients are: mealed powder, saltpeter, sulphur, rosin, turpentine, with pitch, tow, naphtha. &c., as circumstance dictate. *Chambers' Encyclopedia* (London: W. and R. Chambers, 1876) vol. IV, 339.

33. Sulphur [*sic*] Matches consisted of wooden splints or sticks of cardboard coated with sulphur and tipped with a mixture of sulphide of antimony, chlorate of potash, and gum. The treatment with sulphur helped the splints to catch fire, and the odor was improved by the addition of camphor. Match, Wikipedia, accessed November 14, 2017, https://en.wikipedia.org/wiki/Match.

34. These are barrels filled with various kinds of combustibles, intermixed with small shells, grenades, and other fire-works. Charles James, *The Universal Military Dictionary in English and French* (London: T. Egerton, 1816), 38.

35. The carcass is a hollow cast-iron projectile filled with burning composition, the flame of which issues through four fuze holes to set fire to combustible objects. Boatner, 122.

36. A howitzer is a type of artillery piece characterized by a relatively short, chambered barrel which used a small charge to lob a shell a considerable distance. Howitzers were made of bronze and manufactured in three sizes to fire charges on 12, 24, or 32 pounds. Howitzer, Garrison, *Civil War Usage*, 113–114.

37. The perfection of the percussion cap in the mid-nineteenth century revived interest in the grenade. Thousands were used during the Civil War, over 90,000 of Ketcham's grenades were bought by the U.S. government. There were other types: the Adams, and the ingenious but dangerous "Excelsior." In addition, many thousands of rounds of six-pounder spherical case were used as grenades, either thrown or rolled down inclines after the fuse had been lit. Jack Coggins, *Arms and Equipment of the Civil War* (Garden City: Doubleday, 1962), https://books.google.com/books?id=9kLCAgAAQBAJ&pg=PT179&dq=Grenades+Civil+War&hl=en&sa=X&ved=0ahUKEwjMtLiWg8bXAhUmjlQKHe75B58Q6AEILDAB#v=onepage&q=Grenades%20Civil%20War&f=false.

38. A petard is a shell or half-cone of iron filled with powder and balls and used to blast open walls, doors, and other enemy obstructions. John D. Wright, *The Language of the Civil War* (Westport: Oryx Press, 2001), 227.

39. A smoke ball is a hollow paper sphere like a light ball, filled with a composition which emitted a dense, nauseous smoke. The smoke ball was used to suffocate enemy miners at work, or to conceal one's own operations. The smoke ball burned from 25 to 30 minutes. Francis A. Lord, *Civil War Collector's Encyclopedia* (Harrisburg: Stackpole Company, 2004), 199.

40. Suffocating Balls—Suffocating balls were used to drive an enemy from galleries or mines. They are thrown by hand. Henry Wagner Halleck, *Elements of Military Art and Science* (Bedford: Applewood Books, 1861), 285.

41. The Congreve rocket is an artillery rocket developed by Sir William Congreve and first used in 1806. It was used by both the British and Americans during the War of 1812. Congreve rockets bursting during the Battle of Ft. McHenry created "The Rockets' Red Glare," which inspired Francis Scott Key to compose "The Star-Spangled Banner," later adopted

as the national anthem of the United States. Congreve rockets varied in weight from 25 to 60 pounds and could carry either an incendiary or an antipersonnel warhead. The Congreve was a stick-guided rocket, with a range of 0.5 to 2 miles, depending upon its size. Congreve rocket, April 15, 2017, https://www.britannica.com/technology/Congreve-rocket.

42. Parachute rockets were used to illuminate an area of the battlefield or as a signaling device. The parachute opens when the fired rocket explodes. George A. Zinn, "Seacoast Defense," *Proceedings of the Engineers' Club of Philadelphia* (Philadelphia: The Engineers' Club, 1916), vol. XXXIII,44.

43. *Centennial*, vol. I, 428.

44. Battery is a term applied to one or more pieces of artillery. In the Union army a battery was made up of six cannons. In the Confederate army a battery was made up of four cannons. Batteries were normally under the command of a captain. Definitions, USA Civil War Web Site (U.S.A.C.W.W.S.), accessed April 15, 2017, http://www.usa-civil-war.com/Civil_War/definitions.shtml#A.

45. Movements, positions, and spacing of gun batteries. John Gore, *Evolutions of a Field Battery* (London, Simpkin, Marshall and Co., 1846), table of contents.

46. Cannon is a generic term for all firearms larger than small arms. It is a metal tube. If put on a mount, it becomes artillery. The basic artillery piece during the war was the Napoleon, a smooth-bore, muzzle-loading, 12-pounder-gun howitzer. Boatner, 119.

47. As used by ordnance departments and armories, an *eprouvette* is a one-piece, fixed elevation mortar used to test the strength of gunpowder. It went out of general use by the middle of the 19th century. In use, a carefully weighed quantity of powder (charge) was placed inside, followed by a standard weight shot. The charge was fired and the distance the shot flew was measured and compared to the expected standard distance. It was first introduced in the middle of the 1600s. Eprouvettes were also used to test the strength of small-arms powder, starting in the second half of the 1500s. These evolved into pistol-size devices which were used until the end of the black powder era, at the close of the 1800s. Eprouvette, Wikipedia, accessed April 15, 2017, https://en.wikipedia.org/wiki/Eprouvette.

48. Spring (traction) *Eprouvette*—An *Eprouvette* which uses a spring to measure the force created by the combustion of a sample of gunpowder. Eprouvette (Gunpowder tester)—V-spring type, Hagley Museum, accessed November 14, 2017, https://museumcollection.hagley.org/objects/29094.

49. A ballistic pendulum is a device for measuring a bullet's momentum, from which it is possible to calculate the velocity and kinetic energy. Ballastic pendulum, Wikipedia, accessed November 10, 2017, https://en.wikipedia.org/wiki/Ballistic_pendulum.

50. A rotary cannon, rotary autocannon, or Gatling-type cannon is a rapid-firing weapon, which uses multiple barrels in a rotating cluster to produce a sustained rate of fire greater than single-barreled machine guns or automatic cannon of equivalent caliber. Rotary cannon, Wikipedia, accessed November 9, 2017, https://en.wikipedia.org/wiki/Rotary_cannon.

51. A percussion cap is a device containing a material that explodes on being struck and is used to ignite powder or other explosive material. Taylor, 191.

52. The principal operations in manufacturing arms are welding, turning, drilling, tapping, milling, cutting, filing, grinding, case-hardening, tempering, and polishing. Edward S. Farrow, *Farrows Military Encyclopedia* (New York: Edward S. Farrow, 1885), vol. II, 602.

53. A shell is an artillery projectile containing a bursting charge of powder. Boatner, 738.

54. *Centennial*, vol. 1, 428.

55. Hollow projectiles included shells for guns, howitzers, and mortars. These are made of iron. and are classified according to the diameter of the bore of the piece or their weight. Farrow, vol. II, 42.

56. A caisson is two-wheeled cart designed to carry ammunition for a field gun. In Federal batteries, a single gun required two caissons, each of which carried up to 150 projectiles. A caisson carried two ammunition chests and a limber carried one. Garrison, *Civil War Usage*, 41.

57. Spiking a cannon involved driving a spike into the vent, breaking the spike off flush with the cannon surface, clinching the spike inside the cannon by using the rammer, and wedging shot inside the barrel. Unspiking a cannon was done by several methods: placing a charge in the barrel and exploding it to force the spike out of the vent, unscrewing the vent piece, and drilling out the spike or drilling a new vent hole. Boatner, 782.

58. When the charge of gunpowder contained in a gun is fired, the sudden expansion of the powder into many times its former bulk acts with equal force in every direction. The resistance offered by the ball. Which moves easily in the bore, being far less than the bulky and heavier gun carriage, the ball is forced to a great a distance; but the gun with its carriage, must nevertheless feel the reaction, and is driven backward a certain space, ordinarily a few feet. This retrograde motion is called the recoil, and dangerous accidents sometimes take place from it. Farrow, 643.

59. Aiming (of guns, howitzers, mortars, and stone mortars)—Point and shoot was the order of the day. Aiming became important in the Civil War with the use of rifled muskets. Rifled muskets have enough accuracy and aiming became a profitable exercise. Patrick Sweeney, *The Gun Digest Book of Smith & Wesson* (Iola: kp Books, 2004), 37.

60. Grapeshot is a projectile assembled with iron plates and rings and holding a cluster of shot together. Grapeshot was highly effective against troops at short range. Garrison, *Civil War Usage*, 98.

61. Battering in Breach—A gap or opening made by breaking or battering, as in a wall or, fortification. Definitions, USA Civil War Web Site (U.S.A.C.W.W.S.), accessed November 10, 2017, http://www.definitions.net/definition/breach.

62. Coast batteries or coast artillery are fixed or mobile artillery weapons placed close to harbors, cities, or strategic waterways, in positions from which they can fire on approaching enemy ships. Taylor, 57.

63. *Centennial*, vol. I, 428–429.

64. Garrison are infantry, or other units assigned to occupy a fort with permanent quarters and specific duty areas. Military personnel, assigned to man a fort or fortress. Garrison, *Civil War Usage*, 91.

65. Shrapnel is a hollow cast-iron projectile filled with lead bullet set in a sulphur matrix and equipped with a time or percussion fuse, which would set off a bursting charge and scatter the balls. Shrapnel is often

called case shot or spherical case shot. Shrapnel, Shotgun's Home of the American Civil War, http://civilwarhome.com/terms.htm.

66. *Centennial*, vol. I, 429.
67. *Centennial*, vol. I, 426.
68. Brevet rank is regarded as an honorary title, awarded for gallant or meritorious action in time of war, and having none of the authority, precedence, of pay or real or full pay. Boatner, 84
69. *Centennial*, vol. I, 426.
70. *Centennial*, vol. I, 427.
71. *Centennial*, vol. I, 430–431.
72. *Centennial*, vol. I, 432–433.
73. *Centennial*, vol. I, 433.
74. *Centennial*, vol. I, 434.
75. *Centennial*, vol. I, 438.

The Department of Tactics

1. Military science is the study of military processes, institutions, and behavior, along with the study of warfare, and the theory and application of organized coercive force. It is mainly focused on theory, method, and practice of producing military capability in a manner consistent with national defense policy. Military science serves to identify the strategic, political, economic, psychological, social, operational, technological, and tactical elements necessary to sustain relative advantage of military force; and to increase the likelihood and favorable outcomes of victory in peace or during a war. Military science, Wikipedia, accessed August 24, 2017, https://en.wikipedia.org/wiki/Military_science.

2. Donald Stoker, *The Grand Design—Strategy and the U.S. Civil War* (New York: Oxford University Press, 2010), 5.

3. Materials of war in 1861–1864 include weapons, ammunition, wagons, horses, food, tents, and uniforms.

4. Clausewitz was a professional combat soldier who was involved in numerous military campaigns, but he is famous primarily as a military theorist interested in the examination of war, utilizing the campaigns of Frederick the Great and Napoleon as frames of reference for his work. https://en.wikipedia.org/wiki/Carl_von_Clausewitz—cite_note-12 He wrote a careful, systematic, philosophical examination of war in all its aspects. The result was his principal book, *On War*, a major work on the philosophy of war. Carl von Clausewitz, Wikipedia, accessed December 12, 2017, https://en.wikipedia.org/wiki/Carl_von_Clausewitz#Theory_of_war.

5. Sir Basil Henry Liddell Hart (October 31, 1895—January 29, 1970), commonly known throughout most of his career as Captain B. H. Liddell Hart, was an English soldier, military historian and military theorist. B. H. Liddell Hart, Wikipedia, accessed December 12, 2017, https://en.wikipedia.org/wiki/B._H._Liddell_Hart.

6. Antoine-Henri, Baron Jomini (March 6, 1779–March 24, 1869) was a Swiss officer who served as a general in the French and later in the Russian service, and one of the most celebrated writers on the Napoleonic art of war. Jomini's ideas were a staple at military academies, the United States Military Academy at West Point being a prominent example. His theories were thought to have affected many officers who later served in the American Civil War. Antoine-Henri Jomini, Wikipedia, accessed December 12, 2017, https://en.wikipedia.org/wiki/Antoine-Henri_Jomini.

7. Antoine Henri baron de Jomini, *The Art of War* (Philadelphia: J. B. Lippincott, 1862), 13.
8. Stoker, 9.
9. DOD Dictionary of Military and Associated Terms, May 2017, accessed May 26, 2017, http://www.dtic.mil/doctrine/new_pubs/dictionary.pdf.
10. Military tactics is the science (or art) of directing soldiers in combat. Tactics were delegated to division and brigade commanders. Tactics, Garrison, *Civil War Usage*, 245.
11. Jomini, 69.
12. *Centennial*, vol. I, 44.
13. Morrison, 100.
14. William Calvin Oates, *The War Between the Union and the Confederacy* (New York: The Neale Publishing Group, 1905), 302.
15. John Waugh, *The Class of 1846* (New York: Warner Books, Inc., 1994), 512.
16. Robert I. Girardi, *The Civil War Generals* (Blaine: Voyager Press, 2013), 24.
17. Girardi, 19.
18. Cleaves, 13.
19. Seven-up is a card game for three to seven players using a standard deck of fifty-two cards. Cards are played out to form a layout of sequences going up and down in suit from the sevens. The game is won by emptying one's hand before the other players. All cards are dealt to the players, even if as a result some players have one card more than others. The owner of the seven of hearts begins by playing it. The other three sevens may later be played as the first cards of their respective suits. After that, cards may be added in sequence down to the ace and up to the king. A player who cannot place a card passes. Sevens card game, Wikipedia, accessed August 8, 2017, https://en.wikipedia.org/wiki/Sevens_%28card_game%29.
20. A sutler was a civilian licensed or allowed to operate a shop at a military camp or post. Sutlers often offered foodstuffs not included in official rations and other small items, such as buttons and personal items. Sutler, Garrison, *Civil War Usage*, 243.
21. Dabney Herndon Maury, *Recollections of a Virginian in the Mexican, Indian, and Civil Wars*, 3rd ed. (New York: Charles Scribner's Sons, 1984), 229.
22. Alvin C. Voris and Jerome Mushkat, *A Citizen-Soldier's Civil War: The Letters of Brevet Major General Alvin C. Voris* (Dekalb: Northern Illinois University Press, 2002), 128.
23. Waugh, 510.
24. Paddy Griffith, *Battle Tactics of the Civil War* (New Haven: Yale University Press, 1987), 23.
25. Worthington Chauncey Ford, ed., *A Cycle of Adams Letters* (Boston: Houghton Mifflin Company, 1920), vol. II, 7.
26. Archer Jones, *Civil War Command and Strategy—The Process of Victory and Defeat* (New York: The Free Press, 1992), 232.
27. *Citizen Soldier* (Norwich: Swett & Jackman, 1840–1841), 56.
28. Griffith, 124.
29. Totten was appointed Chief Engineer of the United States Army in 1838, and served in the position for twenty-five years until his death in 1864, the longest tenure of any Chief Engineer. As Chief Engi-

neer he was intimately involved with every aspect of the Army Corps of Engineers' activities from fortifications to harbor improvement. Joseph Gilbert Totten, Wikipedia, accessed December 12, 2017, https://en.wikipedia.org/wiki/Joseph_Gilbert_Totten.

30. David S. Heidler and Jeanne T. Heidler, *Encyclopedia of the American Civil War* (Santa Barbara: ABC-CLIO, Inc., 2000) vol. 4. 1967–1968.

31. Superintendent is the title of the commanding officer at the United States Military Academy. Taylor, 239.

32. Lance Betros, *West Point—Two Centuries and Beyond* (Abilene: McWhiney Foundation Press, 2004), 27.

33. Cameron gave his support to Abraham Lincoln, and became his secretary of war. He served only a year before resigning amidst allegations of disorganization and corruption during the early stages of the Civil War. Simon Cameron, Wikipedia, accessed December 13, 2016, https://en.wikipedia.org/wiki/Simon_Cameron.

34. "Major Barnard Reviews the Opinions of Secretary Cameron," *The New York Times*, July 19, 1861, 3.

35. "Thirty-Seventh Congress—House," *National Republican*, December 5, 1862, 2.

36. Volo, 93.

37. *Centennial*, vol. I, 374. [Colonel S. M. Mills prepared the historical sketch of the Department of Tactics in 1896 for the report of the superintendent for 1896. Since 1896, the department has been very materially expanded, changed, and improved. The development and improvement are exemplified by the full extracts from the reports of the commandants who have succeeded Colonel Mills.]

38. *Centennial*, vol. I, 374–375.

39. The School of the Company was a tactics class on the various movements and firing operations used in platoon and company size units. (See section on Hardee's *Rifle and Light Infantry Tactics*)

40. Target practice refers to any exercise in which projectiles are fired at a specified target, usually to improve the aim of the person or persons firing the weapon. Target practice, Wikipedia, accessed December 21, 2017, https://en.wikipedia.org/wiki/Target_practice.

41. Equitation is the art or practice of horse riding or horsemanship. More specifically, equitation may refer to a rider's position while mounted, and encompasses a rider's ability to ride correctly and with effective aids. Equitation, Wikipedia, accessed May 12, 20–17, https://en.wikipedia.org/wiki/Equitation.

42. An outpost is a detachment of guards or sentries posted outside a stationary military force to protect it against surprise by the enemy. Taylor, 186.

43. *Centennial*, vol. I, 380–381.

44. *Centennial*, vol. I, 375.

45. *Centennial*, vol. I, 375.

46. Robert Cowley and Thomas Guinzburg, ed., *West Point—Two Centuries of Honor and Tradition* (New York: Warner Books, 2002), 18.

47. Cowley, 18.

48. Cowley, 19.

49. *Centennial*, vol. I, 375.

50. Joseph G. Swift was the first graduate of the U.S. Military Academy (Class of 1802 and Cullum Number 1) who was chief engineer of the U.S. Army and superintendent of the Academy. Cullum, vol. I, 51–56.

51. Cowley, 19.

52. *Centennial*, vol. I, 376.

53. Cowley, 34.

54. *Centennial*, vol. I, 376–377.

55. *Centennial*, vol. I, 377.

56. Cowley, 34.

57. *Centennial*, vol. I, 377.

58. Cowley, 35.

59. *Centennial*, vol. I, 377.

60. Evolutions of the line refers to movements of a line of soldiers (See section on Hardee's *Rifle and Light Infantry Tactics*).

61. *Centennial*, vol. I, 377.

62. *Centennial*, vol. I, 377.

63. The term "carver" comes from cutting or dividing as in *carving* a turkey or *carving* wood into a figure. In this case, carver may refer to someone who carries the knives for carving into the mess room. Accessed August 11, 2017, http://www.thefreedictionary.com/Carver.

64. *Centennial*, vol. I, 378.

65. Cowley, 35.

66. Cowley, 35.

67. *Centennial*, vol. I, 377.

68. *Centennial*, vol. 1, 378.

69. *Centennial*, vol. I, 379–380.

70. *Centennial*, vol. I, 379

71. Military gymnastics refers to a specific exercise program designed to ensure the fitness of cadets. For more information, please see Whitfield B. East, *A Historical Review and Analysis of Army Physical Readiness and Assessment* (Fort Leavenworth: Combat Studies Institute Press, 2013).

72. *Centennial*, vol. I, 382–383.

73. *Centennial*, vol. I, 380.

74. In 1860, there were forty-three cadets at the Academy from Southern states. Seventeen were members of the Fourth and First Classes. After 1861, there were no Southerners in the graduating classes. *Official Register of the Officers and Cadets of the U.S. Military Academy*, June 1860, 7–16.

75. *Centennial*, vol. I, 381.

76. *Centennial*, vol. I, 223.

77. *Centennial*, vol. I, 377.

78. *Centennial*, vol. I, 379.

79. *Centennial*, vol. I, 380.

80. Wayne Hsieh, *West Pointers and the Civil War* (Chapel Hill: University of North Carolina Press, 2009), 37.

81. A battalion has from 500 to 1,000 troops and is usually commanded by a lieutenant colonel. Taylor, 30–31.

82. Manual of Arms—instructions for handling and using weapons in formation—(See section on Hardee's *Rifle and Light Infantry Tactics*).

83. There are two kinds of wheelings: from halts, or on fixed pivots, and in march or on movable pivots. Wheeling on a fixed pivot takes place in passing a corps from the order in battle to the order in column, or from the latter to the former. Wheels in marching take place in changes of direction in column, as often as this movement is executed to the side opposite to the guide. In wheels from a halt, the pivot-man only turns in his place, without advancing or receding. In the wheels in marching, the pivot takes steps of nine or eleven inches, according as the squad is marching

in quick or double-quick time, to clear the wheeling-point, which is necessary, in order that the subdivisions of a column may change direction without losing their distances, is explained in the School of the Company. The man on the wheeling-flank will take the full step of twenty-eight inches, or thirty-three inches, according to the gait. "Wheeling," 64th Illinois Volunteer Infantry, Company E, "Yates Sharp Shooters," accessed august 8, 2017, http://www.64thill.org/drillmanuals/caseys_infantrytactics/volume1/part05.htm.

84. A platoon is usually composed of 25–50. An infantry company may have 100–200 men. A battalion contains 500–1,000 men. Taylor, 31, 64, and 195.

85. William J. Hardee, *Rifle and Light Infantry Tactics for Exercises and Maneuvers of Troops When Acting as Light Infantry or Riflemen* (Philadelphia: J. B. Lippincott, 1861), Vol. I Schools of the Soldier and Company; Instruction for Skirmishers.

86. A defile is a march in single file or a column of files or to march in single file or a column of files. Taylor, 79.

87. A flanking attack is an attack at the flank of an enemy force. a flank is one of the sides (right or left) of a military formation or position. Taylor, 105.

88. Hardee, Vol. II, 7–8.

West Point in the Civil War

1. *Centennial*, Vol. I, 488.
2. *Centennial*, Vol. I, 489.
3. Total number of general officers in both armies from West Point (448) = graduates who became general officers in the regular and volunteer armies of the United States (294) + graduates who served as general officers in the Confederate Army (151) + graduates who became general officers in foreign armies (3).
4. *Centennial*, Vol. I, 492.
5. *Centennial*, Vol. I, 490.
6. *Centennial*, Vol. I, 493–494.
7. John Whiteclay Chambers II, ed., *The Oxford Companion to American Military History* (New York, Oxford University Press, 1999), 129.
8. Excluding promotions on or after March 13, 1965.
9. Chambers, 129.
10. James Marshall-Cornwall, *Grant as Military Commander* (New York: Barnes & Noble Books, 1970), 23–24.
11. W. J. Wood, *Civil War Generalship—The Art of Command* (Boston: Da Capo Press, 2000), 10.
12. Morrison, 96.
13. List of American Civil War Generals, Wikipedia, Accessed October 31, 2017, https://en.wikipedia.org/wiki/list_of_american_civil_war_generals
14. Waugh, 514.

Commandant of Cadets

1. *Centennial*, Vol. I, 393.
2. Ambrose, 289.
3. Ambrose, 87.
4. Ambrose, 87.
5. The Congress approved and recognized the title and created the Department of Tactics by a law approved on June 12, 1858. Stanley P. Tozeski, *Preliminary Inventory of the Records of the United States Military Academy* (Washington: General Services Administration, 1976), 31.
6. Mesch, 23.
7. Winfield Scott, *Rules and Regulations for the Exercise and Maneuvers of the United States Infantry* (New York: H. W. Mercein, 1815).
8. Morrison, 98–99.
9. Mesch, 23.
10. "The President shall be authorized to appoint a Board of Visitors, of not less than [unspecified] persons versed in Military Science, whose duty it shall be to visit the Academy at the times of examination of the Cadets, for the purpose of ascertaining the progress and improvement of the Cadets, and of examining into, and reporting everything connected with the management and Police of the Institution. The Superintendent shall lay before the Board of Visitors at each examination, the Registers of Police and Instruction, and those Cadets who shall be there noted for irregularities, or inattentive shall be particularly examined before the Board, and if the Board so determine, the Superintendent shall dismiss them from the Academy." *Annual Report of the Board of Visitors to the United States Military Academy, Made to Congress and the Secretary of War for the Year 1819* (West Point: U.S. Military Press and Bindery, 1894), 8.
11. Mesch, 23.
12. Plebes are new cadets or freshman at the U.S. Military Academy. Plebe, Garrison, *Civil War Usage*, 193.
13. Mesch, 27.
14. Barone, Laureen M., "Evolution of the Cadet Disciplinary System: From Confusion to Clarity (1802–1833)," U.S. Military Academy, 4 December 1990, Tactical Officer Education Program Papers, Special Collections, U.S. Military Academy Library, 6.
15. Ambrose, 78.
16. Henry Coppee, *Grant and His Campaigns* (New York: Charles Richardson, 1866), 72.
17. Nathaniel Cheairs Hughes, Jr., *General William J. Hardee—Old Reliable* (Baton Rouge: Louisiana State University Press, 1965), 67.
18. Barone, 9–10.
19. Barone, 11.
20. Jeffrey D. Wert, *General James Longstreet: The Confederacy's Most Controversial Soldier* (New York: Simon & Schuster, 1993), 29.
21. Mesch, 29.
22. Richard M. McMurry, *John Bell Hood and the War for Southern Independence* (Lincoln: University of Nebraska Press, 1982), 9–10.
23. Mesch, 25.
24. Ethan Allen Hitchcock, *Fifty Years in Camp and Field* (New York: G. P. Putnam's Sons, 1909), 48.
25. Symonds, 50.
26. Ulysses S. Grant, *Personal Memoirs* (New York: The Modern Library, 1999), 17.
27. Hughes, 67.
28. Peter S. Michie, *The Life and Letters of Emory Upton*, 247, quoted in Sidney Forman, *West Point: A History of the United States Military Academy* (New York: Columbia University Press., 1950), 153.
29. *Centennial*, vol. I, 379–381.
30. *Centennial*, vol. I, 382–383.
31. *Centennial*, vol. I, 389.
32. *Centennial*, vol. I, 392.

33. Cullum, vol. I, 21.
34. Cullum, vol. I, 22.
35. Cullum's *Officers and Graduates of the U.S. Military Academy* presents the achievements of Union officers who graduated from West Point. The actions of West Pointers who joined the Confederate Army are limited to the sentence, "Joined in the rebellion of 1861–66 against the United States." Ezra J. Warner's *Generals in Gray*, Bruce S. Allardice *More Generals in Gray*, Joe A. Mobley *Confederate Generals of North Carolina*, Gerard A. Patterson *Rebels from West Point*, and James S. Robbins *Last in Their Class* provided information on the military achievements of Confederate commanders.

George W. Gardiner

1. Cullum, vol. I, 83–86.
2. General Hitchcock, who passed over the battleground, February 22, 1836, reports: "Along the north and west faces of the triangular breastwork, formed by felled trees, were about thirty bodies, mere skeletons, although much of the clothing was left upon them. They were lying, almost every one of them, in precisely the position they must have occupied during the fight,—their heads next to the logs over which they had delivered their fire, and their bodies stretched with striking regularity parallel to each other. They had evidently been shot dead at their posts, and the Indians had not disturbed them, except by taking the scalps of most of them ... the advanced guard, doubtless, fell during the first attack. It was during a cessation of fire that the little band still remaining, about thirty in number, threw up time triangular breastwork, which, from the haste with which it was constructed, was necessarily defective, and could not protect the men in the second attack."

The action lasted from 8 a.m. to 4 p.m. There were 108 U.S. troops engaged with an enemy force of 800 Seminole Indians and 100 African Americans. While a man could load a musket, the firing was continued. Captain Gardiner, next to the last surviving officer, fell, pierced by five or six shots, his mortal wound being in the breast.

The Military Academy erected a beautiful, white Italian marble monument at West Point to "Dade and His Command." Cullum, vol. I, 112.

3. Cullum, vol. I, 111–112.

John Bliss

1. Centennial, vol. II, 77.
2. "Books About West Point by John Ward, '64," accessed November 1, 2107, http://www.west-point.org/parent/wppc-wa/2011/08/01/books-about-west-point-by-john-ward-64/.
3. The *Chargé d'Affaires* is a diplomat who heads an embassy in the absence of the ambassador. *Chargé d'Affaires*, Wikipedia, accessed December 22, 2017, https://en.wikipedia.org/wiki/Charg%C3%A9_d%27affaires.
4. Cullum, vol. I, 28.
5. *Centennial*, vol. II, 77.
6. Cullum, vol. I, 28.

John R. Bell

1. John H. B. Latrobe, *West Point Reminiscences—From September, 1818, to March, 1882*, accessed November 1, 2017, http://penelope.uchicago.edu/Thayer/E/Gazetteer/Places/America/United_States/Army/USMA/LATREM*.html, 14.
2. *Centennial*, vol. I, 377.
3. Cullum, vol. I, 104.
4. Cullum, vol. I, 104.

William J. Worth

1. Hitchcock, 48.
2. Cullum, vol. I, 28–29.
3. Symonds, 50.
4. *Centennial*, vol. II, 88.
5. *Aide-de-Camp* is French expression meaning *Helper in the [Military] Camp*). The *Aide-de-Camp* acts as a personal assistant or secretary to a person of high rank, usually a senior military, police or government officer, a member of a royal family, or a head of state. *Aide-de-Camp*, Wikipedia, accessed December 1, 2017. https://en.wikipedia.org/wiki/Aide-de-camp.
6. On May 2, 1847, Congress presented Worth a Sword of Honor. The sword was "...in testimony of the high sense entertained by Congress of his gallantry and good conduct in Storming Monterey." The State of New York presented him with a sword in 1848. He also received swords from Columbia, his native county, in 1842 and from the State of Louisiana in 1848. The City of New York erected a monument to his memory facing Madison Square at the junction of Broadway and Fifth Avenue. William Jenkins Worth, accessed September 11, 2017, http://www.aztecclub.com/bios/worth.htm.
7. Cullum, vol. I, 28–29.
8. In 1841, President John Tyler appointed Spencer to be secretary of war in his administration as war secretary, he proposed a chain of posts extending from Council Bluffs, Iowa, to the Columbia River. He also recommended the government adhere to arrangements made by Army commanders in the field for compensation of the Creek Indians, who had been forced to move west of the Mississippi. John Canfield Spencer, Wikipedia, accessed December 12, 2017, https://en.wikipedia.org/wiki/John_Canfield_Spencer.
9. William Raymond, *Biographical Sketches of the Distinguished Men of Columbia County* (Albany: Weed Parsons and Company, 1851), 55–61.

Ethan A. Hitchcock

1. Cullum, vol. I, 167–169.
2. Poinsett served as secretary of war from March 7, 1837, to March 5, 1841, and presided over the continuing removal of Indians west of the Mississippi and over the Seminole War; reduced the fragmentation of the Army by concentrating elements at central locations; equipped the light batteries of artillery regiments as authorized by the 1821 army organization act. Joel Roberts Poinsett, Wikipedia, accessed December 12, 2017, https://en.wikipedia.org/wiki/Joel_Roberts_Poinsett.
3. When the newly elected President Harrison organized his cabinet in 1841, he offered the position

of secretary of war to Bell, following the advice of Daniel Webster. After Bell accepted, he was blasted as a hypocrite by Democrats, who said he had railed against the spoils system throughout the 1830s. After Harrison's death, his successor, John Tyler, agreed to keep all cabinet appointments, though many members of the cabinet were skeptical Tyler would support Whig initiatives. In May 1841, Secretary Bell issued his report on the nation's defenses, suggesting they were outdated. He also recommended replacing civilian superintendents of national armories with military professionals, fearing civilian superintendents lacked adequate knowledge of munitions storage. John Bell (Tennessee politician), Wikipedia, accessed December 12, 2017, https://en.wikipedia.org/wiki/John_Bell_(Tennessee_politician).

4. Don Carlos Buell graduated from the U.S. Military Academy in 1841 and was commissioned a second lieutenant in the Third Infantry Regiment. Two years after he graduated, Buell faced court-martial for striking a soldier with the flat of his sword, but was acquitted. The incident earned him a reputation for being a harsh disciplinarian. Don Carlos Buell, Wikipedia, accessed November 2, 2017, https://en.wikipedia.org/wiki/Don_Carlos_Buell.

5. William S. Harney commanded the Army's Department of the West at Jefferson Barracks in St. Louis, Missouri, in 1861. William S. Harney, Wikipedia, accessed December 12, 2017, https://en.wikipedia.org/wiki/William_S._Harney#Civil_War.

6. Cullum, vol. I, 169–179.

John Fowle

1. Cullum, vol. I, 109–110.
2. *Centennial*, vol. I, 502–503.
3. *Centennial*, vol. II, 96.
4. Cullum, vol. I, 29–30.

Charles F. Smith

1. Cullum, vol. I, 180–186.
2. Cullum, vol. I, 355.
3. Grant, 17.
4. *Centennial*, vol. I, 502–503.
5. *Centennial*, vol. II, 97.
6. Cullum, vol. I, 353–355.
7. Earthworks are fortifications composed of banks of earth and wood, rather than brick or stone, facing the enemy. Definitions, USA Civil War Web Site (U.S.A.C.W.W.S.), accessed November 3, 2017, http://www.usa-civil-war.com/Civil_War/definitions_2.shtml.
8. Erysipelas is an acute infection typically with a skin rash, usually on any of the legs and toes, face, arms, and fingers. Erysipelas, Wikipedia, accessed November 3, 2017, https://en.wikipedia.org/wiki/Erysipelas.
9. Cullum, vol. I, 355–357.
10. Cullum, vol. I, 353–355.

John A. Thomas

1. Waugh, 24.
2. *Centennial*, vol. I, 502–503.

3. Cullum, vol. I, 547.
4. An advocate of the United States is an official elected or appointed to advance the interests of the United States, especially by investigating complaints concerning public authorities. Accessed December 1, 2016. https://en.oxforddictionaries.com/definition/public_advocate.
5. Cullum, vol. I, 547.

Bradford R. Alden

1. Cullum, vol. I, 488–489.
2. *Centennial*, vol. I, 502–503.
3. *Centennial*, vol. II, 105.
4. *Centennial*, vol. II, 107–108.
5. Cullum, vol. I, 489–490.
6. Cullum, vol. I, 489.
7. An artesian aquifer is a confined aquifer holding groundwater under positive pressure. This causes the water level in a well to rise to a point where hydrostatic equilibrium has been reached. A well drilled into such an aquifer is called an *artesian well*. These types of wells use water pressure to force petroleum to the surface. Artesian aquifer, Wikipedia, accessed November 3, 2017, https://en.wikipedia.org/wiki/Artesian_aquifer.
8. Cullum, vol. I, 489–491.

Robert S. Garnett

1. Cullum, vol. I, 420–421.
2. Cullum, vol. II, 93–94.
3. Ezra J. Warner, *Generals in Gray* (Baton Rouge: Louisiana State University Press, 1959), 100.
4. Cullum, vol. II, 93–94.
5. Warner, 100.
6. Cullum, vol. II, 93–94.
7. Cullum, vol. II, 93–94 and Warner, 100.

William H. T. Walker

1. Sappers were workmen who dug trenches in a zigzag pattern, connecting with trenches dug parallel to a defensive works. Garrison, *Civil War Usage*, 220.
2. Pontoniers were officers or soldiers in charge of bridge equipment for the construction of pontoon bridges. Pontonier, Dictionary.com, accessed December 3, 2017, http://www.dictionary.com/browse/pontonier.
3. Cullum, vol. I, 530–535.
4. *Centennial*, vol. II, 110.
5. *Centennial*, vol. I, 502–503.
6. Cullum, vol. I, 694–695.
7. Warner, 323–324.
8. Cullum, vol. I, 694–695.
9. Warner, 323–324.
10. Cullum, vol. I, 694–695.
11. Clement Anselm Evans, *Confederate Military History* (Atlanta: Confederate Publishing Company, 1899), 449–451.

William J. Hardee

1. Cullum, vol. I, 718.
2. Hughes, 67–68.

3. *Centennial*, vol. II, 113.
4. *Centennial*, vol. II, 111.
5. *Centennial*, vol. II, 111.
6. *Centennial*, vol. II, 114.
7. Hughes, 57–58.
8. Jeffry D. Wert, *The Controversial Life of George Armstrong Custer* (New York: Simon & Schuster, 1996), 35.
9. When the war began in April 1861, many cadets at West Point resigned their appointment and enlisted in the Confederate States Army. These men were excluded from the lists of Notable West Point Graduates Who Served in the Civil War.
10. When the war began in April 1861, many cadets at West Point resigned their appointment and enlisted in the Confederate States Army. These men were excluded from the lists of Notable West Point Graduates Who Served in the Civil War.
11. Cullum, vol. I, 717–718.
12. Horatio Bateman, *Biographies of Two Hundred and Fifty Distinguished National Men* (New York: John T. Giles & Co., 1871), 233.
13. Cullum, vol. I, 717–718.
14. Bateman, 233.
15. Cullum, vol. I, 717–718.
16. William Joseph Hardee, accessed November 27, 2017, http://www.aztecclub.com/bios/hardee.htm, Cullum, vol. I, 717–718 and Bateman, 233.

John F. Reynolds

1. Cullum, vol. I, 341–342.
2. Edward J. Nichols, *Toward Gettysburg—A Biography of General John F. Reynolds* (College Station: Pennsylvania State University Press, 1958), 72–73.
3. Nichols, 75.
4. When the war began in April 1861, many cadets at West Point resigned their appointment and enlisted in the Confederate States Army. These men were excluded from the lists of Notable West Point Graduates Who Served in the Civil War.
5. When the war began in April 1861, many cadets at West Point resigned their appointment and enlisted in the Confederate States Army. These men were excluded from the lists of Notable West Point Graduates Who Served in the Civil War.
6. Cullum, vol. II, 91–93.

Christopher C. Augur

1. Cullum, vol. I, 341–342.
2. When the war began in April 1861, many cadets at West Point resigned their appointment and enlisted in the Confederate States Army. These men were excluded from the lists of Notable West Point Graduates Who Served in the Civil War.
3. When the war began in April 1861, many cadets at West Point resigned their appointment and enlisted in the Confederate States Army. These men were excluded from the lists of Notable Wes Point Graduates Who Served in the Civil War.
4. Cullum, vol. II, 167–169.
5. Cullum, vol. II, 167–169.

Kenner Garrard

1. Parole is a pledge or oath under which a prisoner of war is released under the understanding he will not again bear arms until exchanged. Boatner, 620.
2. When the war began in April 1861, many cadets at West Point resigned their appointment and enlisted in the Confederate States Army. These men were excluded from the lists of Notable West Point Graduates Who Served in the Civil War.
3. When the war began in April 1861, many cadets at West Point resigned their appointment and enlisted in the Confederate States Army. These men were excluded from the lists of Notable West Point Graduates Who Served in the Civil War.
4. Cullum, vol. II, 441–443 and Anna Russell des Cognets, *Governor Garrard, of Kentucky* (Lexington: James M. Byrnes, 1898), 31–32.
5. Cullum, vol. II, 441–443 and des Cognets, 31–32.

Henry B. Clitz

1. Cullum, vol. II, 243–243.
2. Cullum, vol. II, 243–245.

The Commandant's Role in Preparing Civil War Generals

1. *Congr. Globe*, 37th Cong. 1st Sess. 89 (1861).
2. "Worst Generals of the Civil War," Georgia's Blue and Gray Trail, accessed November 20, 2017, http://blueandgraytrail.com/features/worstgenerals.html and "The Worst Civil War Generals and Commanders," Warfare History Network, accessed November 20, 2017, http://warfarehistorynetwork.com/daily/civil-war/the-worst-civil-war-generals-and-commanders/.
3. Girardi, 21.
4. Lew Wallace, *Lew Wallace: An Autobiography* (New York: Harper & Brothers, 1906), vol. I, 344.
5. Girardi, 25.
6. Hitchcock, 322.
7. John Gibbon, *Recollections of the Civil War* (New York: G. P. Putnam's sons, 1928), 38.
8. Girardi, 8–9.
9. Griffith, 23.
10. Wood, 26.
11. Girardi, 18.
12. Girardi, 18.
13. Griffith, 114–115.
14. Jones, *Civil War Command*, 274.
15. Betros, 26.
16. Clayton R. Newell, *The Regular Army Before the Civil War—1845–1860* (Washington: Center of Military History, 2014), 22.
17. Newell, 48–49.
18. Alan Axelrod, *Armies South, Armies North* (Lanham: Rowman & Littlefield, 2017), 13.
19. Symonds, 34.
20. Griffith estimates the Civil War armies had 3,050,000 soldiers. With one thousand men per regiment, that translates to 3,050 regiments. Griffith estimates the pre-war pool of potential officers was 3,000

officers. This estimate includes 1,292 men from serving, resigned, and retired officers; men educated at private military schools; and those with experience in the Mexican and Indian wars. This optimistic estimate equates to one officer per unit compared to the thirty-nine authorized positions. This means 97.5% of the regimental openings had to be filled by untrained commanders. (39 officers/regiment × 3,050 regiments = 118,950 required authorized officers, subtracting the 3,000 pool of available officers yields the need for 118,950 – 3,000 = 115,950 additional officers or 97.5% of the required officer corps had to added to the ranks, 115,950/118,950 × 100% = 97.5%), Griffith, 97.

21. Ken Dougherty, *Civil War Leadership and Mexican War Experience* (Jackson: University Press of Mississippi, 2007), 13.
22. *Congr. Globe*, 37th Cong. 1st Sess. 89 (1861).
23. Wood, 27.
24. *Centennial*, vol. I, 486–487.
25. List of wars involving the United States, Wikipedia, accessed October 30, 2017, https://en.wikipedia.org/wiki/List_of_wars_involving_the_United_States
26. *Centennial*, vol. I, 500.
27. "West Point Military Academy," *Public Ledger*, July 13, 1859, 2.
28. Jones, *Civil War Command*, 5.
29. *Centennial*, vol. I, 602.
30. Dugard, 375.
31. Quote from Luther Giddings, *Campaigns in North America*, New York, 1853. Nichols, 47.
32. Quote from John R. Kenly, *Memoirs of a Maryland Volunteer*, Philadelphia, 1873. Nichols, 47.
33. Allan R. Millett, Peter Maslowski, and William B. Feis, *For the Common Defense* (New York: Free Press, 2012), Third Edition, 134.
34. Elizabeth Brown Pryor, *Reading the Man* (New York: Penguin Group, 2007), 177.
35. Martin Dugard, *The Training Ground—Grant, Lee, Sherman, and Davis in the Mexican War, 1846–1848* (New York: Little, Brown and Company, 2008), 59.
36. A turning movement is an enveloping maneuver, which passes around the enemy's main forces to strike at a vital point in the rear. Taylor, 251.
37. Dougherty, 184–186.
38. "Mexican War: The Proving Ground for Future American Civil War Generals," HistoryNet, accessed November 8, 2017, http://www.historynet.com/mexican-war-the-proving-ground-for-future-american-civil-war-generals.htm.
39. Grant, 96–97.
40. Dugard, 125.
41. Minié Bullet—A bullet-shaped, lead projectile designed to be fired from a muzzle-loading rifle. The bullet improved the accuracy, range, and rate of fire of small arms fire. Boatner, 552.
42. "Civil War Innovations," History Detectives, accessed November 19, 2017, http://www.pbs.org/opb/historydetectives/feature/civil-war-innovations/.
43. A smoothbore is a cannon or musket without rifling; having a smooth tube. Definitions, USA Civil War Web Site (U.S.A.C.W.W.S.), accessed April 15, 2017, http://www.usa-civil-war.com/Civil_War/definitions_3.shtml
44. "Minie Ball," Historynet, accessed October 24, 2017, http://www.historynet.com/minie-ball.
45. Newell, 41–42.
46. "Minie Ball," Historynet, accessed October 24, 2017, http://www.historynet.com/minie-ball.
47. A rifle is a gunpowder weapon with spiral grooves cut into the surface of its bore, so the projectile will leave the weapon with a spinning motion which provides greater accuracy and stability to its flight. Taylor, 211.
48. Terry L. Jones, *Historical Dictionary of the Civil War* (Lanham: The Scarecrow Press, 2011), vol. I, 373.
49. Jomini, 359.
50. Jones, *Civil War Command*, 273.
51. Pryor, 67–68.
52. Ambrose, 509.
53. Dugard, 6.
54. D. H. Mahan, *Advanced-Guard, Out-Post, and Detachment of Services of Troops with the Essential Principles of Strategy and Grand Tactics* (New York: John Wiley, 1864), 32.
55. Wert, *General James Longstreet*, 30.
56. Morrison, 94.
57. Cullum, vol. I, 319–322.
58. Waugh, 514.
59. Cullum, vol. I, 321–322.
60. Cullum, vol. I, 319–325.
61. Wood, 26.
62. Ambrose, 289.
63. Cullum, vol. I, 22.
64. Morrison, 99.
65. "The Best School" comes from the following quote by Andrew Jackson: "I Believe [The U.S. Military Academy Is] the Best School in the World." Morrison, title pages.
66. Donald Cartmell, *Civil War 101* (New York: Gramercy Books, 2001), 88–89.

Appendices

1. Civil War Battle Summaries by Campaign, CWSAC, accessed December 24, 2017, https://www.nps.gov/abpp/battles/bycampgn.htm.
2. Class A and B battlefields represent the principal strategic operations of the war. Civil War Battle Summaries by Campaign, CWSAC, accessed December 24, 2017, https://www.nps.gov/abpp/battles/bycampgn.htm.
3. Cullum, *Officers and Graduates of the U.S. Military Academy*, vols. I and II, Patterson, Gerard A., *Rebels from West Point* (Mechanicsville: Stackpole Books, 2002), 159–163 and West Point Officers in the Civil War, accessed April 4, 2016, http://civilwarintheeast.com/west-point-officers-in-the-civil-war/.
4. New York Volunteers
5. Virginia Volunteers
6. Pennsylvania Militia
7. Ohio Volunteers
8. Michigan Volunteers
9. Not commissioned because of deafness
10. New York Volunteers
11. Colorado Volunteers
12. New York Volunteers
13. Maryland Volunteers
14. Indiana Volunteers
15. Kentucky Volunteers
16. United States Postmaster General
17. Veteran Reserve Corps

18. West Virginia Militia
19. District of Columbia Militia
20. Missouri Militia
21. Inspector General
22. Ohio Volunteers
23. Declined Commission
24. Kentucky Volunteers
25. Ohio Volunteers
26. Vermont Volunteers
27. Indiana Legion
28. Missouri Militia
29. Pennsylvania Volunteers
30. New Mexico Volunteers
31. Inspector General of the Army of the Potomac
32. New York Volunteers
33. Pennsylvania Volunteers
34. Iowa Volunteers
35. Indiana Volunteers
36. Provost Marshall
37. Ohio Volunteers
38. Maryland Volunteers
39. New York Volunteers
40. Massachusetts Volunteers
41. Judge Advocate General
42. Maryland Volunteers
43. Alabama Militia
44. Massachusetts Volunteers
45. Massachusetts Volunteers
46. Vermont Volunteers
47. New York Volunteers
48. Pennsylvania Volunteers
49. Maine Volunteers
50. New York Volunteers
51. New York Volunteers
52. West Virginia Volunteers
53. Massachusetts Volunteers
54. Ohio Volunteers
55. New York Volunteers
56. Wisconsin Volunteers
57. California Volunteers
58. Pennsylvania Volunteers
59. New York Volunteers
60. New York Volunteers
61. Kentucky Volunteers
62. New York Volunteers
63. Indiana Volunteers
64. California Volunteers
65. Ohio Volunteers
66. Pennsylvania Volunteers
67. Missouri Volunteers
68. New Jersey Volunteers
69. Ohio Volunteers
70. California Volunteers
71. New York Volunteers
72. Connecticut Volunteers
73. North Carolina Volunteers
74. Maryland Volunteers
75. Cullum, vol. I, 21.
76. Cullum, vol. I, 171–172.
77. Cullum, vol. I, 174–176.
78. Cullum, vol. I, 181–182.
79. Cullum, vol. I, 190–191.
80. Cullum, vol. I, 196–197.
81. Heidler, vol. 4, 2136–2137.
82. Cullum, vol. I, 201–202.
83. Cullum, vol. I, 210.
84. Dimmock, Charles H., Social Networks and Archival Context (SNAC), accessed May 10, 2017, http://socialarchive.iath.virginia.edu/ark:/99166/w64t6n9h.
85. Cullum, vol. I, 221–222.
86. Webb Garrison, *2,000 Questions and Answers About the Civil War* (New York: Gramercy Press, 1992), 50.
87. Bruce S. Allardice, *More Generals in Gray* (Baton Rouge: Louisiana State University Press, 1995), 110–111.
88. Heidler, vol. 4, 1975–1976.
89. Cullum, vol. I, 231–232.
90. Cullum, vol. I, 232–233.
91. Cullum, vol. I, 233–234.
92. Cullum, vol. I, 238–239.
93. Cullum, vol. I, 240–241.
94. Allardice, *More Generals in Gray*, 34–35.
95. Cullum, vol. I, 308–310.
96. Cullum, vol. I, 319–325.
97. Cullum, vol. I, 326.
98. Cullum, vol. I, 337–341.
99. Randy Bishop, *Civil War Generals of Tennessee* (Gretna: Pelican Publishing Co., 2013), 74–76.
100. *National Cyclopedia*, vol. IV, 361–363.
101. Cullum, vol. I, 347–352.
102. Cullum, vol. I, 353–357.
103. Cullum, vol. I, 361–362.
104. *Handbook of Texas Online*, Jeanette H. Flachmeier, "Johnston, Albert Sidney," accessed December 03, 2017, http://www.tshaonline.org/handbook/online/articles/fjo32.
105. Cullum, vol. I, 372–374.
106. Cullum, vol. I, 375.
107. Bruce S, Allardice and Lawrence Lee Hewitt, eds., *Kentuckians in Gray* (Lexington: University Press of Kentucky, 2008), 117–123.
108. Cullum, vol. I, 381–382.
109. Cullum, vol. I, 383–385.
110. Cullum, vol. I, 389–390.
111. Joe A. Mobley, *Confederate Generals of North Carolina: Tar Heels in Command* (Charleston: The History Press, 2011), 136–139.
112. Mobley, 143–148.
113. Cullum, vol. I, 397–398.
114. Cullum, vol. I, 404–406.
115. Evans, 434–435.
116. Jefferson Davis, Civil War Trust, accessed December 221, 2017, https://www.civilwar.org/learn/biographies/jefferson-davis.
117. John S. Bowman, *The Civil War* (East Bridgewater: World Publications Group, 2006), 276.
118. Emory M. Thomas, *Robert E. Lee—A Biography* (New York: W. W. Norton, 1995), 191–379.
119. Cullum, vol. I, 423–424.
120. Cullum, vol. I, 424.
121. Alan Axelrod, *Generals South and Generals North* (Guilford: Lyons Press, 2011), 14–26.
122. Cullum, vol. I, 429–432.
123. Cullum, vol. I, 433–434.
124. Cullum, vol. I, 438–439.
125. "Distinguished Biographers," ed. *The National Cyclopedia of American Biography* (New York: James T. White & Company, 1897), vol. IV, 178.
126. Cullum, vol. I, 445.
127. Mobley, 91–93.
128. William Nelson Pendleton (1809–1833), Encyclopedia of Virginia, Virginia Foundation for the Humanities, accessed November 29, 2017, https://

www.encyclopediavirginia.org/Pendleton_William_Nelson_1809–1883.

129. *Handbook of Texas Online*, Thomas W. Cutrer, "Magruder, John Bankhead," accessed December 3, 2017, http://www.tshaonline.org/handbook/online/articles/fma15.

130. Albert Taylor Bledsoe, Wikipedia, accessed October 19, 2017, https://en.wikipedia.org/wiki/Albert_Taylor_Bledsoe. Terry A. Barnhart Albert Taylor Bledsoe,

131. Allardice, *More Generals in Gray*, 61–63.
132. Cullum, vol. I, 462–465.
133. Cullum, vol. I, 475–476.
134. Cullum, vol. I, 476–481.
135. Cullum, vol. I, 481–483.
136. Cullum, vol. I, 485–486.
137. Lucius Northrop, National Park Service, accessed December 22, 2017, https://www.nps.gov/people/lucius-northrop.htm.
138. Cullum, vol. I, 498.
139. Cullum, vol. I, 491–493.
140. *National Cyclopedia*, vol. IV, 181.
141. Cullum, vol. I, 510–511.
142. Allardice, *Kentuckians in Gray*, 69–75.
143. Cullum, vol. I, 521–522.
144. Mobley, 65–66.
145. Allardice, *Kentuckians in Gray*, 187–193.
146. Cullum, vol. I, 530–535.
147. Cullum, vol. I, 535–537.
148. Cullum, vol. I, 537–540.
149. Francis Henney Smith, Wikipedia, accessed October 19, 2017, https://en.wikipedia.org/wiki/Francis_Henney_Smith.
150. Cullum, vol. I, 548–549.
151. Cullum, vol. I, 550–551.
152. Cullum, vol. I, 553–558.
153. Cullum, vol. I, 560–561.
154. Abraham C. Myers, Wikipedia, accessed May 28, 2017, https://en.wikipedia.org/wiki/Abraham_Myers.
155. Bowman, 351.
156. Cullum, vol. I, 568–569.
157. Thomas W. Cutrer, "Allen, Robert Thomas Pritchard," *Handbook of Texas Online*, accessed May 28, 2017, http://www.tshaonline.org/handbook/online/articles/fal58.
158. Cullum, vol. I, 575–577.
159. Evans, 400–403.
160. Cullum, vol. I, 583–585.
161. Cullum, vol. I, 587.
162. Cullum, vol. I, 588–589.
163. Cullum, vol. I, 597–601.
164. Cullum, vol. I, 601–608.
165. Cullum, vol. I, 609–610.
166. Cullum, vol. I, 612–613.
167. Cullum, vol. I, 614.
168. Heidler, vol. 4, 2140–2141.
169. West Point Officers in the Civil War—Class of 1835, accessed October 20, 2017, http://civilwarintheeast.com/west-point-officers-in-the-civil-war/class-of-1835/
170. Cullum, vol. I, 622–623.
171. Cullum, vol. I, 625–627.
172. Spencer C. Tucker, *American Civil War: The Definitive Encyclopedia and Document Collection* (Santa Barbara: ABC—CLIO, 2013), 1105.
173. Joseph R. Anderson (1813–1892), Encyclopedia of Virginia, Virginia Foundation for the Humanities, accessed November 29, 2017, https://www.encyclopediavirginia.org/Anderson_Joseph_Reid_1813–1892.
174. Cullum, vol. I, 631–633.
175. Cullum, vol. I, 633–634.
176. Cullum, vol. I, 637–641.
177. Cullum, vol. I, 642–643.
178. Cullum, vol. I, 645.
179. Cullum, vol. I, 646–647.
180. Cullum, vol. I, 651–653.
181. Cullum, vol. I, 654.
182. Cullum, vol. I, 658.
183. Heidler, vol. 4, 1954.
184. Cullum, vol. I, 660–623.
185. Axelrod, 63–69.
186. Cullum, vol. I, 664–667.
187. William W. Mackall, Wikipedia, accessed December 3, 2017, https://en.wikipedia.org/wiki/William_W._Mackall.
188. Cullum, vol. I, 668–669.
189. Cullum, vol. I, 669–670.
190. Cullum, vol. I, 670–671.
191. Cullum, vol. I, 671–672.
192. Cullum, vol. I, 673–674.
193. Axelrod, 125–135.
194. Cullum, vol. I, 676.
195. Cullum, vol. I, 676–679.
196. Cullum, vol. I, 680–683.
197. Cullum, vol. I, 683.
198. Wooster, 166–167.
199. Cullum, vol. I, 684–687.
200. Esmeralda Boyle, *Biographical Sketches of Distinguished Marylanders* (Baltimore: Kelly, Piet & Company, 1877), 309–318.
201. Cullum, vol. I, 601–602.
202. Heidler, vol. 4, 2054–2055.
203. Robert H. Chilton, Wikipedia, accessed December 3, 2017, https://en.wikipedia.org/wiki/Robert_H._Chilton.
204. Axelrod, 2–3.
205. Garrison, *Questions and Answers*, 233.
206. Tucker, 1980.
207. Henry C. Wayne, Wikipedia, accessed December 3, 2017, https://en.wikipedia.org/wiki/Henry_C._Wayne#Civil_War_service.
208. Cullum, vol. I, 703–707.
209. Milton Andrews Haynes, Find a Grave, accessed October 12, 2017, https://www.findagrave.com.
210. Cullum, vol. I, 710–711.
211. Cullum, vol. I, 711–717.
212. Warner, 124–125.
213. Cullum, vol. I, 719–720.
214. *Handbook of Texas Online*, Jerry Thompson, "Sibley, Henry Hopkins," accessed December 03, 2017, http://www.tshaonline.org/handbook/online/articles/fsi01.
215. Edward "Allegheny" Johnson, Civil War Trust, accessed May 5, 2017, https://www.civilwar.org/learn/biographies/edward-allegheny-johnson.
216. Bowman, 349.
217. Cullum, vol. I, 724–725.
218. Cullum, vol. I, 726–727.
219. Heidler, vol. 4, 1863–1864.
220. Cullum, vol. I, 730.
221. Cullum, vol. I, 733–734.
222. Garrison, *Questions and Answers*, 50.
223. Mobley, 67–68.

224. Cullum, vol. I, 746.
225. Bowman, 314.
226. Cullum, vol. II, 1–6.
227. Cullum, vol. II, 6–9.
228. Cullum, vol. II, 9–13.
229. Cullum, vol. II, 15–16.
230. Cullum, vol. II, 18–19.
231. *Handbook of Texas Online*, Thomas W. Cutrer, "Hebert, Paul Octave," accessed December 03, 2017, http://www.tshaonline.org/handbook/online/articles/fhe09.
232. Cullum, vol. II, 27–30.
233. Cullum, vol. II, 31.
234. Bishop, 138–140.
235. Cullum, vol. II, 33–40.
236. Donald C. Pfanz, *Richard S. Ewell—A Soldier's Life* (University of North Carolina Press, 1998) and Bateman, 186.
237. Mobley, 120–122.
238. Cullum, vol. II, 41–43.
239. Cullum, vol. II, 44–46.
240. Bishop, 114–120.
241. *National Cyclopedia*, vol. IV, 207.
242. Allardice, *More Generals in Gray*, 148–149.
243. Tucker, 1203.
244. *National Cyclopedia*, vol. IV, 486.
245. Cullum, vol. II, 59–61.
246. Cullum, vol. II, 61–64.
247. Cullum, vol. II, 65–66.
248. Robert Wooster, *Civil War 100* (Secaucus: Press Book, 1998), 79–80.
249. Cullum, vol. II, 71–73.
250. Cullum, vol. II, 74–79.
251. Cullum, vol. II, 80.
252. *National Cyclopedia*, vol. IV, 466.
253. Cullum, vol. II, 85–86.
254. Cullum, vol. II, 86–88.
255. Cullum, vol. II, 88–89.
256. Cullum, vol. II, 89–90.
257. Cullum, vol. II, 90–93.
258. Robert S. Garnett (1819–1861), *Encyclopedia of Virginia*, Virginia Foundation for the Humanities, accessed November 29, 2017, https://www.encyclopediavirginia.org/Garnett_Robert_S_1819–1861.
259. *Encyclopedia of Virginia*, Virginia Foundation for the Humanities, accessed November 29, 2017, https://www.encyclopediavirginia.org/Garnett_Richard_B_1817–1863.
260. Claudius W. Sears, Wikipedia, accessed December 3, 2017, https://en.wikipedia.org/wiki/Claudius_W._Sears.
261. Cullum, vol. II, 95–96.
262. Cullum, vol. II, 96.
263. Cullum, vol. II, 101.
264. John M. Jones, Wikipedia, accessed December 3, 2017, https://en.wikipedia.org/wiki/John_M._Jones.
265. Cullum, vol. II, 105–107.
266. Allardice, *Kentuckians in Gray*, 49–55,
267. Cullum, vol. II, 109–110.
268. Cullum, vol. II, 110–113.
269. Cullum, vol. II, 115–116.
270. Allardice, *Kentuckians in Gray*, 224–250.
271. *National Cyclopedia*, vol. IV, 352.
272. *National Cyclopedia*, vol. IV, 502.
273. Martin Luther Smith, Aztec Club of 1847, accessed December 22, 2017, http://www.aztecclub.com/bios/smithml.htm.
274. Cullum, vol. II, 126–127.
275. Cullum, vol. II, 131.
276. Cullum, vol. II, 132–134.
277. Mobley, 79–84.
278. Cullum, vol. II, 136.
279. Cullum, vol. II, 140–141.
280. *National Cyclopedia*, vol. IV, 295.
281. Captain W. Gordon McCabe, Graduates of West Point Serving in the CSA Army, 1902 [From the Richmond, Va., Dispatch, March 30, April 6, 27, and May 12, 1902], accessed May 29, 2017, http://www.civil-war.net/searchshsp2.asp?search=Graduates%20of%20West%20Point%20Serving%20in%20the%20CSA%20Army.
282. *National Cyclopedia*, vol. IV, 317.
283. *National Cyclopedia*, vol. IV, 208 and Wooster, 227–228.
284. Wert, *General James Longstreet*, 52–406.
285. Cullum, vol. II, 153.
286. Cullum, vol. II, 156–157.
287. Heidler, vol. 4, 1655.
288. Cullum, vol. II, 158–159.
289. Cullum, vol. II, 161–162.
290. Samuel G. French, *Two Wars—An Autobiography of Gen. Samuel G. French* (Nashville: Confederate Veteran, 1901), 135–310.
291. Cullum, vol. II, 168.
292. Franklin K. Gardner, Civil War Trust, accessed December 22, 2017, https://www.civilwar.org/learn/biographies/franklin-gardner.
293. Cullum, vol. II, 170–178.
294. Cullum, vol. II, 181–182.
295. Cullum, vol. II, 183–184.
296. Cullum, vol. II, 185–187.
297. Cullum, vol. II, 189–190.
298. Michael E. Banasik, ed., *Duty, Honor and Country—The Civil War Experiences of Captain William P. Black, Thirty-Seventh Illinois* (Iowa City: Press of the Camp Pope Bookshop, 2006), 159.
299. Cullum, vol. II, 196–197.
300. Allardice, *Kentuckians in Gray*, 43–48.
301. Cullum, vol. II, 201–205.
302. Cullum, vol. II, 205–206.
303. Heidler, vol. 4, 2099–2101.
304. Colonel Louis Hébert, Pea Ridge National Military Park Arkansas, accessed December 22, 2017, https://www.nps.gov/peri/learn/historyculture/colonel-hebert.htm.
305. Cullum, vol. II, 210–211.
306. Cullum, vol. II, 211–213.
307. Cullum, vol. II, 214–219.
308. Cullum, vol. II, 219–220.
309. Cullum, vol. II, 225–227.
310. *Handbook of Texas Online*, Thomas W. Cutrer, "Smith, Edmund Kirby," accessed December 03, 2017, http://www.tshaonline.org/handbook/online/articles/fsm09.
311. Cullum, vol. II, 230–232.
312. *Handbook of Texas Online*, Thomas W. Cutrer, "Hawes, James Morrison," accessed December 05, 2017, http://www.tshaonline.org/handbook/online/articles/fhafd.
313. *Handbook of Texas Online*, Thomas W. Cutrer, "Bee, Barnard Elliott, Jr.," accessed December 05, 2017, http://www.tshaonline.org/handbook/online/articles/fbe22.
314. Cullum, vol. II, 237–242.
315. Cullum, vol. II, 242–245.
316. Cullum, vol. II, 246–247.

317. Cullum, vol. II, 248–249.
318. Cullum, vol. II, 250–255.
319. Cullum, vol. II, 256–260.
320. "The Four Horsemen of the Point" were Ambrose E. Burnside, John G. Foster, John G. Parke, and Jesse L. Reno, Garrison, *Questions and Answers*, 135.
321. Cullum, vol. II, 262–264.
322. "The Four Horsemen of the Point" were Ambrose E. Burnside, John G. Foster, John G. Parke, and Jesse L. Reno, Garrison, *Questions and Answers*, 135.
323. Cullum, vol. II, 266–267.
324. Donald A. Davis, *Stonewall Jackson* (New York: Palgrave Macmillan, 2007), 47–187.
325. Cullum, vol. II, 270–272.
326. Cullum, vol. II, 272–273.
327. *National Cyclopedia*, vol. IV, 397.
328. Cullum, vol. II, 280–282.
329. William Duncan Smith, Wikipedia, accessed December 3, 2017, https://en.wikipedia.org/wiki/William_Duncan_Smith.
330. *National Cyclopedia*, vol. IV, 35.
331. Cullum, vol. II, 285–286.
332. David R. Jones, Hollywood Cemetery, accessed December 21, 2017, https://www.hollywoodcemetery.org/david-r-jones.
333. Cullum, vol. II, 288–291.
334. Cullum, vol. II, 291–292.
335. Mobley, 182–186.
336. Evans, 417–418.
337. *Handbook of Texas Online*, Louise Horton, "Maxey, Samuel Bell," accessed December 03, 2017, http://www.tshaonline.org/handbook/online/articles/fma85.
338. Robbins, 239–254 and 272–277.
339. Cullum, vol. II, 310–311.
340. Cullum, vol. II, 311–312.
341. Cullum, vol. II, 314–315.
342. Bateman, 120.
343. Cullum, vol. II, 318–322.
344. "The Four Horsemen of the Point" were Ambrose E. Burnside, John G. Foster, John G. Parke, and Jesse L. Reno, Garrison, *Questions and Answers*, 135.
345. Cullum, vol. II, 323–324.
346. Cullum, vol. II, 325–329.
347. Cullum, vol. II, 329–331.
348. Cullum, vol. II, 336–337.
349. Cullum, vol. II, 338.
350. James S. Robbins, *Last in Their Class* (New York: Encounter Books, 2006), 231–233.
351. Walter H. Stevens, Hollywood Cemetery, accessed December 21, 2017, https://www.hollywoodcemetery.org/walter-h-stevens.
352. Warner, 166–167.
353. Cullum, vol. II, 350–352.
354. Cullum, vol. II, 353–355.
355. William Nelson Rector Beall (1825–1883), The Encyclopedia of Arkansas History & Culture, accessed December 22, 2017, http://www.encyclopediaofarkansas.net/encyclopedia/entry-detail.aspx?entryID=7849.
356. Patterson, 20 and 29.
357. George H. Steuart (brigadier general), Wikipedia, accessed December 3, 2017, https://en.wikipedia.org/wiki/George_H._Steuart_(brigadier_general).
358. Cullum, vol. II, 367–370.
359. Cullum, vol. II, 370–372.
360. "The Four Horsemen of the Point" were Ambrose E. Burnside, John G. Foster, John G. Parke, and Jesse L. Reno, Garrison, *Questions and Answers*, 135.
361. Johnson K. Duncan, Wikipedia, accessed December 3, 2017, https://en.wikipedia.org/wiki/Johnson_K._Duncan.
362. Cullum, vol. II, 376–378.
363. Allardice, *More Generals in Gray*, 168–169.
364. Cullum, vol. II, 385–386.
365. Beverly Robertson, Wikipedia, accessed December 3, 2017, https://en.wikipedia.org/wiki/Beverly_Robertson.
366. Allardice, *Kentuckians in Gray*, 89–95.
367. Seth Barton, Wikipedia, accessed December 3, 2017, https://en.wikipedia.org/wiki/Seth_Barton.
368. List of Confederate States Army officers educated at the United States Military Academy, Wikipedia, accessed November 17, 2017, https://en.wikipedia.org/wiki/List_of_Confederate_States_Army_officers_educated_at_the_United_States_Military_Academy.
369. Cullum, vol. II, 391–393.
370. Evans, 409–412.
371. Robbins, 205–220.
372. Cullum, vol. II, 401–409.
373. Garrison, *Questions and Answers*, 51.
374. Cullum, vol. II, 410–411.
375. Cullum, vol. II, 415–416.
376. Cullum, vol. II, 416–417.
377. Bishop, 214–216.
378. Tucker, 1154.
379. Heidler, vol. 4, 1602–1603.
380. Cullum, vol. II, 419–421.
381. Cullum, vol. II, 421–423.
382. Cullum, vol. II, 423–424.
383. Heidler, vol. 4, 2135–2136.
384. McCabe, http://www.civil-war.net/searchshsp2.asp?search=Graduates%20of%20West%20Point%20Serving%20in%20the%20CSA%20Army.
385. Tucker, 1343.
386. Cullum, vol. II, 436–437.
387. Cullum, vol. II, 437–438.
388. Cullum, vol. II, 441–443.
389. Allardice, *Kentuckians in Gray*, 138–144.
390. Cullum, vol. II, 443–449.
391. Cullum, vol. II, 463.
392. Cullum, vol. II, 463–465.
393. Mobley, 60–62.
394. Robbins, 208–220.
395. Cullum, vol. II, 476–477.
396. Cullum, vol. II, 478–480.
397. *National Cyclopedia*, vol. IV, 418.
398. Cullum, vol. II, 482.
399. Allardice, *Kentuckians in Gray*, 63–68.
400. Cullum, vol. II, 484–490.
401. Cullum, vol. II, 490–492.
402. Tucker, 655.
403. Cullum, vol. II, 499–500.
404. Cullum, vol. II, 504–506.
405. Cullum, vol. II, 504506.-
406. Cullum, vol. II, 508–512.
407. Cullum, vol. II, 515–519.
408. Cullum, vol. II, 521–522.
409. Evans, 398–399.

410. Cullum, vol. II, 523–524.
411. Cullum, vol. II, 524–526.
412. John S. Bowen, Wikipedia, accessed December 3, 2017, https://en.wikipedia.org/wiki/John_S._Bowen.
413. Cullum, vol. II, 532–534.
414. Cullum, vol. II, 537–542.
415. John R. Chambliss, Wikipedia, accessed December 3, 2017, https://en.wikipedia.org/wiki/John_R._Chambliss.
416. Bishop, 67–69.
417. Cullum, vol. II, 550–560.
418. Tucker, 2060.
419. Cullum, vol. II, 565–567.
420. *Handbook of Texas Online*, Thomas W. Cutrer, "Hood, John Bell," accessed December 03, 2017, http://www.tshaonline.org/handbook/online/articles/fho49 and Bateman, 239.
421. Bishop, 179–181.
422. General Reuben R. Ross (1830–1864), Montgomery County War Records, accessed November 20, 2017, http://www.tngenweb.org/montgomery/soldiers/rrrosssol.html.
423. George Washington Custis Lee, Arlington House, Robert E. Lee Memorial, accessed December 22, 2017, https://www.nps.gov/arho/learn/historyculture/george-lee.htm.
424. Cullum, vol. II, 572–574.
425. Cullum, vol. II, 574–575.
426. Cullum, vol. II, 576–577.
427. *Handbook of Texas Online*, Thomas W. Cutrer, "Deshler, James," accessed December 22, 2017, http://www.tshaonline.org/handbook/online/articles/fde46.
428. John Pegram, Hollywood Cemetery, accessed December 21, 2017, https://www.hollywoodcemetery.org/john-pegram.
429. Axelrod, 92–102.
430. Archibald Gracie III, Wikipedia, accessed December 3, 2017, https://en.wikipedia.org/wiki/Archibald_Gracie_III.
431. Stephen D. Lee, Civil War Trust, accessed December 22, 2017, https://www.civilwar.org/learn/biographies/stephen-d-lee.
432. Mobley, 126–131.
433. John Bordenave Villepigue, Wikipedia, accessed December 3, 2017, https://en.wikipedia.org/wiki/John_Bordenave_Villepigue.
434. Cullum, vol. II, 591.
435. Cullum, vol. II, 604–605.
436. Cullum, vol. II, 605–609.
437. Cullum, vol. II, 613–614.
438. Francis T. Nicholls, Wikipedia, accessed December 3, 2017, https://en.wikipedia.org/wiki/Francis_T._Nicholls.
439. Cullum, vol. II, 618–619.
440. Cullum, vol. II, 619–621.
441. Jones, *Historical Dictionary*, vol. I, 317–318.
442. Cullum, vol. II, 625–627.
443. Cullum, vol. II, 630–631.
444. Cullum, vol. II, 632–636.
445. Cullum, vol. II, 643–645.
446. Cullum, vol. II, 646–647.
447. Cullum, vol. II, 647–648.
448. Allardice, *Kentuckians in Gray*, 180–186.
449. Lunsford L. Lomax, Wikipedia, accessed December 3, 2017, https://en.wikipedia.org/wiki/Lunsford_L._Lomax.
450. *Handbook of Texas Online*, Thomas W. Cutrer, "Major, James Patrick," accessed December 22, 2017, http://www.tshaonline.org/handbook/online/articles/fma19.
451. Cullum, vol. II, 658–659.
452. Bishop, 111–113.
453. Cullum, vol. II, 668.
454. Cullum, vol. II, 670–671.
455. Fitzhugh Lee (1835–1905), Encyclopedia of Virginia, Virginia Foundation for the Humanities, accessed November 29, 2017, https://www.encyclopediavirginia.org/Lee_Fitzhugh_1835–1905.
456. Evans, 389–391.
457. Flag semaphore is the telegraphy system conveying information at a distance by visual signals with hand-held flags, rods, disks, paddles, or occasionally bare or gloved hands. Information is encoded by the position of the flags; it is read when the flag is in a fixed position. Flag semaphore, Wikipedia, accessed December 21, 2017, https://en.wikipedia.org/wiki/Flag_semaphore.
458. Garrison, *Questions and Answers*, 15.
459. Cullum, vol. II, 677–678.
460. Cullum, vol. II, 682–683.
461. Boatner, 277.
462. Bowman, 322.
463. *National Cyclopedia*, vol. IV, 352.
464. Cullum, vol. II, 706–707.
465. Bryan M. Thomas, Wikipedia, accessed December 3, 2017, https://en.wikipedia.org/wiki/Bryan_M._Thomas.
466. Cullum, vol. II, 723–725.
467. Cullum, vol. II, 729.
468. Joseph Wheeler, Encyclopedia of Alabama, accessed December 7, 2017, http://www.encyclopediaofalabama.org/article/h-2140.
469. Cullum, vol. II, 740–742.
470. Patterson, 54–55, 105, 107,109–111.
471. Cullum, vol. II, 755–757.
472. When the war began in April 1861, many cadets at West Point resigned their appointment and enlisted in the Confederate States Army. These men were excluded from the lists of Notable Graduates.
473. Cullum, vol. II, 772–773.
474. Cullum, vol. II, 774–779.
475. Cullum, vol. II, 784–790.
476. Cullum, vol. II, 813–814.
477. When the war began in April 1861, many cadets at West Point resigned their appointment and enlisted in the Confederate States Army. These men were excluded from the lists of Notable Graduates.
478. Cullum, vol. II, 813–814.
479. Cullum, vol. II, 837–840.
480. When the war began in April 1861, many cadets at West Point resigned their appointment and enlisted in the Confederate States Army. These men were excluded from the lists of Notable Graduates.
481. Cullum, vol. II, 840–844.
482. When the war began in April 1861, many cadets at West Point resigned their appointment and enlisted in the Confederate States Army. These men were excluded from the lists of Notable Graduates.
483. Cullum, vol. II, 866–867.
484. When the war began in April 1861, many cadets at West Point resigned their appointment and enlisted in the Confederate States Army. These men were excluded from the lists of Notable Graduates.

Bibliography

Allardice, Bruce S. *More Generals in Gray.* Baton Rouge: Louisiana State University Press, 1995.
Allardice, Bruce S., and Lawrence Lee Hewitt eds. *Kentuckians in Gray.* Lexington: University Press of Kentucky, 2008.
Ambrose, Stephen E. *Duty, Honor, Country: A History of West Point.* Baltimore: Johns Hopkins University Press, 1996.
Annual Report of the Board of Visitors to the United States Military Academy, made to Congress and the Secretary of War for the Year 1819. West Point: U.S. Military Press and Bindery, 1894.
Annual Report of the Secretary of War. United States War Department. Washington: Government Printing Office, 1896.
Axelrod, Alan. *Armies South, Armies North.* Lanham: Rowman & Littlefield, 2017.
_____. *Generals South and Generals North.* Guilford: Lyons Press, 2011.
Aztec Club of 1847. "Martin Luther Smith." http://www.aztecclub.com/bios/smithml.htm.
_____. "William Joseph Hardee." http://www.aztecclub.com/bios/hardee.htm.
Banasik, Michael E., ed., *Duty, Honor and Country—The Civil War Experiences of Captain William P. Black, Thirty-Seventh Illinois.* Iowa City: Press of the Camp Pope Bookshop, 2006.
Barone, Laureen M. "Evolution of the Cadet Disciplinary System: From Confusion to Clarity (1802–1833)." US Military Academy. 4 December 1990. Tactical Officer Education Program Papers. Special Collections.US Military Academy Library.
Bateman, Horatio. *Biographies of Two Hundred and Fifty Distinguished National Men.* New York: John T. Giles & Co., 1871.
"Beall, William Nelson Rector (1825–1883)." *The Encyclopedia of Arkansas History & Culture,* http://www.encyclopediaofarkansas.net/encyclopedia/entry-detail.aspx?entryID=7849.
Betros, Lance. *West Point—Two Centuries and Beyond.* Abilene: McWhiney Foundation Press, 2004.
Bishop, Randy. *Civil War Generals of Tennessee.* Gretna: Pelican Publishing Co., 2013.
Boatner, Mark M. III. *Civil War Dictionary.* New York: David Key Company, Inc., 1988.
Bowman, John S. *The Civil War.* East Bridgewater: World Publications Group, 2006.
Boyle, Esmeralda. *Biographical Sketches of Distinguished Marylanders.* Baltimore: Kelly, Piet & Company, 1877.
"Burbridge, Stephen G." Arlington National Cemetery Website. http://www.arlingtoncemetery.net/sgburb.htm.
Cartmell, Donald. *Civil War 101.* New York: Gramercy Books, 2001.
The Centennial of United States Military Academy at West Point, New York, 2 vols. Washington: Government Printing Office, 1904.
Chambers, John Whiteclay II, ed. *The Oxford Companion to American Military History.* New York, Oxford University Press, 1999.
Chambers' Encyclopedia (London: W. and R. Chambers, 1876) vol. IV.
The Citadel Alumni Association, http://www.citadelalumni.org/s/1674/alumni/index.aspx?sid=1674&gid=1001&pgid=535.
"Civil War Battle Summaries by Campaign." CWSAC, https://www.nps.gov/abpp/battles/bycampgn.htm.
Civil War Trust. "Davis, Jefferson." https://www.civilwar.org/learn/biographies/jefferson-davis.
_____. "Gardner, Franklin K." https://www.civilwar.org/learn/biographies/franklin-gardner.
_____. "Hoke, Robert F." https://www.civilwar.org/learn/biographies/robert-f-hoke.
_____. "Johnson, Edward 'Allegheny.'" https://www.civilwar.org/learn/biographies/edward-allegheny-johnson.

_____. "Lee, Stephen D." https://www.civilwar.org/learn/biographies/stephen-d-lee.
Citizen Soldier. Norwich: Swett & Jackman, 1840–1841.
Cleaves, Freeman. *Rock of Chickamauga—The Life of General George H. Thomas.* Norman: University of Oklahoma Press, 1948.
Coggins, Jack. *Arms and Equipment of the Civil War.* Garden City: Doubleday, 1962.
Congr. Globe, 37th Cong. 1st Sess. (1861).
"Congress—House of Representatives." *Buffalo Journal,* December 25, 1821.
"Congress—House of Representatives." *Hartford Courant,* December 15, 1834.
"Congress—House of Representatives." *The Hillsborough Recorder,* March 29, 1820.
"Congressional Proceedings." *New York Tribune,* January 13, 1844.
"Congressional Proceedings." *New York Tribune,* February 28, 1844.
Coppee, Henry. *Grant and His Campaigns.* New York: Charles Richardson, 1866.
Cowley, Robert, and Guinzburg, Thomas ed. *West Point—Two Centuries of Honor and Tradition.* New York: Warner Books, 2002.
Cullum, George W. *Biographical Register Officers and Graduates of the U.S. Military Academy at West Point, N.Y. from Its Establishment in 1802 to 1890 with the Early History of the United States Military Academy.* Cambridge: Riverside Press, 1891. Third Edition, Vol. I Nos. 1 to 1000 and Vol. II Nos. 1001 to 2000.
Cutrer, Thomas W. "Allen, Robert Thomas Pritchard." *Handbook of Texas Online.* http://www.tshaonline.org/handbook/online/articles/fal58.
_____. "Bee, Barnard Elliott, Jr." *Handbook of Texas Online.* http://www.tshaonline.org/handbook/online/articles/fbe22.
_____. "Deshler, James." *Handbook of Texas Online.* http://www.tshaonline.org/handbook/online/articles/fde46.
_____. "Hawes, James Morrison." *Handbook of Texas Online.* http://www.tshaonline.org/handbook/online/articles/fhafd.
_____. "Hebert, Paul Octave." *Handbook of Texas Online.* http://www.tshaonline.org/handbook/online/articles/fhe09.
_____. "Hood, John Bell." *Handbook of Texas Online.* http://www.tshaonline.org/handbook/online/articles/fho49.
_____. "Magruder, John Bankhead." *Handbook of Texas Online.* http://www.tshaonline.org/handbook/online/articles/fma15.
_____. "Major, James Patrick." *Handbook of Texas Online.* http://www.tshaonline.org/handbook/online/articles/fma19.
_____. "Smith, Edmund Kirby." *Handbook of Texas Online.* http://www.tshaonline.org/handbook/online/articles/fsm09.
Davis, Donald A. *Stonewall Jackson.* New York: Palgrave Macmillan, 2007.
des Cognets, Anna Russell. *Governor Garrard, of Kentucky.* Lexington: James M. Byrnes, 1898.
"Dimmock, Charles H." Social Networks and Archival Context (SNAC). http://socialarchive.iath.virginia.edu/ark:/99166/w64t6n9h.
"Distinguished Biographers." *The National Cyclopedia of American Biography.* New York: James T. White & Company, 1897, vol. IV.
DOD Dictionary of Military and Associated Terms. http://www.dtic.mil/doctrine/new_pubs/dictionary.pdf.
Dougherty, Kevin. *Civil War Leadership and Mexican War Experience.* Jackson: University Press of Mississippi, 2007.
Dugard, Martin. *The Training Ground—Grant, Lee, Sherman, and Davis in the Mexican War, 1846–1848.* New York: Little, Brown and Company, 2008.
East, Whitfield B. *A Historical Review and Analysis of Army Physical Readiness and Assessment.* Fort Leavenworth: Combat Studies Institute Press, 2013.
"Edmund Rice, #92 Edmund Rice Received the Medal of Honor for Bravery at Gettysburg." Norwich University. http://bicentennial.norwich.edu/92-0/.
Ellis, William Arba. *Norwich University 1819–1911—Her History, Her Graduates, Her Roll of Honor.* Montpelier: Capital City Press, 1911.
Encyclopedia of Virginia, Virginia Foundation for the Humanities. "Anderson, Joseph R. (1813–1892)." https://www.encyclopediavirginia.org/Anderson_Joseph_Reid_1813–1892.
_____. "Garnett, Richard B. (1817–1863)." https://www.encyclopediavirginia.org/Garnett_Richard_B_1817–1863.
_____. "Garnett, Robert S. (1818–1861)." https://www.encyclopediavirginia.org/Garnett_Robert_S_1819–1861.
_____. "Lee, Fitzhugh (1835–1905)." https://www.encyclopediavirginia.org/Lee_Fitzhugh_1835–1905.

_____. "Pendleton, William Nelson (1809–1883)." https://www.encyclopediavirginia.org/Pendleton_William_Nelson.
Evans, Clement Anselm. *Confederate Military History*. Atlanta: Confederate Publishing Company, 1899.
Farrow, Edward S. *Farrows Military Encyclopedia*. New York: Edward S. Farrow, 1885. vol. II.
Flachmeier, Jeanette H. "Johnston, Albert Sidney." *Handbook of Texas Online*. http://www.tshaonline.org/handbook/online/articles/fjo32.
Ford, Worthington Chauncey ed. *A Cycle of Adams Letters*. Boston: Houghton Mifflin Company, 1920.
Forman, Sidney. *West Point: A History of the United States Military Academy*. New York: Columbia University Press, 1950.
French, Samuel G. *Two Wars—An Autobiography of Gen. Samuel G. French*. Nashville: Confederate Veteran, 1901.
French, William H., William F. Barry, and H.J. Hunt, *The 1864 Field Artillery Tactics*. Mechanicsburg: Stackpole Books, 2005.
Garrison, Webb. *The Encyclopedia of Civil War Usage*. New York: Castle Books, 2001.
_____. *2,000 Questions and Answers about the Civil War*. New York: Gramercy Press, 1992.
Geiger, Rodger L., ed. *The American College in the 19th Century*. Nashville: Vanderbilt University Press, 2000.
Gibbon, John. *Recollections of the Civil War*. New York: G.P. Putnam's Sons, 1928.
Girardi, Robert I. *The Civil War Generals*. Blaine: Voyager Press, 2013.
Gore, John. *Evolutions of a Field Battery*. London, Simpkin, Marshall and Co., 1846.
Grant, Ulysses S. *Personal Memoirs*. New York: Modern Library, 1999.
Griffith, Paddy. *Battle Tactics of the Civil War*. New Haven: Yale University Press, 1987.
Halleck, Henry Wagner. *Elements of Military Art and Science*. Bedford: Applewood Books, 1861.
Hardee, William J. *Rifle and Light Infantry Tactics for Exercises and Maneuvers of Troops When Acting as Light Infantry or Riflemen*. Philadelphia: J.B. Lippincott, 1861.
"Haynes, Milton Andrews." Find a Grave. https://www.findagrave.com.
"Hébert, Colonel Louis." Pea Ridge National Military Park Arkansas. https://www.nps.gov/peri/learn/historyculture/colonel-hebert.htm.
Heidler, David S., and Jeanne T. Heidler. *Encyclopedia of the American Civil War*. Santa Barbara: ABC-CLIO, Inc., 2000, vol. 4.
History Detectives. "Civil War Innovations." http://www.pbs.org/opb/historydetectives/feature/civil-war-innovations/.
Hitchcock, Ethan Allen. *Fifty Years in Camp and Field*. New York: G.P. Putnam's Sons, 1909.
Hofstadter, Richard. *Anti-Intellectualism in American Life*. New York: Vintage, Alfred A. Knopf, 1963.
Holland, Lynwood Mathis. *Pierce M.B. Young: The Warwick of the South*. Athens: University of Georgia Press, 1964.
Hollywood Cemetery. "Jones, David R." https://www.hollywoodcemetery.org/david-r-jones.
_____. "Pegram, John." https://www.hollywoodcemetery.org/john-pegram.
_____. "Stevens, Walter H." https://www.hollywoodcemetery.org/walter-h-stevens.
Horton, Louise. "Maxey, Samuel Bell." *Handbook of Texas Online*. http://www.tshaonline.org/handbook/online/articles/fma85.
Hsieh, Wayne. *West Pointers and the Civil War*. Chapel Hill: University of North Carolina Press, 2009.
Hughes, Nathaniel Cheairs, Jr. *General William J. Hardee—Old Reliable*. Baton Rouge: Louisiana State University Press, 1965.
James, Charles. *The Universal Military Dictionary in English and French*. London: T. Egerton, 1816.
Jomini, Antoine Henri baron de. *The Art of War*. Philadelphia: J.B. Lippincott, 1862.
Jones, Archer. *Civil War Command and Strategy—The Process of Victory and Defeat*. New York: Free Press, 1992.
Jones, Terry L. *Historical Dictionary of the Civil War*. Lanham, MD: Scarecrow Press, 2011.
Katcher, Phillip, and Tony Bryan. *American Civil War Artillery—1861–1865 Field Artillery*. Botley: Osprey Publishing, 2001.
Latrobe, John H.B. *West Point Reminiscences—From September, 1818, to March, 1882*. http://penelope.uchicago.edu/Thayer/E/Gazetteer/Places/America/United_States/Army/USMA/LATREM*.html, 14.
"Lee, George Washington Custis." Arlington House, Robert E. Lee Memorial. https://www.nps.gov/arho/learn/historyculture/george-lee.htm.
"Legislative." *Buffalo Daily Gazette*. March 13, 1843.
Lord, Francis A. *Civil War Collector's Encyclopedia*. Harrisburg: Stackpole Company, 2004.
Mahan, D.H. *Advanced-guard, Out-post, and Detachment of Services of Troops with the Essential Principles of Strategy and Grand Tactics*. New York: John Wiley, 1864.
"Major Barnard Reviews the Opinions of Secretary Cameron." *New York Times*. July 19, 1861.

Marshall-Cornwall, James. *Grant as Military Commander*. New York: Barnes & Noble Books, 1970.

Maury, Dabney Herndon. *Recollections of a Virginian in the Mexican, Indian, and Civil Wars*. 3rd ed. New York: Charles Scribner's Sons, 1984.

McCabe, Captain W. Gordon. "Graduates of West Point Serving in the CSA Army." 1902 [From the Richmond, Va., Dispatch, March 30, April 6, 27, and May 12, 1902]. http://www.civil-war.net/searchshsp2.asp?search=Graduates%20of%20West%20Point%20Serving%20in%20the%20CSA%20Army.

McMurry, Richard M. *John Bell Hood and the War for Southern Independence*. Lincoln: University of Nebraska Press, 1982.

Mesch, Allen H. *Teacher of Civil War Generals*. Jefferson, NC: McFarland, 2015.

"Mexican War: The Proving Ground for Future American Civil War Generals." HistoryNet. http://www.historynet.com/mexican-war-the-proving-ground-for-future-american-civil-war-generals.htm.

Millett, Allan R., Peter Maslowski, and William B. Feis. *For the Common Defense*. New York: Free Press, 2012, Third Edition.

"Minie Ball." HistoryNet. http://www.historynet.com/minie-ball.

Mobley, Joe A. *Confederate Generals of North Carolina: Tar Heels in Command*. Charleston: History Press, 2011.

Mordecai, Alfred. *Report on Experiments in Gunpowder Made at Washington Arsenal in 1843 and 1844*. Washington: J. and G.S. Gideon, 1845.

Morrison, James L., Jr. *"The Best School"—West Point, 1833–1866*. Kent: Kent State University Press, 1998.

National Park Service. "Northrop, Lucius." https://www.nps.gov/people/lucius-northrop.htm.

Newell, Clayton R. *The Regular Army Before the Civil War—1845–1860*. Washington: Center of Military History, unknown.

Nichols, Edward J. *Toward Gettysburg—A Biography of General John F. Reynolds*. College Station: Pennsylvania State University Press, 1958.

Norton, Mary Beth, et al. *A People and a Nation: A History of the United States, Volume I: To 1877*. New York: Houghton-Mifflin Company, 2007.

Oates, William Calvin. *The War Between the Union and the Confederacy*. New York: Neale Publishing Group, 1905.

Official Register of the Officers and Cadets of the U.S. Military Academy, June 1850, Digital Archives, US Military Academy Library.

Official Register of the Officers and Cadets of the U.S. Military Academy, June 1860, Digital Archives, US Military Academy Library.

Park, Rosewell. *A Sketch of the History and Topography of West Point and the U.S. Military Academy*. Philadelphia: Henry Perkins, 1840.

Patterson, Gerard A. *Rebels from West Point*. Mechanicsville: Stackpole Books, 2002.

Pfanz, Donald C. *Richard S. Ewell—A Soldier's Life*. Chapel Hill: University of North Carolina Press, 1998.

Pryor, Elizabeth Brown. *Reading the Man*. New York: Penguin Group, 2007.

"Pyrotechnic Projects: Black Match Fuse & Quickmatch." https://www.cannonfuse.com/store/pc/Pyrotechnic-Projects-Black-Match-Fuse-Quickmatch-d6.htm.

Rafuse, Ethan S. *George Gordon Meade and the War in the East*. Abilene: McWhiney Foundation Press, 2003.

"Ransom, Thomas Edward Greenfield." Vermont in the Civil War. http://www.vermontcivilwar.org/get.php?input=4869.

Raymond, William. *Biographical Sketches of the Distinguished Men of Columbia County*. Albany: Weed Parsons and Company, 1851.

Robbins, James S. *Last in their Class*. New York: Encounter Books, 2006.

"Ross, General Reuben R. (1830–1864)." Montgomery County War Records. http://www.tngenweb.org/montgomery/soldiers/rrrosssol.html.

Scheel, Heinrich Otto. *De Scheel's Treatise on Artillery*. Bloomfield: Museum Restoration Service, 1984.

Scott, H.L. *Military Dictionary*. New York: D. Van Nostrand, 1861.

Scott, Winfield. *Rules and Regulations for the Exercise and Maneuvers of the United States Infantry*. New York: H.W. Mercein, 1815.

"Shrapnel." Shotgun's Home of the American Civil War. http://civilwarhome.com/terms.htm.

"Spring (Traction) *Eprouvette*, Eprouvette (Gunpowder Tester)—V-spring Type." Hagley Museum. https://museumcollection.hagley.org/objects/29094.

Stoker, Donald. *The Grand Design—Strategy and the U.S. Civil War*. New York: Oxford University Press, 2010.

Sweeney, Patrick. *The Gun Digest Book of Smith & Wesson*. Iola: kp Books, 2004.

Symonds, Craig. *Joseph E. Johnston—A Civil War Biography*. New York: W.W. Norton & Company, 1992.

Taylor, Priscilla S., and John M. Taylor. *Dictionary of Military Terms*. New York: H.W. Wilson Company, 2003.
"Thirty-Seventh Congress—House." *National Republican*. December 5, 1862.
Thomas, Emory M. *Robert E. Lee—A Biography*. New York: W.W. Norton, 1995.
Thompson, Jerry. "Sibley, Henry Hopkins." *Handbook of Texas Online*. http://www.tshaonline.org/handbook/online/articles/fsi01.
Tozeski, Stanley P. *Preliminary Inventory of the Records of the United States Military Academy*. Washington: General Services Administration, 1976.
Tucker, Spencer C. *American Civil War: The Definitive Encyclopedia and Document Collection*. Santa Barbara: ABC-CLIO, 2013.
USA Civil War Web Site (U.S.A.C.W.W.S.). "Battering in Breach." http://www.definitions.net/definition/breach.
____, "Battery." http://www.usa-civil-war.com/Civil_War/definitions.shtml#A.
____, "Earthworks." http://www.usa-civil-war.com/Civil_War/definitions_2.shtml.
____, "Smoothbore." http://www.usa-civil-war.com/Civil_War/definitions_3.shtml.
"VMI Civil War Generals." Virginia Military Institute. http://www.vmi.edu/archives/civil-war-and-new-market/vmi-civil-war-generals/.
Volvo, James M., and Dorothy Dennen Volvo. *The Antebellum Period*. Westport: Greenwood Press, 2004.
Voris, Alvin C., and Jerome Mushkat. *A Citizen-Soldier's Civil War: The Letters of Brevet Major General Alvin C. Voris*. Dekalb: Northern Illinois University Press, 2002.
Wallace, Lew. *Lew Wallace: An Autobiography*. New York: Harper & Brothers, 1906, vol. I.
Ward, John. "Books About West Point by John Ward, '64." http://www.west-point.org/parent/wppc-wa/2011/08/01/books-about-west-point-by-john-ward-64/.
Warner, Ezra J. *Generals in Gray*. Baton Rouge: Louisiana State University Press, 1959.
Waugh, John. *The Class of 1846*. New York: Warner Books, 1994.
Wert, Jeffry D. *The Controversial Life of George Armstrong Custer*. New York: Simon & Schuster, 1996.
____. *General James Longstreet—The Confederacy's Most Controversial Soldier*. New York: Simon & Schuster, 1993.
"West-Point Military Academy." *The People's Press*, January 9, 1835.
"West Point Military Academy." *Public Ledger*. July 13, 1859.
"West Point Officers in the Civil War." http://civilwarintheeast.com/west-point-officers-in-the-civil-war/.
"West Point Officers in the Civil War—Class of 1835." http://civilwarintheeast.com/west-point-officers-in-the-civil-war/class-of-1835/.
"What Is Jacksonian Democracy?" Reference.com. https://www.reference.com/government-politics/jacksonian-democracy-6194d7e044d1cd33#.
"Wheeler, Joseph." Encyclopedia of Alabama, http://www.encyclopediaofalabama.org/article/h-2140.
"Wheeling, 64th Illinois Volunteer Infantry, Company E." Yates Sharp Shooters. http://www.64thill.org/drillmanuals/caseys_infantrytactics/volume1/part05.htm.
Wood, W.J. *Civil War Generalship—The Art of Command*. Boston: Da Capo Press, 2000.
Wooster, Robert *Civil War 100*, Secaucus: Citadel Press Book, 1998.
"The Worst Civil War Generals and Commanders." Warfare History Network. http://warfarehistorynetwork.com/daily/civil-war/the-worst-civil-war-generals-and-commanders/.
"Worst Generals of the Civil War." Georgia's Blue and Gray Trail. http://blueandgraytrail.com/features/worstgenerals.html.
Wright, John D. *The Language of the Civil War*. Westport: Oryx Press, 2001.
Zinn, George A. "Seacoast Defense." *Proceedings of the Engineers' Club of Philadelphia*. Philadelphia: Engineers' Club, 1916.

Index

Numbers in ***bold italics*** indicate pages with illustrations

Academic Board 17–*18*, 20, 54
academic performance 42
Academic Regulations 15, *18*, 20, 29
Adams, John 31
Advance on Little Rock 168, 233–234, 240
Advanced Guard and Outposts 14
Advanced Guard, Outpost, and Detachment Service of Troops 155, 157, 158
Aide-de-Camp 68, 93, 96, 97, 102, 103, 108, 109, 126, 127, 130, 262
Alden, Bradford R. 98, 161; assignments 102; biographical sketch 103–105; cadet 181; Civil War service; notable cadets 99–102; promotions 102; service at the Academy 98; significant contributions 98; superintendent 98
Allen, Ethan 145, 261
Alvord, Benjamin *73*, 104, 222
American Colonization Society 75
American Journal of Education 27
ammunition 17, *18*, 255, 257, 258, 259
annual review *48*
antebellum 5, 6, *10*, 27, 42, 146, 147, 157
Appomattox Campaign 166, 220–223, 227–229, 232–233, 236–240, 242–243, 245–*250*
Army and Navy Chronicle 11
Army of Northern Virginia *154*, 218, 219, 220, 221, 222, 223, 225, 227, 228, 229, 230, 231, 232. 234, 235, 236, 237. 238, 239, 240, 242, 243, 244, 245, 247, 248
Army of Occupation 70, 76, 122, 141
Army of Tennessee 116, 123, 136, *154*, 219, 220, 223, 224, 225, 226, 228, 229, 230, 231, 232, 233, 236, 239, 243, 244, 245, 246, 247, 248
Army of the Cumberland 123, 136, 137, *154*, 218, 224, 225, 226, 228, 229, 230, 231, 232, 233, 234, 235, 235, 236, 239, 240, 241, 241, 242, 243, 244, 246
Army of the Ohio 220, 221, 228, 229, 230, 234, 235, 236, 237, 238, 239, 240, 241, 242, 243, 246, 247
Army of the Potomac 15, 127, 128, 135, 137, 141, *154*, 218, 219, 220, 221, 222, 223, 224, 225, 226, 227, 228, 229, 230, 231, 232, 233, 234, 235, 236, 237, 238, 239, 240, 241, 242, 243, 244, 245, 246, 247, 248, 249, *250*
Army of the Tennessee *154*, 224, 225, 226, 228, 229, 233, 241, 242, 244, 245, 246, 248
Art of War: book 33, *154*, 157, 259, 273; subject *6*, 15, 23, 25, 26, 43, 44, *47*, 155, *156*, 259
artillery 7, 8, *13*, *17*, *18*, 19, 20, *21*, 24, 25, *28*, 29, 30, 32, 33, 42, 50, 52, 54, **55**, 56, 57, *63*, 64, 68, *73*, 75, *85*, 87, 88, 89, 90, 91, 96, 97, *99*, 108, 109, *118*, 121, 124, *125*, 126, 127, 131, 134, 135, 137, 138, 147, 150, 158, 159, 160, 161, 164, 169, 220, 225, 226, 227, 228, 229, 230, 240, 247, 255, 258, 262
Atlanta Campaign 41, 114, 116, 121, 123, 136, 137, 167, 219, 220, 225, 226, 227, 228, 229, 230, 231, 234, 236, 239, 240, 241, 242, 243, 244, 246, 247, 248
Augur, Christopher C. *39*, 45, 52, 87, 95, 159, 164; assignments 130–132; biographical sketch 132; Civil War service 192, 232, 251; notable cadets *129*–130; promotions 130; service at the Academy *129*; significant contributions *129*; superintendent *129*
Aztec Club of 1847 90, 132, 268, 271

Baily, Jacob W. 25
Barnard, Henry 27
Barnard, John G. *16*, 51, *73*, 111, 117, 182, 222, 256, 260, 273
battalion of cadets *28*, 30, 31, **55**, **66**
Battle of Fredericksburg 127–128, 135
Battle of Shiloh 89, 91, 121, 123, *153*
Battle of the Bad Axe 61
battlefields *13*, 24, 26, 30, *34*, 50, 91, 111, 132, 137, 143, 145, 152, *154*, 160, 265
bayonets *35*, 111, *154*
Bell, John R. 44, 52, 76, 158, 159, 262–263; assignments *63*, 64; biographical sketch 64; notable cadets 62, *63*; promotions *63*; service at the Academy 62; significant contributions 62; superintendent 62
Black Hawk War 60, 61, 169
Bliss, John 30, 44, 52, 58, 263; assignments 59–60; biographical sketch 60–61; notable cadets 59; promotions 59; service at the Academy 58; significant contributions 58; superintendent
Bowman, Alexander H. *16*, 51, 124, *129*, *133*, 138, 175, 182
Brewerton, Harry 51, 93, 98, 171
Buell, Don Carlos *39*, 41, 76, 86, *144*, 190, 230, 251, 263
Bureau of Topographical Engineers **55**, *59*, *217*
Butler, Ben 25, 41, *144*

cadet balls 49, 119, 163
cadet mess 49, 160
caissons 19, *21*, 258

277

Index

Cameron, Simon 27, 260, 273
campaigns 23, 24, 41, 42, 43, 51, 53, *63*, 64, 68, 69, 74, 75, 76, 81, 82, 114, 115, 116, 121, 122, 123, 126, 127, 128, 130, 131, 132, 135, 136, 137, 141, 150, 152, *154*, *156*, 165, 166, 167, 168, 169, *217*, 218, 219, 220, 221, 222, 223, 224, 225, 226, 227, 228, 229, 230, 231, 232, 233, 234, 235, 236, 237, 238, 239, 240, 241, 242, 243, 244, 245, 246, 247, 248, 249, *250*
canister *18*–19, 257
Cannon, Newton 11
Carlisle Barracks 32, 74, 77, 88, 135
Carolinas Campaign 121, 123, 168, 220, 226–228, 231–232, 239–242, 244, 246, 248–249
cartridges *18*, 19
cavalry tactics 20, 29, 32, 35, 50, *118*, 121–122, 126, 138, 160–161
Centennial *3*, 50, 255, 256, 257, 258, 259, 260, 261, 262, 263, 264, 265, 271, 272
Chattanooga-Ringgold Campaign 121, 167, 221, 223, 224, 225, 226, 228, 229, 231, 232, 233, 234, 235, 239, 240, 241, 242, 243, 244, 246, 248, 249
Chickamauga Campaign 114, 116, 167, 219, 224, 225, 228, 229, 230, 231, 232, 233, 234, 235, 239, 240, 241, 242, 243, 244, 245, 246, 247, 248
Citizen Soldier 259
citizen-soldiers 12, 25, *34*, *144*
civil engineering *14*, 15, *156*, 157, 160
Civil War *3*, 8, 9, *10*, 15, 26, *28*, 29, 33, *34*, 37, *40*, 42, 43, 44, 45, 46, 53, *55*, *59*, 62, 66, 72, 77, 79, 84, *85*, 90, 92, 93, *94*, 98, *99*, 104, 106, 110, 111, 115, 117, 119, 121, 122, 123, 124, *125*, 127, *129*, 132, *133*, 134, 136, 137, 138, 141, 143, *144*, 145, 146, 147, 148, *151*, 152, *153*, 155, 157, 158, 159, 159, 161, *162*, 163, 164, 165, 169, *170*, 171, 172, 173, 174, 175, 176, 177, 178, 179, 180, 181, 182, 183, 184, 185, 186, 187, 188, 189, 190, 191, 192, 193, 194, 195, 196, 197, 198, 199, 200, 201, 202, 203, 204, 205, 206, 207, 208, 209, 210, 211, 212, 213, 214, 215, 216, *217*, 230, 251, 252, *253*; *see* Rebellion of the Seceding States
civilians 29, 43, 46
classroom 8, 30, 33, 43, 44, 145, 146, *149*, 158
Clausewitz, Carl von 23, 259
Clitz, Henry B. 45, 52, 138, 244; assignments *139*–140; biographical sketch 140–142; cadet 235, 96, 100; Civil War service 96, *139*, 141, 194, 235; notable cadets 138; promotions *139*; service at the Academy 138; significant contributions 138; superintendent 138
colleges *5*, *6*, 8, *10*, 26, 29, 43, 44, 70, 103, 143, 157
combat *13*, 24, 71, 113, 136, 146, 150, *151*, *154*, 169, 214, 215, 216, *217*, 247, 255, 259, 260, 272
commissary duty 56
commission 12, 20, 27, 32, 33, 42, 50, 51, 69, 77, 78, 89, 90, *94*, 104, 109, 110, 113, 115, 117, 122, 131, 146, 147, 150, *151*, 160, 161, 169, 218, 223, 225, 230
competitive environment 44, 46, 159
conduct 46, *48*, 49, 68, 69, 70, *73*, 87, 89, 106, 108, 109, 113, 115, 120, 122, 128, 137, *139*, 141, 145, *153*, 158, 262
Confederacy 25, 27, 42, 43, 44, 45, 115, *144*, *154*, 164, 240
Confederate Heartland Offensive 167, 219, 222, 224, 226, 228, 231, 233, 234, 236, 237, 240, 243, 244, 246, 248
Confederate States Army 33, 113, 115, 117, 120, 122, *144*, 169, 222, 223, 225, 227, 233, 244, 245
Congress *10*, 11, 12, *13*, 29, 32, 70, 76, 79, 84, *94*, 98, 111, *118*, 260, 261, 262, 271, 272, 275
Coppee, Henry *48*, 261
corps *3*, 15, *16*, *17*, 20, 27, *28*, 30, 31, 32, 33, 37, *38*, 42, 46, *47*, *48*, 49, 50, 51, 52, 53, 56, 57, 58, 60, 65, 68, 70, *71*, *73*, 75, 79, *99*, 116, 117, 121, 123, 124, 126, 127, 128, 131, 132, 134, 136, 146, *149*, 152, *156*, 160, 169, 195, *217*, 218, 222, 227, 229, 236, 243
Corps of Cadets *3*, 30, 31, 32, 37, 46, 49, 50, 53, 58, 60, 65, *71*, 79, *99*, 117, 134, 160
Corps of Engineers 15, *16*, 124, *149*, *156*, 169, 215, *217*, 218, 222, 229
courts-martial 31, 49, 58, 76, 140, 263
Court of Inquiry 58, 75
Cox, Jacob 25
Crockett, Davey 10
Cullum, George 16, *17*, 53, 54, 73, 92, 164, 222
Cullum number 52, 53, 54, 58, 62, 65, 71, 79, 84, 93, 98, 106, 111, 117, 124, 129, 133, 138, 169–217
curriculum *5*, 7, 24, 25, 26, 27, 31, 32, 43, 54, 65, 143, 148, *154*, 158, 159

Dade's Massacre 44, 56, 75
Davis, Jefferson 67
Delafield, Richard 51, *55*, *59*, 79, 84, 93, 117, 124, *217*
demerits *6*, *48*, 49, 160
Democratic Party (Democrats) *10*, 235, 263
Department of Artillery *13*, *17*, *18*, 19, *20*
Department of Engineering *13*, *14*, 15, *18*, 33, 50, *118*
Department of Ordnance and Gunnery *13*, 20, 21
Department of Practical Military Engineering *13*, 15, *16*
Department of Tactics *13*, *17*, 22, 23–*36*, 52, *118*, 161, 256, 260, 261
DeRussy, Rene E. 51, 79, 84
deviation in firing 17, 19, 256
discipline 2, *6*, 7, 15, 29, 30, 31, 43, 44, 46, *47*, 48, 49, 50, 51, 54, *55*, 62, 76, *85*, 90–92, *118*, 119, 141, 143, 145, *149*, 152, *156*–160
divisions 37, *38*, 64, 69, 70, 74, 77, 90, 91, 115, 116, 123, 127, 128, 131, 132, 136, 137, 146, 155, 227, 230, 234, 239, 241, 243, 245, 247, 249, 259, 261
dragoons 32, 42, *85*, 120, 122, 134, 135, 137, 169
drill *1*, *3*, 7, 8, *17*, 20, *28*, 30, *34*, *36*, 46, *47*, 49, 50, 51, 53, 72, 76, *85*, *99*, 103, 141, *153*, 155, 158, 159, 160, 164

enemy *1*, *2*, *10*, 23, 24, *36*, 51, 70, 76, 91, 120, 128, 136, 146, 152
Enfield rifles 153
engagements 24, 37, 109, 123, 136, *154*
engineering *1*, 7, 8, 11, 12, *13*, *14*, 15, *18*, 20, 24, 26, 27, 32, 33, 42, 43, *47*, 50, 67, 79, 111, *118*, 124, *149*, 150, *156*, 157, 158, 159, 160, 218, 223, 224, 227, 231, 245, 246, 248, 249, *250*
evolutions *18*, 31, 32, *47*, 65, 76, 155, 159, 255, 258, 260, 273
examinations 29, 33, *85*
expedition to, and capture of, New Orleans 166, 224, 231, 239, 245
expedition to the Red River of the North 89, 90

faculty *6*, 25, 43, 46, 54, 143, 146, *149*, 157, 158, 159
federal (U.S. Government, Union Government) *10*, 11, 110, 114, 116, 137, 143, *153*
Federal Penetration Up the Cumberland and Tennessee Rivers 89, 167, 219, 220, 221, 222, 223, 224, 225, 226, 227, 228, 229, 230, 231, 233, 234,

235, 236, 237, 239, 240, 241, 242, 243, 244, 246, 248,,
field fortifications *14*, 15, 43, *156*, 157
field pieces *17*, *28*
Florida Expedition 167, 231, 236, 237, 249, *250*, 267
Florida War 56, 57, 68, 74, 75, 113, 114, 120, 169
Foote, Andrew H. 90
forces 23, 24, 33, 37, *40*, 43, 68, 70, 90, 91, 104, 110, 116, 123, 127, 128, 145, 148, 150, *154*, 223, 227, 228, 232, 240
Forrest's Defense of Mississippi 168, 226, 230
Fort Sumter 33, *40*, 166, 218, 219, 225, 226, 231, 232, 235, 236, 243, 248
fortifications *13*, *14*, 15, 24, 43, 79, *156*, 157, 218, 263
forts 11, 90, 91, 92, 106, 111, 132, 146, 147; Adams 126; Armstrong 60; Augur 132; Blakely 136, 168, 226, 227, 233, 235, 241, 244, 248; Brady 82; Brooke 102; Brown 121, 122, 126, 127, *139*, 140, 141; C. F. Smith 92; Columbus 56, 57, 88, 89, 90, 109, 130; Conrad 135; Crawford 74, 75, 82, 88; Dalles 131; Davidson 169; Dearborn 82; Defiance 140; Delaware 56, 57, 88, 89; De Russy 169, 226; Donelson *40*, 89, 90, 91, 92, 164, 167, 219, 226, 228, 233, 242, 244, 246; Edwards 82; Fisher 42, 166, 234, 244, 249; Gaines 122; George 63; Gibson 113; Graham 121, 122; Gratiot 82; Hamilton 141, 234; Hatteras 222; Heiman 90; Henry 89, 90, 167, 224, 233, 242; Hoskins 131, 132; Howard 60; Inge 121, 122; Jackson 56, 57, 166, 224, 231, 239; Jesup 74, 76, 120; Jones 103, 104; King 102; Lafayette 126, 234; Laramie 132; Leavenworth 60, 61, 126; Macon 237, 239; Marion 56, 57, 88, 90; Mason 121, 135; McAlister 168, 228, 246; McHenry 126; McKavett 140; Mifflin 56, 57, 135; Mitchell 56, 57; Monroe 68, 108, 109, 126; Morgan 122, 126; Moultrie *63*, 64, 126, 232; Niagara 130; Ontario 108, 109; Orford 126, 131; Pickens 56, 57, 126, 141, *217*, 224; Pierre 77; Pillow 167, 230, 232; Preble 126; Pulaski 166, 218, 224, 239, 246, 248; Ripley 114, 115; St. Philip 166, 224, 231, 239; Sanders 223, 232; Simcoe 109, 167; Snelling 60, 61, 82, 88, 89; Stansbury 74; Stedman

166, 220, 221, 223, 227, 238, 239, 244; Sumter 33, 166, 218, 219, 225, 231, 232, 235, 236, 242, 243, 248; Towson 113; Trumbull 126; Union 140; Vancouver 103, 126, 131; Wagner 41, 167, 224, 226, 236, 239, 246, 247, 249, *250*; Wayne 140; Winnebago 60, 61; Wolcott 93, 96, 97; Wood 126; Yakima 131; Yuma 126
Fowle, John 44, 52, 79, 263; assignments 83–84; biographical sketch 82–83; notable cadets 79–81; promotions 81; service at the Academy 79; significant contributions 79; superintendent 79
Franklin-Nashville Campaign 168, 224, 226–232, 234, 235, 239, 241–244, 248
Freemason 70
Frémont, John C. 88, 89
front *14*, 24, 26, 35, *36*, 90, 114
frontier duty 60–61, 74, 83. 88–89,89, 103, 108–109, 113–115, 120–124, 126, 131, 135–136, 140–141

Gardiner, George W. *17*, 20, 30, 33, 52, 54, 158, 159, 262–263; assignments 56; biographical sketch 56–57; cadet 200, 241; Civil War service 44; notable cadets: promotions *55*–56; service at the Academy 54; significant contributions 54–55; superintendent 54
Garnett, Robert S. 106–110, 158, 159, 161, 164, 263, 268, 272; assignments 108–109; biographical sketch 109–110; cadet 190, 241; Civil War service 45, 86; notable cadets 106–108; promotions 108: service at the Academy 106; significant contributions 106; superintendent 106
Garrard, Kenner 45, 52, *133*–137, 159, assignments 135–136; biographical sketch 136–137; cadet 101, 200, 241; Civil War service 101, 136, 137; notable cadets 134; promotions 134–135; service at the Academy *133*; significant contributions *133*–134; superintendent *133*
garrison 19, *21*, 31, 33, 46, 56, 57, *59*, 60, 61, 64, 65, 68, *71*, 72, *73*, 74, 75, 88, 90, 96, 97, *99*, 102, 103, 108, 109, 120, 121, 122, 126, 127, 130, 131, 135, 140, 141, 147, 243, 258
Georgia Military Institute 9
Georgia State Militia 113, 115
Gettysburg Campaign 127–128,

136, 166, 218, 219–241, 243–*250*
graduating classes: 1818 169–*170*; 1819 171; 1820 171–172; 1821 172; 1822 173; 1823 173–174; 1824 174–175; 1825 175; 1826 176–177; 1827 177; 1828 178; 1829 178–179; 1830 179–180; 1831 180–181; 1832 181–182; 1833 182–183; 1834 183–184; 1835 184–185; 1836 185–186; 1837 186–187; 1838 187–188; 1839 188–189; 1840 189–190; 1841 190–191; 1842 191–192; 1843 192–193; 1844 193; 1845 193–194; 1846 194–196; 1847 196; 1848 197; 1849 197–198; 1850 198–199; 1851 199–200; 1852 201; 1853 202–203; 1854 203–204; 1855 204; 1856 205–206; 1857 206–207; 1858 207; 1859 207–208; 1860 208–209; May 1861 209–210; June 1861 210–211; 1862 211–212; 1863 212; 1864 213; overall summary 213–214; valedictorians 214–*217*
grand strategy 23
grand tactics *14*, 15, 24, 32, 33, 43, *47*, 50, *118*, 145, 146, 155, *156*, 158, 159
Grant, Ulysses S. *39*, *40*, 41, 42, 50, 84, 87, 90, 91, 92, 95, 114, 145, *151*, 152, 161, 164, 192, 251, 263, 265, 272, 273, 274; operations 115, 136, *154*, 161, 166, 167, 219, 220, 221, 222, 223, 224, 225, 226, 227, 228, 229, 230, 231, 232, 233, 234, 235, 236, 237, 238, 239, 240, 241, 242, 243, 244, 245, 246, 247, 248, 249, *250*, 272; operations against Vicksburg 114, 155, 167, 219, 221, 224, 225, 226, 227, 228, 230, 231, 232, 233, 234, 235, 236, 237, 238, 239, 240, 242, 243, 245, 246, 247, 248; Overland Campaign *154*, 166, 220, 221, 222, 223, 225, 226, 227, 228, 229, 230, 231, 232, 233, 234, 235, 236, 237, 238, 239, 240, 241, 243, 244, 245, 246, 247, 248, 249, *250*
grapeshot 19, 69, 258
Greeley, Horace 12
grenades *18*, 19, 257, 90, 91
gunnery 8, *13*, *18*, 19, 20, *21*, 22, 30, 255

habits of obedience 48
Hale, John P. 11
Halleck, Henry W. *39*, 69, 78, 81, *85*, 92, 164, 188, 222, 227, 252, 273
Hardee, William J. 26, 158, 159, 161, 163, 164, 166; assignments 117, 120–121; biograph-

ical sketch 121–123; cadet 81, *85*; Civil War service 114, 116, 122, 123, 188, 226; notable cadets 119–120; promotions 120; service at the Academy 117; significant contributions 117, *118*, 119; superintendents 117; tactics 117, 122, 164
Harney, William S. 77, 263
Hart, B.H. Liddell 23, 259
Hawes, Albert G. 11,268
Hitchcock, Ethan Allen 44, 45, 49, 52, 148, 158 159, 161 163, 261, 262, 273; assignments *73–75*; biographical sketch 75–77; cadet 75; Civil War service *39*, 251, 252; notable cadets 72–73; promotions *73*; service at the Academy 71, *118*, 145; significant contributions 71; superintendent *71*
hops 119
House Committee on Military Affairs 11
House of Representatives 11, 27, 256, 272
Hutchens, John 27

initial velocity *17*, *18*, 256
innovations in military technology 43
Iuka and Corinth operations 167, *217*, 224, 226, 227, 228, 229, 231, 232, 233, 234, 236, 241, 242, 243, 248

Jackson, Andrew *10*; democracy 9, 256, 274
Jackson's Valley Campaign 165, 218, 220, 225, 226, 228, 229, 230, 234, 235, 236, 237, 238, 239, 241, 242, 244, 245, 246, 247
Jefferson, Thomas 29
Jefferson Barracks 60, 61, 74, 76, 82, 103, 121, 135, 221, 263
Johnston, Albert S. 67, *133*, 163, 219
Johnston, Joseph E. *38*, *40*, 41, 42, 49, *66*, 67, 72, 115, 121, 123, 148, 163, 179, 220, 226, 228, 239, 240, 241, 243. 244, 246
Joint Operations Against New Madrid, Island No. 10, and Memphis 167, 219, 224 227, 229, 231, 235, 241, 243
Jomini, Antoine Henri baron de 23, 24, 33, 44, *154*, 259
Kentucky Military Institute 9, 221, 222

laboratory *17*, 20
Larned, Charles W. *1*, 2, *3*
Latrobe, John H. B. 62
leave of absence 60, 61, 74, 76, 77, 82, *94*, 97, 109, 109, 113, 114, 115, 121, 122, 132, 140, 141

Lee, Robert E. *38*, *40*, 41, 42, 51, 67, 72, 98, 106, 110, 111, *133*, 137, 145, 148, *151*, 163, 178, 220, 221, 222, 223, 225, 227, 228, 229, 233, 236, 237, 238, 239, 242, 243, 244, 246, 249, *250*
Levy, Simon Magruder 29
Lincoln, Abraham 132, 218 227, 241, 242, 260
liquors *99*
loading *18*, 19, 35, 104, 257, 258, 265
Longstreet's Knoxville Campaign 167, 223, 228, 232, 237, 238

Mahan, Dennis. H. *14*, 15, 33, 43, 44, *47*, 67, *154*, 155, *156*, 157, 158, 159, 160, 163, 174, 215, 218
Maine 11, 64, 126
Manassas Campaign 165, *217*, 218, 219, 220, 221, 222, 224, 225, 226, 227, 228, 229, 230, 231, 232, 234, 235, 236, 237, 238, 239, 240, 241, 242, 244, 245, 246, 247, 249, *250*
maneuvers *13*, 19, 24, 31, 33, *34*, *36*, *47*, 65, 123, 155
manual of arms 24, *35*, *48*
mathematics *1*, *5*, 7, 8, 27, 67, *85*, 98, 103, *149*, *156*, 160, 220,
McClellan, George B. *39*, *40*, 41, 91, 96, 98, 100, *144*, *151*, 161, 194, 235, 252,
McIntire, Samuel B. *118*, 211
McWhiney, Grady 26
Meridian and Yazoo River expeditions 167, 243
mess 30, 31, 32, 49, *55*, 160
Mexican War 15, 69, 74, 77, 88, 97, 106, 108, 111, 114, 115, 120, *125*, 126, 127, 128, 130, *139*, 141, 142, 147, 148, 150, *151*, 152, *162*, 164, 169, 255
Michie, Peter 50, 134, 138, *250*, 261
Military Academy *1*, *3*, *5*, *6*, 7, 8, 9, *10*, 11, *13*, 15, 19, 24, 25, 26, 27, *28*, 29, 30, 31, 33, *36*, 37, *38*, 42, 43, 44, 46, *48*, 51, 52, 53, 54, *55*, 56, 57, 58, *59*, 60, 62, *63*, 64, 65, 67, 68, 69, *71*, *73*, 74, 75, 82, 84, 88, 89, 93, *94*, 96, 97, 98, 102, 103, 106, 108, 109, 111, 113, 114, 115, 117, *118*, 120, 121, 122, 126, 127, 130, 131, *133*, 135, 137, 138, *139*, 140, 141, 143, 146, 147, 148, *149*, 150, 155, *156*, 163, 169, *217*, 218, 220, 225, 226, 230, 232, 235, 240, 241
military boards 50
Military Committee 11
military engineering 8, *13*, *14*,

15, 27, 32, 33, 43, *47*, 111, *156*, 157, 218
Military Occupation of Texas 74, 103, 120, 126, 130, *139*
military schools 2, 8, *14*, 157
military science *1*, 11, 12, *18*, 23, 259
military training 8, *13*, 15, *17*, 19, *21*, 25, 26, *35*, 46, *144*, 148, 159
militia *34*, 113, 115, *118*, 121, 128, 169, 218, 219, 222, 224, 226, 227, 228, 229, 232, 239, 243, 247, 248
miners 111
minor tactics 15, 24, 43, *47*, 146, 147, *156*, 158, 159
Mobile Campaign 136, 138, 226, 227, 230, 233, 235, 248
mortars *17*, 19, *28*
muskets *3*, *18*, 19, *28*, 30, *35*, 43, 91, 104, 111, *151*, 152, *153*, *154*, 159, 255, 258, 265

Napoleon 26, 43, 255, 258, 259
New Hampshire 11, 56, 60
New York *1*, 11, 29, 30, 56, 57, *59*, 60, 68, 69, 70, 74, 75, 88, 89, 90, 97, 108, 109, 110, 126, 130, 132, *133*, 134, 137, 140, 141, 157, *217*, 227, 228, 234, 244, 262
New York Tribune 12, 256, 272
Norwich University 9, 255, 256, 272
notable graduates 53, *55*, *59*, 62, 66, 72, 79, *85*, *94*, 98, *99*, 106, 111, 119, 124, *125*, *129*, 134, 138, 160, 161, 163; 1818 169–*170*; 1819 *170*–171; 1820 171–172; 1821 172; 1822 173; 1823 173–174; 1824 174–175; 1825 175–176; 1826 176–177; 1827 177; 1828 178; 1829 178–179; 1830 179–180; 1831 180–181; 1832 181–182; 1833 182–183; 1834 183–184; 1835 184–185; 1836 185–186; 1837 186–187; 1838 187–188; 1839 188–189; 1840 189–190; 1841 190–191; 1842 191–192; 1843 192–193; 1844 193; 1845 193–194; 1846 194–196; 1847 196; 1848 197 1849 197–198; 1850 198–199; 1851 199–200; 1852 201; 1853 202–203; 1854 203–204; 1855 204; 1856 205–206; 1857 206–207; 1858 207; 1859 207–208; 1860 208–209; May 1861 209–210; June 1861 210–211; 1862 211–212; 1863 212; 1864 213

Oates, William C. 27, 259, 274
obedience 7, 11, 44, *48*, 51, 145, 155
offensive in Eastern Kentucky 167, 221, 222, 228, 238, 241, 247

Ohio 11, 27, 82, 83, 110, 136, 137, *144*, 148, 220, 221, 224, 225, 226, 228, 229, 230, 233, 234, 235, 236, 237, 238, 239, 240, 241, 242, 243, 246, 247, 265, 266
operations: against Baton Rouge 166, 225, 232, 240; against Charleston 166, 224, 227, 229, 236, 247; against Fort Fisher and Wilmington 166, 234, 244, 245, 249; against Fort Pulaski 218, 224, 239, 246, 248; against Galveston 168, 221; against the Defenses of Charleston 167, 224, 229, 236, 239, 246, 249; in Mobile Bay 168, 240, 241; in Western Virginia 165, 220, 224, 229, 231, 232, 235, 237, 238, 239, 242, 243, 244, 246; to blockade the Texas Coast 168, 232, 245; to control Missouri 168, 229, 230, 233, 235, 236, 239, 240, 241, 243, 247
ordnance 8, *13*, *17*, *18*, 20, *21*, 22, 230, 67, 68, 77, 80, 117, 121, 169, 190, 218, 219, 221, 223, 224, 229, 230

parole *133*, 135, 141, *217*, 226, 264
Partridge, Alden 30, 58
Pea Ridge Campaign 168, 221, 232, 236, 240
Pegram, John 107, 110, *112*, 244
personal discipline 44
petroleum deposits 104
philosophical studies 50
plains 131
Poinsett, Joel Roberts 76, 262
politicians 12, 25, 43, 77, *144*
pontoniers 111, 265
Porter, Horace *3*, 24, 208, 255
Prairie Grove Campaign 168, 233, 246, 248
projectiles *18*, 19, *21*, 218, 255, 257, 258, 260
promotions 11, 53, *55*, 56, 57, *59*, 60, 61, *63*, 64, 68, 69, 70, *73*, 75, 77, 81, 82, 87, 89, 91, 96, 102, 106, 108, 113, 115, 120, 122, 125, 130, 131, 134, 136, 137, 138, *139*, 141, *144*, 147, 148, *151*, 159, 164, *250*, 251, 261
proof of gunpowder *17*, 19
pyrotechny *17*, *18*, 19, *21*, 257

Quartermaster's Department 32, 223
quick match *18*, 19

Rathbun, George O. 11
Rebellion of the Seceding States 75, 89, 114, 121, 126, 131, 135, 140, 142; *see also* Civil War
recoil 19, 258

reconnaissance 91, *151*, 152, 242
recruiting service 60, 61, 64, 68, *71*, *73*, 74, 75, 82, 89, 103, 108, 114, 115, 120, 122, 130, 135, 140
Red River Campaign 169, 221, 226, 229, 232, 234, 237, 240, 241, 247, 248
regiments: Cavalry Corps 243; Confederate Fiftieth Virginia Infantry 226; Confederate First Georgia Infantry 239; Confederate First Maryland Infantry 225; Confederate First North Carolina Infantry 231; Confederate Ninth Texas Infantry 237; Confederate Tenth Georgia Infantry 232, 239; Confederate Twentieth Georgia Infantry 236; Confederate Twenty-first Louisiana Infantry 231; Confederate Virginia Infantry 225; Corps of Artillery 20, 30, 56, 57, *73*; Eighth Infantry 68, 69, *73*, 75, 76; Eleventh Infantry *59*, 60; Fifth Cavalry 108, 134; Fifth Infantry 60, 81, 126; First Artillery 30, *55*, 56, 68, 87, 90; First Cavalry 120; First Dragoons 134; First Infantry 52, *59*, 61, *73*, 75; 46th New York 134, 137; Fourteenth Infantry *125*, 127; Fourth Artillery 20, *63*, 64, 108, 109, 134; Fourth Infantry 52, 102, 103, 130; Light Artillery *63*, *64*; 164th Illinois Volunteer Infantry 261, 275; Second Artillery 56, 57, 87, 89, 120; Second Cavalry 52, 122, 134, 136, Third Cavalry 137; Second Infantry 52, *73*, 77, 130, 140; Second Kentucky Cavalry 234; Seventh Infantry 52, 108, 109, *139*; Seventh Texas Cavalry 228; Sixth Infantry 30, 52, *59*, 60, 61, 81, 83, 113, 114, 115, *139*; Tenth Infantry 88, 90, 113, *139*, 140, 141; Third Artillery 20, 52, 96, 97, *125*, 126; Third Infantry 52, 60, *73*, 76, 81, 82, 88, *139*, *263*; Thirteenth Infantry 52, 130; Twelfth Infantry 52, 130, *139*, 141; ;
Regular Army *34*, 72, 104, 137, 148, 150, 152; soldiers 29, 46
regulations *5*, *6*, 12, 15, *18*, 19, 20, 27, 29, 30, 31, 32, 33, 46, *47*, 49, 50, 65, *118*, 140, 145, 157
retreat 26, *36*, 56, 57, 123
Reynolds, John F.: assignments 126–127; biographical sketch 127–128; cadet 86, 190; Civil War service *40*, 45, 230, 252; notable cadets *125*; promotions *125*–126; service at the Academy 52, 119, 124, 158, 159, 164; significant contributions 124–*125*; superintendent 124
Richmond-Petersburg Campaign 166, 220, 221, 222, 223, 224, 225, 226, 227, 228, 229, 230, 231, 232, 233, 234, 235, 236, 237, 238, 239, 241, 242, 243, 244, 245, 246, 247, 248, 249, *250*
Rifle and Light Infantry Tactics *34*, 117, 121, 122, 161, 164, 226
rifled muskets 43, 152, *153*, *154*, 258
rifles *18*, 19, *34*, 35, 42, 43, 67, 117, 121, 122, 152, *153*, *154*, 159, 161, 164, 171, 226, 238, 257, 265
rifling *17*, 19, 265
Rogue River 103, 104, 126, 127, 131, 132
role model 46, 49, 158, 160, 163
Rosecrans, William S. 12, 23, *40*, 41, 84, 87, *94*, 110, 123, *144*, 161, 164, 191, 252
Rules and Regulations for the Exercise and Maneuvers of the United States Infantry 47

sappers 111, 263
Savannah Campaign 168, 228, 242, 244, 246
School of the Battalion 31, 33, *36*, 65
School of the Battery *18*, 255
School of the Company 28, 31, 33, 35, *47*, 65, 260
School of the Gunner *18*
School of the Piece *18*, 255
School of the Soldier 31, 33, *35*, *47*, 51, 65, 159
science *1*, *5*, 8, 11, 12, *13*, *14*, 15, *18*, 20, *21*, 23, 32, 33, 37, *47*, 58, 104, *149*, *156*
science of war *1*, 8, *13*, *14*, 15, *47*, 58, *156*, 159
Scott, Winfield *34*, *47*, 49, 68, 69, 70, 74, 76, 77, 78, 84, 89, 90, 102, 103, 104, 115, 122, 141, 148, 150, *151*, 152, 164, 225, 261
Second Class 7, 32, 33, 46, 53, 255
Second Dragoons 120
self-control 7, 48
Sheridan's Valley Campaign 166, 221, 225, 227, 229, 235, 236, 240, 242, 243, 246, 247, 248, 249, *250*
Sherman, William T. *39*, 41, 80, 84, 86, 91, 92, 121, 123, 136, 137, 146, 161, 164, 189, 223, 228, 251
Sibley's New Mexico Campaign 168, 223, 224, 226, 227, 229, 236

Siege of Port Hudson 131, 132, 167, 221, 224, 232, 233, 234, 237, 238, 240, 241, 245
slavery 77
slow match *18*, 257
Smith, Charles Ferguson 145; assignments 88–89; biographical sketch 89–92; cadet 67, 175, 219; Civil War service 39, 44, 45, 252; notable cadets *85*–87; promotions 87–88; service at the Academy 48, 49, 52, 84, 158, 159, 160, 161, 163, 164; significant contributions 84–*85*; superintendent 84
smoothbore muskets 152, *153*, *154*
South Carolina Military Academy (The Citadel) 9
Spencer, John C. 70, 262
spiking and unspiking 19
Springfield rifles *154*
staffs *6*, 15, 24, 29, 30, *34*, 37, *48*, *63*, 64, 76, 104, 143, 146, 147, 159, 161, 169, 222, 225, 227, 229, 239
Stones River Campaign 121, 167, 219, 221, 223, 224, 226, 228, 230, 231, 234, 239, 240, 241, 242, 243, 244, 246, 247, 248
strategy *6*, 8, 15, 23, 24, 29, 32, 33, 43, 50, 51, *118*, 146, 152, 155
study and recitation 20
summer encampment *47*, *48*, 49, 54, *94*, 119, *156*, 158, 160
Swift, Joseph Gardner 29, 30, 58, 260

tactical defensive 43
tactics 7, 8, *13*, *14*, 15, *17*, *18*, 19, 20, *21*, 22, 23, 24, 25, 26, *28*, 29, 30, 31, 32, 33, *34*, *36*, 43, 46, *47*, 50, 52, 53, 54, *55*, 56, 57, 58, *59*, 60, 62, 64, 65, *66*, 68, 70, *71*, 74, 75, 79, 82, 83, 84, *85*, 88, 89, 93, 96, 97, 98, *99*, 103, 106, 108, 109, 111, 114, 115, 117, *118*, 121, 122, 124, 126, 131, 134, 135, 138, 140, 141, 145, 146, 152, *154*, 155, *156*, 158, 159, 160, 161, 163, 164, 226, 255, 259, 260, 261, 265, 273
target practice *17*, 19, *28*, 30, 260
Taylor, Zachary 70, 76, 89, 108, 109, 122, 128, 148, *151*

technology *17*, 26, 29, 43, 145, 152, *154*
Tennessee 11, 12, 88, 89, 90, 91, 97, 116, 121, 123, 124, 135, 136, *154*, 167, 219, 220, 221, 222, 223, 224, 225, 226, 227, 228, 229, 230, 231, 232, 223, 234, 235, 236, 237, 238, 239, 240, 241, 242, 243, 244, 245, 246, 247, 248, 263, 266, 271
Thayer, Sylvanus 11, 29, 30, 31, *48*, 49, 51, 54, *55*, 58, 60, 62, 65, `*71*, 84, 88, 89, 146, 155, 163, 256
Thayer Hotel 29
theory of artillery 17
Thomas, George H. 20, *40*, 42, 84, 86, 123, 137, 161, 164, 189, 228, 252
Thomas, John Addison: assignments 96–97; biographical sketch 97; notable cadets 94–96; promotions 96; service at the Academy 44, 52, 93–*94*; significant contributions 93; superintendent 93
Thomas, Pierre 30
Totten, Joseph 27, 259–260
Treatise on Field Fortification 157
Twiggs, David E. 127, 137

Union 9, *17*, 37, *38*, *40*, 41, 42, 43, 44, 45, 53, *55*, *59*, 62, *63*, *66*, 67, 68, 72, *73*, 77, 79, 80, *85*, 86, 87, 89, 90, 91, 92, *94*, 95, 96, 98, *99*, 100, *253*, 262
U.S. Army *3*, *34*, 218, 222, 224, 225, 227
U.S. Military Academy at West Point *1*, 2, *3*, *5*, *6*, 7, 8, 11, 12, 15, *18*, 24, 25, 26, 27, *28*, 29, 32, *36*, 37, *38*, 42, 43, 44, 46, *47*, *48*, 49, 51, 53, 54, *55*, 56, 57, *59*, 60, 62, 66, 67, 69, 71, 72, 75, 79, 82, 84, *85*, 88, 89, 90, *94*, 97, *99*, 102, 103, 104, 106, 109, 111, 113, 114, 117, *118*, 119, 122, 124, *125*, 126, 127, *129*, 132, *133*, 134, 137, 138, 141, 143, *144*, 145, 146, 147, 148, *149*, 150, *151*, 152, *154*, 155, *156*, 157, 158, 159, 160, 161, *162*, 163, 169, *217*, 218, 220, 225, 226, 230, 232, 235, 240, 241, *250*
Utah Expedition 89, 90, 126, 127, 169

Virginia Military Institute 8, 222, 255, 275
Virginia Peninsula Campaign 126, 127, 141, *154*, 165, 218, 219, 220, 221, 222, 223, 224, 225, 226, 227, 228, 229, 230, 231, 232, 233, 234, 235, 236, 237, 238, 239, 240, 241, 242, 243, 244, 245, 246, 247, 248, 249
volunteers *34*, 74, 90, 104, 132, 134, 137, 146, 150, 152, *154*, 169, 224, 265, 266; California 88, 90; Indiana 222, 229; Missouri 229; New Jersey 219; Ohio 225; Pennsylvania 127, 128, 218; U.S. *39*, *40*, *73*, 78, 88, 126, 127, 130, 135, 137, 169, 219
Voris, Alvin 25, 259, 275

Walker, William H.T.: assignments 113–114; biographical sketch 114–116; cadet 187; Civil War service 81, 225; notable cadets 111–113; promotions 113; service at the Academy 45, 52, 111, 159; significant contributions 111; superintendent 111
Wallace, Lew 91, 264, 275
Wallace, W.H.L. 91
War Department 70, 74, 78, *118*, 147, *156*, 220
War of 1812–1815 (War of 1812) 30, 56, *59*, 60, *63*, 64, 68, 69, 79, 81, 82, 147, 150, 163
war with Mexico *see* Mexican War
Welles, Gideon 25
Western Military Institute 9
West Point *see* U.S. Military Academy at West Point
Williams, Jonathan 29, 209
Wilson's Raid in Alabama and Georgia 168, 230, 248, 249
Wool, John E. 27, 93, 96, 97, 108, 109
Worth, William J. 262; assignments 68–69; biographical sketch 69–70; notable cadets *66*–68; promotions 68; service at the Academy 31, 44, 49, 52, 65, 158, 159, 160, 161, 163, 164; significant contributions 65–*66*; superintendent 65

www.ingramcontent.com/pod-product-compliance
Lightning Source LLC
Chambersburg PA
CBHW081543300426
44116CB00015B/2739